SUBSTANCE AND SHADOW

SUBSTANCE
AND SHADOW

WOMEN AND ADDICTION
IN THE UNITED STATES

STEPHEN R. KANDALL
with the assistance of Jennifer Petrillo

HARVARD UNIVERSITY PRESS
Cambridge, Massachusetts, and London, England 1996

Library of Congress Cataloging-in-Publication Data

Kandall, Stephen R.
    Substance and shadow : women and addiction
in the United States / Stephen R. Kandall.
        p.   cm.
Includes bibliographical references and index.
ISBN 0-674-85360-1 (alk. paper)
1. Women—Drug use—United States—History.
2. Drug abuse—United States—History.
3. Narcotic addicts—United States—History.
4. Narcotic addicts—Rehabilitation—United States—
    History. I. Title.
HV5824.W6K35   1996
362.29′082—dc20   96-10207

Designed by Gwen Frankfeldt

With the hope that the generations do learn
To my mother, Sophie, and the memory of my father, Charlie
my wife, Judy
the children, Marlene and Larry

PREFACE

On a steamy day in July 1989, I found myself sitting in the air-conditioned Central Florida courtroom of Judge O. H. Eaton, Jr., testifying as an expert witness for the defense in the case of Jennifer Johnson. Ms. Johnson, a young African American woman, had been charged with two counts of delivery of a controlled substance (through the umbilical cord) to a minor (her newborn infant) and one count of abuse of her infant based on the supposedly deleterious effect of that alleged "drug delivery."

My appearance as an expert witness was reasonable, since I had cared for over a thousand drug-exposed babies in my twenty-four years of specialized practice, had published over seventy articles and book chapters on the effects of maternal drug use during pregnancy, and had lectured on the subject throughout the United States (and subsequently also in Australia, Italy, and Belgium). In addition, I was serving as a consultant on the effects of addiction during pregnancy to the National Institute on Drug Abuse, the American Civil Liberties Union, the March of Dimes, Bank Street College of Education in New York, the Scott Newman Foundation in Los Angeles (founded by Paul Newman and Joanne Woodward), and many other agencies and foundations, and was to chair a national consensus panel on treatment of drug-exposed infants.

None of my experience was of any help to me in that courtroom, where so many aspects of the legal proceedings seemed illogical. I knew that Ms. Johnson had sought treatment for her cocaine use during her pregnancy but had been unable to secure a treatment slot in the few available programs in Florida. It was hard for me to believe that passive transfer of a tiny amount of cocaine, which *might* have occurred in the short time between the birth and the clamping of the umbilical cord, could be legally construed as "delivery of a controlled substance to a minor." Although I was not allowed to hear the prosecution's case, I knew that the obstetrician could not even recollect the time interval between birth and cord clamping, and that no scientific data had been presented to document the passage of any cocaine. I also knew that both of Ms. Johnson's other children, born in 1987 and 1989, had looked normal after birth and were doing well on medical follow-up. My own work and that of many others had shown that the effects of fetal cocaine exposure were, at best, controversial and poorly understood—although ironically, the detrimental, even devastating effects of legal drugs such as alcohol were certainly known. When I met her, it was clear to me that neither putting her in jail nor taking away her children would really address her situation.

Yet there I was, trying to help Ms. Johnson, whom I found to be a caring, concerned woman, attempting to be a good mother under difficult personal and economic circumstances. We were very different—she a mother facing prosecution and I a pediatrician concerned with the problems associated with drug use—but we shared the same, perhaps unrealistically optimistic, hope that the legal system would resolve the issue in a way best for mother and child.

After a brief trial, however, in a legal first, Ms. Johnson was convicted under a U.S. drug-trafficking statute. Although she did not go to jail, she was sentenced to one year in a drug treatment program (which she had already voluntarily started), fourteen years probation, and two hundred hours of community service; she was to be placed under court-supervised prenatal care if she became pregnant again; and she was forbidden to go to bars and use drugs or alcohol herself, or to associate with those who did. The Appellate Court upheld the lower court finding by a vote of two (male) to one (female), but in 1992, the conviction was unanimously overturned by the Florida Supreme Court, which stated: "The Court declines the State's invitation to walk down a path that the law, public policy, and common sense forbid it to tread" (*Johnson v. State*, 602 So. 2d 1288 [Fla 1992]).

During my preparation for the trial and after Ms. Johnson's initial conviction, I became aware of a number of similar prosecutions going forward across the United States. I asked myself how we, as a country fighting a well-publicized "war on drugs," had reached the sorry point where the case of a disadvantaged minority woman, one of many thousands of drug users in the state of Florida, had become a battle zone. I knew from my own medical and advocacy work that addiction in women had been increasing since the beginning of the "crack" epidemic in the mid-1980s. But, I wondered, how far back in American history could the problem of women and addiction be traced? What was the magnitude of the problem? If it had been significant, what treatments, if any, had been successful? How did this and other prosecutions fit into the general history of women and addiction in the United States? Could we learn important lessons from looking back over many years? The result of my attempt to answer these questions is this book.

Jennifer Petrillo, my principal research assistant, diligently developed many of our concepts and relentlessly hounded the librarians in her search for original material. When Jennifer went off to medical school, Anna Lisa Raymundo continued this important effort. Wendy Chavkin, Loretta Finnegan, Mary Jeanne Kreek, and especially David Courtwright made extremely valuable suggestions in the formative stages of the book. Herman Joseph, John Langrod, Joyce Lowinson, Barbara and Ira Marion, Robert Newman, and Lynn Paltrow proved to be accessible and knowledgeable tutors, influencing my ideas about addiction. My director, Richard Bonforte, gave me time and encouragement, and my professional colleagues, Tatiana Doberczak, Kendall Jenkins, Ramesh Jhaveri, Lucy Perrotta, Aimee Telsey, and Julie Topsis, took care of the babies in the Beth Israel Medical Center Neonatal Intensive Care Unit. Larry Gartner first suggested that I explore the area of perinatal addiction and remains an admired teacher. Jennifer Johnson provided me the opportunity to ask the original question. Mary J. Peck and her staff of librarians at the Seymour J. Phillips Health Sciences Library of the Beth Israel Medical Center, and Arthur Downing and his staff, especially Lois Fischer Black, at the New York Academy of Medicine, were very gracious with their time and accepting of my many unreasonable demands. Angela von der Lippe of

Harvard University Press provided encouragement and sage advice from her senior editorial perspective. I am extremely grateful to Linda Howe, my editor, who molded the manuscript with consummate skill and good humor into its present form. My brother, Geoff, and all the children—Marlene, Larry, Wendy, Jon, Bob, Lauren, Jim, and even Averi—and most important, my wife, Judy, gave me much encouragement and shared my excitement every step of the way.

CONTENTS

ILLUSTRATIONS

SUBSTANCE AND SHADOW

one

A HISTORICAL PERSPECTIVE

Beginning in the mid-1980s, America witnessed a media blitz on the horrors of drug abuse, especially of "crack" cocaine. Banner headlines, such as "Crack, a Disaster of Historic Dimensions, Still Growing" (*New York Times,* May 28, 1989) and "Crack's Destructive Sprint across America" (*New York Times Magazine,* October 1, 1989), focused attention on the relationship between drug use and the social and economic conditions that were ravaging society: poverty, violent crime, overcrowded prisons, hospital emergency rooms overrun with cases of drug-related violence and illness, homelessness, and sexually transmitted diseases. By the early 1990s, it was estimated that the aggregate costs of this devastation, including crime, health care, and reduced work productivity, exceeded 300 billion dollars annually (Califano 1992).

The often sensationalistic coverage of the "crack epidemic" by television, radio, weekly news magazines, and daily newspapers conveyed the false impression that drug use is a relatively recent phenomenon in American society. In fact, however, the legal use of opiates in America dates back well over two hundred years. A considerable amount of opium, for example, was produced in the colonies during the Revolutionary War (Wilbert 1908), and the colonial militias relied on gum opium for its narcotic effects (Kremers and Urdang 1976: 166). Such use was not unaccompanied by warnings. *The American Dispensatory* noted that "the habitual use of opium produces . . . tremors, paralysis, stupidity, general emaciation . . . [and] can scarcely ever be relinquished" (Coxe 1818: 410). Despite concern about their dangers, the medicinal and recreational use of opiates grew rapidly, especially during the latter half of the nineteenth century. Although medicinal use subsequently abated as physicians, pharmacists, and patent medicine manufacturers heeded published warnings or came under regulatory control, recreational use of more powerful opiates continued into the twentieth century, along with the development of newer and more potent methods of administration.

Like opiates, cocaine in the United States can be traced back over decades, in this case, to the 1870s. At that time it was medically useful as a topical anesthetic, it served as a common ingredient in patent medicines, and it was used recreationally by society's upper classes. Nonmedicinal use of cocaine by Southern Negroes[1] from the 1880s through the early part of the twentieth century, however, prompted a wave of national concern and near-hysteria. President William Howard Taft proclaimed: "The misuse of cocaine is undoubtedly an American habit, the most threatening of the drug habits that has ever appeared in this country" (Wright 1910: 50).

During the latter part of the nineteenth century and well into the early twentieth, a number of factors—the changing social demographics of drug users, growing concern about the effects of chronic drug dependence, increasing knowledge among physicians and pharmacists about the dangers of opiates, early attempts at regulating the pharmaceutical industry, and the nation's emergence as a true international power—led to dramatic changes in the country's "drug policy." Where once quiet tolerance of most drug use had been the order of the day, municipal legislation against opium smoking by Chinese immigrants in 1875 and 1876 foreshadowed the powerful societal forces that would come together over the next forty years to create a new "anti-drug policy." This "supply side" policy began formally with the passage of the Harrison Anti-Narcotic Act of 1914, a tax act, and with the 1919 *Webb* (*Webb et al. v. U.S.,* 249 U.S. 96) and *Doremus* (*U.S. v. Doremus,* 249 U.S. 86) Supreme Court decisions, which allowed federal and state governments to initiate new drug-fighting policies, such as increasingly strict legislation, harsh repression of addicts, and national and international drug interdiction measures. These tougher measures overshadowed "demand side"–driven initiatives, such as the drug treatment clinics that operated primarily between 1919 and 1923, the inpatient federal treatment facilities at Lexington, Kentucky, and Fort Worth, Texas, that operated from 1935 to 1971, the therapeutic communities and other innovative programs introduced in the mid-1950s, and methadone maintenance programs, which began in the mid-1960s. The composite result of these strategies, however, was little more than a "patchwork quilt" approach to the problem of drug use in America. Over the last fifteen to twenty years, continuing stress on drug interdiction and policing has driven up the national drug budget, from just under one billion dollars in 1978 to over fourteen billion dollars in 1995, without producing a clear consensus on the long-range benefits of these policies.

Over the past twenty-five years, amid an atmosphere of escalating fear and growing frustration with America's inability to win the "war on drugs," a "new" issue has emerged, one that previously received little attention: the use of illicit substances by women. As early as 1782, de Crevecoeur (1981) reported that it was common practice for the women of Nantucket Island to take "a dose of opium every morning." Over the ensuing decades women's use of opiates and other drugs increased, and by the end of the nineteenth century, close to two-thirds of the nation's opium and morphine addicts were women.

During most of the second half of the nineteenth century, women addicted to opiates, as well as those who used cocaine, chloral hydrate, and cannabis, were generally tolerated in an atmosphere of silent acceptance. But many lived in the shadow of guilt and shame, concealing their drug use even from close family members. They maintained their drug habits either through self-medication with easily obtainable proprietary, or "patent," medicines or through the collusion of physicians and pharmacists, as overzealous, ignorant, or condescending as they were greedy. Women were medicated excessively not only for a wide range of organic complaints but also for a vague set of nonorganic complaints labeled "neurasthenia" or "nervous weakness." In fact, women's addictions were to some degree responsible for the growth of an entire branch of the American pharmaceutical industry at the turn of the century. Although drug use was known to exist among women of all social classes, the stereotypical picture was that of a genteel white, middle- or upper-middle-class Southern lady much like the ennobled morphine-addicted Mrs. Henry Lafayette Dubose portrayed in Harper Lee's novel, *To Kill a Mockingbird*.

By the beginning of the twentieth century, the composition of American society was changing dramatically. Pressure to reform

United States drug policy or, more accurately, to develop a drug policy for the first time, had been building since the 1870s. Much of this pressure was the result of a growing national perception of economic and social danger to white America. Part of the campaign to change America's drug policy was predicated on the fear that drug use was corrupting women, but many were now convinced that "opium dens," a white "slave trade" in prostitution, and Negro violence against white women posed a serious threat to the established social order.

The connection between drugs and female sexuality has existed for thousands of years and is widely represented in the art of ancient cultures. The use of drugs by prostitutes, the power of certain drugs to intensify sexual feeling, and the perceived relationship between the "nature of femininity" and the "special states of consciousness" enacted by women as oracles, witches, midwives, and herbal healers (Palmer and Horowitz 1982: 13), all reinforced the association between women's sexuality and mind-altering substances. Women have traditionally been cast as "Eves," whose mystery and innate wisdom, in combination with particular substances (in Eve's case, an apple) can be dangerous to society (p. 21). Iconography of various kinds, for example, the long-haired female nude leaning on a bottle of the popular tonic Vin Mariani in a late-nineteenth-century advertisement, and the image of seductive, bare-breasted "Cocaine Lil"; the body-shaped cocaine spoon in common use during the 1920s; and later, the theme of women as victims of drugs in American movies, echoed and exploited the connection. Even today, many drugs retain highly "sexed" female nicknames—cocaine (Girl, Girlfriend, Her, Lady, White Lady, La Dame Blanca, Aunt Nora), heroin (Aunt Hazel, White Girl), marijuana (Aunt Mary), and depressants (Pink Ladies). Contemporary advertising, such as the full-page photograph of a sensuous woman in an Opium perfume ad, perpetuates this long-time association between drugs and alluring sexuality.

The Harrison Anti-Narcotic Act of 1914, the Supreme Court decisions of 1919, and the closure of the short-lived drug treatment clinics ushered in the Classic Era of drug control. Addicted women moved farther into the shadows. The general lack of attention to female drug users can be explained in part by the relative decline in the percentage of female addicts during these years. Certainly, rich women and the "smart, chic set" could maintain their drug habits through private physicians, private clinics, and sanitariums. An increasing number of female addicts, however, were poor urban women, who became increasingly dependent on male suppliers and the criminal underworld for drugs.

During the Second World War, when international supply lines were abruptly cut, both male and female addicts scrambled to procure drugs by any means available. Between 1941 and 1971, about fifteen thousand women, both voluntary admissions ("vol") and convicts serving sentences ("con"), found treatment at the federal drug treatment facility in Lexington, Kentucky. By the 1950s, the scientific community slowly began to recognize that the repressive measures of the previous thirty or forty years had done more harm than good. The election of John F. Kennedy to the presidency in 1960 reordered national priorities on many mental health issues, including drug abuse. Integrated into the more enlightened approach of this period was the development of many new kinds of treatment for narcotic addiction, including therapeutic communities, outpatient treatment, medical detoxification, correctional treatment programs, and methadone maintenance. These programs, however, were almost exclusively male-oriented and male-dominated and thus generally unsuited to the treatment of addicted women, although female drug users participated.

Just as some strides were being made in bringing female addicts out of the shadows, the counterculture of the 1960s produced a new population of drug-using women. Drawn largely from America's youth culture, these women had been challenged to "drop out and turn on," and they began to experiment with drugs like marijuana and LSD. In addition, many physicians at the time, convinced like their predecessors a century earlier that few female complaints could not be adequately managed with pharmaceuticals, began prescribing the newly available tranquilizers, sleeping pills, and diet pills to their female patients.

As a result, by the early 1970s, the percentage of female "hard drug" users had risen from less than 20 percent to over 30 percent. Although for many years drug abuse had been viewed as a "man's disease," the Women's Movement drew increased attention to women and drugs. Both the National Institute on Alcohol Abuse and Alcoholism (NIAAA) and the National Institute on Drug Abuse (NIDA) initiated projects intended to provide gender-specific assistance to substance-abusing women and to evaluate targeted treatment. Many drug-addicted women responded to these tentative, if inadequate, overtures toward drug treatment.

In spite of these efforts, the percentage of female drug abusers rose again during the "crack" epidemic of the mid-1980s. The association of drugs and sexuality produced a bitter harvest: HIV-associated disease was spread through needle sharing, engaging in unprotected sex while using drugs, and trading sex for drugs. HIV-infected women gave birth to HIV-infected babies, and by the early 1990s, this mode of transmission began to account for the overwhelming majority of pediatric AIDS cases.

Much of the initial effort to help drug-addicted women focused on the specific issue of drug use during pregnancy. Although it was generally agreed that the problem was increasing, there was no agreement on its true extent. In the late 1980s, despite a variety of studies that produced substantially lower estimates of the number of drug-exposed infants, the press chose to sensationalize the issue by dwelling on the study that claimed the highest number. Thus, although national estimates of the number of drug-exposed infants born in 1988 ranged from a low of about 13,000 to a high of about 100,000 (Dicker and Leighton 1991), press reports consistently quoted the less representative but higher figure of about 375,000 infants (Chasnoff 1989).

Not only was the number of drug-exposed infants increasing, but such exposure, it was claimed, caused permanent, irreparable harm. The media invented the label "crack babies," and with little medical evidence, characterized these infants as undergrown, brain damaged, and congenitally stigmatized,[2] who as children would be unlovable, unadoptable, and unteachable.[3] They were the "innocent victims" of selfish and uncaring women who had lost their maternal instincts under the influence of drugs.[4] Other news stories branded babies exposed to "crack" as "genetic inferiors," "troubled," "tormented," and unable to cope with kindergarten.[5] These reports, coupled with society's stated (but often unactualized) concern for children, contributed to a groundswell of anger against "crack"-using mothers.[6]

Over the last decade, given the broad options of legalizing drugs, expanding the role of child protective agencies, and increasing the number of gender-specific treatment programs, society has instead responded by prosecuting women for substance use during pregnancy. Despite condemnation from medical, public health, and legal organizations, by September 1994 over two hundred women in twenty-four states had been prosecuted for drug-related behavior during pregnancy. Ironically, throughout the 1980s most of these women had been caught "between a rock and a hard place" (Kandall and Chavkin 1990). Sexually and physically abused as children, they grew up in environments incompatible with learning to be an adequate parent. They desperately and often unsuccessfully sought treatment, yet, having revealed their drug-taking histories to health professionals, they found themselves facing prosecution (Chavkin et al. 1993b). During this period, less than 1 percent of federal antidrug funding was directed at treatment for addicted women, and even smaller amounts were earmarked for drug treatment during pregnancy.

The inability of contemporary society to deal with addiction in women in effective and comprehensive ways recapitulates the failures of the past. Historical information on women and drug use in the United States is far less accessible than comparable information on men. Precise statistical data on female addicts for the last half of the nineteenth century is lacking, and much of the available information is buried in physicians' anecdotes and pharmacy records. A few early surveys provide limited, if sometimes contradictory, information on this population. Given the primitive epidemiology of the time, the easy accessibility of unregulated "patent" medicines, and the fact that women's opiate addiction was often unknown to their families, or if known, quietly tolerated, this scarcity is not surprising.[7]

This book will trace women's use of opiates (opium and its derivatives), cocaine, marijuana, prescription drugs, and psychedelics in the United States over the past century and a half. Although addiction to cigarettes and alcohol has caused much more disease in women and presents an enormous public health challenge to our society, a discussion of these substances is beyond the scope of this book. Those wishing to explore the subject of women and alcoholism might consult Vandor's (1991) *Alcohol and Drugs Are Women's Issues* and Sandmaier's (1980) *The Invisible Alcoholics: Women and Alcohol Abuse in America*. The latter, based on fifty interviews with women of varied age, occupation, sexual orientation, and social, racial, and ethnic backgrounds, provides telling analogies to women's use of other substances: high prevalence rates (about one-third of the estimated ten million alcoholics in the mid-1970s were women, and in 1977 Alcoholics Anonymous reported that one-third of their new members were women); wide representation of societal types; large-scale concealment of alcohol consumption; and the relation between drinking and self-medication. As Sandmaier notes,

> Not all women suffer drinking problems, but the acute frustration and self-negation that alcohol can temporarily blunt is not the exclusive property of women who drink. In a culture that cuts off women from many of their own possibilities before they barely have had a chance to sense them, that pain belongs to all women. Outlets for coping may vary widely, and may be more or less addictive, more or less self-destructive. But at some level, all women know what it is to lack access to their own power, to live with a piece of themselves.

A number of major themes recur throughout the following chapters. The central one is that in a society where drugs have been available from early times, women have always made up a significant portion, and at times a majority, of America's drug users and addicts. Popular stereotypes notwithstanding, addicted women have come from a variety of racial, geographic, and socioeconomic backgrounds, and these factors have affected individual patterns of drug use. If these women share any common bond, it is that their addiction has not yielded to treatment. Despite their best intentions, guilt and shame, both self-imposed and societal, have pushed them to the margins of society.

A second theme is the inappropriate and often excessive medication of women by physicians and pharmacists, which, along with women's own self-medication, has been a significant component of the female addiction problem. Voltaire once said that "doctors pour drugs, of which they know little, for diseases, of which they know less, into patients—of whom they know nothing." Throughout recent history, women have been thought to need "special protection" and regarded as less able to bear pain and psychic discomfort, whether because of "women's diseases" and "neurasthenia," as in the Victorian era, or the modern-day stresses of running a busy household, competing in a male-dominated workforce, or attempting to conform to society's slender, youthful ideal. The fact that physicians, physicians' wives, and nurses have been disproportionately afflicted by addiction, and are thus less likely to view it as a "problem," has resulted in the underestimation of its gravity. In addition, the number of female physicians, who might be expected to be more sensitive to women's needs and life stresses, has increased only in recent years.

A third theme is the unique role of women as childbearers, child rearers, and child medicators. Throughout the nineteenth century, concerned voices called attention to the dangers of the opiate-laden homeopathic and allopathic (or "conventional") medications[8] mothers and nurses gave to children at home. Until such drugs were regulated in the early years of this century, women were held increasingly responsible for their inappropriate administration. (This theme resurfaces with new virulence in the prosecution of women for drug use during pregnancy in the 1980s.)

A fourth theme is the link between female sexuality and drug use. As I have noted, the association is an ancient one. Within the context of the past century and a half, it has pervaded the issues of prostitution, the perceived or proclaimed sexual threats to women from minorities, the glamorization of drug-associated sex, the connection between psychedelic drug use and "free love," and the contemporary drug-using mother's "triple curse": minority status, HIV-positive diagnosis, and children who are "drug babies."

A fifth theme is that, although concern about women's drug use has been raised, and to some degree acknowledged, for over a century, the specific issue of helping drug-addicted women was not directly confronted until the early 1970s. Before the Second World War, much of the attention focused on women and drugs came from the less-than-objective press and from the movie industry, which, by sensationalizing the threat posed to women by socially marginalized groups such as Chinese immigrants, Southern black males, and Mexican migrant workers, both mirrored and shaped society's attempts to control these "socially deviant" groups. While it is true that some women were passive beneficiaries of such drug treatment efforts as sanitariums, drug clinics, and methadone maintenance programs, not until the 1970s, following the emergence of the Women's Movement and various self-help initiatives, did addicted women finally begin to receive attention in their own right. Even then, drug-using women, especially those belonging to racial and ethnic minorities, faced hostility, prejudicial reporting to legal and child protection authorities, and criminal prosecution for drug-related conduct during pregnancy. The story of women and drugs in the United States is an ongoing one and there is, unfortunately, no end in sight.

two

THE DRUG PROBLEM

The geographic landscape of the United States has changed dramatically over the last century and a half, but the landscape of drug addiction has altered very little. Today, as in the past, drugs with the potential for abuse are available in wide variety, drug use and drug addiction occur at all levels of society, and the illegal status of many drugs, which leads to trafficking and clandestine use, frustrates attempts to determine the actual number of drug addicts. Physicians faced a similar situation in the mid-nineteenth century, when the use of drugs, and in particular, opiates, first came to be seen as a cause for concern. In their classic work *The Opium Problem,* C. E. Terry and Mildred Pellens (1928) acknowledged that opiate use was a "major medico-social problem," but they also admitted that "no one is possessed of an accurate knowledge as to the exact number of individuals regularly using opium in this country today" and that "under present conditions it is impossible to obtain such a figure" (p. 1).

Available figures on opiate imports provided one means of estimating the use of these drugs in America. Although opium had been grown in Virginia, Tennessee, South Carolina, and Georgia during the Civil War (Culbreth 1903), and was subsequently cultivated in Vermont, New Hampshire, Connecticut, Florida, Louisiana, California, and Arizona (Oliver 1872), the failure to convert this cultivation into an economically feasible enterprise insured that the national opium supply would continue to be imported, primarily from the Orient and

Turkey, as it had in the past. The historian David Courtwright (1982) has pointed out, however, that importation figures would almost certainly have been underestimates, since the imposition of high tariffs on "smoking opium" from the 1840s on led to smuggling on a "massive scale," which increased still further following the ban on imports of smoking opium in 1909 and the passage of the Harrison Anti-Narcotic Act in 1914. Using importation data from the U.S. Department of Commerce, Lawrence Kolb and A. G. Du Mez (1924) reported that annual imports of opium for consumption, excluding opium alkaloids, rose steadily, from over 131,481 pounds in the 1860s to over 628,177 pounds during the decade from 1900 to 1909. During that same fifty-year period, the importation of opium for smoking increased sevenfold, from 21,176 pounds to 148,168 pounds. Assuming an average daily consumption of these drugs, Kolb and Du Mez estimated that, between 1860 and 1909, the number of opium smokers in America rose from almost 8,500 to almost 60,000, and the total number of opiate addicts by a factor of 4.4, from just over 44,000 to over 195,000. These increases exceeded the growth in the U.S. population, which increased over the same period by a factor of 2.4, from about thirty-four million to eighty-three million.

Anecdotal reports appeared to confirm the fact that opiate use was rapidly increasing. In 1867 Fitzhugh Ludlow, a self-confessed hasheesh eater, wrote in *Harper's Magazine* that "the habit is gaining fearful ground . . . All our classes from the highest to the lowest are yearly increasing their consumption of the drug" (cited in Day 1868: 283). The same concern was expressed by Horace Day in *The Opium Habit*: "The number of confirmed opium-eaters in the United States is large, not less, judging from the testimony of druggists in all parts of the country as well as from other sources, than eighty to a hundred thousand" (1868: 6–7). In 1872 F. E. Oliver wrote in the annual report of the State Board of Health that the "opium habit" was prevalent in many parts of Massachusetts. In a survey of "eighteen prominent apothecaries of New York City," supplemented by anecdotal evidence from Portland, Maine, New Jersey, Indiana, Boston, St. Louis, and the Mississippi Valley, Alonzo Calkins concluded that "opium-mania, far from being restricted within the purlieus of our cities and rural centres, is fast pervading the country-populations" (1871: 40). Another commentator concluded that the opium habit had made "extraordinary headway" and that opium eaters were reportedly "counted by the thousands" (Nolan 1881) and totaled perhaps a quarter of a million people.

The first known epidemiological survey of opiate use was conducted by Orville Marshall, in Michigan, in 1877. Although this survey suffered from serious methodological flaws—Marshall, for example, included information gathered from physicians but not pharmacists—it identified 1,313 opium eaters, a figure that Marshall boldly extrapolated to 7,763 statewide. In an even more tenuous extrapolation, based on population figures from 1874, Terry and Pellens (1928) estimated that there were slightly over 250,000 opiate addicts living in the United States at that time. Marshall, however, assumed that about one-fifth of imported opium met medicinal needs and, using average consumption figures, he reasoned that there were 93,654 nonmedicinal opium users nationwide, a figure that more closely approximated the estimate of 82,696 by an "able writer" in the *New York Times*.

Other small, limited surveys offered other estimates, but these shed little further light on the true extent of the opiate problem in America. In his 1880 survey of fifty Chicago pharmacists, Dr. Charles Warrington Earle, a physician at the Washington Home for the care of opium addicts, identified 235 opium users in Chicago. Two years later, a "careful statistician report[ed] more than a quarter of a million confirmed opium inebriates in the United States" (Winterburn 1882: 509). J. M. Hull's Iowa survey, based on 123 replies from pharmacists, identified 235 opium users, from which he extrapolated a statewide figure of about six thousand. Accounting for the likelihood of underreporting, Hull concluded: "I feel safe in saying there are in this State over ten thousand people who are constantly under the influence of an opiate" (1885: 540).

Estimates of opiate use varied even within a single geographic area, such as New England. A broad-based 1888 survey of 600 druggists in 190 Massachusetts cities and towns, and 260 physicians in 100 cities and towns, revealed that opium use was extensive, but neither the physicians nor the druggists felt that it was increasing (Hartwell 1889). In Vermont, however, a physician noted that "the habit is growing from year to year" (Shipman 1890: 72). A report in 1900, based on a polling of Vermont druggists and general stores, estimated that 3,300,000 doses of opium were sold every month, enough to supply "one and one-half doses of opium to every man and woman in the State of Vermont above the age of 21 years, every day of the year" (Grinnell 1905).

Even given the lack of sound epidemiology, some estimates of the amount of opiate addiction appear inflated. A New York physician, George Wheelock Grover, proclaimed in 1894, without providing any evidence, that two million lives were "bound in the steel chains of the drug bondage" (p. 9). More reputable national organizations exhibited similar credibility problems. A committee of the American Pharmaceutical Association, after conducting a survey of pharmacists and physicians, reported in 1902 that there were at least two hundred thousand drug users—not restricted to opium—in the United States (Hynson 1902). But when the same committee conducted a more extensive survey the next year, it reported that "the habitual use of opium in its various forms is increasing," and claimed that there were over a million opium smokers alone (Eberle and Gordon 1903).

Heroin, a synthetic derivative of morphine, which had been developed in London in 1874 but was first marketed by the Bayer Company in Germany in 1898, never approached the wide nonspecific medicinal applications of opium and morphine. Its use did not contribute significantly to addiction figures prior to the 1920s (Courtwright 1982), nor were women heavily represented among heroin users during this period. A Board of Health report by C. E. Terry of Jacksonville, Florida, in 1913 found that 54.5 percent of the heroin addicts registered in the previous year were women; a year later the figure was only 32 percent, which was more consistent with reports from other areas. In contrast, studies of hospitalized addicts found that in Cleveland (Drysdale 1915) 80 percent, and in Brooklyn (Leahy 1915) 95 percent, of the heroin users were men.

These published estimates were based on anecdote, personal experience, and small, methodologically flawed surveys, which assayed highly selected and truncated samples. It is probably safe to assume, however, that the amount of opiate use rose from the middle to the end of the nineteenth century, and possibly into the early twentieth, and that in the mid-1880s there were between 150,000 and 200,000 chronic opium users in the United States. This number is consistent with the more conservative estimate of Terry and Pellens (1928), who used Hull's lower figures to calculate a nationwide estimate of 182,215 chronic opium users for the year 1884. Courtwright (1982) agrees that the number of opiate addicts increased from the 1840s to the end of the century and then began to decline, never exceeding approximately 313,000 between 1900 and 1914. Nonetheless, lacking a national survey or national registry, it is impossible to do more than estimate the extent of opiate use and addiction during these years.

Women and Opiates

For much of the twentieth century addiction has been known as a "man's disease," yet the majority of morphine and opium addicts in the nineteenth century were women. This fact certainly did not go unnoticed at the time. A. T. Schertzer (1870), a Baltimore physician, in warning his medical colleagues that "this dangerous habit is easily acquired," cited one case of a twenty-eight-year-old woman who had reportedly consumed 5,840 ounces of laudanum over a two-year period. F. E. Oliver's 1871 survey in Massachusetts cited a response from one physician that "the use of opium has slightly increased, mostly among females" and from another that "the use of opium has greatly increased, especially among women." Dr. J. B. Mattison, who wrote and lectured extensively about addiction from his vantage point as superintendent of the Brooklyn Home for Habitués, remarked of laudanum addiction: "How many women are to-day sitting in a similar shadow is beyond our knowing; but it is known that they swell largely the ranks of opium habitués . . . My personal experience is entirely confirmatory of this statement" (1879: 332). In 1894, Dr. Joseph Pierce noted: "We have an army of women in America dying from the opium habit—larger than our standing army. The profession is wholly responsible for the loose and indiscriminate use of the drug" (p. 631). By that time, opiate addiction had already become transgenerational. Charles W. Earle (1880) reported on one family in which both the sixty-five-year-old mother and her thirty-year-old daughter were addicted to gum opium. At the turn of the century, medical textbooks by James M. Anders (1899) and James French (1903) both noted the fact that women were more commonly victims of morphinism than men.

Quantitative data on the extent of women's opiate use in the nineteenth century was limited and, if available, poorly documented. But contemporary surveys consistently indicated that women comprised the majority of opium addicts. In Orville Marshall's 1878 Michigan study, 56 percent of the 630 opium users and 66 percent of the 683 morphine users were women. The same study also revealed that women constituted the majority of addicts in eighty-eight of the ninety-six individual towns in Michigan reporting statistics on addiction. Charles W. Earle (1880) found that 72 percent of the 235 opium eaters he identified in Chicago were women. J. M. Hull's 1885 survey in Iowa revealed that 63 percent of the identified opiate users were women but, he added, "not a prostitute among them" (p. 540). Another commentator estimated that 80 percent of the opium eaters in Albany, New York, were women (Nolan 1881). If the approximate number of opiate addicts in the United States in the late nineteenth century reached a total of 150,000 to 200,000, and reports consistently indicate that between two-thirds and three-quarters of them were women, it is likely that more than 100,000 women were involved in the chronic use of opiates during that time.

One difficulty in establishing accurate numbers is the secrecy with which many women treated their addiction. A case report in 1833 noted about one female addict: "No one had ever suspected this lady of using opium or any other stimulus, for she had *never*, in any one instance, been in the least degree *overexcited* by it. She had never taken more than she found necessary to enable her to attend properly to her family and friends. Her husband even knew it not" ("Opium eating" 1833). According to Earle (1880), female opium eaters "have done this for years without imparting their secret to their nearest friends . . . The lady I referred to as being under treatment for morphia and chloroform, took the first-named drug for four years before her husband was aware of it" (cited in Morgan 1974: 59). D. W. Nolan (1881) pointed out that since "no person detests the vice or despises its victim more than does the opium-eater himself," the addict "zealously guards his secret" (p. 828). J. B. Mattison (1898) observed that women often concealed their drug habit "due to the desire . . . to protect [themselves] from unkind and unjust judgment" (p. 202). A Baltimore physician noted that a woman's drug use was "not always to be detected . . . by the user's most intimate friends or relations" (Howard 1904: 132), but that "intuition and mental notes of experience" were to be employed to tear female morphinists from the "tentacles of this octopus" (p. 113).

Because of the nature of their clientele, many physicians considered addiction more common among the upper classes. Alonzo Calkins

(1871) wrote that "in the division of sex the women have the majority" (p. 164), and mentioned one physician's findings that "the aggregate of instances among women in high place is incredibly large" (p. 165). Calkins described the typical addict as "the lady of haut-ton, idly lolling upon her velvety fauteuil and vainly trying to cheat the lagging hours that intervene ere the 'clockwork tintinnabulum' shall sound the hour for opera or whist, the quasi-lady of the demi-monde as well" (p. 163). A pharmacist in Atlanta also recorded that, of the large number of his customers who were addicts, there were "a great many more ladies" ("The Opium Habit" 1878: 40). As further evidence of increasing use, an Albany druggist reported that to supply his customers, 80 percent of whom were women, "where twenty-five years ago he made it [laudanum] by the gallon, he now prepares it by the barrel." This he reported reluctantly, however, since "inclination and gallantry" would prompt a denial of the fact of women's addictions (Nolan 1881: 835). A physician in Trinity, Alabama, echoed his colleagues: "the weaker sex are slightly in the majority, and of these it [opiate use] is confined mostly to the higher and middle class" (Duncan 1885).

Other writers were well aware, however, that addiction among women was not confined only to the upper classes. In *Harper's Magazine* Fitzhugh Ludlow remarked on the increase in drug use among "our weary sewing-women and . . . our disappointed wives" (Day 1868: 283). Horace Day identified "women obliged by their necessities to work beyond their strength" as among the most common users of opiates (p. 7). William Pepper's 1886 textbook, *A System of Practical Medicine,* warned, "To the overworked and underfed mill-operator it [opium addiction] is a snare more tempting than alcohol, and less expensive" (Wilson 1886: 649).

Isolated and lonely rural women resorted to opium, just as their male counterparts turned to alcohol. Rural farming families, lacking easy access to physicians, often relied on mail-order catalogs and popular magazines to procure home remedies, many of which contained opiates, for pain relief. F. E. Oliver's 1872 report found that many Massachusetts women took to opium because they were "doomed, often, to a life of disappointment . . . and in the smaller and more remote towns, not unfrequently, to utter seclusion, deprived of all wholesome social diversion . . . opium being discreetly selected as the safest and most agreeable remedy" (p. 168). In many cases, because these remedies were inadequately labeled, women were probably maintaining themselves on opiates, unaware of their own addiction.

Prostitutes constituted a particular subgroup among lower-class, opium-using women. Alonzo Calkins noted that New York prostitutes "are reliant upon laudanum" and that "two-thirds of the class become habituated, eventually to opium in some form." Corroborating evidence of opium use among the "courtesans of Savannah" (1871: 165) and the prostitutes of Massachusetts (Oliver 1872) appeared in the medical literature. In his Michigan survey of 1878, Orville Marshall reported that "the prostitute, broken in health and exhausted by disease and debauchery, is a willing victim to a new vice [opium eating]" (cited in O'Donnell and Ball 1966: 52). Charles W. Earle (1880) noted that while most of the women in his Chicago survey of opiate users were housewives, one-third were prostitutes. H. S. Duncan (1885), an Alabama physician, also noted that opium use was common in "women of idleness and prostitution" (p. 247). Yet, as J. M. Hull (1885) observed, "we may count out the prostitutes so much given to this vice, and still find females far ahead so far as numbers are concerned" (p. 537).

Opium use was common among the Chinese women brought to California as prostitutes during the midcentury Gold Rush. Significant quantities of opium entered the country when large numbers of Chinese laborers immigrated to dig for gold or work on the railroads, which would eventually extend from coast to coast. Opium dens and prostitution flourished in such a setting, where men outnumbered women by thirteen to one in 1870 and by twenty-one to one a decade later (Helmer 1975: 23). Prostitutes relied on opium to combat fatigue, stress, boredom, physical ailments, and homesickness. The owners of opium dens frequently owned brothels and often lent money to the prostitutes to initiate and maintain their drug habit. For some of these women, opium offered a final escape: they committed suicide by swallowing raw opium (Hirata 1979: 232).

Women's drug use also fed into nativist fears about the "white slave trade," which reportedly drugged and kidnapped women into a life of prostitution. Such forced prostitution was allegedly common, yet William Sanger revived an old theme when he noted in 1858 that 25 percent of his sample of two thousand prostitutes had entered the business "by inclination." According to Sanger's reasoning, drugs and alcohol must have produced such a high level of sexual arousal in these women that they resorted to sexual overactivity. His conclusion reflects a general belief that women's drug use was dangerous because addiction led women to behave in a sexually promiscuous manner quite unacceptable in nineteenth-century America.

Women of high social standing frequented opium dens for recreational purposes. In her 1879 story "Opium Dream," Santa Louise Anderson recorded a visit to an opium den in San Francisco's Chinatown. Anderson made it clear that she was "at no loss in the preparation" of the opium, since she had visited the den often (Palmer and Horowitz 1982: 84). In his book *Shadows Lifted* (1894), George Wheelock Grover wrote of the opium dens: "Here the cultured woman of society, the opium smoker *par excellence,* whose system is as saturated as his pipe, the Chinaman, the laborer, and 'longshoreman, the young man in society, all herd in nerveless companionship together" (p. 98). Although the number of such women who visited opium dens was never as large as the sensationalistic press liked to report, popular lithographs and news stories of the time depicted the practice, and early silent films portrayed upper-class women as opium eaters in these settings.

The opium-induced dreams of English writers such as Thomas De Quincey, Samuel Taylor Coleridge, and Robert Southey inspired some women to try opium recreationally. Literary "habitués," who wrote of the pleasant stimulation of opiates, were reportedly responsible for initiating many new addicts: "Men and women who had never heard of such a thing, stimulated by curiosity, their minds filled with the vivid pictures of a state of dreamy bliss, a feeling of full content with the world and all about, tried the experiment, gradually wound themselves in the silken meshes of the fascinating net" (Kane 1881: 22). Jane Addams, later a renowned social reformer and Nobel Peace Prize winner, tried to recapture De Quincey's drug-induced reveries as a seventeen-year-old seminary student by drugging herself with opium (Palmer and Horowitz 1982).

Despite the admonitions of the Woman's Christian Temperance Union, founded in 1874, hypodermic syringes for a time replaced hip flasks and decanters as respectable social paraphernalia. The Temperance Movement, which flourished from the mid-nineteenth century into the 1920s, might in fact be said to have played a role in creating female addicts, in that it kept some addicted women from using alcohol as a possible substitute for narcotics. As one upstate New York physician noted, "some perhaps use it in preference to alcohol because of its greater secrecy [sic] and less degrading effects" (Hamlin 1882: 427). Upper-class "society" women found it more socially acceptable to use narcotics than to indulge in alcohol to relieve emotional stress. The more acceptable use of opiates afforded Victorian women of higher status a temporarily blissful refuge from the demands of modern society.

Opiate Consumption and Medications

Whatever the extent of nonmedicinal recreational use, the major reason for the increase in opiate consumption and addiction during the nineteenth century was the overprescribing and dispensing of legal opiates by physicians and pharmacists. Possessing a severely limited therapeutic armamentarium, medical practitioners used opiates and narcotics,[1] in allopathic medicines and homeopathic remedies, to control an extraordinarily wide range of somatic complaints (Pickard and Buley 1946). Opium, in its many applications, was ranked in 1834 as the most widely used drug in the materia medica (Wood and Bache 1834). It was employed by physicians and pharmacists during the mid to late nineteenth century in preparations such as laudanum (a solution of opium dissolved in alcohol or water) and paregoric (camphorated tincture of opium) as well as in gum and powdered form; it could also be administered rectally. Morphine, an opium derivative first isolated in 1817, could be taken orally in powder, tablet, or liquid form, as well as rectally. In addition, hypodermic syringes, introduced into this country from Great Britain in 1856, rendered the administration of morphine by injection feasible (Kane 1881).

Many historians have concluded that the Civil War played a crucial role in the spread of opiate use in America. During the war, approximately ten million opium pills and nearly three million ounces of opium powders and tinctures were distributed to Union forces alone to combat diarrheal diseases and relieve the pain of battlefield wounds (Courtwright 1978). In *The Opium Habit*, Horace Day (1868) declared that the "maimed and shattered survivors from a hundred battle-fields, diseased and disabled soldiers released from hostile prisons" were most susceptible to opiate addiction (p. 7). In Massachusetts, F. E. Oliver (1872) noted opium smoking "among soldiers retired from the army." Charles W. Earle (1880) acknowledged that "wounds received during the war, painful stumps after amputation, injuries to nerves, etc." were contributing to the growing number of addicts in Chicago. Although their exact numbers are not known, sick and wounded Civil War veterans swelled the ranks of America's addicts.

Opiates were used to treat an almost limitless list of illnesses:[2] painful injuries; intestinal illnesses such as cholera, lead colic, food poisoning, parasites, dysentery, stomachache, and gallstones; headaches; musculoskeletal problems such as rheumatism, neuralgia, and nerve injuries; respiratory conditions such as pneumonia, asthma, bronchitis, influenza, and consumption; cardiac conditions such as palpitations, neuralgia of the heart, and dropsy (generalized swelling); typhus, typhoid, and yellow fever; infections such as syphilis, eye inflammations, inflammation of the kidneys and bladder, ulcerated throat, rabies, gangrene, and lockjaw; mental disorders such as delirium tremens and insanity; and miscellaneous conditions such as bleeding, wax in the ear, earache, hemorrhoids, suppression of urine, and impotence. J. Milner Fothergill (1877) called opium "our favorite remedy and our most trusted analgesic" (p. 287). Teaching textbooks such as *A System of Medicine* by J. Russell Reynolds (1876) and *Lectures on the Principles and Practice of Medicine* by Nathan S. Davis (1884), both widely used in medical schools by 1891, validated many of these applications.

In many cases, physicians' use of opiates was logical and medically appropriate. Opiates have strong analgesic (pain-controlling) and intestinal antispasmodic properties, which explains their efficacy in treating painful conditions as well as common nineteenth-century illnesses, such as cholera and dysentery, marked by severe diarrhea. Although he railed against the overuse of medications, the Boston physician and writer Oliver Wendell Holmes (1888) exempted opium, which, he said, "the Creator himself seems to prescribe." D. W. Cathell (1905) also cautioned his medical colleagues: "Above all else, carry a supply of morphia granules or tablets, and give the proper number of them in an ounce or two of hot water as soon as you reach either of the thousand cases in which great pain is a symptom" (p. 297).

In many other cases, however, such as the treatment of asthma, heart palpitations, wax in the ear, and minor musculoskeletal problems, the use of opiates was inappropriate, but physicians relied on the drug in the absence of specific remedies because it was all they had at hand to make the patient feel better. Virgil G. Eaton (1888), who reported on the opium habit in *Popular Science Monthly*, pointed out that opiates were being used in "every ailment which flesh is heir to." S. Weir Mitchell (1888), a physician widely known for his rest cures, and himself an opium user, cautioned that the use of opiates to control pain seemed to be considered part of our "right to escape pain, however brief." A lay reformer, Charles B. Towns (1912), attributed opiate use to the human wish to "ease pain and stimulate ebbing vitality."

Whether appropriate or not, treatment with opiates often continued too long. Orville Marshall claimed that, "undoubtedly in many instances physicians are directly responsible for the habit" (O'Donnell and Ball 1966: 52). Blaming the physicians who were "criminally careless in placing the instrument [syringe] in the hands of the patient or her friends," H. H. Kane (1881) believed that doctors should have been well aware of the dangers of opiates and that lack of knowledge rendered them "culpably ignorant, and certainly deserving of punishment" (p. 219). He also indicted druggists "who, in many cases, sell the drug without a physician's prescription, and without any reasonable excuse on the part of the patient, in direct violation of the law" and singled out the "charlatans, . . . utterly without conscience," who used deceitful advertisements and lies to snare hapless victims in the web of addiction (pp. 219–220).

Dr. Leslie E. Keeley, a well-known but controversial nineteenth-century entrepreneur who established a series of drug treatment sanitariums, claimed that "hundreds have been brought to poverty by *frauds* calling themselves 'Doctors' and beguiling the poor wretches with solutions of morphia at fearful prices" (1881: 146). Another writer noted that "the careless manner in which physicians prescribe opiates, and the prevailing custom among druggists of duplicating prescriptions, are prolific sources of the evil" (Nolan 1881: 829). As late as 1913, Charles Douglas, writing in the *New York Medical Journal*, warned that "there are many individuals in the profession who, through carelessness or a failure to appreciate its dangers, are recklessly prescribing this drug, with the result that morphinism is often acquired" (p. 882). Standard medical textbooks advised physicians of the dangers of unnecessarily administering morphine. Pepper (1886),

Osler (1894), and French (1903) all pointed out the great extent to which physicians were responsible for opiate addiction in the United States.

The general population, especially those who did not consult physicians, had ready access to opiates in a multitude of other ways. Many Americans relied on patent medicines, which were available without prescription in pharmacies and through Sears Roebuck and similar mail-order catalogues.[3] The number of brands of nostrums listed in a Boston catalogue increased from less than a hundred in 1804 to between five and six hundred in 1857 (Young 1967: 19). Americans consumed opiates in a vast array of patent medicines with names like Dover's Powder, Jayne's Expectorant, Jackson's Pectoral Syrup, Allen's Lung Balsam, Shilo's Consumptive Cure, King's New Discovery, Mrs. Winslow's Soothing Syrup, Edison's Polyform, Boschee's German Syrup, Bateman's Pectoral Drops, and Dewee's Carminative.[4] They could purchase syringes and needles through the mail; in 1897 the Sears Roebuck catalog offered a standard syringe kit for $1.50 and a deluxe model for $2.75.[5]

Opium and morphine were also primary ingredients in home remedy liniments such as St. Jacob's Oil, Good Samaritan Liniment, and Seeley's Pile Ointment (Faulkner and Carmichael 1892). Although labels rarely listed the concentrations of ingredients, it is likely that the homeopathic principles espoused by the German physician Samuel Hahnemann—diluting ingredients by the thousandfold—were seldom followed, and that these remedies contained high concentrations of opiatelike compounds.

R. V. Pierce, a retired U.S. congressman who established the Invalids' Hotel and Surgical Institute in Buffalo, New York, and ran an ever-expanding homeopathic business, promoted his own remedies in his book, *The People's Common Sense Medical Adviser in Plain English* (1895).[6] A variety of ailments—rheumatism, skin diseases, nasal catarrh, bronchitis, diarrhea, gallstones, dyspepsia, hepatitis, constipation, and piles (hemorrhoids)—would yield, he claimed, to his preparations. Pierce denied that his remedies, "in most instances," contained "a single ingredient which enters into the composition" of opiate-containing remedies, yet *The Cottage Physician* listed opium as an ingredient in Pierce's Golden Medical Discovery and Pierce's Favorite Prescription (Faulkner and Carmichael 1892: 535). According to the progressive reformer Samuel Hopkins Adams, who published a series of articles on the "nostrum evil and quacks" in *Collier's Weekly,* "gullible Americans will spend this year some seventy-five millions of dollars in the purchase of patent medicines" containing, among other things, "an appalling amount of opiates and narcotics." Pierce's Golden Medical Discovery Adams declared "an unqualified fraud" (1907: 51).

The enormous and profitable industry supplying these patent medicines remained completely unregulated until the passage of the Pure Food and Drug Act of 1906. This legislation was the first federal attempt to regulate patent and proprietary medicines by requiring that product labels list dangerous and addictive ingredients. It passed over the vigorous objections of special interest groups, which for years had proved remarkably effective in preventing legislation requiring commercial preparations to list potentially harmful compounds (Young 1961).

Women and Medications

The predominance of women among the addicted population is largely the result of Victorian medical practice. Like men, women were treated for nonspecific painful conditions and diarrheal disease, but they were considered less capable of managing their condition and more in need of medication—specifically opiates. In *Our Family Doctor,* Dr. Henry S. Taylor advised that of women, "there is more of delicacy and feebleness" (1869: 276). S. Weir Mitchell thought it necessary to medicate women more than men, since "their lives are likely, nay, certain, to bring them a variety of physical discomforts, and perhaps pain in its gravest forms" (1888: 83). And R. V. Pierce opined in his *Medical Adviser:*

> Physically, and mentally, woman is man modified, perfected—the last and crowning handiwork of God. When, therefore, this structure so wonderfully endowed, so exquisitely wrought, and performing the most delicate and sacred functions which God has ever entrusted to a created being, is disturbed by disease, when the nicely-adjusted balance of her complex nature deviates from its true and intended poise, the most efficient aid should be extended, in order that the normal equilibrium may be regained, her health restored, and her divine mission, on which human welfare so largely depends, be fulfilled. Its importance should

elicit . . . the most scientific administration of the choicest, rarest, and purest medicinal elements in the whole range of nature. (1895: 684)

In a widely read professional text, D. W. Cathell urged his medical colleagues to be especially attentive to the complaints of "woman, noble woman! as true to duty as Diana, with voice soft, gentle, and kind, and the look of heaven in her face" (1905: 73).

The most common use of opiates to alleviate women's organic troubles, however, was in the treatment of "female complaints." Proprietary concoctions and opiate-containing prescription drugs were considered "women's friends" in the relief of gynecological problems. At least one female physician, the avid hydrotherapist and pharmacological nihilist Mrs. R. B. Gleason (1871), advised the use of laudanum to treat dysmenorrhea, irregular uterine contractions during childbirth, the after-pains of childbirth, pelvic pain after miscarriage, and hemorrhoids.

In his 1878 Michigan survey Orville Marshall noted that "the most frequent cause of the opium-habit in females is the taking of opiates to relieve painful menstruation and diseases of the female organs of generation. The frequency of these diseases in part accounts for the excess of female opium-eaters over males" (O'Donnell and Ball 1966: 52). Dr. Horton Howard pronounced in *Domestic Medicine* that "no organ of the female system is perhaps so liable to become diseased, or to fail to perform its healthy functions, as the uterus" (1879: 9). On the same subject, J. B. Mattison remarked, in a letter to the editor of the *Medical Bulletin,* that "a large proportion of the deviations from health which induce the use of some form of opiate, are dependent on disorders peculiar to [the female] sex" (1879: 332). J. Milner Fothergill (1877) advised the use of opium to treat abnormal uterine bleeding and "nocturnal excitement." Dr. T. Gaillard Thomas, the august president of the American Gynecological Society, declared that, "for the relief of pain, the treatment is all summed up in one word, and that is *opium.* This divine drug overshadows all other anodynes . . . you can easily educate her to become an *opium-eater,* and nothing short of this should be aimed at by the medical attendant. There is a natural tendency in the human race to take to opium" (1879: 316). Thomas's medical textbook (1880) advised using opium to treat inflammation of the vulva, endometrium, peritoneum, and ovaries as well as for "uterine degeneration," cancer, and abnormal uterine bleeding.

Dr. R. V. Pierce joined this all-male chorus in his *Medical Adviser:* on the basis of his "vast experience" in treating "many thousands of cases annually," he claimed that "every organ of the system is in *intimate* sympathy with the uterus, or womb" (1895: 685). Not surprisingly, Pierce recommended his own Golden Medical Discovery and Favorite Prescription for ulceration of the womb and vaginal discharge, and advised that "use of these blood cleansing and invigorating tonic medicines should be kept up *persistently* for several weeks; for you must not expect a perfect cure too soon in a malady that has become chronic and seated" (p. 720).

In their textbook *The Cottage Physician,* Thomas Faulkner and J. H. Carmichael (1892) recommended morphia for "painful menstruation" and laudanum for sensitivity associated with "falling of the womb" and for gonorrhea. A bedtime pill "composed of one grain of opium and two grains of sugar of lead" would induce abortion or miscarriage. William K. David's handbook, *Secrets of Wise Men, Chemists and Great Physicians* (1896), listed tincture of opium as the first ingredient in the remedy for "difficult menstruation" and a morphine salt as the first ingredient in the remedy for gonorrhea. In his textbook, *Psychiatry,* Stewart Paton remarked that "not a few patients gradually become habituated to the vice from the fact that the drug is too often prescribed for long periods of time . . . in women for dysmenorrhoea" (painful menstruation) (1905: 317). As late as 1913, C. C. Wholey could observe in the *Pennsylvania Medical Journal* that "women suffering from dysmenorrhea . . . pass on the word that paregoric, laudanum, etc., is a specific" (p. 724).

In *A Physician's Counsels to Woman,* Dr. Walter C. Taylor (1872) reminded women: "When she fails to become a mother, the wife stops short of full womanly development and happiness" (p. 319). Late nineteenth-century physicians clearly recognized the importance of the events surrounding pregnancy to the developing fetus. In *The Cottage Physician,* Faulkner and Carmichael remarked that "to women is entrusted a most sacred charge—the germ of a new being, whose position and usefulness in life will be greatly influenced by her prudence or indiscretion" (1892: 266). Their concern, however, extended less to pharmacology than to vague considerations of psychic health: the authors recommended opium for the diarrhea associated with morning sickness (p. 284). Dr. R. V. Pierce freely recommended Pierce's Favorite Prescription for *all* pregnant women:

It soothes and strengthens the nerves and acts directly on the feminine organism in a way which fits it for the proper and regular performance of all its functions at all times. Taken during gestation it robs childbirth of its dangers to both mother and child, by preparing the system for delivery, thereby shortening labor, lessening pain and abbreviating the period of confinement. The Favorite Prescription also promotes the secretion of an abundance of nourishment for the child, if taken after confinement, besides building up the mother's strength and making her recovery more perfect. (1895: 681–682)

The prescribing practices of physicians and pharmacists, advertisements, the endorsements of public figures, and the testimonials of success published in women's magazines encouraged women to buy and use patent medicines, many of which contained addictive substances (Haller and Haller 1974: 284–285). Pierce's *Medical Adviser* contained page after page of such personal testimonials, along with photographs and addresses, not only about the wonderful care offered at his Institute in Buffalo, but also about the miraculous cures his remedies effected for "falling of the womb," "paralysis and uterine disease," "indigestion, constipation, and uterine disease," "female weakness," "womb disease," "dropsy," "severe flowing," "dyspepsia," "vaginitis," "suppressed menstruation and nervous debility," "terrible pain and fainting spells," "thick neck" (probably goiter), "ovarian disease," and "impoverished blood." Other testimonials were introduced with vivid titles, such as "Just a Mere Skeleton," "At Death's Door," "Mother's Relief," "A Mother's Friend," "Shortens Labor," and "Childbirth Made Easy." Articles in *Ladies' Home Journal* and other popular magazines, however, warned women of the dangers of taking unregulated proprietary medicines: "How the Game of Medical Advice Is Worked" and "How the Private Confidences of Women Are Laughed At" (Starr 1982).

In his comic novel *The Road to Wellville* (1993), T. Coraghessan Boyle has achieved an antic send-up of the goings-on at John Harvey Kellogg's Battle Creek, Michigan, "health sanitarium" in the year 1907. At the end of the novel, having been swindled and abused at the hands of charlatan "health cereal" promoters, Charlie Ossining finds economic salvation—as well as fabulous wealth—with Ossining's Per-To (Perfect Tonic), a product similar to Lydia E. Pinkham's Vegetable Compound—*A Sure Cure for Prolapsis Uteri and All Fe-*

male Weaknesses, a thirty-proof female remedy. In a satiric poke at the entire patent medicine industry, Boyle explains its instant success:

> It had an attractive and eye-appealing label of shiny embossed silver-and-gold paper, it was celery-impregnated, it made active blood, sturdy legs and sound lungs, and it was a specific for pleurisy, heart ailments, diphtheria, the flu, general weakness, men's troubles, women's troubles, and rectal itch. Charlie floated its active ingredients—"Celeriac, Gentian, Black Cohosh, True & False Unicorn Life & Pleurisy Root"—in a forty-percent-alcohol solution ("Added solely as a Solvent and Preservative"). (pp. 469–470)

Neurasthenia

Opiates were also widely prescribed for "neurasthenia," "la névrose," or nervous weakness, a vague disorder most often attributed to the excitement, prosperity, and intellectual challenges of an urbanizing America: civilization seemed to be synonymous with nervousness. H. H. Kane opens his book, *Drugs That Enslave,* with the observation that "a higher degree of civilization, bringing with it increased mental development among all classes, increased cares, duties and shocks, seems to have caused the habitual use of narcotics" (1881: 17).

Neurasthenia encompassed a vast array of symptoms: tenderness of the scalp, tenderness of the spine and of the whole body, vague pains and flying neuralgias, flushing and fidgetiness, tremulous and variable pulse and occasional palpitations, strength giving out or legs giving way, sensitivity to cold or hot water, sensitivity to weather changes, a feeling of profound exhaustion unaccompanied by positive pain, ticklishness, a desire for stimulants and narcotics, insomnia, nervous dyspepsia, partial failure of memory, sexual exhaustion, deficient mental control, changes in the expression of the eyes and countenance, mental depression with general timidity, morbid fears of various kinds, fear of society, "sick headache" and various forms of head pain, pain and heaviness, disturbances of the nerves and organs of special sense, floating specks before the eyes, noises in the ears, localized peripheral numbness and hyperaesthesia, crawling or creeping sensations under the skin, general and local chills and flashes of heat, and local spasms of muscles (Beard 1878; Mortimer 1901).

Neurasthenia was regularly treated with tonics, elixirs, and patent medicines containing alcohol or opiates or both. In 1867, Fitzhugh Ludlow, an opium user, commented on the use of opiates to relieve modern-day anxieties: "The terrible demands made in this country on modern brains by our feverish competitive life, constitute hourly temptations to some form of the sweet, deadly sedative" (Day 1868: 283). H. H. Kane attributed much of the excessive prescribing of narcotics to the fact that "pain, 'nervousness' and hysteria" were occupying physicians' attention, and opiates provided an easy remedy (1881: 18). B. H. Hartwell listed "increased mental and emotional strain" as one of the causes of "the opium evil" (1889: 19–20). Henry G. Cole ascribed the increasing number of "opiate eaters" to the mental strain caused by

> our mechanical inventions, the spread of our commerce . . . our ambition for political honors; and grasping for petty offices for gain; our mad race for speedy wealth, which entails feverish excitements, . . . a growth so rapid, and in some respects so abnormal, that in many directions the mental strain has been too much for the physical system to bear; till finally the overworked body and the overtaxed brain must . . . find rest in the repeated use of opium or morphine. (1885: 6–7)

The American Pharmaceutical Association's Committee on the Acquirement of Drug Habits also blamed the widespread use of opiates on modern social demands and pressures. As late as 1915, an article by L. L. Stanley in the *Journal of the American Institute of Criminal Law and Criminology* linked the opiate problem with "Mania Americana," which caused individuals to rely on narcotics to escape from the rigors of modern life (1915–1916: 586).

Since women were disproportionately affected by these new nervous complaints, they were disproportionately medicated for them, often with unfortunate results. One physician wrote of a patient who allowed "no visit to terminate without entreaties that something may be done to break up this habit to which she has been many years a bound and servile slave. The drug was originally prescribed to her to quiet some slight degree of nervous irritation" ("Opium Eating" 1833: 66–67). Dr. Walter C. Taylor observed that "nervous affections are more apt to attack" women and an "undue stimulus . . . applied to the nervous system" during the formative years would lead to a "nervous system morbidly sensitive" (1872: 278). As George M. Beard, a contemporary authority on neurasthenia, observed in 1871,

"The general law is that the more nervous the organization, the greater the susceptibility to stimulants and narcotics. Woman is more nervous, has a finer organization than man, [and] is accordingly more susceptible to most of the stimulants" (p. 511). A few years later, however, Beard noted that although opium had been extensively used to treat neurasthenia, "now we scarcely think of using it for that purpose in the treatment of the nervous, except when there is severe pain to be relieved" (1878: 7). Others found that opiate use continued. In 1879 Mattison diagnosed a woman who had endured six years of pain and nervous exhaustion as suffering from the "combined action of neurasthenia proper and the opiate tincture" (1879: 332).

In explaining why women "opium eaters" outnumbered men by three to one, Charles W. Earle concluded: "This is undoubtedly due to the fact that women more often than men are afflicted with diseases of a nervous character, in which narcotic remedies are used sometimes for a long period." In Chicago, Earle noted, opiate use was more common in the more "Americanized" immigrant groups, especially "those neurasthenic people who bear pain badly, and demand relief from some source . . . a certain class of ladies . . . [who] constantly demand to be relieved from pain" (Morgan 1974: 54). T. Gaillard Thomas commented that the effects of "excessive development of the nervous system were more especially exerted upon the female sex" (1880: 44). A physician in upstate New York concurred with the general opinion that women were more prone to opium addiction because of their "more nervous organization and tendency to hysterical and chronic diseases" (Hamlin 1882: 427). In his study of the opium habit in Boston, Virgil Eaton remarked on the common use of opium-containing patent medicines. One woman became addicted to an opium-containing "cough balsam," which "quieted her nerves." When the pharmacist ran out of that preparation, he substituted one "containing about the same amount of morphine . . . and from that time on she was a constant morphine-user" (1888: 664–665). S. Weir Mitchell devoted his attention to women with "the petty moral deformities of nervous feminine natures" (1888: 10–11).

In some cases, women's opiate abuse began with the death of loved ones in the Civil War. Opiate addiction was common among the "anguished and hopeless wives and mothers, made so by the slaughter of those who were dearest to them, [who] have found, many of them, temporary relief from their sufferings in opium" (Day 1868: 7). In other cases, women used opiates to "self-tranquilize" in response to domestic stress; one woman reported that she took opium "because her husband was dissipated, and as he made night hideous, she wanted something to give her rest" (Shipman 1890: 75). Charles W. Earle (1880) told the story of another woman, "an octoroon, [who] commenced using it [opium] when 13 years of age. Away from her friends, she became downhearted and homesick, when an elderly lady, herself a morphia-eater, offered the young girl a powder, with the remark that it would cheer her up and cause her to forget her sorrows. This was repeated for several days, the morphia habit was established, which has clung to the woman to this day" (Morgan 1974: 55).

According to H. H. Kane, "opium and morphine are most commonly used . . . in neurasthenic patients," and once a woman has experienced relief from opiates, she "insists upon the further use of the drug, sometimes feigns illness, in order to procure it, finally obtains some herself, and in guilty secrecy drifts rapidly into the habit" (1881: 18). A contributor to Pepper's *System of Practical Medicine* stated: "To women of the higher classes, ennuyée and tormented with neuralgias or the vague pains of hysteria and hypochondriasis, opium brings tranquility and self-forgetfulness" (Wilson 1886: 649). George Wheelock Grover offered his explanation of why women overused opiates in *Shadows Lifted*:

> The mother whose well ordered household, whose bright-eyed family move the admiration of all who come into that pleasant family circle grows careless in her home, unresponsive even to the touch of the baby fingers that once were the plectrum that played upon the strings of her heart as the fingers of the night wind touch those of the Eolian harp. What does all this mean? Nervous prostration. (1894: 90–91)

Dr. R. V. Pierce heartily recommended his Favorite Prescription and his Golden Medical Discovery to those many women who "suffer from nervous prostration, or exhaustion, owing to congestion of the uterus and ovaries, caused by overindulgence; again by overwork, the strain of too many household cares, or too frequent childbirths" (1895: 626–627). Pierce attributed neurasthenia to "the wear, tear and strain of modern life . . . concentrated upon the nervous system" (p. 619). When Harriet Beecher Stowe's daughter, Georgiana May, fell into a loosely characterized "depression," she was treated by a physician who apparently restored her to "her old self," but with disastrous consequences:

> Only gradually it became apparent that there was something false about her brightness, a feverish quality in her liveliness. The doctor had prescribed morphine to lift her from the original depression. It was quite a customary prescription, except that it had not worked quite as it should have with Georgiana. The cure had become its own illness. Georgie burned with a flame that was lighted only by the drug. In its absence, she plummeted into a state from which she could only be rescued by more morphine. (cited in Courtwright 1982b: 164)

There were others who believed that neurasthenia was due not to intellectual challenges but rather to listlessness and boredom. F. E. Oliver (1872) took note of opium use among the socially isolated women in small, remote Massachusetts towns. "A lady doctor," Arabella Kenealy (1899), claimed that boredom, born of modern conveniences, accounted for this nervous affliction in "the girl of today." In *What a Young Woman Ought to Know* Mary Wood-Allen concluded that "much of the neurasthenia . . . now so common in that portion of the female sex who have ample means and leisure to indulge in any luxury agreeable to their taste . . . is due to narcotics" (1905: 232). But "a lady of culture and distinction" described this "leisure" quite differently:

> I am the last woman in the world to make excuses for my acts, but you don't know what morphine means to some of us, modern women without professions, without beliefs. Morphine makes life possible. It adds to truth a dream. What more does religion do? Perhaps I shock you. What I mean is that truth alone is both not enough and too much for us. Each of us must add to it his or her dream, believe me. I have added mine; I make my life possible by taking morphine. I have managed to prevent it from disfiguring my life, though I know other women who botched it horribly. I am really morphine mad, I suppose, but I have enough will left not to go beyond my daily allowance. (Collins and Day 1909: 4–5)

Boyle echoes these themes in *The Road to Wellville*. John Harvey Kellogg has designed exotic cures for the treatment of neurasthenia, a frequent diagnosis: "Some people are just higher keyed than others, too sensitive and thoughtful for their own good, too intellectual, poetical, too urbane and aesthetically minded" (p. 113). Although both men and women are treated at Kellogg's sanitarium, women are in the majority, and "being of feebler constitution and hence less able to bear these terrible shocks, the result runs the gamut from mild hysteria and nervous exhaustion to cancer, marasmus and death. Little wonder that Midulet characterizes our era as 'The Age of Womb Diseases'" (p. 189). One of the main characters finds her way to a "doctor" who practices "womb manipulation," because "this is the seat of the hysterical passions in the female anatomy and the key, many feel, to neurasthenic disorders" (p. 341). D. W. Cathell (1905) roundly condemned this kind of charlatanism and admonished fellow physicians: "God only knows how many young women in our land are at this moment tormented with apparitions of 'womb complaint' which have no existence except in Dr. Spayer's imagination or in Dr. Squinteye's opinion, who, had not the Womb Bugaboo been suggested to their minds, would have lived a lifetime with scarcely a thought about the womb!" (p. 222).

During the Victorian era, physicians and pharmacists prescribed opiate-containing medications frequently and often inappropriately. Self-administration of opiates, widely available in patent medicines, was also common. Women received treatment for a wide range of somatic, especially gynecological complaints, as well as perceived psychic distress. Addiction to opiates touched all social levels—society women identifying with the artistic or intellectual set, rural and working-class women coping with long hours and loneliness, and prostitutes in city streets and opium dens. It is hardly surprising that such a large proportion of America's opiate addicts were women.

Other Drugs

Cocaine

Just as the rapidly escalating use of opiates began to arouse public concern, cocaine was introduced from Europe. American physicians used it in a limited way following an enthusiastic article by Dr. G. Archie Stockwell in an 1877 issue of the *Boston Medical and Surgical Journal,* which extolled the virtues of its stimulant properties. In the *Detroit Therapeutic Gazette,* W. H. Bentley, a Kentucky physician, recommended cocaine for "'wasting diseases,' tardy convalescence from acute maladies, in certain forms of dyspepsia; and . . . in the 'opium habit'" (1880: 253). In 1884, shortly after Dr. Carl

Koller's successes in Austria using cocaine as a topical anesthetic for the eye, Dr. Herman Knapp, a prominent New York ophthalmologist, promoted cocaine as a general topical anesthetic, and within a short time, its medical applications expanded rapidly. Cocaine was hailed as a wonder drug and found wide acceptance as an anesthetic, a physical stimulant (especially for the heart), and a mental stimulant, as a treatment for dyspepsia (gastric upset, such as nausea and vomiting), as a diuretic in conditions such as typhoid fever and kidney disease, and, most notably, in the treatment of hay fever, colds, and sinus conditions.[7]

The therapeutic application of cocaine for a variety of medical conditions did not overlook women. Case reports document, for example, painless eye surgery under topical cocaine anesthesia on a woman who, after a previous unsuccessful surgery, was prepared to undergo general anesthesia with ether (Walker 1884). Another reported successful nasal surgery on an "intractable" patient (Jarvis 1884). In the less than fully objective *Therapeutic Gazette,* a publication of the Parke-Davis Pharmaceutical Company, Laurence Turnbull described the successful use of cocaine in four women with various ear, nose, and throat problems, such as deafness, congestion, cough, and hoarseness.

Medical practitioners also promoted cocaine as a cure for opiate addiction. A report by Professor E. R. Palmer in the *Louisville Medical News* evoked an editorial response in the *Detroit Therapeutic Gazette:* "One feels like trying coca, with or without the opium habit. A harmless remedy for the blues is imperial" ("Erythroxylon Coca as an Antidote to the Opium Habit" 1880: 172). W. H. Bentley found cocaine useful in treating three opiate-addicted women (1880: 253–254). In New York, J. P. Marsh (1883) employed coca in successfully treating a woman with a twelve-year morphine habit. James T. Whittaker (1885), a Cincinnati physician, reported using a three-day regimen of injected cocaine to cure a twenty-five-year-old opiate-addicted woman who had first tried morphine at age twenty-two for "obstinate neuralgia" and had become addicted to it during a bout of pneumonia.

Supplies of coca and coca products in America were extremely limited prior to the mid-1880s. Realizing how rapidly cocaine was becoming accepted by physicians, E. R. Squibb and Company and McKesson and Robbins began to market the drug domestically. In an 1885 pamphlet, *Coca Erythroxylon and Its Derivatives,* Parke-Davis advertised that cocaine would be "the most important discovery of the age, the benefits of which to humanity would be incalculable." The pamphlet also proclaimed coca "a drug which through its stimulant properties, can supply the place of food, make the coward brave, the silent eloquent, free the victims of alcohol and opium habit from their bondage, and, as an anaesthetic render the sufferer insensitive to pain, and make attainable to the surgeon heights of what may be termed, 'aesthetic surgery' never reached before" (p. 4).

Even E. R. Squibb, a much-respected physician and chemist who had earlier criticized the promotion of cocaine, came to praise its use enthusiastically. Although by 1886 Freud had become disillusioned with cocaine, its general popularity and acceptance, if questioned by some American physicians, remained high, and both the pharmaceutical and chemical industries responded to the demand. Unfortunately, since pharmaceutical companies did not release information on cocaine production, no accurate figures on the amount of cocaine consumed either by men or by women are available. Importation figures for coca leaf, however, reveal an upward trend in the years from 1885 to 1905, and calculations show that consumption of cocaine increased fivefold from the early 1890s through the next decade (Spillane 1994). Much of this growth was due to the aggressive marketing of cocaine, especially in patent medicines or proprietary remedies.

Cocaine had its public advocates. Dr. William Hammond, a neurologist and later Surgeon General of the Army, wrote in some detail of his own self-administration of cocaine as well as the experience of other physicians in treating sciatica, painful intercourse, hemorrhoids, eye infections, and opium addiction. Hammond (1886a) also lauded cocaine in the treatment of women with goiter but found it unsuccessful "for the relief of masturbation." Like Freud, who had treated his own "neurasthenia" with cocaine, Hammond recommended a claret-glassful of "wine of coca" with each meal for neurasthenia and general debility.

Cocaine was a boon to society women suffering from neurasthenia. A case report in the *Therapeutic Gazette* claimed that coca had reversed the chronic exhaustion that had kept a woman bedridden for almost a year (Hole 1880). W. A. Hammond (1886a, 1886b) found cocaine to be efficacious in treating women with melancholia, one of whom reportedly had not spoken for nine months. At a meeting of the New York Neurological Society in 1886, another physician confirmed Hammond's experience: he had administered coca leaves to a despondent woman and achieved "happy results." In his *History of Coca* (1901), W. Golden Mortimer almost offhandedly acknowledged that "women are more commonly the sufferers of neurasthenia," which he defined as "troubles produced from a possible nervous perversion, engendered through overtaxing the powers mentally or physically in the modern whirl and bustle of a busy life." Extolling the virtues of cocaine, Mortimer pointed out its widespread use among physicians:

> fully one-half of those who went at all into detail advocated the use of Coca for cases of neurasthenia, and for the various symptoms of nerve and muscle depression grouped under that title. The whole train of ills, resulting from debility, exhaustion, overwork, or overstrain of nerve or mind, recalls the early designation given to the classification of this long group of symptoms by some of the European physicians as "the American disease," the derangement of an overworked and overhurrying people. (pp. 390–391)

Cocaine, like opiates, was also used to treat gynecological complaints: "If the patient be a woman," Mortimer noted, "the gynaecologist locates the concentration of troubles in predominant functions" (1901: 384). Case reports of the Medical Society of Virginia in 1887 document the use of cocaine to treat painful intercourse and uterine diseases (Byck 1974). Dr. Charles Thomas (1885) wrote of the benefits of topical cocaine in treating cervical endometritis, painful irritation and inflammation of the female urethra, and dysmenorrhea, in which cocaine was "capable of producing excellent results when applied to the os uteri and to the cervical cavity by means of a small cotton tampon" (pp. 649–650). Other physicians found cocaine efficacious in the management of painful spasms of the vagina ("Minutes of the Clinical Society of the New York Postgraduate Medical School and Hospital" 1884) and cervical lacerations following childbirth (Roeth 1886). William H. Byford (1885b, 1886) successfully treated a case of cracked nipples and another of vomiting during pregnancy with cocaine.

Professionals, writers, and other intellectuals who desired to work long hours used cocaine for its stimulant properties. Physicians, represented most notably by William Halsted[8] and his research assistants, formed an identifiable group of cocainists in the 1880s and 1890s

(Spillane 1994). Women relied on cocaine in social situations: one doctor claimed that he "had fashionable ladies come to him to get hypodermic injections of cocaine to make them lively and talkative" (Whittaker 1885b: 177–178).

The general public encountered coca and cocaine in "commercial folk medicines," home remedies, and tonics with names like Coca Beef Compound, Lambert's Wine of Coca, Nyal's Compound Extract of Damiana, Coca Calisaya, Coca Cordial, Nichols Compound Coca Cordial, Metcalf Coca Wine, and Maltine with Coca, and in soft drinks such as John Styth Pemberton's "French Wine of Coca, the Ideal Tonic," developed in 1866 and eventually marketed under the brand name Coca-Cola. Vin Mariani, another coca preparation formulated in Paris by Angelo Mariani, a Corsican chemist, quickly gained wide acceptance in the United States. "In the way of medication and as an adjunct to the food," wrote W. Golden Mortimer, "I know of no better remedy than Coca, preferably the original wine of Coca prepared by Mariani" (1901: 397). Dr. J. Leonard Corning endorsed Vin Mariani as "undoubtedly the most potent for good in the treatment of exhaustive and irritative conditions of the central nervous system" (cited in Byck 1974: 275).

During the 1880s, women of the more privileged classes turned to cocaine for medical and recreational purposes. Cocaine was also found, however, among lower-class women. In an article entitled "Cocaine Debauchery," E. R. Waterhouse described a raid on a drugstore that in reality served as a "cocaine joint" frequented by a "lower class of fallen women" and "lower class prostitutes, black as well as white" (1886: 464–465). According to Thomas G. Simonton (1903), cocaine-addicted prostitutes were well represented, for example, among the women in one workhouse in western Pennsylvania.

During the 1880s, cocaine use spread to the Negro stevedores working in New Orleans and other Southern ports. It quickly gained popularity, and by the end of the century Southern Negroes were heavy cocaine users. Exaggerated reports of the wildfire progress of cocaine among Southern Negroes would galvanize a demand for anti-drug legislation.

Hypnotics
Ether, chloroform, and chloral hydrate were considered fashionable in some social circles toward the end of the nineteenth century. Dr.

Henry S. Taylor recommended that "ladies who visit Europe or elsewhere by sea" could alleviate their sea-sickness by taking "a teaspoonful of ether in a glass of water" (1869: 305–306). Physicians prescribed chloroform, which came into use as an anesthetic in the 1840s (Pickard and Buley 1946), more or less nonspecifically, for example, in treating nervous headaches (Taylor 1872: 379). As one chloroform habitué noted in the *Detroit Lancet*, "Doctors sometimes advise patients to use chloroform for the relief of trifling ailments, or they fail to remonstrate against the practice when they hear of it among their patients" ("The Chloroform Habit" 1884: 254). *The Cottage Physician* listed chloroform as an ingredient in such remedies as Shilo's Consumptive Cure, King's New Discovery, and Edison's Polyform, as well as in liniments, such as St. Jacob's Oil, Hamlin's Wizard Oil, and Good Samaritan Liniment (Faulkner and Carmichael 1892). The reformer Samuel Hopkins Adams (1907) tried to expose the dangers of these medications, which, he claimed, "hasten the progress of the disease" being treated.

By the 1850s, chloroform had evolved into a nonmedicinal agent. An undercover female reporter for the *New York Herald* wrote in an 1894 article that, in treating her for "nervousness," a doctor had told her "there was probably no form of disease where this gas had been so beneficial as in nervous troubles of all descriptions, and he was convinced that I could and would be cured." In 1901 the *Boston Globe* reported that upper-class women were flocking to "oxygen parties," gatherings at which they inhaled a nitrous oxide mixture to liven up the festivities (Silver 1979: 681).

Chloral hydrate could be purchased at most local drugstores beginning in 1869. It relieved tension and pain, helped alcoholics sleep, and served as a general sedative ("Abuse of Chloral Hydrate" 1880); it was also used to treat delirium tremens in insane asylums. By 1872, J. H. Etheridge, a physician, expressed reservations about the expanding use of chloral hydrate: "Men and women who suffer from sleeplessness habitually, are easily tempted to resort to it, and many, very many do it." He noted, however, that the drug enjoyed wide use among "school-teachers, bookkeepers, [and] invalid women made weaker by family cares" and that "in obstetric practice, many physicians have used chloral hydrate with the happiest effect" (1872: 525). In reviewing replies to a questionnaire distributed to medical personnel, H. H. Kane found that women, especially those taking the drug for "painful uterine complaints," but also prostitutes and hospital nurses, made up about one-third of the total chloral users (Kane 1881). Kane also reported the unconfirmed experience of Quintius C. Smith, a West Coast physician, who found that chloral hydrate was common among prostitutes on the Pacific coast.

Not surprisingly, chloral hydrate was also used in the treatment of neurasthenia (Tyson 1900). Edith Wharton's novel *The House of Mirth* (1905) poignantly described the fall from grace of Miss Lily Bart, who, like many of her contemporaries, turned to chloral hydrate to ease life's pains and disappointments. The novel sold thirty thousand copies within ten days of publication and was widely read. As Lily sank into a life of reduced circumstances and social isolation, chloral hydrate became her chief solace:

> Nothing but the silence of her cheerless room—that silence of the night which may be more racking to tired nerves than the most discordant noises: that, and the bottle of chloral by her bed. The thought of the chloral was the only spot of light in the dark prospect: she could feel its lulling influence stealing over her already. But she was troubled by the thought that it was losing its power—she dared not go back to it too soon. Of late the sleep it had brought her had been more broken and less profound; . . . What if the effect of the drug should gradually fail, as all narcotics were said to fail? She remembered the chemist's warning against increasing the dose; and she had heard before of the capricious and incalculable action of the drug. (pp. 299–300)

Cannabis

Cannabis, or marijuana, entered the country in 1611 with the first settlers in the Jamestown Colony (Grinspoon 1971). The plant became widely cultivated: its fibrous trunk was used in making rope, paper, and cloth and its seed in birdseed. Hemp production continued through the nineteenth century, although the Civil War, which interrupted cotton production, and the decline of the shipbuilding industry greatly reduced the need for rope to bind cotton bales or secure sails.

Between 1840 and the end of the century, doctors and other dispensers of drugs prescribed cannabis for many ailments, and it was entered into the *United States Pharmacopoeia*, a list of all drugs, in 1850. In 1860 R. R. M'Meens reported to the Ohio State Medical Society that cannabis was recommended in the treatment of tetanus, neuralgia, convulsions, rheumatism, asthma, and chronic bronchitis, and in women specifically for uterine hemorrhage, dysmenorrhea, labor pains, postpartum psychoses, and gonorrhea. In the story "Perilous Play," written by Louisa May Alcott in 1869, Dr. Meredith, obviously quite knowledgeable about the drug, reassures a young upper-class picnicker to whom he is introducing "hashish bonbons": "I use it for my patients. It is very efficacious in nervous disorders, and is getting to be quite a pet remedy with us" (Palmer and Horowitz 1982: 72). J. Milner Fothergill (1877) recommended the use of cannabis as a stimulant and in treating gout, epilepsy, neuralgias, and abnormal menstrual flow. Cannabis was also widely prescribed for headaches, especially in women. George M. Beard wrote in the *Virginia Medical Monthly* in 1879 that *cannabis indica* was one drug by which "the treatment of sick headache . . . [has been] . . . revolutionized" (p. 270). T. Gaillard Thomas, a gynecologist, found cannabis beneficial in treating fibroids and polyps, painful menstruation, and unusual vaginal bleeding, for which he considered the drug "one of the best at our command" (1880: 632). A physician's wife noted other applications:

> I had been in the habit of taking the drug for a neuralgic headache, to which I am subject, and had never experienced any other effect from its use than relief of pain. During the summer, however, I contracted a severe cold, and when my menstrual epoch arrived, the flow was very profuse, accompanied by severe pain in the left ovary. For the relief of these symptoms my husband gave me cannabis indica. ("An Effect of Cannabis Indica" 1885: 107)

J. B. Mattison (1891) considered cannabis beneficial in the treatment of opium addiction as well as headache, which he referred to as "the bane of American women." Cannabis, like so many other drugs, was also reputedly useful in the treatment of neurasthenia, and at least one major text, found in almost a third of American medical schools in 1891 (Strumpell 1888), suggested *cannabis indica* as a safer treatment alternative to chloral and morphine. Although noteworthy physicians such as Sir William Osler (1913) continued to regard cannabis as "probably the most satisfactory remedy" for migraine, the drug fell into disrepute in the medical profession by the end of the century because of its variable results, the difficulty of regulating dosage, and the risk of abuse and habitual use.

Fitzhugh Ludlow's book, *The Hasheesh Eater* (1857), traces recreational use of marijuana to the 1840s and 1850s. In Alcott's "Perilous Play," one young woman takes "hashish bonbons" to escape the "ennui" of her restrictive social life and another because she is "tired of being a lonely statue" (Palmer and Horowitz 1982). An article revealing a "hasheesh hell on Fifth Avenue" in the December 2, 1876, issue of *Illustrated Police News* was accompanied by a drawing of five well-dressed, noticeably intoxicated women (*New York Times Magazine,* Dec. 13, 1970: 26). In *Harper's Monthly* in 1883, H. H. Kane wrote of his experiences in a New York hashish house, which catered to "both male and female [clients] . . . of the better classes." Kane described heavily curtained rooms "magnificently fitted up . . . reserved for persons, chiefly ladies, who wish to avoid every possibility of detection, and at the same time enjoy their hashish and watch the inmates of this room."

In Kane's (1881) opinion, hashish posed a lesser problem than morphine, opium, or chloral hydrate, and its use was "due more to moral depravity than to any special morbid craving for the substance used" (p. 207). The only cannabis habitué he had known, Kane noted, was a woman who "began to use the drug through curiosity, having read of its peculiar effects, and being extremely desirous of finding something to supply the place of the alcohol, to which she had become a slave" (pp. 208–209). In the first known report of a true psychedelic experience, May C. Hungerford wrote in 1884 of taking an overdose of hasheesh, which she had begun using for headaches on the orders of her physician (Palmer and Horowitz 1982). She was reported to have a nineteenth-century "American Christian consciousness."

Marijuana opened the Pandora's box of sexuality. In 1869, after taking cannabis, Horatio C. Wood noted "a good deal of priapism during the night, and a state of venereal excitement . . . lasting several days." Victor Robinson, a physician who practiced in Harlem, wrote in 1910 of a sensual vision he experienced when he was introduced to marijuana:

> I hear the songs of women. Thousands of maidens pass near me, they bend their bodies in the most charming curves, and scatter beautiful flowers in my fragrant path. Some faces are strange, some I knew on earth, but all are lovely. They smile, and sing and dance. Their bare feet glorify the firmament. It is more than flesh can stand. I grow sensual unto satyriasis. The aphrodisiac effect is astonishing in its intensity. I

enjoy all the women of the world. I pursue countless maidens through the confines of heaven. A delicious warmth suffuses my whole body. (cited in Strasbaugh and Blaise 1991: 138)

The Landscape of Drugs

By the close of the nineteenth century, drugs had become an everyday presence in American life. It is hard to imagine that anyone managed to avoid exposure to narcotics. They were legally prescribed and used without prescription, in conventional and homeopathic remedies and patent medicines. Opium smoking had been taken up by white society. Cocaine was widely accepted in medical circles, and common among Southern Negroes and other socially marginalized groups. Chloroform, chloral hydrate, cannabis, and related substances were available for medical and recreational use. Women—from high society to the urban and rural poor—comprised the majority of America's opiate addicts. Through advertisements and endorsements, the pharmaceutical industry encouraged women to turn to drugs to ease their minds and bodies. Women were disproportionately medicated for organic complaints by physicians limited therapeutically to the control of pain, and even more disproportionately for casually diagnosed nonorganic complaints.

Despite its high prevalence, the problem of drug addiction among women went largely unaddressed, although it was documented in anecdotes, physician and pharmacy records, and sensationalized newspaper stories. Women's exalted status in Victorian society and "social responsibility for fostering morality" (Coontz 1992: 97) resulted in a public unwillingness to admit the extent of narcotic addiction and drug use. At the same time, women's desire to conceal their own drug use and the dulling effects of drugs over time kept addicted women in the shadows and diffused early legislative attempts to control drug use. Treatment for addiction, an option only for those who could afford it, was generally ineffective, and was certainly less accessible to women than to men.

The nation's approach to drug use was—and still is—defined by its sociodemographic perceptions. As long as the addicted population remained an "acceptable" segment of the mainstream population, drug use was quietly tolerated, although this conveniently obscured the fact that working-class women, farmers' wives, and prostitutes also lived in the shadowy world of addiction. When the drug landscape began to change radically—when racial and ethnic minorities sought further social and economic opportunities, and women were cast as vulnerable "sexual victims" of these groups, the national approach to the vexing problem of drug use in America shifted.

three

AMERICA'S RESPONSE

During the Victorian era, the American public tolerated and even accepted drug use. Physicians who followed the medical literature were undoubtedly aware of the horrors of addiction and the iron grip in which it held its victims. But the prevailing stereotype of the opiate addict—female, middle- or upper-class, and white—coupled with the fact that these women had largely become addicted through medical intervention and remained nonthreatening to society, dissuaded most physicians from crusading for reform.

Lawrence Kolb, the first medical director of the federal drug treatment facility in Lexington, Kentucky, recalled an image from his youth: "A respectable woman in the neighborhood often came in to buy laudanum. She was a good housekeeper and the mother of two fine sons. Everybody was sorry about her laudanum habit, but no one viewed her as a sinner or a menace to the community. We had not yet heard the word 'addict,' with its sinister modern connotations" (1956: 19). Increasing disclosures of opiate, ether, chloroform, bromide, and alcohol use among Victorian women tarnished their shining image as the special "guardians of moral 'purity' and social standards" (Worth 1991: 3). This, along with a clearer understanding of the impact of opiates during pregnancy and the common practice of treating children with opiates, helped convince American society that it had a drug problem in need of serious examination.

The number of addicts actually began to decline toward the end of the century, just as public concern about addiction intensified. Significant sociodemographic changes were well under way, contributing to growing fears over drug use: the number of drug users among the black and Chinese populations was on the rise; urban addicts were beginning to outnumber rural addicts; drug use was increasingly associated with poverty; and the press began reporting links between drug use and crime more frequently. Within a relatively short time, the prototypical drug addict had become a poor urban male with links to the underworld. The traditional association of female sexuality and drug use would prove extremely useful in passing legislation to extend social and economic control over racial and ethnic minorities. In the decades leading up to the Harrison Anti-Narcotic Act of 1914, repeated portrayals of the threat these "drug-crazed minorities" posed to white women in the more sensationalist press proved to be powerful instruments in moving America toward a national antidrug policy.

One Response: Physician Education

Even without a national antidrug policy, the number of addicts in the United States would have declined simply because of gradual changes in the prescribing practices of physicians and pharmacists. In an effort to reduce the excessive, often inappropriate, medicinal use of opiates, cocaine, chloral hydrate, and cannabis, medical journals and other publications provided more accurate information on their dangers. In a lecture before the Massachusetts Medical Society in 1860, Oliver Wendell Holmes declared that "the community is still overdosed" with a variety of medications (1888: 184). Horace Day described the familiar progression in *The Opium Habit:*

> The frequent, if not the usual history of confirmed opium-eaters is this: A physician prescribes opium as an anodyne, and the patient finds from its use the relief which was anticipated. Very frequently he finds not merely that his pain has been relieved, but that with this relief has been associated a feeling of positive, perhaps of extreme enjoyment. A recurrence of the same pain infallibly suggests a recurrence to the same remedy. The advice of the medical man is not invoked, because the patient knows that morphine or laudanum was the simple remedy that proved so efficacious before, and this he can procure as well without as with the direction of his physician. He becomes his own doctor, prescribes the same remedy the medical man has prescribed, and charges nothing for his advice. The resort to this pleasant medication after no

long time becomes habitual, and the patient finds that the remedy, whose use he had supposed was sanctioned by his physician, has become his tyrant. (1868: 58)

In his book on practical family medicine, Dr. A. W. Chase warned that opium and morphine were "equally as dangerous as the Sedatives." "I never use [opium or morphine] if I can possibly avoid it, as they so quickly establish an appetite, or craving necessity for their repetition" (1873: 596). A homeopathic text called opium one of the "violent poisons," which was "disused in the new practice of medicine" (Howard 1879: 106). Harry Hubbell Kane (1881) devoted extensive sections of *Drugs That Enslave* to the symptoms of opiate usage and the dangers of morphine. In the *Boston Medical and Surgical Journal*, J. A. Loveland (1881) reported the first known case of death during withdrawal in a thirty-five-year-old female morphine addict.

Advances in public health and sanitation, reductions in serious diarrheal diseases, the introduction of vaccination and chemotherapy, more precise diagnosis, and the availability of safer analgesics, such as aspirin, all contributed to a decrease in doctors' administration of opiates. The press also called attention to the extent of iatrogenic addiction. A Hearst newspaper story from 1893, reporting on the injudicious prescribing patterns of physicians, was headed "Doctors Are Largely Responsible for Drunkenness and the Opium Habit" and subheaded "Alcohol and Opiates Are Too Frequently and Carelessly Prescribed by Medical Men" (cited in Silver 1979: 25). George Wheelock Grover remarked on the changing scene:

> The old physician, with his gig and his trunk, so useful in his day, with his case full of remedies which have done this and have done that and which are administered because of the accumulation of mere individual experience, the old familiar figure of our grandfathers' days, is passing into that of the alert modern scientist, who uses remedies as an astronomer uses instruments that pierce the sky road of the stars, or the surgeon directs with accuracy his keen-edged tools. (1894: 119)

Although publications like the *New York Medical Journal* (Manges 1900) sounded a note of warning about heroin and its dangers almost as soon as the drug was introduced, many physicians initially viewed heroin as a safe, nonaddicting alternative to morphine and prescribed it "in the sincere belief that it would not create a habit" (Towns 1912).

Later writers, such as George Pettey (1902–1903) and Charles Atwood (1905), however, warned physicians about the dangers of its excessive use. D. W. Cathell also advised his fellow physicians that indiscriminate use of all opiates would lead to addiction, and that physicians would "surely and *deservedly* incur the blame" (1905: 255). In 1906, the American Medical Association Council on Pharmacy and Chemistry endorsed the use of heroin in small amounts, warning, however, of the possibility of addiction (Morgan 1981: 94).

But if general medical practice was changing, other aspects of medical practice were not. Some in the medical community continued to prescribe opiates for "female complaints." The 1865 edition of William H. Byford's standard gynecological text on "diseases and accidents incident to women" recommended opium for the treatment of dysmenorrhea. The 1888 edition, co-authored by Byford's son, continued to recommend opiates to control the pain of dysmenorrhea, as well as uterine inflammation, cancer of the uterus and ovary, rectovaginal lacerations, and uterine displacement. Other physicians disavowed the routine administration of morphine to women. H. S. Duncan, an Alabama physician, condemned it as a form of "malpractice" and claimed that "many otherwise noble women will be driven to prostitution from its effects" (1885: 248). Another warned that the danger of forming a morphine habit was "a consideration not to be overlooked" (Davenport 1889: 155). One text advised that opium should be "employed with the utmost caution" (Allbutt and Playfair 1897: 364). J. M. Baldy's *American Text-Book of Gynecology* condemned the use of such drugs in the treatment of dysmenorrhea: "He who is compelled to resort frequently to opium and stimulants must be considered devoid in diagnostic ability, and consequently ought not to be entrusted with the management of such cases" (1898: 105).

For the most part, society viewed women addicted to opiates with sympathy and blamed their addictions on the physicians and pharmacists who prescribed the drugs. As H. H. Kane advised, "Pity, then, rather than blame" (1881: 33). Overrepresented among the addicted women in some surveys were doctors' wives, who spent long hours alone while their husbands attended the sick, and nurses, who also had easy access to drugs. As a Massachusetts physician reported, "Not long ago, I had under my care the wife of a noted physician; she had taken morphine for seven years without her husband's knowledge" (Russell 1887: 144). S. Weir Mitchell, who commented on the issue of women's weaknesses and the temptation to overmedicate, warned that if the physician was too quick to prescribe, the patient would soon be "on the evil path of the opium, chloral, or chloroform habit" (1888: 93). He agreed that "if there be one set of women more liable than another to become victims of morphia or chloral, it is the wives of physicians. Every winter I see four or five, and always it is true that the habit has arisen out of the effort of the husband to attend medically on his wife" (p. 99).

Toward the end of the nineteenth century, the tendency to treat neurasthenia with addictive drugs diminished. As William Pepper advised in his medical textbook, "all drugs hold a secondary position [to rest] in the relief of a pure neurasthenia" (1886: 357). William Osler (1901), the most widely read physician in American medical schools at the time, condemned the use of drugs for neurasthenia, especially morphine, chloral hydrate, and cocaine. And James French's textbook also warned that "powerful opiates should be avoided" in the treatment of neurasthenia (1903: 699).

Cocaine, although popular, also had its detractors and critics. In his lectures, J. B. Mattison acknowledged the value of cocaine in eye surgery but added that "a potency for good implies a potency for harm." It was time, he said, to "revoice a warning as to the use and abuse of this valued, but at times, toxic drug," which, he felt, was more dangerous than alcohol or opium (1887a: 1). From his own experience and reports from physicians in New York, Chicago, and the Northwest, Mattison described cases of cocaine toxicity in women treated for gynecological disease, chronic bladder infection, dental problems, and hay fever. One female patient died from "cocaine poisoning" after "freely using a four per cent solution of cocaine, for toothache" (p. 5). An eleven-year-old girl succumbed after an injection of cocaine to treat her fainting fits. Cases of cocaine toxicity provided by a New York City physician mentioned women who had received treatment for lacerated cervix and neuralgic headache.

Mattison, directly at odds with W. A. Hammond over the dangers of cocaine, challenged him on "cocaine toxaemia" before the American Association for the Cure of Inebriates in November 1887, where he presented further case histories of cocaine poisoning: a woman who suffered "violent general convulsive movements [and] . . . entire loss of consciousness for about five minutes" following the administration of cocaine for hemorrhoids; a seventy-year-old woman who developed breathing problems after the instillation of cocaine into her eye; a twelve-year-old girl who became toxic after treatment for an unspecified condition (Mattison 1887b).

The warnings continued (Spillane 1994). An article in the *New York Medical Journal* in 1891 reported six cocaine-related fatalities and noted that the medical literature reported over four hundred poisonings (Gay 1981: 312). Several observers cautioned that in women cocaine could produce an unwanted aphrodisiac effect, resulting in "unseemly" behavior or indecent exposure.[1] A dentist reported the case of a sixteen-year-old patient, who, after being injected in the gum with cocaine, had experienced "a paroxysm of the most intense pleasurable excitement" that was due to its "aphrodisiac quality" (Cornell 1891: 152). A comprehensive review article a few years later also alerted physicians to the many dangers of cocaine (Scheppegrell 1898).

By the 1890s physicians more readily accepted the dangers of cocaine abuse. Increasingly concerned about how rapidly use proceeded to abuse, the deterioration in mental and physical health induced by cocaine, and the difficulty in breaking patients of the cocaine habit, physicians had largely discarded cocaine "for every purpose except the one of producing local anaesthetization" (Grover 1894: 68). As one historian has recently argued, however, although many physicians understood that cocaine abuse frequently began iatrogenically, through medical treatment, and that cocaine was commonly taken together with morphine, they continued to use and prescribe it because they believed that its usage could be controlled through proper dosing, that its toxicity was due in some part to unpredictable idiosyncracy, and that the majority of cocaine users were socially acceptable people of middle-class and professional status (Spillane 1994).

As evidence of cocaine's baleful effects mounted and other topical anesthetic substitutes were developed, medicinal use of the drug declined. Ironically, however, cocaine imports increased, largely to supply manufacturers of patent medicines. By 1900, medicines for colds, sinus ailments, and asthma, including the much-in-demand Birney's Catarrhal Powder, Dr. Cole's Catarrh Cure, and Crown Catarrh Powder (Adams 1907: 42), were widely sold, resulting in many new cases of cocaine overuse (Spillane 1994). Uncontrolled use of patent medicines began to decline after the turn of the century, aided by the Pure Food and Drug Act of 1906, which was passed through the combined efforts of muckraking journalists who sought to expose the dangers of patent medicines; physicians, pharmacists, and chemists intent on limiting or eliminating the use of dangerous medications; and the federal government.

Some physicians likewise warned about the dangers of chloral hydrate. According to J. B. Mattison (1879b), "the laity look upon chloral with less distrust and as less dangerous than opium; and therefore are more disposed, when in pain or sleepless, to act as their own medical advisers." Mattison catalogued a number of cases of toxicity: a thirty-eight-year-old woman who developed partial paraplegia (limb weakness), a sixty-nine-year-old woman and a forty-six-year-old woman who suffered skin eruptions, a nineteen-year-old girl whose complexion became "dull and pasty," and a thirty-three-year-old woman who exhibited pallor, double vision, a staggering gait, and stupor. For treatment, Mattison advised either a "heroic plan" using amelioration with morphine or hemp (marijuana) or one of "more gradual abandonment" (1879b: 12). Later, he extended his cure to treatment with opiates such as morphine and codeine, botanic preparations, and "an eight minutes bed-time galvanic seance" (1892: 13)

In *Drugs That Enslave*, H. H. Kane also warned about the dangers of chloralism, noting that the habit "*causes a more complete ruin of mind and body* than either opium or morphine" (1881: 163). He found chloralism to be common among women with rheumatism, facial neuralgia, cancer of the breast, "reflex uterine irritation," "insomnia and nervousness of prolapsis uteri," "periodical mania," and "cardiac disease, hemiplegia, and dementia." Kane also cautioned that excessive intake of chloral hydrate could be fatal: one of his patients, diagnosed with "dipsomania in a hysterical female," had continued the medication in an unsupervised fashion when he was no longer personally attending her, with tragic results.

Physicians themselves were not above using drugs for various physical and psychological purposes and, like their patients, becoming "hooked." In *The Morphine Eater*, Leslie E. Keeley, director of the Keeley Institute in White Plains, New York, published letters from physicians who had succumbed to addiction. One physician-addict wrote movingly of his exhaustion and humiliation: "I have acquired a profound contempt for myself, and believe I do *really despise* myself more thoroughly, (if possible), than anybody else does" (1881: 149). John Harvey Kellogg (1898) commented on the number of physicians who came to his Battle Creek, Michigan, facility seeking treatment for addiction. J. B. Mattison claimed that "in a certain New England city, containing upward of one hundred medical men, between thirty and forty are addicted to some form of opium," and ascribed their addiction to easy access to drugs, knowledge of their uses, "some form of neurotic disorder," and a search for relief from the "anxious hours, the weary days, and wakeful nights" (1883: 621). A decade later Mattison (1892), still writing about opiate addiction in the medical profession, provided case histories of seven physicians who had been addicted to morphine for periods of one to ten years. He also noted two physicians with "multiple inebriety" to morphine, cocaine, and rum, an early recognition of the modern concept of "polydrug abuse." Grover's treatise on drug addiction is also replete with stories of physicians' addictions. One such physician-addict was "a man of eminent Christian character, an honored member of the Congregational church, a Sir Knight who stood high in the regard of his fellow-Knights" (1894: 15).

Estimates of morphine and opium addiction among physicians during this period ranged from 6 percent to 10 percent (Crothers 1899), to nearly 16 percent (Happel 1900). The *Philadelphia Medical Journal* estimated in 1899 that physicians and dentists made up 30 percent of the "cocainists" in America (Gay 1981: 313). The high prevalence of opiate addiction among physicians and druggists did not go unnoted in two commonly used medical textbooks (Anders 1899; French 1903). In the *American Journal of Public Health,* Lucius Brown blamed physicians for their indiscriminate prescription of opiates and commented that "in most instances the physicians are themselves addicts" (1915: 332).

Despite warnings in the medical literature, many physicians remained ignorant of the dangers of opium addiction. In *The Opium Habit,* an anonymous addict graphically detailed his own successful attempt to wean himself off drugs without the help of physicians, not one of whom "had made the opium disease a special study, or who knew very much about it" (Day 1868: 35). Horace Day later commented that "the profession generally is not well informed on the subject. In my own case I certainly found no one who seemed familiar with the phenomenon pertaining to the relinquishment of opium, or whose suggestions indicated much more than vague, empirical ideas on the subject" (p. 60). A physician-addict, unable to find help for his own addiction, asked: "Why is it that practitioners, as a rule, have never made a study of the opium disease?" (Keeley 1881: 153). "All the doctors in this part of the State are in absolute darkness" (p. 148). Another commentator noted that "a very large proportion of the medical profession has either lost sight of the fact that the habitual use of an opiate produces a true disease, or never knew it" (Brown 1915: 323) and that "certain physicians unhappily leave behind them a sad trail of addicts" (p. 332).

Childbearers and Child Rearers

In view of their unique role as mothers—bearers and rearers of children—women who suffered from opiate addiction aroused particular public concern. In the mid-nineteenth century little was known about the fetal effects of maternal opiate use during pregnancy. One physician minimized the risks: "It is claimed that it injures the foetus. This can only be, however, when it is used in large and frequently repeated doses" (Frost 1869–1870: 143). H. H. Kane showed more circumspection when he commented that "the excessive use of this drug by one or both parents, but especially the mother, in case she is able to carry her child to full term, will modify disadvantageously the physical, mental, or moral development of the child thus born." Kane related an anecdotal report from a Southern physician: an opium-using mother gave birth to a child who grew up to be "very simple and childish" (1881: 44). F. H. Hamlin, in the *Medical Gazette*, was more dogmatic about the drug's ill effects, writing that in cases where pregnancy had been completed, "the children have been sadly deficient, mentally and physically" (1882: 429).

The earliest mention of "congenital addiction" in the American medical literature is thought to be F. B. Earle's (1888) case report of a full-term baby, born to a chronic opium user, who died three days after birth. T. J. Happel (1892) accurately described what we now call "neonatal withdrawal" or "neonatal abstinence," noting the characteristic signs of restlessness, fretfulness, and cyanosis (lack of oxygen) in an opiate-exposed newborn infant. He pointed out, quite correctly, that such babies become dependent on the opiate during their intra-uterine life and need attentive care with an opiate after birth. Louis Fischer, a New York physician, also noted that infants born to morphine-addicted women require treatment with morphine after birth or "they are apt to suffer collapse, and their condition may end in death" (1894: 199).

In its discussion of infant morphinism, the *American Text-book of Applied Therapeutics* recognized the need for treatment after birth but noted frankly that "the ultimate prognosis as to the child's growing up is . . . bad" (Wilson and Eshner 1896: 610). An infant born to a morphine-addicted woman, J. B. Mattison concluded, must receive "special care . . . lest it die in collapse, which so often proves fatal in such cases" (1898: 207).

Other writers, such as Thomas Clifford Allbutt (1895), Harrington Sainsbury (1909), and C. C. Wholey (1912), also published descriptive case histories of congenital opiate addiction in books and journals. One of the more comprehensive descriptions of "congenital morphinism" was provided by George E. Pettey, who stated the symptoms to be expected in the newborn infant, the relationship of those symptoms to the mother's dose of narcotic, and an appropriate regimen of treatment. Pettey also recorded the case of a woman who came to him for treatment, having taken McMunn's Elixir of opium for thirty-one years. Of eighteen children born alive, the only ones to survive were the two she bore before she became addicted. "All of the children," he wrote, "died within three days from their birth . . . The same physician attended her in all these confinements, and both the mother and the physician looked upon the death of the children, as a natural consequence of the mother's condition and inevitable." In her last confinement, however, she was attended by another physician "who appreciated the conditions under which the child was being brought into the world" (1913: 331–332) and successfully treated the infant with paregoric, a form of opium still used for this purpose today (Kandall 1993). Not until the late 1950s and early 1960s were careful studies of such infants gathered together and published in national medical journals.

Much more concern, however, was voiced about mothers' administration of opiates to their young children. In many pediatric illnesses, opiates proved to be extremely useful therapy. Benjamin Rush, the renowned eighteenth-century pediatrician, teacher of several generations of doctors, and signer of the Declaration of Independence, undertook a systematic investigation of cholera and concluded that in severe cases, when emetics and purges were no longer sufficient treatment, "recourse must be had to opiates. A few drops of liquid lauda-num combined in a testaceous julip, with pepper-mint or cinamon-water would soothe the stomach and bowels." To relieve the abdomi-nal pain and spasms of the bowel associated with cholera, Rush recommended "glysters made of flaxseed tea, or of mutton broth, or of starch dissolved in water, with a few drops of liquid laudanum in them" (1789: 112).

In the first formal paper on a pediatric subject published in the United States, Edward Miller, a physician, wrote that for the treatment of cholera, in addition to washing the patient and "discharging" the contents of the stomach and intestines, a "pill" consisting of one-sixth of a grain of opium should be administered every two to six hours, or "sometimes oftener according to the urgency of the symptoms" (1798: 60). Miller also realized, however, that "opiates alone, so generally used, and so much confided in, afford only a short-lived, delusive repose in the tumult of the system" (p. 62).

Opiates were commonly used for the medical problems of infancy and childhood, most of which were treated by mothers at home (Sharp 1986; Baker 1994). Such illnesses included teething, worms, diarrhea, colic, bowel pain, fever, smallpox, measles, whooping cough, croup, colds, thrush (a fungal infection of the mouth), difficulty voiding, urinary incontinence, and irritability in infants. During the westward migration of the mid-nineteenth century, women turned to opium preparations for basic therapy, especially for diarrheal diseases like dysentery and cholera, which ravaged many wagon trains. Despite their usefulness, however, the unsupervised availability of these medi-cations could prove dangerous: in one case, a young child drank a "whole bottle of laudanum" and died (Schlissel 1982).

The potential for inappropriate and dangerous use of opiates on children had been noted early. In 1832, W. G. Smith had observed that

the youthful, inconsiderate mother and the idle nurse, too frequently resort to opium to hush the infant's cries, which might have been done, by the ordinary and only best means of nursing . . . The gay and youthful mother, rather than forego the pleasures of a crowded assem-bly, or the gaudy charms of a dramatic scene, a single evening, not unfrequently commits the unfortunate infant to its cradle under the influence of opium, in the form, either of Darby's Carminative, the Paregoric Elixir, or Godfrey's Cordial, and even laudanum itself. (p. 21)

Shortly thereafter, a contributor to the *Boston Medical and Surgical Journal* commented: "It is remarkable, when we consider with what unguarded rashness medicines containing opium are given by mothers and nurses to young children, that fatal accidents do not more frequently occur." In describing a case of narcotism in an infant, the same writer cautioned, "how much more practitioners should be on their guard when administering this article to such delicate subjects" ("Dangers of Giving Opiates to Children" 1834: 174). Thomas Pollard, a Richmond physician, suggested that practitioners proceed more cautiously with children, using smaller doses not too frequently repeated. As he advised his fellow doctors, "it is our duty to apprize [sic] mothers of these effects, and warn them against this unjustifiable use of Opium" (1858: 134). An article in *Godey's Magazine* discouraged the practice of "drugging" children with opiates and counseled mothers and nurses to use drugs very sparingly" ("Diet and Drinks of Nursing Women" 1860: 558). Horace Day, a Philadelphia physician, writing in *The Opium Habit,* recalled that "paregoric, too—combining two of the most dangerous of all substances, alcohol and opium—was a favorite medicine of my excellent mother, and in all the little ailments of childhood was freely administered" (1868: 199). Dr. Henry S. Taylor directed his message about the care of children to "ill informed mothers" whose love for children he acknowledged while "seriously deprecat[ing] the manner in which that love sometimes shows itself" (1861: 42).

Warnings about medicating children with opiates continued over the following decades. In *A Physician's Counsels to Woman,* Dr. Walter C. Taylor considered the "dangerous remedy" opium:

The extreme susceptibility of young children to the action of this substance is a fact well known to physicians. Many refuse to prescribe it . . . A single drop of laudanum has been known to destroy the life of an infant at the breast. It is necessary, also, to be careful of the use of this drug in external applications, for it is readily absorbed by the delicate skin of a child, and may thus occasion alarming, or even fatal, narcotism. The various "soothing syrups," sold so largely in the market, contain opium. Their employment has much to do in increasing the ailments and mortality of infant life. A mother who gives, or permits to be given to her little one, an opiated preparation, in order to check its cries, places its life in peril. (1872: 258–259)

F. E. Oliver (1872) attributed some of the excessive adult use of opium in Massachusetts to the "taste implanted in infancy and child-hood by nursery medication." In *Dr. Chase's Family Physician, Farrier, Bee-Keeper and Second Receipt Book*, A. W. Chase declared of opi-ates: "their extensive use in the form of 'Soothing Sirup' has been an outrage upon the incredulous and unwary, that has resulted in the untimely deaths of thousands of children" (1873: 596).

In his 1878 survey of the "opium habit" in Michigan, Orville Marshall criticized the "indiscriminate use of medicines without intel-ligent medical advice" and warned about the risks of administering opiate-containing medicine to young children: "it is claimed that over three-quarters of a million of bottles of Mrs. Winslow's soothing-syrup are sold annually" and that calculating the known amount of morphine in the medication, it would be enough "to kill a half million of infants not accustomed to its use" (cited in O'Donnell and Ball 1966: 51). Marshall himself attended a seven-year-old child who had been given morphine since birth by his mother, a morphine-eater; the child died after "suffering all that any old opium-eater would when deprived of his accustomed stimulus" (1878: 53).

In an 1880 issue of the *Chicago Medical Review*, Charles W. Earle reported a doleful case:

> an infant at two weeks of age was given its first dose of soothing syrup. It took two bottles during the first month, six bottles during the second and third months, and four bottles each month during the remaining four months of its life. It died during its seventh month. During the last three months it was constantly nervous, it gradually became pale and slightly yellow. (cited in Morgan 1974: 55)

Earle also described untreated opiate withdrawal in the infant, an eyewitness description that could stand in a modern pediatrics text-book: "upon the rapid withdrawal of its morphia . . . it was taken with terrible diarrhoea, incessant vomiting, apparent unbearable mus-cular pains, prostration, and death" (cited in Morgan 1974: 55–56). Another report, this one in the *Southern Clinic: A Monthly Journal of Medicine, Surgery and New Remedies*, noted the case of a three-year-old child who had drunk one-third of a bottle of the opium-containing Dr. Bull's Cough Syrup; the hapless parents assumed that the medication was harmless and deferred calling a physician "until almost too late" (Bryce 1880: 400). In an address to the National Eclectic Medical Association, Dr. George W. Winterburn lectured about the "triad of infant murderers . . . Godfrey's Cordial, Paregoric, and Mrs. Winslow's Soothing Syrup," which were commonly used "because they are supposed to be harmless" (1882: 510–511). Winterburn even advocated labeling these opium-containing preparations and warned of the dangers of their inappropriate use. John Broadhead Beck (1884), also a physician, regarded opium as an "admirable" agent for treating infants, but its use in "unskillful hands," he noted, could produce great harm.

Cautionary warnings continued to accumulate. Faulkner and Carmichael's *Cottage Physician,* citing a report in the *Pacific Medical and Surgical Journal,* warned of the dangers of administering the morphine-containing Mrs. Winslow's Soothing Syrup to children: "It would be scarcely possible to estimate the number of children which it sends to the grave before their second year. Another still graver question is: How much of the physical disease, drunkenness, degradation, and vice, and how many of the weakened intellects are due to the use of the soothing syrup in infancy?" (1892: 535). Citing four case studies, Louis Fisher concluded that "we have more instances of children and infants addicted to the opium habit than we might otherwise suppose." Physicians, he wrote, had to "contend with ignorant mothers, stupid nurses, and careless women, who in order to get sleep at night feed their nurslings with soothing syrups, teething cordials, and other soothing liquids, not to mention the most common and also the most easily obtainable paregoric" (1894: 197).

Dr. George Wheelock Grover echoed Fischer's frustation:

> The writer has seen sound and healthy children born in families of opium eaters when it was the father that was using the drug. When, however, it is the mother who is the habitue, the child is very likely to exhibit the peculiar symptoms that follow in the wake of this deadly agent . . . The writer has seen children six months old exhibit all the peculiar and specific restlessness, general appearance, nervous unrest, of the adult opium eater. These morphinized miniatures of humanity take to the soothing syrup or the dose of paregoric which is given to them to quiet their uneasiness, as the duck sails into the embrace of the waters of the lake. (1894: 114)

Samuel Hopkins Adams wrote in his *Collier's Weekly* exposés of "Opium-containing soothing syrups, which stunt or kill helpless infants" (1907: 11). The Hearst newspapers also kept the issue in the public eye with dramatic headlines: "Mothers Giving Children Narcotics May Cause Formation of Drug Habit," "Demure Nurse-Maid Drugs Helpless Little Ones," and "Tiny Baby a Drug Addict" (cited in Silver 1979: 128, 129). Some adult addicts actually attributed their addiction in adulthood to being treated in infancy with paregoric, the "nemesis of the nursery" (Cobbe 1895).

Commenting on breastfeeding by opiate-using women, the American Pharmaceutical Association concluded that "the nursing babe absorbs medicine from its mother's breast as it draws its nourishment; it becomes an habitue with its birth" (Eberle and Gordon 1903: 479–480). Women, as the primary caretakers of children, were held inherently accountable for the effects of drugs and medications they administered. A 1909 newspaper report claimed that, despite the passage of the Pure Food and Drug Act three years earlier, the cocaine alkaloid, "beyond a doubt, one of the most dangerous of known poisons," was still being sold to mothers and children in thirty-nine soft beverages and "not only as beverages, but as headache remedies and nerve tonics" (cited in Silver 1979: 56). In 1912, the *Journal of the American Medical Association* decried the fact that patent medicines capable of "poisoning babies with opium mixtures or of killing women with headache powders" were still largely unregulated ("Property Right versus Public Health" 1912). Moralistic preaching in popular magazines warned parents to remember the derelict opium pipe smoker if tempted to give their children "any medicine, patent or otherwise, that contains opium, morphine, laudanum, heroin or any of their kindred alkaloids" ("A Modern Opium Eater" 1914).

The Search for Cures

As physicians learned more about the dangers of drugs, efforts were also under way to reduce the number of addicts through treatment. The self-confessed opium eater Fitzhugh Ludlow described a fictitious treatment facility, Lord's Island, which was surrounded by "fences, bolts, and bars . . . with more or less miles of deep water as the barrier" to keep the addict from "the poison by which he is imperilled" (Day 1868: 286). The range of proposed available treatments, "capable of indefinite combinations," included: bedrest with hot bricks and blankets at the extremities; galvanic currents; Russian baths ("a most admirable appliance" consisting of a steam room and 70 degree baths); concentrated beef tea (a dietary staple administered orally and by enema); graded doses of Magendie's Solution of Morphia, when needed, supplemented by bromide of potassium; exercise "carried to the extent of healthy fatigue"; hydrotherapy; shampoo treatments; Turkish baths; "movement cure"; and drugs as varied as cannabis, chloroform, and botanics such as capsicum. Women caught in the clutches of addiction (and able to afford treatment) could also find sanctuary in this "delightful refuge."

Many claimed that treatment for opiate addiction could be successful, although "cures" often involved the simple substitution of one drug for another. Case reports published by W. H. Bentley in the *Detroit Therapeutic Gazette* attested to successful treatment of opium addiction with coca.

> Miss M., a sprightly, intelligent blonde, age thirty . . . Eight years previous she had a protracted attack of pneumonia, during which she contracted the habit of using morphine which she still retained . . . She had tried nostrums and had visited some advertising quack in another State, to no purpose. I then suggested the erythroxylon . . . I prescribed a pound for her . . . She was much encouraged and had ordered two pounds more. This quantity completed the cure. I saw her recently when she assured me that she had no desire for morphine.

> July 1878, was called to a case . . . "in the hills." I was quite astonished to find about one tenth of an acre in poppies . . . the lady of the house, a widow, age forty, told me that she was an "opium eater" . . . she used about half a pound of the drug a year . . . I sent her one half-pound fluid extract coca to begin with. When used, she sent for half the quantity, stating that she thought it would complete the cure. I sent her a half pound. She sent me her opium crop that winter, with the message that the medicine had cured her.

> An old lady, age seventy-two. Had been addicted to the habit for thirty-five years. I persuaded her to try the coca. She was then taking 1/2-drachm doses of opium three times a day . . . Sometimes she does not taste opium for a fortnight, using the coca during the time, then she returns to her opium, and thus she alternates. Her doses of opium have

been reduced to as little, I think, as 10 grs., and her general health has greatly improved. Before using the coca, she was a great sufferer from duodenal dyspepsia. She has so far improved, in this respect, that she rarely suffers in this particular, and it is a wonder, too, for she is a ravenous feeder and as fond of "cake and pastry" as a child.

H. H. Kane concurred: "Great advances have been made in the treatment of this affliction in the last few years . . . The suffering incident to the breaking of this habit can, in a great measure, be relieved" (1881: 106). He listed a variety of treatments, including "baths of various kinds," electricity ("a powerful continued current . . . is the most serviceable"), drugs such as bromides, strychnia, capsicum, belladonna, and cannabis indica (but not coca or chloral hydrate), diet, stimulants, and alcohol ("never more than ten days"). Anticipating modern thinking on the subject, Kane was careful to stress that "the thorough cure of an opium or morphine habitue does not consist alone in stopping the use of the drug" (p. 140).

One particular difficulty, Kane pointed out, was treating "hysterical females," who were most likely to interfere with their own treatment at home, and thus to require committal to an institution. Other authorities echoed his concern. Dr. Roberts Bartholow felt that among those most difficult to treat were "women condemned to a life of constant invalidism, and ladies immersed in the gayeties of societal life" (Kane 1881: 145). F. H. Hamlin likewise warned that "the dangers of relapse are greatest in hysterical females" (1882: 431). In Maria Weed's (1895) novel *A Voice in the Wilderness,* of the three morphine-addicted women portrayed, one died despite treatment, one required treatment with stimulants and chloroform to effect a cure following failure after a slow, three-month detoxification, and the third remained addicted, cajoling physicians into giving her drugs or stealing them from their offices.

But these opinions were at variance with that of J. B. Mattison (1892), who felt that women were easier to cure than men and cited the recovery of two sisters who had been morphine addicts for ten years. Mattison also mentioned a case report by Dr. Albert Day, who cured a thirty-six-year-old woman of a thirteen-year morphine addiction acquired during treatment for a "uterine disorder." Gratefully, the woman wrote: "I can think of but one thing only, my happy deliverance from an iron bondage; and I now appreciate and enjoy this bright, beautiful world, as one who having long groped in thick darkness" (p. 9). Other examples from Dr. T. D. Crothers, the director of a sanitarium in Hartford, Connecticut, and editor of the *Quarterly Journal of Inebriety*, included six women, ages twenty-eight to sixty-two, who had been cured of opiate addictions ranging from six months to twelve years.

Applying new scientific ingenuity to an old problem, D. W. Nolan wrote that opium addiction was "a diseased condition to be remedied, like other diseases, by those physical and moral agencies which reason and experience show to be efficacious" (1881: 832). Successful treatment, although difficult, could be accomplished either by "immediately giving up the drug and suffering the consequences" or by the preferable regimen of a "gradual lessening of the dose until a barely perceptible quantity is taken" (p. 833). Others believed that opiates were a cellular poison and induced a state of treatable "toxemia." This theory, proposed by C. L. Seeger in the *Boston Medical and Surgical Journal* as early as 1833, relied on intestinal purgatives and emetics, good food, rest, and fresh air, treatments that would form the foundation of the sanitarium movement. Further refinements were proposed by physicians like Dr. William Waugh in Chicago and, most prominently, Dr. George E. Pettey, who ran a drug-treatment sanitarium in Memphis.

Not all physicians believed that opiate addiction required the attentions of a specialist. In *The General Practitioner as a Specialist*, J. D. Albright claimed that the generalist was quite capable of treating opiate addiction, a "cruel merciless monster whose almost relentless grasp holds in a thraldom infinitely worse than slavery, its legion of victims in all parts of the world" (1900: 5). With remarkable confidence, Albright offered a forty-eight-hour cure for opiate addiction, a four- to six-day cure "which will show fully ninety per cent. [sic] of cures in curable cases," and a more gradual treatment that might take up to twenty or thirty days. In defining addiction as a chronic relapsing disease, perhaps in an effort to explain the large number of treatment failures that certainly occurred, Albright cautioned that relapse should be interpreted not as a sign of failure but rather as an incentive for the physician to pursue a rational course of treatment as for any other medical condition.

Sanitariums provided another alternative for the treatment of addiction. These private facilities, sometimes part of a series of similar institutions, increased in popularity as the century advanced, and by

1910, they numbered around a hundred. Most of them relied on the provision of a quiet, therapeutic setting in a bucolic landscape and were generally open only to middle- and upper-class addicts—who could afford their fees. Some "treatment experts," such as John Harvey Kellogg, who ran a renowned sanitarium in Battle Creek, Michigan, developed elaborate therapeutic regimens, for which they claimed great success. Although his regimen called for up to six months of bed rest, in *Modern Medicine and Bacteriological Review,* published (coincidentally) in his hometown, Kellogg (1898) advocated rapid drug withdrawal lasting only one or two days, believing that a "short, sharp fight" was preferable to the "long-drawn-out agony" of gradual dosage reduction. The mainstays of Kellogg's acute treatment approach included avoiding drugs, except for the occasional use of morphia, atropine, minerals, or botanicals such as fluid extract of Coto bark; a fluid diet consisting of buttermilk, malted nuts, or unfermented fruit juices; enemas, repeated as often as every four hours; "hydrotherapy," an elaborate ritual of hot and cold baths; and the liberal use of strong galvanic currents applied in specific ways (in the treatment of diarrhea, for example, "the negative pole should be applied at the back, the positive in front"). Attesting to Kellogg's popularity but not necessarily to his success, his sanitarium was still offering the same regimen five years later.

The best-known sanitariums were the national "chain" of Keeley Institutes.[2] Leslie E. Keeley published his pamphlet *The Opium Habit; Its Proper Method of Treatment and Cure, Without Suffering or Inconvenience* because he was concerned that "the use of this drug is alarmingly on the increase . . . the habit has been largely unchecked, the evil has been unhindered" (1880: 3–4). Opium, Keeley wrote, caused a change in the structure of the nerves. His famous bichloride of gold "cure" would "*develop* nerves," and "the effect of gold upon nerve tissue, restoring it to a natural condition, is perfectly marvelous." The Keeley Institutes offered hot baths, exercise, fresh air, and a "plain and wholesome" diet. Keeley also developed a slow, nine-day opium discontinuation regime.

Between September 1892 and September 1893, almost fifteen thousand addicts sought treatment at Keeley's popular centers, where women enjoyed separate facilities. For morphine or opium addiction, treatment lasted four to eight weeks, "dependent on the amount of the drug used daily, and the general condition of the patient." In the

White Plains, New York, facility, treatment cost twenty-five dollars a week for the cure and medical attendance (payable four weeks in advance) and between six and fifteen dollars a week for room and board at a local boardinghouse (*The Keeley Institute, White Plains,* undated pamphlet). Some patients suffering from neurasthenia received Keeley's special treatment, which contained "Kola" (Albright 1900), while others received Gold Neurotine (Keeley 1880).

Given the extent of opiate addiction in America, it is not surprising that sharp-eyed entrepreneurs soon sought to cash in on it. Vendors' uncanny ability to capitalize on addicts' desperation, shame, and gullibility, bolstered by endless testimonials of miraculous cures, fed a thriving home remedy industry. Many addicts undertook their own treatment using the unregulated "cures" advertised in newspapers, magazines, and pamphlets mailed out in great quantities by quacks and charlatans. Most of these cures contained morphine or another opiate combined with herbal or sweetened preparations for palatability. Some were even "specifically prepared" for individual addicts, who answered a questionnaire detailing their opium consumption. This allowed the entrepreneur to prepare substitute opiates in an amount that would sustain addiction safely and without discomfort (Haller and Haller 1974). An advertisement in the *New York Herald* for October 5, 1902, offered a free bottle of a "St. James Society curative nostrum" with the come-on, "Morphine, Laudanum, Opium and All Drug Habits, Cured Free" (cited in Silver 1979). Samuel Hopkins Adams, however, debunked the Society's "cure," calling it a "swindle" and noting that he knew of "two unfortunates who got the St. James' habit more firmly fixed than the original morphine habit" (1907: 116).

Charles B. Towns, a failed stockbroker, enjoyed great success with his popular "secret" formula, which, it was eventually discovered, consisted of prickly ash bark, hyoscyamus, and belladonna. This remedy, given in conjunction with cathartics, castor oil, and other substances, reportedly cured thousands of addicts before physicians were able to challenge Towns's claims (Musto 1973). Towns's formula was also used by Dr. Alexander Lambert, a New York physician "of high repute," who was former President Theodore Roosevelt's private physician for many years (*New York Times,* October 7, 1909). Dr. Lambert was also successful in treating addicts, such as a fifty-nine-year-old woman with a twenty-year morphine addiction, who, although "feeble and nervous" on admission, was discharged in good condition after only thirteen days of treatment with Towns's formula. Another cure for addiction, developed by a physician at Bellevue Hospital in New York City, could reportedly "restore victims in 72 hours." After administration of seven grains of morphine, patients received a "corrective dose," which was described only as a formula that "awakens and gives back life to the secretive and excretive powers that have been partially paralyzed by the use of the drug" (*New York Times,* March 28, 1908).

Amid similar overstated claims, there were many who recognized the general lack of success in curing opiate addiction. Horace Day graphically depicted the horrors of addiction and the extreme difficulty the addict faced if he resolved to free himself from "these protracted and apparently hopeless disorders" (1868: 6). Fitzhugh Ludlow noted "how impracticable in the large majority of cases is any cure of a long-established opium habit" (Day 1868: 285). The robust entrepreneurial promotion of these so-called cures for addiction soon encountered rebuttals: these "cures" were useless. Recidivism rates were almost certainly high, and many patients who could not be treated successfully, or who relapsed after discharge from a treatment program, probably did not return to that facility. Horatio C. Wood, Jr. (1893), a professor of "therapeutics" at the University of Pennsylvania, wrote: "I have seen the whole body of a woman almost as black as a man's coat from the beating she had received to keep her awake in narcotic poisoning." In acknowledging the past failures of treatment regimens, George Wheelock Grover explained that most treatments, including the sanitariums, had not succeeded for several reasons:

> They fail first in their ability to sustain the system of the patient in such a manner that he can pass through his weeks of treatment without shock in any way to the already shocked and weakened system. They fail, secondly, in the fact that they leave the patient in such a condition that his future abstinence is largely, if not wholly, a matter of sheer volition, with the system still calling for the well known nepenthe and with the resistance to that craving a mere matter of the will. The time is sure to come when the patient will lapse again into the arms of his old bondage. (1894: 48)

Sanitarium advertisements and patient testimonials boasted of success, but since they neither kept nor published records, there is no real evidence to show how effective Keeley's Institutes, or any other sanitariums, were in curing addictions. Although many hailed the sanitarium movement as a progressive innovation that attempted to individualize and humanize care for addicts, claims of success were greatly exaggerated. The *New York Times* (April 15, 1915) reported Dr. Perry Lichtenstein's opinion that many of the sanitariums simply dispensed drugs to addicts and "pretended to cure the drug habit while really existing for the purpose of supplying drugs to those who wanted them." It was also subsequently shown by Chauncey F. Chapman (1893) that Keeley's bichloride of gold contained no gold at all. The popularity of Keeley's facilities peaked in the late 1890s and thereafter declined. The last Keeley facility, in Dwight, Illinois, was acquired by the federal government in 1920 for use as a Veterans Administration hospital.

Viewed through the prism of history, these therapies represent the first attempt to confront a national problem most physicians either avoided or dealt with ineffectually. Long before the medical profession appreciated the addict's sense of hopelessness, opiate addicts themselves recognized their physical and psychological imprisonment. But treatments were tried and discredited, one after another, creating among the public a sense of frustration over the medical establishment's inability to provide a solution.

The Legislative Response

Alongside the campaign to educate physicians about the dangers of addictive drugs and the many failed attempts to find effective treatment, another drug control strategy was emerging. Although some of the nation's antidrug feeling was prompted in part by a desire to improve women's lives, the antidrug agenda was more solidly based in fear of the growing minority population. During the late nineteenth century the Hearst-dominated tabloid press began to highlight the plight of female addicts, who were often portrayed as targets of sexually predatory racial groups. An 1895 article, for example, told of "Eight Men and Two Women Who Lay at a Gotham Gate of a Hundred Sorrows"; an 1899 article that "well dressed visitors arrive in cabs and automobiles at an opium den"; an 1893 headline that "Slave to Morphine Dies from Drug: Mary J. Holmes Passed from Deep Sleep to Death While a Friend Watched beside Her" (cited in Silver 1979: 28).

The press also linked drug-related urban crime committed by minority youths to the sexual vulnerability of young women. As one historian noted, "Tracts and broadsides, lurid articles, and pious 'eyewitness' accounts of degenerate, drug-sodden, sex-crazed dope fiends fascinated and horrified the public" (Blum 1969: 53). These graphic depictions, which focused on a small but growing segment of the addicted population, would be an important factor in mobilizing public support for antidrug statutes.

During the same period, an emerging Hollywood that attracted silent film fans by the millions, had discovered that opium smoking and opium dens were popular movie subjects.[3] In 1894, Thomas Edison made a kinetograph, a half-minute film, entitled *Chinese Opium Den.* Edison's company went on to produce *Rube in an Opium Joint,* probably the earliest surviving film dealing with drugs, in 1905. *Morphia—The Death Drug,* filmed in 1914, told the story of a physician who forced his secretary into morphine addiction. Other films portrayed women as addicts: in the two-reeler *The Drug Traffic,* two women died from morphine poisoning, and in *The Secret Sin* (1915), a physician hooked the heroine on morphine after she had experimented with opium in a Chinese opium den. A flood of similar films followed: *The Rise of Susan* (1916), in which a drug-crazed woman threw herself to her death, *The Devil's Needle* (1916), in which a model took narcotics to relieve the boredom of posing, *The Girl Who Didn't Care* (1916), *The Devil's Assistant* (1917), featuring a heroine who became addicted to drugs after her child's death, and *Romance of the Underworld* (1918). Even Charlie Chaplin took up the theme: in *Easy Street* (1917), he was accidentally injected with drugs and transformed into a mob-conquering hero.

Society's growing unease toward cocaine use was reflected in movies like *Cocaine Traffic* (1914), *Bondwomen* (1915), *Black Fear* (1916), *The Mystery of the Leaping Fish* (1916), a parody of Sherlock Holmes whose main character was named Coke Ennyday, and D. W. Griffith's *For His Son* (1912), in which a physician who sought to make his beloved son wealthy by developing a soft drink called Dopokoke inadvertently turned him into a cocaine addict. More than two hundred films featuring addicts, peddlers, and smugglers were produced during the silent era.

Published reports claimed to document cases of women waking out of drug-induced stupors to find themselves in brothels (Sanger 1858).

Rumors of hypodermic-wielding men in search of female victims in amusement parks, crowded streetcars, and dance halls circulated widely (Banner 1974). Public concern about the white slave trade eventually resulted in the passage of the White Slave Traffic Act, or Mann Act, in June 1910, which was intended to regulate "interstate and foreign commerce by prohibiting the transportation therein for immoral purposes of women and girls" (S. Doc. 702, serial 5943, 61–63). Even so, a newspaper story of December 7, 1913, reported that "hundreds of respectable girls" were drugged in darkened movie houses by poisoned-needle-wielding white slave traffickers (cited in Silver 1979: 141). Hollywood films also depicted male procurers of the white slave trade, employed, presumably, by international syndicates. Silent films such as *Traffic in Souls* (1913), *White Slave Traffic* (1913), *The White Slave* (1913), and *The Great White Trail* (1917) exemplify Hollywood's lurid treatment of women's enslavement through drugs.

Much of the flurry of attention focused on women and opium reflected a desire to control the "Oriental" presence in America. The historian John Helmer argues that the first wave of Chinese immigrants were not opium smokers and that opium smoking increased because Chinese producers pushed to expand their market in America. Estimates of the number of opium smokers who either brought the drug with them from China or took up the practice in the United States show an increase to 30 or 40 percent of the Chinese population by the end of the century (Helmer 1975; Courtwright 1982).

Opium smoking spread to white America in the 1870s, primarily through underworld contacts, and after 1875 to the upper classes (Courtwright 1982). It was commonly believed that opium was used to seduce young girls and to reduce sexual inhibitions. San Francisco authorities learned that "many women and young girls . . . were being induced to visit the [Chinese opium smoking] dens, where they were being ruined morally and otherwise" (Kane 1882: 1). The same writer reported: "Many females are so much excited sexually by the smoking of opium during the first few weeks that old smokers with the sole object of ruining them have taught them how to smoke. Many innocent and over-curious girls have thus been seduced" (p. 8). In 1883, the Hearst newspapers told of working women taking lunch breaks in Chinatown opium dens (cited in Silver 1979).

Many, like the Englishman Norman Kerr (1894), knew that opiates sedated rather than stimulated users, that "opium soothes, alcohol maddens," but the lay mythology that opiates induced erotic parox-ysms, rape, and seduction persisted (cited in Morgan 1974: 22–23). Dr. Hamilton Wright, one of the early architects of international U.S. drug policy, played on this mythology to advance his campaign for sweeping antidrug legislation. Wright claimed that "one of the most unfortunate phases of the habit of smoking opium in this country [was] the large number of women who have become involved and were living as common-law wives or cohabitating with Chinese in the Chinatowns of our various cities" (Wright 1910: 44). The tabloid press continued to feature the theme, publishing pictures with captions like "A Dirty Opium Den in New York's Chinatown, Where Men and Women of All Grades of Society Meet in Common Degradation as Slaves of the Drug" (cited in Silver 1979: 38–39). Such images persist today: Caleb Carr's novel *The Alienist*, set in New York in 1896, tells of a young waif abandoned by a mother "who put an opium habit above caring for her son and finally became the mistress of a Chinese purveyor of the drug" (1994: 10).

In other cases, women were portrayed not as hapless victims but as drug ring organizers. A San Francisco newspaper reported on Mrs. Rose Mentor, a "woman arrested for dealing in opium." Another story told of a "woman taken in a $1,000,000" Mexican border drug smuggling ring, and still another detailed the arrest of the Bennetts, "self-styled world's greatest dancers," in a "big opium raid in hotel room of tango pair" (cited in Silver 1979: 36). It was apparent, however, that these rings were run by men, and they were easily viewed as further examples of women's ruin in the drug trade.

The first anti-opium legislation, passed in San Francisco in 1875, was intended to keep whites from associating with opium-smoking Chinese. But the ordinance, which prohibited opium smoking in smoking-houses or "dens," was inspired less by concern for public health than by racism. Although opium smoking among the Chinese population in California had been increasing since 1850, there was little outcry for legislation until the mid-1870s, when an economic depression, job competition between whites and Chinese, and a con-comitant campaign to curtail "Oriental" immigration coincided (Hel-mer 1975). Similar laws were passed in Virginia City, Nevada, in 1876 and in New York State in 1882.

Additional state antidrug laws were passed between 1882 and 1915, but their general lack of success in controlling drug use was soon apparent. The limited jurisdiction of local laws could not check sales to buyers who crossed state lines or used the mail or parcel post. These limitations, as well as the lax wording and inconsistencies characteristic of much of the early state legislation, contributed to the impetus for a more comprehensive federal response.

Typical of early municipal legislative efforts was an 1898 Houston, Texas, ordinance, which imposed a fine of twenty-five to a hundred dollars for any unauthorized sale of cocaine, morphine, or opium (Courtwright 1982). Many states made exceptions for various types of drugs, however, including decocainized coca leaves, extremely small amounts of narcotics, certain so-called household remedies, and some liniments, ointments, and similar topical preparations (Terry and Pellens 1928). By 1912, every state except Delaware, as well as many large cities, had passed laws or ordinances against either opiates or cocaine or both (Kolb 1962). New York, whose addicted population was growing rapidly, passed an anti-cocaine law in 1913 and broadened the legislation in the Boylan Law the following year to include opium and its derivatives. National legislation to control opium smoking was introduced in 1880 and 1884, and although both bills died in committee, these efforts suggested that taxing mechanisms could be used to control the flow of opiates, a strategy that would bear fruit with the passage of the Harrison Anti-Narcotic Act.

Changing demographics also affected cocaine use. Where once the typical cocainist had been a professional, upper-middle-class male, nonmedicinal use of cocaine created new populations of users. Cocaine became popular as a stimulant in New England textile mills and Western mining towns (Spillane 1994). In the *Quarterly Journal of Inebriety*, Thomas Crothers wrote that cocaine users were increasingly "persons of the tramp and low criminal classes," especially in urban areas (1898: 370). By the 1890s cocaine was linked to the criminal underworld, and dens, first seen only in New Orleans, became commonplace in other American cities. By the turn of the century, Atlanta, Chattanooga, Dallas, and Houston were reporting cocaine epidemics. In New York, Chicago, Pittsburgh, and Kansas City, cocaine came to be associated with specific areas of urban vice. The drug was never cheap: drug habits costing more than two dollars a week, a substantial amount for the time, were common, and many users turned to criminal activity to support drug purchases (Spillane 1994). In many cases this activity was thought to be violent in nature—assaulting or shooting people, resisting arrest, or committing arson (Crothers 1910).

Cocaine use among blacks played a prominent role in antidrug legislative efforts. Due in large part to the conditions of rural poverty, blacks suffered more illness than whites and, lacking easy access to physicians, often resorted to Tucker's Asthma Cure, Agnew's Powder, Anglo-American Catarrh Powder, and similar cocaine-containing patent medicines (Helmer 1975). In addition, nonmedicinal cocaine, imported in the 1880s through Southern ports, had become an increasingly popular stimulant among black stevedores, levee construction crews, and plantation workers (Spillane 1994). In 1860 the great majority of the country's 4.5 million blacks, who constituted 14 percent of the population, were Southern slaves. Following the Civil War, the federal government provided some protection to the newly freed blacks, but Jim Crow laws prompted a heavy exodus from the South in the late 1870s, and the "Black Belt" became more diffuse thereafter. In the early twentieth century, the major migration of blacks to Northern industrial centers headed largely to cities like Chicago, Detroit, Pittsburgh, and New York.

Although Freud and others had long since recognized the dangers of cocainism, there were some who continued to extol the virtues— even the wonders—of cocaine. In his encyclopedic history of coca, W. Golden Mortimer called the drug "Nature's best gift to man" (1901: 22). Once cocaine became more closely associated with minority urban populations, however, its use became a matter of urgent concern. Cocaine reputedly gave blacks superhuman strength and cunning, and even invulnerability to bullets, beliefs that played into increasing racial and ethnic fears. By 1908, stories in the *New York Times* characterized cocaine as "the most insidious of deadly drugs" associated with slovenly, disreputable characters in tenderloin areas of the nation's cities (Fixx 1971: 159–161). On September 29, 1913, a Hearst newspaper printed the headline: "10 Killed, 35 Hurt in a Race Riot Born of a Cocaine 'Jag,'" followed by "Drug Crazed Negroes Fire at Every One in Sight in Mississippi Town" (cited in Silver 1979: 55). Such inflammatory rhetoric only added to the perception that blacks were a threat to white society, although there was little evidence to support these claims. In fact, in the *Journal of Nervous and Mental Disease*, E. M. Green reported the findings of a Georgia study that psychoses induced by cocaine were much more common in whites

(1914: 702). And of 2,119 admissions of blacks to the Georgia State Sanitarium between 1909 and 1914, only one could be ascribed to cocaine toxicity.

In the South, where during the Temperance Movement the consumption of cocaine-laced drinks increased, whites feared that cocaine would promote black sexual violence against white women. Professional pronouncements fueled this belief. The Committee on the Acquirement of the Drug Habit of the American Pharmaceutical Association claimed that "the negros, the lower and immoral classes" were easily influenced and took more drugs because "they give little thought to the seriousness of the habit forming" (Eberle and Gordon 1903: 480). A 1907 report by the committee noted that both women and blacks were "particularly vulnerable to cocaine" (Worth 1991: 4). The Shanghai International Commission declared in 1909 that "cocaine is often the direct incentive to the crime of rape by the Negroes of the South and other sections of the country" (Wright 1910; Musto 1973: 43–44). Testimony before the House of Representatives in 1910 claimed that Southern blacks "would just as leave rape a woman as anything else and a great many of the southern rape cases have been traced to cocaine" (Morgan 1981: 93). Hamilton Wright reported that "[cocaine] is used by those concerned in the white slave traffic to corrupt young girls, and when the habit of using the drug has been established, it is but a short time before such girls fall to the ranks of prostitution" (*New York Times*, March 12, 1911). Another article (*New York Times*, August 1, 1914) reported that a young man crazed by cocaine had "seized several women" in Battery Park. That same year, in the *Medical Record*, Edward Huntington Williams noted that "the cocain habit has assumed the proportions of an epidemic among the colored people" and that "sexual desires are increased and perverted" (1914: 247–249).

Cocaine also became increasingly associated with prostitution. While journalists wildly overstated the role of cocaine in luring women into the "white slave trade," cocaine use among prostitutes, as indicated by police reports from New York City, was certainly growing. In 1903 the American Pharmaceutical Association reported that cocaine was displacing morphine as the drug most widely used by prostitutes. In a survey of the Baltimore City Jail, black women reported that cocaine was the drug they used most often. The same report noted that "almost every colored prostitute [was] addicted to cocaine" (Eberle and Gordon 1903: 478). Chicago prostitutes were serviced by "runners" who delivered cocaine to them and their customers from local drugstores (Spillane 1994).

Just as cocaine use appeared to be dropping from peak usage (Helmer 1975), pressure from many different directions came together to promote significant anti-cocaine legislation. Cocaine sales were restricted in Oregon in 1887, in California in 1907, and in Louisiana in 1911. In New York State, anti-cocaine laws were passed in 1907, 1908, 1910, and 1913 (the Delahanty measure). Other states, such as Kentucky, Illinois, and Ohio, pressed pharmacists to restrict cocaine sales through state regulations and pharmacy codes (Spillane 1994). Yet many of the measures intended to control the cocaine trade proved ineffective.

International Pressures

At the turn of the century, the United States was seeking recognition as an international power and attempting to solidify its future influence in global politics. International opium traffic had not been ignored during the nineteenth century. Early treaties with Siam in 1833 and 1856, with Japan in 1858, and with China in 1844, 1858, 1880, and 1903 attempted to impose restrictions. In 1842, tariffs had been levied on opium imports for the first time and were periodically increased over the next sixty years. But if the United States hoped to shape international drug policy in the new century, it became clear that the nation needed both a coherent internal drug policy and a strong presence at international drug conferences. Politicians and the press joined together to influence the national mood in support of strong and effective action, despite the self-interested objections of those, such as physicians and pharmacists, whose livelihoods would be seriously threatened by a program of drug control.

The United States thus committed itself to promoting a campaign to control the international flow of drugs.[4] The Spanish-American War of 1898 had left the nation with control of Puerto Rico, Cuba, Guam, and the Philippines. Many American servicemen returned from the Philippines addicted to opium. Some acquired opiate habits through medical administration. One veteran recounted a typical experience:

a bout with dysentery, treatment with C&O (camphor and opium pills) for four months, and addiction to increasing amounts of laudanum on his return home (Stanley 1919). Others acquired the habit of smoking opium from "natives of foreign countries" (Eberle and Gordon 1903). In response to pressure from Charles Henry Brent, the first Episcopal bishop in the Philippines, a special committee appointed by President Taft urged that opiates be entirely prohibited there, except for medicinal purposes.

Beginning in 1909, the pace of international drug control accelerated. Coincident with the first international Shanghai Commission, the United States felt pressured to "clean up its own house" and in February 1909 passed "an Act to prohibit the importation and use of opium for other than medicinal purposes" (Terry and Pellens 1928). The principles enunciated at the International Opium Conference in Shanghai in 1909 were formalized by the Hague Opium Convention and signed by twelve countries, including the United States, on January 23, 1912. Two subsequent meetings in 1913 and 1914 led to the signing of the completed international agreement, which formalized international control of the opium trade. To many, however, the treaty seemed constructed to protect the interests of opium-producing countries and leaked "like a sieve" (La Motte 1924: 175). The onset of the First World War soon after temporarily drew attention away from the issue of opium control. At the same time, the actualization of international agreements and the passage of a national antidrug tax act moved America into the Classic Era of drug control.

Culmination

Early in the century, American society had come to regard addiction as contrary to its own best interests. Drug use had no place in a country that valued action, rationality, and predictability. Addicts—viewed as enslaved, unproductive, inefficient, escapist, and self-centered—were a threat to American society. It has been observed that "the sinister transmogrification of narcotic addiction was a critical precondition for the legal developments that followed. It would have made no sense—politically, culturally, morally, or in any other way—to repress addicts who were mainly sick old women" (Courtwright, Joseph, and Des Jarlais 1989: 5). The emergence of socially deviant groups evoked a legislative response that relied on the police power of the state to restrict or eliminate objectionable behavior and "social deviance."

The mythology that "Negroes" and "Orientals" threatened white women with violence, seduction, rape, and enslavement, which was promulgated by the government, dramatically overstated in the press, and glamorized in the movies, served the national agenda well. As the nation moved toward a policy of restriction and repression, the "women in danger" scare tactics presented convincing reason for legislation. Increasingly efficient forms of mass communication, such as newspapers and the movies, sent graphic images to a public hungry for sensation and increasingly intoxicated by Hollywood. In turn, the media's sensationalistic reporting on women's drug addiction furthered the national agenda.

Ultimately, the vigorous campaign against addictive drugs was political rather than medical. The inappropriate medicinal use of opiates had already been largely curtailed: infectious diseases once treated with opiates were controlled through improving sanitary conditions, older addicts were dying off, conscientious physicians were better informed about opiates and about the newer, milder analgesics, and unscrupulous physicians faced a measure of regulatory control. Some physicians called for reform. One claimed that "the opium habit would die out of the land" by more strictly controlling the sale of opiates, preventing pharmacists from refilling prescriptions, and labelling proprietary preparations (Winterburn 1882: 513). Charles B. Towns (1912) railed against druggists who organized to overturn or amend legislation that would curtail their drug-related income.

National anti-opium legislation, along with the Shanghai Conference in 1909, created a momentum for comprehensive federal action. Dr. Hamilton Wright drafted a national drug control plan that relied on federal powers of taxation. The proposed legislation would require all dealers in opiates, cocaine, chloral hydrate, and cannabis to register with the government, pay taxes on the drugs, keep records, and use revenue stamps on drug containers or face severe penalties. No exemptions were made for small quantities of drugs, and patent medicines and household remedies were included.

Introduced in April 1910 by Representative David Foster of Vermont, chairman of the House Committee on Foreign Affairs, the bill was debated for weeks. Both Wright and Foster referred specifically to the problems of women and children (Morgan 1981). But under pressure from drug manufacturers and pharmacy lobbying groups, the Sixty-first Congress failed to pass the Foster Bill. In its wake, however, would come one of the major legislative antidrug initiatives of the twentieth century.

four

THE HARRISON ANTI-NARCOTIC ACT

Although the Foster Bill went down to defeat, Hamilton Wright remained determined to pass comprehensive antidrug legislation. As the American delegates to the Second International Opium Conference in 1912 had noted, "the one nation which has not been vitally affected by the international movement initiated by the United States is the United States itself . . . the Congress so far has failed favorably to consider carefully drafted measures aimed to bring the continental United States into line and in accord with the principles now embraced by the International Opium Convention" (cited in Terry and Pellens 1928: 646). To that end, Wright searched out a sponsor for a new antidrug bill after Foster's death: Representative Francis Burton Harrison, a New York Democrat. The resulting legislation, like the earlier bill, attempted to control and regulate nonmedicinal narcotics, operationally defined as opium and coca-based drugs, but the statute was in essence a tax revenue measure. It required those involved in the production, importation, manufacture, or dispensation of these drugs to register and pay an occupational tax. Violators risked penalties of up to five years in prison.

At the National Drug Trade Conference in 1913, the most vocal opposition to the proposed bill came from the American pharmaceutical industry, which resented governmental intrusion into the legal drug market. The two conference representatives from the American Medical Association, however, supported passage (Musto 1973). The Harrison Anti-Narcotic Bill, drafted by a joint committee of the departments of State and Treasury, was passed by the House in June 1913 and by the Senate in August 1914, and was signed into law by President Woodrow Wilson in December 1914.

Passage of the Harrison Act generated considerable confusion. Some regarded it simply as an information-gathering act whose provisions the states would enforce. Others believed that it empowered federal police to regulate narcotics sales within the states. U.S. Surgeon General Rupert Blue, representing the Public Health Service, declared that the Harrison Act fit the former description, and that physicians could continue to write narcotic prescriptions for patients. The American Medical Association also supported the contention that patients could continue to receive narcotics, although their sale for nonmedicinal use was prohibited. But the Bureau of Internal Revenue, the agency responsible for enforcing the Harrison Act, held a markedly different view. Intent on enforcing the underlying moral message of Harrison—that using narcotics for any purpose other than medical treatment was harmful and should be punished—the Bureau interpreted the Act to mean that providing narcotics to addicts solely for addiction maintenance was also illegal. Relying on this more rigid interpretation, the Bureau pursued strict enforcement through expanded police activity (Musto 1973).

Addicts who were accustomed to obtaining drugs from street sources found themselves in desperate straits after March 1, 1915, when the act went into effect. Drug prices skyrocketed. On April 16, the *World* reported that "drug slaves" were being admitted to New York hospitals in large numbers; in one day Bellevue alone admitted "nineteen drug slaves, some of whom were physical wrecks. They told pitiful tales of the suffering they had undergone after they had been cut off from their usual supplies of morphine, cocaine, or heroin" (Silver 1979: 85). In a *New York Times* interview (April 15, 1915), the head of the city's "dope squad" stated that "the poorer people, the men and women we call the 'bums,' who have always bought from street peddlers, are really up against it. The suffering among them is terrible."

By 1916, illicit markets for controlled drugs had sprung up in most of the nation's cities, and stronger law enforcement only pushed drug prices higher. In 1915, the price of street heroin in New York City, according to police reports published in the *New York Times*, had risen from just over six dollars an ounce to twelve dollars for an eighth of an ounce, a sixteenfold rise. Writing for the *New Republic*, Pearce Bailey (1916), who served as the army's chief neuropsychiatrist during the First World War, recorded an eightfold rise, from eighty-five cents a drachm to over seven dollars a drachm, "and it is adulterated at that." Opium addicts seeking a less expensive substitute for smoking opium, whose importation was barred in 1909, intensified the demand for heroin, which further inflated prices. Bailey also took note of a growing subculture of urban gangs of "boys and young men" with links to criminal activity, such as heroin possession, stealing, and destruction of property. This ominous development helped to reinforce society's view that addiction was a problem not for medicine but for the criminal justice system.

Despite initial judicial uncertainty, Treasury Department rulings and two Supreme Court decisions validated the government's power to regulate drug use, thus dictating the restricted options that would be available to addicts over the next forty years. In *U.S. v. Doremus*, the Court held that the Harrison Act was constitutional: the government could restrict drug use in medical practice. In *Webb et al. v. U.S.*, the Court ruled that physicians could not prescribe narcotics solely for addiction maintenance. Over the previous years, physicians had routinely prescribed maintenance doses of opiates to patients, usually those with chronic or terminal illnesses who had become addicted in the course of treatment. Suddenly, physicians found themselves treating "criminals" rather than "patients." Just thirty-six days after the *Webb* and *Doremus* decisions, federal agents in New York City arrested six physicians, four druggists, and two hundred addicts for violation of the Harrison Act (*New York Times*, April 9, 1919). Once physicians recognized the implications of the Supreme Court decisions, they were increasingly reluctant to treat addicts.

By 1919, of the addicts surveyed in penal institutions and almshouses, state, county, and municipal hospitals, and insane asylums, a majority reported that they had acquired the drug habit through association with another addict rather than through a physician. Patients in private hospitals and sanitariums, in contrast, reported that they acquired their addiction through the activities of physicians or in "other ways" than "association with other addicts" ("Traffic in Narcotic Drugs" 1919). Charity and private patients listed "self-medication of proprietary medicines" least often, attesting to the impact of federal regulation of narcotic sales and patent medicines. The population of addicts was separating into two distinct groups, those with the economic resources to maintain their iatrogenic habit, and the poor underclass with fewer options, who were being driven into the criminal underworld.

Prevalence of Addiction

Establishing the number of addicts in the United States at the time of the Harrison Act was no easy matter. In what was most likely a sensational propaganda piece about the evils of opium, an anonymous "modern opium eater" reported that "the United States Revenue Service has a roster of over three hundred thousand known users of opium in San Francisco alone. Countless other thousands are unregistered. Every other great city in the country has similar rosters, and numbers its 'fiends' by thousands and tens of thousands" ("A Modern Opium Eater" 1914).

Some limited data from efforts to register narcotic addicts did become available. In Jacksonville, Florida, Charles Terry, the city's health officer, registered 541 opium users, which represented less than 1 percent of the population. Extrapolating these numbers to the United States as a whole, Terry estimated that in a population of more than ninety-seven million, there were 782,118 narcotic users (Terry 1913). Lucius Brown, the food and drug commissioner for the state of Tennessee, however, reported registration of 2,370 addicts statewide in the wake of the Tennessee Anti-Narcotics Law of 1913. Brown's conservative estimate of "not less than 269,000 addicts" nationwide, about one-third that of Terry, was more consistent with the 200,000 estimate provided by the pharmaceutical industry (Wilbert 1915).

An article in *The World* in 1915 claimed that 200,000 "dope fiends" and an additional 10,000 cocaine users lived in New York City alone, but admitted, "there has never been a dope 'survey' of this city, and so estimates differ widely as to the actual number of addicts here." A report in the *New York City Department of Health Monthly* estimated that there were up to 300,000 addicts in the city and over one million addicts in New York State (Collins 1919). But a Joint Legislative Committee investigating the "distribution and sale of so-called habit-forming drugs" suggested that there were perhaps "100,000 people . . . now suffering from this disease" in New York State (cited in Terry and Pellens 1928: 826).

This confusion over numbers was further perpetuated by national surveys, which were considered more comprehensive. Dr. Charles F. Stokes, former surgeon general of the U.S. Navy, estimated that there were two million narcotic addicts in the country (*New York Times,* June 10, 1917), more than four times the estimate of another writer a year later (Scheffel 1918). In 1918, the Special Committee of Investigation appointed by the Secretary of the Treasury issued a preliminary report: basing their figures on questionnaires sent to physicians, they had identified 270,662 addicts, which, if extrapolated to the nation as a whole, would have produced a total of 694,000 addicts. Du Mez claimed that a number like 750,000 would be conservative, while the Bureau of Internal Revenue inflated the number to 1,500,000 (*New York Times,* April 13, 1919). The Treasury Department's final report, however, counted only 73,150 chronic narcotics users or 238,000 addicts nationwide, about 0.25 percent of the population (Kolb and Du Mez 1924). Terry and Pellens (1928) suggested a more likely estimate of about 420,000 addicts. The most inflated estimates went as high as five million users (Chein 1965), a reflection of a political agenda intended to achieve a strong federal approach to drug control.

In an attempt to reconcile these wildly divergent estimates, Lawrence Kolb and A. G. Du Mez (1924) conducted a comprehensive review of epidemiologic data, figures on opium imports, and average daily consumption among addicts. Despite the considerable disparity in much of the data, the authors concluded that the number of opiate addicts had probably peaked at about 246,000 during the years 1890 to 1909, and then declined to "somewhat less than 215,000" in 1915 and "about 110,000 in 1922 to 1924." Data gathered from thirty-four of the forty-four drug treatment clinics in 1920 yielded an estimate of 104,300 addicts nationwide or, if extrapolated only from New York City clinic figures, a slightly higher figure of 140,600. Adjusting for the amount of narcotics used for legitimate medicinal purposes, Kolb and Du Mez put the number of illicit opiate addicts at about 100,000 and of chronic cocaine users at about 9,000. A retrospective estimate by the National Commission on Marijuana and Drug Abuse concluded that there had been about 250,000 addicts in 1914, and that this number had halved over the next decade, due mainly to prohibition and policing (*Drug Use in America* 1973).

The general consensus, therefore, is that the number of opiate addicts in the United States peaked at the end of the nineteenth century and then declined. Using a different quantitative methodology, David Courtwright (1982) concluded that the number of opiate addicts rose from the 1850s to the 1890s, peaked in the 1890s at 4.59 per thousand population, and then declined to 1.97 per thousand in 1920, even assuming 100 percent underreporting. Data from the clinic survey in 1920 suggested a ratio of close to one per thousand (Kolb and Du Mez 1924). As Courtwright also pointed out, even if the numbers of addicts reported from clinics in Tennessee, Pennsylvania, and New York City from 1913 to 1922 were doubled, the rate of addiction in the United States during these years would still be 2.06 to 2.66 addicts per thousand, far fewer than at the end of the previous century.

Female Users

The years surrounding the Harrison Act saw an even greater decrease in the number of female addicts. Just before 1914, the majority of addicts registered in two Southern cities were women. In the Jacksonville, Florida, clinic, which operated from 1912 to 1914, women made up 68 percent of the opium and morphine addicts in 1912 and 58 percent of the addicts in 1913 (Terry 1913). These women were primarily white, although the population was 50 percent black and 50 percent white.

In the statewide drug maintenance program in Tennessee, which began in 1913, women made up two-thirds of the 2,370 opiate addicts registered in the first twelve months of operation, and 90 percent were white. Women formed two-thirds of the morphine and gum opium users, and three-quarters of the tincture of opium (laudanum) users, but only one-quarter of the heroin addicts. The average age of female registrants, which ranged from twenty-two to ninety, was forty-nine years. The average length of addiction, which ranged from one month to fifty years, was eleven and a half years. More than a quarter of these women were judged to have no present organic illness requiring opiate treatment, while 14 percent acquired their narcotism because of "female complaints" (Brown 1915).

These numbers obviously reflected the population surveyed. Subpopulations, such as rural farming families, were not usually included in surveys, despite the fact that, as one writer pointed out, "much-harassed farmers' wives" contributed to the number of opiate addicts (Blair 1919). Among other selected populations, such as addicted prisoners, men would be expected to outnumber women. In his survey of a thousand inmates at City Prison in Manhattan, Perry Lichtenstein, the prison physician, noted that the "male habitues greatly outnumber the female" (1914: 964). Women inmates, Dr. Lichtenstein discovered, had previously been employed as actresses, nurses, saleswomen, and stenographers, and had been arrested for "soliciting, keeping disorderly houses, or shoplifting" (p. 965). He also found that iatrogenic addiction among women was uncommon, accounting for only twenty patients, most of whom were suffering from "[fallopian] tubal disease." When Clifford B. Farr reported on heroin addiction at Philadelphia General Hospital in 1915, he found that 25 percent of the patients were female and most reported that the origin of their drug use was "evil association." Another survey at the same hospital the following year revealed that women, most of whom were prostitutes, still made up only 30 percent of the population (McIver and Price 1916). At San Quentin prison, 15 percent of opiate-using male inmates reported that they had begun using drugs under the influence of "female-outcasts of the underworld, who send them to obtain the drug" (Stanley 1918).

Although an increasing number of narcotic-using women could be found among the poorer segments of society, this subset of women was not entirely representative. Writing in the *Century Magazine*, Charles B. Towns (1912) revealed that among his opiate-addicted patients he counted "exemplary mothers and wives." In New York City, Dr. Lichtenstein was surprised at "how many habitues are of the better class," including nurses, actresses, and "some of the very richest of our people" (1914: 965). Another observer commented that "society women who have undergone a trying season of parties and social functions, ever endeavoring to outrival their neighbor in splendor, often find themselves wrecked in mind and body" (Stanley 1915–1916: 586). In the *American Journal of Clinical Medicine*, George D. Swaine codified the distinction between different types of female drug users. He characterized Class One addicts as "physical, mental and moral defectives," tramps, hobos, criminals and underworld types, and women, "the idle rich, who began taking the drug for the intoxication it produces and have kept it up until they have become slaves to its devilish power." In contrast, Class Two addicts included "many good types of citizens," among them, women and girls who had become addicted because of physicians' prescribing practices (1918: 611).

By 1918 the Treasury Department's Special Committee on Investigation could report that "drug addiction is about equally prevalent in both sexes" ("Traffic in Narcotic Drugs" 1918). As a survey of female opium addiction from 1850 to 1970 concluded, passage of the Harrison Act was indeed "the watershed event that started the change that was to affect the entire complexion of American drug control and the pattern and extent of female drug abuse" (Cuskey, Premkumar, and Siegel 1979: 12).

After 1915, addicted women faced social stigmatization as well as increasing difficulty if they tried to maintain or rid themselves of their addiction. A female addict could switch to other drugs, find a courageous physician who was sympathetic or financially avaricious enough to supply her with drugs, frequent a narcotics dispensary or clinic for maintenance or decreasing doses with the ultimate goal of detoxification, enter a sanitarium for a "cure," quit her drug habit by herself, or enter the drug underworld.

"Patent" or proprietary drugs were still available, despite long-standing attempts at regulation. Although the American Pharmaceutical Association had presented model regulations, which formed the basis for the regulatory laws passed in thirty states in the 1870s and 1880s (Haller 1989), consistent federal legislation was still needed. The landmark Pure Food and Drug Act, spearheaded by Harvey Washington Wiley, chief chemist for the Department of Agriculture, and passed in 1906, required labels only on those over-the-counter products containing opiates, cocaine, marijuana, or chloral hydrate (Young 1967). From 1902 to 1912, the production of patent medicines actually increased—by 60 percent—and industry profits rose from 100 million dollars to 160 million dollars, reflecting these drug use patterns (Young 1961, 1967). Women thus continued to find it relatively easy to obtain drugs, especially patent medicines, from various sources. Some began to take morphine or heroin by injection after importation of smoking opium was banned in 1909.

Women of means, or those who could be maintained on small doses that would not attract the attention of narcotic agents, continued to receive drugs from private physicians without social retribution. Such was the case of a member of the Metropolitan Opera Company, who had managed to reduce her opium habit from twenty-five grains a day to fifteen (*New York Times,* April 15, 1919). But even if physicians attempted to comply with existing law, enterprising patients could procure single prescriptions through subterfuge. A deputy commissioner of the New York State Department of Narcotic Drug Control described the process:

> A woman arrives in New York with letters from the physicians in her home city, in which it is stated that she has a painful facial disease . . . no fewer than four physicians, no one of whom knew of the others prescribing, sent reports and requests concerning her to the department. It appears that when a physician, after prescribing, explains to the woman that she must come under the law and that he can treat her but once on an unofficial blank, she does not return to him, but applies to another doctor, who innocently prescribes for her. (Graham-Mulhall 1921: 107)

Nurses and physicians' wives also continued to have access to addicting drugs. Dr. Lichtenstein noted that he had "treated many nurses addicted to morphine taken hypodermically" (1914: 962). The majority of women seen at the New York City Narcotics Relief Station at Bellevue Hospital in 1919 were nurses, exceeding the numbers of working mothers, college students, and adolescents (Graham-Mulhall 1926). In Iowa, M. C. Macklin (1919) noted that the "bad example which is especially true of physicians' wives" was one of the major causes of female morphine addiction.

Some women undertook the difficult task of self-withdrawal. By going "cold turkey" or gradually reducing their drug use themselves, these women could avoid attending public clinics, begging physicians for maintenance narcotics, or resorting to the underworld. How many women attempted self-managed detoxification—and how many actually succeeded—is unknown.

Women who resorted to underworld sources to procure drugs, if not already involved, risked a life of crime. As in the past, some prostitutes became drug addicts, but a growing number of addicts turned to prostitution to support their habit. For women of higher standing, who "were not likely to follow the prostitutes into that dark and expensive world of the pusher and the black marketeer, if they could avoid it," entry into the underworld drug culture was dangerous (Cuskey, Premkumar, and Siegel 1979). But some women had little choice:

> In respect to female habitues the conditions are worse, if possible. Houses of ill fame are usually their sources of supply, and one has only to think of what repeated visitations to such places mean to countless good women and girls—unblemished in most instances except for an unfortunate addiction to some narcotic drug—to appreciate the terrible menace. (*American Medicine*, 1915)

The Clinics

Cities that opted to treat addiction as a medical and a public health problem offered another option. When the Harrison Act took effect in the spring of 1915, and more acutely after the Supreme Court decisions of 1919, the country faced the problem of what to do with addicts who had been cut off from narcotic supplies. Federal authorities feared they might turn to crime. At the same time, they anticipated that significant numbers of soldiers returning from the First World War had become addicted to drugs in the course of treatment for war-related injuries (*New York Times,* November 28, 1917). Some physicians argued for the right to treat their wealthy private patients, and others advocated the establishment of public treatment facilities for humane purposes. As arrests of drug users and drug suppliers rose throughout the country, the need for a solution to the problems of addicts and doctors became more pressing.

In the summer of 1919, the Internal Revenue Service urged that more clinics, which had existed on a small scale since 1912, should be established. A newspaper headline of August 7, 1919, read "U.S. Clinic to Sell Drugs to Addicts" at one-eighth the cost of street drugs (cited in Silver 1979: 86). Clinics began to proliferate, and although many were set up in response to governmental recommendations, others were established "in cities with little need except a deserving physician with the proper political connections" (Musto 1973: 151). Eventually, forty-four clinics were established in cities across the nation, including New York City; New Orleans, Shreveport, and Alexandria, Louisiana; Augusta, Atlanta, and Macon, Georgia; Los Angeles and San Diego, California; Cleveland and Youngstown, Ohio;

Knoxville and Memphis, Tennessee; Clarksburg, West Virginia; Paducah, Kentucky; and Houston, Texas.

An underlying assumption in the creation of these drug clinics was that making narcotics legally available to clinic registrants would reduce drug-related crime. Male addicts who were resistant to supportive treatment and forced abstinence tended to steal drugs directly or to commit robberies to support their habit. For narcotic-addicted women, who often turned to prostitution or petty crime, the clinics provided maintenance doses of narcotics, free of the threat of arrest. The assumption appeared to be vindicated by the Shreveport clinic, which operated from 1919 to 1923. During those years, theft and robbery "dropped off dramatically" (Waldorf, Orlick, and Reinarman 1974). But those who opposed the clinics concluded that they led directly to increases in criminal behavior and in incarceration, and cited penal facilities such as the U.S. Penitentiary at Atlanta, the New York City Prison, and Sing Sing in New York State (Anslinger and Tompkins 1953).

Another principle underlying the clinic idea was that dispensing legal drugs at low cost would undermine and eventually destroy the black market in regulated drugs. Some clinics wrote prescriptions for drugs, while others dispensed low-cost or no-cost morphine directly to patients. In the Shreveport clinic, addicts could buy morphine for six cents a grain, far less than both the pharmacists' ten to fifteen cents and the peddlers' fifty cents to a dollar. This strategy proved successful: during its years of operation, few if any illegal opiates were available (Waldorf, Orlick, and Reinarman 1974). Another hope was that ending of the black market in drugs would achieve increased safety for addicts and the general population. Instead of rounding up and arresting hundreds of addicts for simple possession, law enforcement personnel would be able to focus on reducing the illicit trade in drugs.

Fear of addicted criminals and a desire to reduce the illegal drug trade were significant factors, but the clinic idea was also promoted as a humane and reasonable approach to the national drug problem. Some physicians continued to support the hard-line position of increased law enforcement and forced abstinence, while others considered addiction a disease that required treatment, so that addicts would not be forced into illicit activities to support their habit. An editorial in *American Medicine* in 1915 called addiction "a medical problem purely and exclusively. The drug addict is sick, with a pathology as definite as that of any toxic disorder" (p. 800). Five years later an article in the same journal still claimed that addiction was "a definite physical disease, characterized by pathologic processes as real as those associated with any other bodily ill" (*American Medicine* 1920: 13). In New York State, the Whitney Committee, charged with reviewing laws on the distribution and sale of drugs, concluded in 1917 that narcotic addiction was a "definite disease" requiring "proper and humane treatment and cure" by means of "a supply of narcotic drugs to which the confirmed addict shall have access" (cited in Terry and Pellens 1928: 827–828). In reaction to the social changes in the addicted population, however, a mood of nontolerance had become dominant. Following the *Doremus* and *Webb* decisions, physicians found it necessary to suppress any compassion they might have felt for addicts in order to comply with the increasingly repressive national attitudes toward drug addiction.

The largest of the drug treatment clinics was based in New York City. Immediately after the Harrison Act went into effect, the New York "dope squad" announced that "anyone absolutely in need of a drug might be treated at any of the city hospitals," which were offering a "gradual reduction of the dosage" rather than a "sudden stopping of the drug" (*New York Times,* April 15, 1915). As the Annual Report of the New York City Department of Health remarked, the clinic had been opened because, "owing to enforcement of prohibition, it was feared that there would be a material increase in the number of persons addicted to the use of habit-forming drugs" (1919: 193). The Department of Health also noted that the change in the prescribing practices of physicians "caused addicts considerable distress" (p. 194). According to one commissioner the clinic was intended "for the humane purpose of saving the addict from the profiteering doctor and the profiteering druggist and to prepare him for hospitalization" (Graham-Mulhall 1921: 109). From its opening in June 1919 to the end of that year, the clinic filled over 216,000 prescriptions for 6,579 patients, dispensing 3,555 ounces of heroin and 1,125 ounces of morphine (p. 194). A total of 1,390 patients, primarily heroin addicts, were committed to hospitals for treatment, which consisted of rapid withdrawal to a level of comfort, followed by hyoscine (a poisonous nerve depressant and a sleep-inducer derived from belladonna) treatment and a four-week period of convalescence (p. 222).

During its operation, from June to December 1919, the New York

City clinic treated 1,532 women, who constituted 23 percent of the 6,579 addicts registered during that time. These women tended to be young—58 percent were under thirty and 90 percent were under forty—and three-quarters of them were white. A list of 264 female patients compiled by S. Royal Copeland, a health department commissioner, on July 31, 1919, included 127 houseworkers, 22 actresses, and 20 maids (*New York Times,* August 1, 1919). Records indicate treatment of women with short- and long-term addictions, among them, a middle-aged woman who had become addicted in the course of treatment for influenza the previous year, and two widows, one addicted to morphine for one year, the other for fifteen years. Writing in 1926, Sara Graham-Mulhall claimed that, at the time of its closure in 1920, the New York clinic had even registered 800 pregnant addicts (p. 29).[1]

Another New York State clinic, this one in Albany, served a more rural population of addicts but almost equal numbers of men and women. The average age of the female addict was thirty; 25 percent of the women but only 10 percent of the men were nonwhite (Musto 1973). Other clinics reported a predominance of males: in six clinics established in Connecticut between 1918 and 1920, 74 percent of the registered addicts (152 of 205) were men.[2] When its clinic opened in 1919, Memphis was still reporting that 57 percent of morphine addicts were female ("Drug Addicts in the South" 1919). In the New Haven, Connecticut, clinic, which operated from 1918 to 1920, twenty-five of the ninety-one patients registered in 1920 were women (Musto and Ramos 1981). Clinics in other parts of the country, such as Cleveland, where 35 percent of approximately two thousand registered addicts were women, and Los Angeles, where one-third of 582 addicts were women (Terry and Pellens 1928), reveal the extent to which men were beginning to outnumber women in the ranks of America's addicted.

The Shreveport clinic was probably the most successful example of a morphine maintenance program and might have served as a model for the rest of the country. Opening on May 3, 1919, under the direction of Dr. Willis Butler, it was modeled after one in New Orleans that had been designed to provide temporary drug relief at a reasonable price, cut down on increasing rates of theft, and drive illegal opiates out of the city. During its four years of operation, until February 10, 1923, the Shreveport clinic enjoyed broad community support, saw the local theft and robbery rate decline dramatically, and essentially ended the black market in drugs in that part of Louisiana. Its patient population was diverse, presumably reflecting the wide variety of addicts who needed help. Just over half had been addicted by physicians, and most were long-term addicts (the mean length of addiction was eight years).

Women composed about 25 percent of the 760 patients in the Shreveport clinic for whom records were still available in the mid-1970s (Waldorf, Orlick, and Reinarman 1974) and generally consumed smaller quantities of drugs than men. Although the occupation women most frequently reported was that of waitress, 35 percent were housewives. Among the female opiate addicts seen at the Shreveport clinic were a young store clerk suffering from syphilis who had used twelve grains of morphine daily for five years; a forty-eight-year-old nurse addicted to morphine for eleven years because of gallstone pain; a thirty-six-year-old nurse who had been in treatment eighteen times; a fifty-seven-year-old woman who had been addicted by her husband, a physician, after she "went insane" at age thirty; an eighty-year-old housewife, an addict for thirty years because of asthma and rheumatism, who was considered by the staff to be a "pitiful, incurable case"; a thirty-six-year-old cotton picker addicted to morphine for twenty-six years; a twenty-one-year-old housewife who had been a morphine addict for eight years after an operation for gangrene; and a seventy-one-year-old widow addicted to morphine for cancer pain.

Of the total clinic population, 89 percent cited some medical reason for their addiction. But not every woman attending the Shreveport clinic fit this picture. One woman, who received ten grains of morphine daily, was described by federal agents as a transient who "looks good and healthy but claims she feels bad if she doesn't get her daily allowance of morphine . . . a typical drug addict with no visible means of support." Other case profiles described a thirty-seven-year-old woman, also with no visible means of support, who had been addicted for eight years, "a good healthy plain everyday drug addict"; a thirty-two-year-old prostitute, an addict for twelve years, who appeared to federal agents to be "the picture of health; strongly built"; and a thirty-year-old woman who had switched from smoking opium to morphine, and when the clinic in Houston closed, had moved to Shreveport "to satisfy her addiction for the drug."[3]

Drug maintenance clinics provided a safe and inexpensive way for female addicts to procure narcotics. If they chose, they could maintain an orderly life without having to rely on the underworld or on men as sex partners or pushers, for their drug supply. During the few years the clinics existed, they enabled women to cope with addiction in a legal and medically supervised way, an option that vanished rapidly as they closed their doors.

The drug treatment clinics were never popular with the Narcotics Unit of the Treasury Department, since they ran counter to its repressive treatment approach. The unit monitored them closely, and in 1920, in an attempt to consolidate federal control over drug policy, it launched a campaign to ensure their closure. To support its case, the government argued that some addicts were receiving more narcotics than they needed and selling the surplus on the street, some were supplementing the free narcotics they received at the clinics with black market drugs, and some were continuing their criminal activities. The respectability of the clinics was further damaged by the revelation that many were hurriedly established, and were understaffed or run by physicians or administrators with little knowledge or training in the treatment of addiction.

Local citizen groups, whose fears had been fueled by sensational press reports on addicts and addiction, also began to pressure authorities to close the clinics. Twenty years earlier, press coverage had helped shape the consensus that achieved state and local regulation; now their convincing if not entirely honest depiction of the clinics drew public support for federal efforts.

In what might seem an ironic twist, physicians played a key role in the demise of the clinics. Although some in the medical establishment supported the concept of drug maintenance either because they recognized that addicts were able to lead a more normal life or because they themselves profited from dispensing drugs, most were opposed to the clinic idea. Opposition arose for a number of reasons: the general philosophical unacceptability of drug maintenance; the bad name poorly run drug clinics were giving organized medicine; pressure from federal authorities; press-driven concern about the effect of ambulatory treatment on local crime rates; and for some, discouraged by clinic failures, a desire to provide more comprehensive treatment for addicts.

The crosscurrents in the move to close the clinics were illustrated by events in New York City. In 1920, the Department of Health claimed in its annual report that the city clinic was being closed because the budgetary appropriation for drug treatment had run out. An article in the *New York Sun* (May 3, 1920), however, carried the headline "Drug Evil Routed. Hospital to Close. No Further Use for Worth Street Clinic Except Registration," a rationale apparently intended to satisfy the somewhat grandiose plan to "solve" the drug problem.

Dr. S. Dana Hubbard (1920b), who worked in the New York City Department of Health, reported at the time of the clinic closure that addicts had obtained excess narcotics, which they sold at a profit, persuaded friends to register to receive narcotics, forged prescriptions, tampered with dosage sheets, and sold registration cards illegally. Hubbard concluded that ambulatory treatment of narcotic addiction was not only a failure but "vicious in principle": "With but a very few possible exceptions, no cures are known to have been effected by means of the reduction system as used at this 'clinic'" (p. 772). Sara Graham-Mulhall (1921a), who became the joint commissioner for drug treatment when the clinic closed, recounted some of the difficulties the city encountered in treating addicts, agreeing that the clinic had been "an enormously expensive and colossal failure." She also revealed that a raid on the apartment of a nurse who worked at a New York hospital had uncovered the names of over four thousand male and female addicts, collected for the "sinister purpose of distributing them to illegal sellers" (1921b: 26).

Reporting in the *American Journal of Public Health*, C. E. Terry (1921) concluded that the New York clinic had failed primarily because its basic philosophy regarded the individual as an "addict" rather than as a "patient." Strongly believing that addicts should be treated humanely as medical patients, Terry was appalled at the clinic's long waiting lines in bad weather, its inability to deliver medical care, and its lack of confidentiality, which allowed easy reproduction of records and illicit sales of narcotics to those seeking help. Terry contrasted the New York clinic with the Narcotic Dispensatory in New Orleans, which was established by the Louisiana State Board of Health in 1918 under the direction of Dr. Marion W. Swords. He lauded the more modest approach taken by Dr. Swords, who realized that a "permanent cure of those afflicted with drug addiction-disease is impossible, in the great majority of cases, unless the addict be placed in a position to secure scientific treatment" (p. 34). The New Orleans clinic did not register patients, which averted the possibility of blackmail, and never revealed the patient's addicted status.

Nor was Terry satisfied when the New York clinic was closed and control of drug treatment passed to Sara Graham-Mulhall. He asserted that she lacked credibility and experience, and that her claims of success (which were at odds with her previous statements of the clinic's failures) were exaggerated.

As outpatient drug addiction treatment lost credibility, public health leaders promoted inpatient treatment. In August 1919, Riverside Hospital in New York allocated seven hundred beds on an emergency basis to treat addicts (New York City, Department of Health Annual Report 1920: 222). Dr. S. Royal Copeland enthusiastically praised this inpatient treatment, having seen "two hundred husky, red-cheeked, bright-eyed and clear-brained young men [women were ignored] who, a month before, were wrecks of humanity" (1920: 23). Most judged this inpatient approach unsuccessful, however, since, as the Annual Report noted, addicts showed "a non-appreciation of the service." The Department of Health, apparently losing patience, recommended that addiction treatment be discontinued and that addicts be "detained in institutions" for "custodial care" (p. 257). As S. Dana Hubbard wrote of the clinics, "they are not desirable and do not satisfactorily deal with the problem" (1920b: 35).

In a lecture in San Francisco in 1920, C. E. Terry also reported that, of the addicts from Riverside Hospital who were considered "statistically cured," all had either smuggled drugs into the hospital, had relapsed within a short period, or were in wretched condition when they were discharged. In fact, at the same conference, Graham-Mulhall herself reported the findings of the resident physician at Riverside Hospital: 90 percent of the 2,600 addicts released from the facility had returned to drug use within a few days after discharge (Terry 1921: 26). According to Graham-Mulhall (1921b), the Riverside Hospital experiment failed because the addicts under treatment became demoralized as their drug dose was lowered and resorted to larceny, lying, and forgery to maintain their supply. Her approach to treatment, however, became far more repressive than Terry's: among other things, she called for an isolation colony for addicts and a constitutional amendment giving Congress the "power to stamp out drug evil in the whole country" (pp. 31–32).

By 1920, public opinion was divided. The Federal Bureau of Internal Revenue, which had been responsible for establishing a few clinics after 1914, always favored drug detoxification over the clinic philosophy of drug maintenance. Although individual physicians dissented, the medical establishment took a unified stance: the clinics seemed difficult to operate and were thus basically unworkable. In 1920 the American Medical Association (AMA) announced its formal opposition to maintenance clinics. The next year the AMA solidified this position in an influential statement urging state and federal governments "to put an end to all manner of so-called ambulatory methods of treatment of narcotic drug addiction, whether practiced by the private physician or by the so-called 'narcotic clinic' or dispensary" (*Report of Committee on Narcotic Drugs* 1921: 1671). This position supported the Bureau's initiative that same year to begin closing the clinics, allowing only the elderly and the medically incurable to receive maintenance narcotics.

Because most of the clinics existed for only a limited period, long-term beneficial—or harmful—effects in the twelve to fifteen thousand addicts who received treatment were never systematically studied. Even had the well-kept records of the Shreveport clinic been carefully analyzed, they would have documented the course of only a selected population of patients, since the clinic tended not to admit "bums" or "loafers," and often refused admission to suspected criminals (Waldorf, Orlick, and Reinarman 1974). According to Terry and Pellens, with the closure of the clinics, important gains slipped away:

> The opportunity to influence individuals to be treated was lost; incurable cases that were being supervised and kept on a minimal dose of drug reverted to larger doses and lost their positions; drug peddlers returned and exerted, as they had before, their influence in spreading addiction among the younger age groups; petty thieving and pocket-picking and other minor crimes, resorted to by addicts of the underworld in order to secure the means to pay the peddlers' prices, were shown by police records in a number of communities to have reached their former frequency. (1928: 91)

Certainly, some addicts did have an opportunity to give up crime, obtain employment, support their families, and prepare for hospitalization and drug withdrawal. One of the side-benefits of drug treatment (which remains relevant today) was the opportunity it gave clinic physicians to treat venereal disease, which was diagnosed in 40 percent of the addicts in the Shreveport clinic alone (Waldorf, Orlick, and Reinarman 1974). Ultimately, however, the short life and rapid demise of the clinics left many important questions unanswered, including the number of men and women who were spared a life of crime to support their drug habit, the clinics' impact on addicts' health, and their role in deterring the rise of the illegal drug trade.

Although by 1921 most of the clinics had closed, some men and women continued to receive maintenance doses of narcotics. The Shreveport clinic existed until February 1923, and the treatment hospital in that city remained open until March 1925. Dr. Willis Butler, a Shreveport staff member, told one interviewer that he subsequently ran a maintenance clinic in San Francisco during the 1930s (Waldorf, Orlick, and Reinarman 1974). Opiate maintenance continued after the Harrison Act well into the 1960s, not only in Kentucky but probably throughout the South. In his study *Narcotic Addicts in Kentucky,* John O'Donnell (1969) found that 87 percent of the women surveyed received narcotics from a physician during at least part of their addiction, and more than half were maintained by physicians for the entire period.

America's experiment with legal, clinic-based drug maintenance ended abruptly when the last clinic closed in 1923. For those who could afford them, limited opportunities for drug treatment remained available in private sanitariums, while the less fortunate found treatment in prisons or state psychiatric hospitals. Most, however, had nowhere to turn but the drug underworld.

With the passage of the Harrison Act and the *Webb* and *Doremus* Supreme Court decisions, physicians were rightly apprehensive about the legal repercussions of maintaining female addicts on narcotics. More enlightened about the dangers of opiates, physicians as well as pharmacists were also turning less often to drugs for organic and nonorganic complaints. These developments ensured that a large number of female addicts would be poor, disadvantaged women relegated to illegal drug use, male dependence and domination, and lives of degradation and shame. It was not until the 1960s that drug maintenance through organized clinics was once again considered seriously.

five

THE CLASSIC ERA

During the Classic Era of drug enforcement, which extended from the
closure of the drug maintenance clinics in the 1920s through the
Second World War, federal policy advocated harsh and punitive law
enforcement efforts in dealing with drug trafficking and sales.
Whereas the original Harrison Act had mandated five years in prison
for violations, state laws numbering "far into the hundreds" increased
penalties to maximums of twenty, forty, and even ninety-nine years
over the next three decades and, eventually, in some states, to life
imprisonment or death (Brecher 1972). In another extension of federal
power, the Narcotic Drugs Import and Export Act of 1922 (Jones-
Miller Act) provided for the creation of a federal Narcotics Control
Board to further regulate imports and exports of opium, cocaine, and
their derivatives. A report to Congress in 1923, however, concluded
that "no domestic law, to say nothing of international agreements or
treaties, which . . . have already proved impotent in dealing with the
question, can control this traffic" (cited in Terry and Pellens 1928).
Although political difficulties with the League of Nations and the
League's Opium Advisory Committee prevented the United States
from serving as a leader in international antidrug activities, American
representatives attended conferences on the traffic in opium, coca
leaves, morphine, heroin, and cocaine in Geneva in 1924 and 1930.
Intra-hemispheric efforts to control the flow of drugs in the Americas
resulted in the Havana Conference in 1928 and agreements with
Mexico in the 1930s (Walker 1981).

In response to governmental regulation of the selling of cocaine—there were as yet almost no laws against possession—an underground distribution network, in existence since 1894, increasingly assumed the task of providing cocaine to addicts (Spillane 1994). The Hearst newspaper columnist and antidrug crusader Winifred Black commented in 1927 that addiction to cocaine had become "an endless chain—and its links reach from the lowest dives in the lowest parts of the big cities, to the beautiful homes in the suburbs, yes, and out to the lonely farm and down into the kitchens, and out into the fields." A year later, she published an article headlined "60 Percent of All Violent Crime Traced to Cocaine" (cited in Silver 1979: 62).

Tightening federal control was also evident in the 1922 Supreme Court decision *U.S. v. Behrman*, which held, by a six to three margin, that physicians could not legally supply opiates to addicts for self-administration. No longer would physicians be able to claim that they were treating addicts "in good faith" by prescribing small amounts of narcotics in maintenance or withdrawal doses (Ashley 1972; King 1953). In 1924, Congress outlawed the importation of opium to manufacture heroin—although, by 1940, in spite of this legislation, heroin had become the principal drug in many cities, and "the heroin mainliner had emerged as the dominant underworld addict type" (Courtwright 1982: 112). The federal government also attempted to standardize the varied state approaches to the drug problem by passing the Uniform Narcotics Act of 1932.[1] Under this legislation, all activity related to drug use—being present in a place where drugs were being used, possessing drug paraphernalia, being an addict, and even, under the "narcotics vagrancy" law, being "likely to use narcotics"—was potentially punishable (*Drug Use in America* 1973). The Act codified prohibitive trends in state legislatures, although it ultimately failed to promote a uniform national approach to the drug problem.

The federal government was not only making and interpreting laws, it was actively enforcing them. The Narcotic Division of the Department of the Treasury, Prohibition Unit, established in 1920 and charged with enforcing the Harrison Act, a decade later turned the responsibility over to the Federal Bureau of Narcotics, a newly created government agency directed by Harry Anslinger, who would serve in that capacity for the next thirty years. Federal authorities pursued a vigorous narcotic-fighting agenda using entrapment, legal harassment, and threats to intimidate physicians and users. This harsh agenda derived in part from the need to justify increases in federal appropriations, which rose from 292,000 dollars in 1915 to a peak of over 1,708,000 dollars in 1932 (*Budget of the U.S. Government* 1945).

Further compounding the national drug problem was Prohibition, launched with the passage of the Volstead Act in 1919. On March 6, 1920, the *San Francisco Examiner* ran the headline "Increase in Use of Drugs Is Alarming: Probation Officer Reports on Spread of Evil Since Prohibition Went into Effect" (cited in Silver 1979: 173). The repeal of Prohibition in 1933 shifted the attention of illicit traffickers away from alcohol and back to narcotics, even as it freed up federal agents engaged in the control of illicit alcohol for narcotic control activities.

In *Linder v. U.S.,* a 1925 Supreme Court case whose important judicial precedents might have reversed the punitive drug policies of the Classic Era, the Court ruled that Dr. Linder, a Seattle physician, had not violated the Harrison Act when he sold one tablet of morphine and three tablets of cocaine to Ida Casey, an informer-addict in a state of partial withdrawal. The doctor, it was alleged, had prescribed these drugs even though "Ida Casey did not require the administration of either morphine or cocaine by reason of any disease other than such addiction." But as the Court ruled, addicts

> are diseased and proper subjects for treatment, and we cannot possibly conclude that a physician acted improperly or unwisely or for other than medical purposes solely because he has dispensed to one of them, in the ordinary course and in good faith, four small tablets of morphine or cocaine for relief of conditions incident to addiction.

According to the Court, the Harrison Act was intended "not to regulate health and morals, but to make regulations with respect to drug traffic." This ruling was further substantiated in 1936 in *U.S. v. Anthony,* when a federal judge ruled that attempts to regulate a physician's prescription of drugs to an addict "would not only be contrary to the law, but would also make the law unconstitutional as being clearly a regulation of the practice of medicine."

Despite these rulings, however, the Federal Bureau of Narcotics continued to harass, threaten, and prosecute physicians who made narcotics available to addicts. The agency justified these activities in part by referring to the statements of reputable organizations, such as the AMA's Committee on Narcotic Drugs, which wrote in 1921 of "the shallow pretense that drug addiction is a disease" (Ashley 1972). Few physicians were eager to risk their careers by challenging zealous federal authorities, nor were lower courts willing to challenge official police and federal propaganda. In spite of the *Linder* ruling, therefore, physicians continued to abide by the repressive interpretations of previous Court decisions. The Classic Era rolled on.

"Moral crusaders," many of them women, also roused antidrug sentiment. Newspapers of the early 1920s featured articles with titles such as "Drugs Wreck Life and Hopes of Girl School Teacher" and continued to associate drugs and crime in lurid headlines: "$20,000,000 in Narcotics Smuggled into U.S. Yearly, Says Government Report," "America Leads in Importation of Narcotics," "U.S. Is Revealed as Supply Base for Narcotics," "America Is World's Biggest Opium Mart," and "America Leads Rest of World in Addiction to Narcotics," the last article quoting a figure of one million to four million dope users. The antidrug campaign was soon joined by congressmen and governors, Lady Astor, the Woman's Christian Temperance Union, the City Federation of Clubs, the American Legion, the Elks Club, the Lions Club, the Knights of Columbus, and the Rotarians (Silver 1979).

Classic Era Users

As in the past, during the Classic Era of federal drug control it was difficult to estimate the number of narcotic addicts in the United States and to judge the efficacy of the measures instituted to control drug use. The availability of drugs had decreased markedly after the turn of the century. Legal imports of smoking opium fell to zero following the 1909 ban. Total annual opium imports, which had fallen from 628,177 pounds (1900–1909) to 366,054 pounds (1910–1919), declined to 144,805 pounds (1920–1923). The annual importation of opium products had peaked at 27,143 ounces between 1910 and 1919, and subsequently fell to about one-fifth of that amount between 1920 and 1923 (Terry and Pellens 1928). International pressure, beginning with the Shanghai meetings and continuing with the Hague Convention and the League of Nations agreements of 1921, was having an effect on the drug trade worldwide. But some, like the anti-opium crusader and writer Ellen La Motte, remained critical of international efforts, which could so easily be subverted. In *The Ethics of Opium,* La Motte claimed that "America is confronted with a drug problem—how to stop the illicit sales of dangerous, habit-forming drugs, which are peddled and smuggled from one end of our country to the other" (1924: 3). In 1923, the U.S. Congress passed a resolution to increase restrictions on international drug trafficking that included a Treasury Department estimate of more than one million addicts (Terry and Pellens 1928). By 1929 it was estimated that addicts consumed five billion dollars' worth of opiates (Silver 1979).

A telling comment on the failure of federal drug policies to stem the tide of addiction appeared in the *St. Louis Post-Dispatch* (May 25, 1930). In an article entitled "A Million Dope Addicts Now in the United States," Senator S. Royal Copeland noted that the "drug curse has increased fifteen times during the fifteen years of restriction by the federal Government" (cited in Silver 1979: 135). By the mid-1930s, the Hearst newspapers were actually looking back to the more "humane" era of the clinics. Accompanying a story about the New York clinic was a photograph of "men and women waiting patiently in line for the dope that will save them from horrible agony, in a New York experiment of over twenty years ago which permitted addicts to get their drug rations by registering with the Municipal bureau. They have no such means of relief now" (cited in Silver 1979: 51).

In his seminal sociological study *Opium Addiction in Chicago,* Bingham Dai (1937) wrote that the number of opiate addicts in that city had increased fivefold, from a conservative estimate of 5,000 in the mid-1920s to about 25,000 in the mid-1930s.[2] This statement was at variance, however, with the report of the Narcotic Law Enforcement Division of the Treasury Department in July 1926, which estimated that the number of addicts nationwide had fallen from about 110,000 two years earlier to about 91,000 (Silver 1979). Harry Anslinger, director of the Federal Bureau of Narcotics, whose figures most likely reflected a political need to show a decrease, estimated the number of nonmedical addicts in the United States at 22,000 in 1937–1938, far below the 250,000 to 300,000 reported at the turn of the century (Anslinger and Tompkins 1953: 266).

Women in the Classic Era

Nationwide, the number of female narcotic addicts declined to about 20 percent of the total addicted population and stayed relatively constant (Musto 1977). A report in the *Journal of the American Medical Association* noted that about 10 percent of the addicts arrested in New York were women, but acknowledged that this was probably an underestimate, since women were less likely to be arrested (Simon 1924). A study of 550 addicts at New York's Metropolitan Hospital between 1927 and 1929 found that 117, or 21 percent, were women (*New York Times,* January 6, 1930). A 1930 report from the Correction Hospital on Welfare Island found that 200 of the 832 patients (24 percent) were women (*New York Times,* October 9, 1930). Bingham Dai's (1937) study found that between 1928 and 1934, 27 percent of the addicts in Chicago were women.

Some surveys from the mid-1920s suggested that female addicts formed a fairly homogeneous population: more than half were over age thirty—most between twenty and forty—white, Protestant, and from small towns, cities, or rural areas in the South (Cuskey, Premkumar, and Siegel 1972). In fact, however, this group was far more heterogeneous: female addicts and drug users came from widely divergent backgrounds and social strata, and obtained and used drugs in different ways. From 1919 to 1925, the *New York Times* chronicled the use of drugs by American youngsters from settings as diverse as New York and Denver (February 2, 1919; April 27, 1922; February 26, 1925). In *No Bed of Roses: The Diary of a Lost Soul,* O.W., an addict-prostitute, noted that unlike addicts from New York, who were heroin "sniffers," "no one in the South sniffs, because no one here seems to use heroin. They always take morphine" (1930: 286).

Studying data derived from various sources during the Depression, Dai found that most female addicts were between twenty and thirty years of age, and almost all (111 of the 115 in the Chicago Reformatory) had left home, many when they were as young as thirteen or fourteen. Slightly over half the women had completed between five and eight years of schooling, and almost one-third between nine and twelve years, while 9 percent had "none or very little," and 7 percent had "thirteen or more years." Sixty percent of the women listed "domestic and personal service" as their occupation, far ahead of "trade industries" (15 percent). Dai also commented that "waitress" and "show-girl," occupations that kept women "on the go," appeared conducive to a drug-taking life. Just over half of the total population of addicted women were married, 22 percent were single, 14 percent were widowed, and 11 percent were separated or divorced. Three-quarters of them began using drugs between the ages of fifteen and twenty-nine, and most became addicted either through other addicts (51 percent) or through self-medication (34 percent); only 6 percent were iatrogenically addicted.

Cocaine also remained accessible in some areas. Lieutenant Henry Scherb of the New York City Police reported that cocaine was widely used by most drug addicts on Welfare Island in 1925 and that 78 percent of the women had previous arrest records (*New York Times,* April 15, 1926). In *Addicts Who Survived,* one woman recounted being introduced to cocaine in the 1930s at "one of those coke joints in Harlem" where "there were blacks and whites sniffing . . . Some were show people, some were ordinary people" (Courtwright, Joseph, and Des Jarlais 1989: 210). Another interviewee described her progression from marijuana to cocaine to heroin in the 1940s through her association with prostitutes.

The medical establishment continued to be well represented among the nation's addicts. Bingham Dai (1937) recounted the observation of someone familiar with Chicago, "I know at least one hundred doctors who are addicted to the use of morphine or cocaine," and he himself found that 60 percent of the addicts who called themselves "professionals" were physicians. When she was admitted to a private sanitarium in the early 1920s, O.W. found that "three-quarters of [the other patients] were doctors . . . They would come for the six weeks' treatment, often as a stall to their wives and families. Few would be in earnest" (1930: 288–289). In another private sanitarium, O.W. met Dr. DuVol, one of the staff, "an incurable heroin addict . . . the saddest case I have ever known" (p. 229).

Nurses, too, continued to fall victim to drug addiction. In 1920, the Committee on the Narcotic Drug Situation of the American Medical Association specifically mentioned the overworked and overstressed "nurse with an epidemic sweeping the city and who must not stop" as being "at high risk for addiction" (cited in Terry and Pellens 1928: 888). O.W. chummed around with a Miss Gray, who, as she recounted in her drug memoir, "was always hopped up to the ears," stole morphine from patients for her own personal use, and used so much cocaine that "one nostril was almost entirely eaten away" (p. 223). When Commissioner Graham-Mulhall raided the apartment of an opiate-addicted nurse, most of whose life "had been spent in the propinquity of the drug," authorities seized "a collection of indescribable instruments, depraved contrivances for inducing the drug influences" (1926: 58–59).

The prevalence of addiction in the medical community probably influenced physicians' prescribing practices. Between 1914 and 1938, some twenty-five thousand physicians were indicted, and three to five thousand went to jail for violations of the Harrison Act (Ashley 1972; Ashbrook and Solley 1979; Goode 1972). O.W. described a familiar ploy: one addict "used to go to various doctors and tell them a hard luck story. Sure as fate, she would emerge from their office with a tube of morphine or cocaine . . . She never went to the same doctor twice, and as there are hundreds of doctors in New York, she had a wide field to operate in" (1930: 235). O.W. herself found a radiologist who took pity on her in the throes of withdrawal and gave her morphine tablets (p. 254). Lawrence Kolb (1962) reported that in 1928, of 119 iatrogenically and self-addicted white patients (115 of whom were morphine addicts), 45 were women. Having studied 120 narcotic-addicted women at the New York Correction Hospital on Welfare Island, M. O. Magid felt it necessary, despite a general awareness of iatrogenic addiction, to warn his colleagues to "exercise greater care in the administration of opium or its alkaloid for the relief of pain or to produce sleep" (1929: 306). Magid also noted a parallel report from the Philadelphia General Hospital, which cited "professional medication" as the largest single factor in producing morphinism (p. 307). A later report from an Illinois reformatory found that of 37 women studied, 13 had become addicted through a physician's pre-scriptions (Hall 1938).

Bingham Dai recounted another example of the harmful conse-quences of prescribed narcotics: a showgirl who became addicted following gynecological surgery and relapsed after each of five at-tempted cures over the next thirteen years. In his opinion, however, her relapses were due more to "mixing with her old associates" and "the influence of her addict-friends" than any other cause (1937: 99–102), which illustrates his hypothesis that addiction was related to personality factors and social context. Another woman became ad-dicted when doctors and her father gave her morphine for kidney problems. Still another, who first received morphine for menstrual cramps at age seventeen, eventually became addicted to the drug at age twenty-six following an automobile accident. Dai concluded that her association with friends who were drug users was a more important influence in her initial addiction and her subsequent relapses than her early initiation. A male addict who became iatrogenically addicted at age nineteen following a spinal injury, later addicted his own wife, who took up drugs "in order to share the habit with him" (p. 113).

Crusaders such as Sara Graham-Mulhall also pressed for more recognition of the dangers of iatrogenic addiction. In *Opium: The Demon Flower,* Graham-Mulhall wrote of the "college girl, with her high-strung mentality . . . [whose] physician may be primarily responsible in carelessly prescribing for a highly nervous temperament" (1926: 43). She also told of addicts, "young women of good families," who were "hiding behind the private prescriptions of physicians in private practice" (p. 66). Despite these dramatic examples, however, Graham-Mulhall absolved physicians: "An erroneous opinion in regard to the physician has been held by the public, that he is solely responsible for the spread of addiction . . . in ninety per cent. [sic] of the cases the addict under thirty acquired the habit through bad association and home environment, and the middleaged and elderly become addicts through selfmedication" (1921: 201).

Drugs and Crime

Despite major federal efforts between the wars to control drug use through legislation and active policing, the drug problem was not contained. More potent forms of opiates were being used by those segments of the population lacking social supports, the legitimate economic means to maintain costly drug habits, and access to any part of the medical system that might provide help. Drug raids and vice squad activities delivered a new set of criminals to an already overburdened criminal justice system. Federal narcotics convictions totaled 6,651 in 1922 (cited in Silver 1979: 127), and averaged 5,000 a year between 1923 and 1930, and 2,500 a year throughout the 1930s (Morgan 1981: 122). When control of drug distribution networks passed from Jewish to Italian hands during the late 1920s, the quality of heroin declined. As William Burroughs wrote in *Junky,* "There should be at least a hundred caps in one-quarter ounce of H before it is cut. But if the wholesaler is Italian he is almost sure to give a short count" (1977: 41). As street heroin became weaker and more adulterated, users switched from sniffing to subcutaneous and intramuscular injection, and later to intravenous injection. In *Addicts Who Survived,* one addict noted that, starting in the early 1930s when she could no longer get opium, she switched to "skin-popping [injecting]" heroin (Courtwright, Joseph, and Des Jarlais 1989: 82).

As the nation began to redefine its view of addicts—no longer "people" but "criminals"—addicted women, less likely to turn to "serious crime" or become a real threat to society, received relatively little attention. Drug use "among . . . women remained 'hidden' unless they had an encounter with the criminal justice system" (Worth 1991: 5). A study of 120 female addicts admitted to the Welfare Island Correction Hospital, either through the courts or voluntarily, found that heroin was the drug of choice for 56 women, followed by combinations of opiates (38 women) and morphine (21 women). Ninety-two of the women were twenty to forty, and forty-two of the women had become addicted in their teens (Magid 1929).

Among Bingham Dai's reformatory population of addicted women, 85 percent were unemployed, 6 percent listed prostitution as their profession, and 37 percent had venereal diseases. Slightly over half of the incarcerated women had IQs over ninety, but eighty-eight of the ninety-five women tested were felt to have psychopathic personalities: "inadequate, egocentric, morally inadequate, or emotionally unstable." Twenty percent of the women used liquor "to a greater or lesser extent" (1937: 59). A later study of thirty-seven women addicts in the Illinois State Reformatory found that their average age was thirty-three, almost all were white and native-born, and all but two were addicted to either heroin or morphine by needle injection (Hall 1938).

Eleanora (Billie) Holiday, the most famous female black jazz and blues singer of her time, provides an insider's view of the prison facility at Alderson, West Virginia. In *Addicts Who Survived,* a male interviewee commented that Holiday "really went down the hill with heroin, but when she was smoking opium she kept herself very good" (Courtwright, Joseph, and Des Jarlais 1989: 95). Holiday, who had a long-standing drug habit, spent ten months at Alderson in the mid-1940s for a narcotics violation. She observed that, although "the place wasn't too bad," providing decent food, "classes in Spanish, woodcraft, cooking, ceramics, and stuff like that," the addicts' lives were strictly controlled and no real drug treatment was provided: "There was no cure. They don't cut you down slow, weaning you off the stuff gradually. They just throw you in the hospital by yourself, take you off cold turkey, and watch you suffer" (Holiday 1956: 133).

Drugs had their major impact on women in the poorer segments of American society, who were without the means to purchase street drugs or pay a physician to prescribe them. During the Depression, their circumstances worsened. An article in a Chicago newspaper for December 7, 1934, told of the "pitiful plight of 13 women narcotic addicts . . . driven to shoplifting and other petty crimes by their great need for money to spend for narcotics" (cited in Silver 1979: 108).

Boxcar Bertha Thompson, a legendary hobo (who may have been a fictional construct of the writer Ben L. Reitman), told of the down-and-out drug-using women who rode the rails: "The only sisters of the road who indulge in it are those whose hoboing is secondary to their racket. Crooks or prostitutes who occasionally hobo their way about sometimes go in for dope. In the south this is much more common than in the north" (cited in Palmer and Horowitz 1982: 133; and Strasbaugh and Blaise 1991: 191).

Other oral histories, like those in *Addicts Who Survived,* provide a further perspective on the survival tactics of female addicts. Emily and Al, the only married couple interviewed, told of making money by stealing and reselling meat. Although Al had been arrested for booking, Emily had always managed to avoid the criminal justice system (Courtwright, Joseph, and Des Jarlais 1989: 147). Another female addict gave up "hooking" after a few years but was later arrested for shoplifting (pp. 164–171). Those not directly involved in crime often relied on men for their drugs. One woman picked pockets to buy drugs while her husband, her usual source of support, was in jail (p. 212). A *New York Times* report (June 21, 1921) noted that two women had smuggled heroin to their jailed husbands by mixing it with perfume and pressing it on to writing paper. Toward the end of *No Bed of Roses,* O.W. laments her life of prostitution, drug use, and dependence on men: "Men . . . men . . . men . . . everywhere men, trying to hound me and trail me like a pack of stray dogs. Men, the only means of earning food and board . . . and I loathe them" (1930: 324).

Prostitution

Women also turned to prostitution to obtain drugs. According to the index of commercialized prostitution issued by the American Social Health Association, which ranged from zero ("no commercialized prostitution") to one hundred ("flagrant prostitution"), the national average score from 1920 to 1929 was ninety-nine, with a slight decline to ninety-two between 1930 and 1938 (Adler 1979). Although many prostitutes worked in brothels under the watchful eyes of madams, who were "generally very alert to and opposed to the use of drugs" (Winick and Kinsie 1971: 67), they were surrounded by customers, friends, and coworkers who were drug users. As a result, in houses of prostitution drug habits spread easily. The rate of addiction among prostitutes in any given city appeared to reflect overall rates of addiction in that city: larger cities generally had more addicts, and urban areas closer to New York City were subject to greater heroin traffic, since heroin use spread outward (Courtwright 1982).

Many female addicts considered prostitution a reasonable option: it was easy to get into, demand was constant, and it produced more cash than women could earn in other ways. In some cases, a woman's initial exposure to drugs was the direct result of her entry into prostitution. Such was the case with Sophia, who was picked up as a runaway by a pimp, and whose drug use began when out of curiosity she tried his opium. As she remarked, many prostitutes were addicts who would "take junk just to forget what they were doing" (Courtwright, Joseph, and Des Jarlais 1989: 166). In other cases, however, women turned to prostitution to support an existing habit. One interviewee in *Addicts Who Survived* was introduced to marijuana and cocaine by a prostitute and ended up supporting her heroin addiction through prostitution because, as she had been told, "you can make yourself some money" (p. 162). O.W., who survived the 1920s as a prostitute, found that many others were also using dope: "Most girls in this business use it. They claim it takes them out of the stark reality that faces them on all sides" (1930: 149). She ended her memoirs with a poignant postscript: although desperate for a "cure," she was released from her ninth treatment failure in five years. A "notorious prostitute and an incurable drug addict," she had a "wasted body," ten cents to her name, and nothing ahead but time to reflect on her misery: "Behind her trailed a short, thick-set man. A dope peddler can always spot a 'junkie,' and after a stretch on the Island, they'll sell their soul for a shot" (p. 329).

Sara Graham-Mulhall devoted an entire chapter of *Opium: The Demon Flower* to lurid stories of victims ensnared by female "opium vampires," often "beauties of dubious theatrical reputation" who lived on the outer edges of crime or women who associated with underworld drug users. Many of these women were believed to come from the upper strata of society, and finding themselves in a state of financial distress, used drugs to ensnare their prey, either as a drug scout or the operator of an opium den. Graham-Mulhall used these poorly documented case histories to stir up an antidrug frenzy:

> Such girls have been trapped by the drug, forced into the degraded adventures of opium vampires, made the narcotic slaves of drug dealers and smugglers. It is a shameful neglect of lawmakers and health authorities that professional procurers of the drug, human monsters who exploit these young women, are so rarely caught, whereas the opium vampires die in shame and disgrace. It is a new form of white slavery, which begins and ends with the power of opium. The white slaves of a former generation were ignorant peasant girls; the white slaves of opium are American born, daughters of good families, young women of intelligence and breeding. (1926: 60–61)

The Rich

At the opposite end of the social spectrum, the "smart set"—chic and stylish movie stars, artists, and the "idle rich"—experimented freely with cocaine and marijuana, and even brought opium smoking back into style in their circle during the 1920s and 1930s. Scandals followed one on another. An Oakland, California, Hearst newspaper headline in 1923 proclaimed "1,000 Drug Addicts in Doctor's Book," including "society women" (cited in Silver 1979: 151). In *No Bed of Roses,* O.W. commented that the showgirl Lilly West's theatrical career was ruined when her admission for addiction to Bellevue Hospital was made public in *Broadway Brevities* and the *Daily News:* "I feel certain that she is through in the theatrical world . . . That kind of publicity doesn't go over the way it used to go. People are beginning to want their stage favorites to live right" (1930: 201–202). The *New York American* for March 25, 1923, told the story of Evelyne Standfield, the daughter of a wealthy gold miner, who had become a morphine addict by the age of nineteen. Miss Standfield was quoted as saying that "there is no difficulty in buying dope if you have the money. In the case of a pretty girl, even money is not essential" (cited in Silver 1979: 143).

Other sensational stories of ensnared society belles also received front-page publicity. "Dixie" Dixon, the daughter of a venerable Virginia family, died in a New York taxicab "in the clutches of a gang of drug dealers" (cited in Silver 1979: 144). Another newspaper headline announced "Frivolous Butterflies of Fast Life Frequently Kill Themselves While in the Depths of Drug Despair" over a story on drug use among the socially prominent. One woman, for example, "instead of giving her tortured nerves the rest and sleep that nature demands, resorted to opiates to quiet them" (p. 145).

Opium smoking parties became common diversions. Bingham Dai's (1937) case histories included a woman who became addicted by going to smoking parties in Cleveland in 1932, a man who ascribed his addiction to "pleasure parties, made up of both men and women," and another man who was led into addiction by a female friend at a smoking party. In *Addicts Who Survived,* one interviewee described the opium parties she attended in the 1930s: "They had a lot of big stars that were on opium. They'd put a mattress on the floor. They wore beautiful silk pajamas and had a big can of opium and a big pipe" (1989: 80). Another reported: "We all went there [the opium parties] and we laid around. We smoked. We had fruit, candy, and everything" (p. 81). Still another recounted that she had been introduced to opium smoking by her husband, a musician, who had smoked with Jean Cocteau in Paris (p. 239). According to Emily and Al, "In the thirties it was all rich people, all wise guys who smoked . . . wealthy people smoked opium, millionaires, rich people . . . Union leaders used to smoke . . . Women smokers were rare . . . they were a very small minority" (pp. 92–95).

The association of drugs with female sexuality was prominent in the popular culture of the time. In *Really the Blues* (1990), his chronicle of the Jazz Age drug scene, Milton "Mezz" Mezzrow described the widespread use of opium and cocaine. Many big bands included songs linking women and drugs in their repertories, for example, Duke Ellington's "Hophead" (1927) and Louis Armstrong's "Muggles" (1929) about marijuana. Leadbelly sang (of cocaine), "Ho, ho, baby, take a whiff on me." Cab Calloway recorded "Minnie the Moocher," in which an opium addict hooks his girlfriend on drugs, "Kicking the Gong Around," in which an opium addict loses his sweetheart to opium, and "Reefer Man," the fantasy world of the marijuana smoker. There were many others—"Sweet Marijuana Brown," "If You're a Viper," and "The Girl in the Blue Velvet Band," in which a man is seduced by sex and drugs and enters a life of crime. In the case of "Cocaine Lil," a popular cult figure of the era who "lived in Cocaine Town upon Cocaine Hill," the drug proved fatal:

> They laid her out in her cocaine clothes.
> She wore a snowbird hat with a crimson rose.
> On her tombstone you'll find this refrain:
> "She died as she lived—sniffing cocaine."
> (cited in Palmer and Horowitz 1982: 122)

A character in Cole Porter's 1934 hit musical *Anything Goes* complains, "I get no kick from cocaine," which became "Some like the perfumes of Spain" when cocaine became less fashionable.

During the 1920s and 1930s Hollywood became one of America's leading industries, one which both dictated and reflected national values.[3] Many film studios capitalized on the subject of women and addiction. *Sowing the Wind* depicted a remorseful mother who kills herself with opium. Other films of the early 1920s included *Reputation*, in which a female addict commits murder and suicide; *The Dungeon*, in which a woman is hypnotized by a drug fiend; *Drifting*, the story of an American girl who is an opium smuggler in China; and *Daughters of the Rich*, in which a female addict commits suicide.

Some films on drug-related themes featured major screen stars. Norma Shearer starred in *Lucretia Lombard* in 1923 as an elderly addict who dies of an overdose. D. W. Griffith's film *That Royale Girl* (1925) starred W. C. Fields as a con man with an addicted wife. In *East of Suez* (1925) a drugged and hypnotized Pola Negri is kidnapped. Toward the end of the 1920s, female addicts were featured in *The Unfair Sex, Sisters of Eve*, and *The Pace That Kills*, in which a country boy follows his sister to the big city, becomes addicted through a relationship with a woman, and eventually discovers his sister, an addicted prostitute. *Cocaine Fiends*, a 1939 film, dealt with drug-associated prostitution and degradation.

Drugs found their way into off-screen Hollywood life as well (Courtwright, Joseph, and Des Jarlais 1989). As one study notes, drugs "had been an integral feature of the movie colony from its inception. The wacky antics of stars on and off the stage owed much to psychoactive drugs" (Starks 1982: 46). In 1923, five well-known actresses pled guilty to heroin possession. Mabel Normand and Tallulah Bankhead developed expensive cocaine habits. One of the more notorious stories involved the drug-induced death of the popular actor

Wallace Reid in 1923 and the downfall of his wife, Dorothy Daven-port Reid, about whom a headline stated "Film Star's Ruin Laid to Narcotic Ring" (cited in Silver 1979). Following Reid's death Dorothy Reid became an antidrug activist and starred in the film *Human Wreckage* (1922), playing a reformer who tries to help addicts get off drugs.

The drug-induced fall of another actress, Juanita Hansen, who "dropped from a thousand dollar a week life of luxury into a New York police station cell," was widely covered in the press. Although addiction ended her career, she eventually won her struggle against drugs and established a foundation to help narcotic addicts (Starks 1982; Silver 1979). The actress Barbara LaMarr used heroin, mor-phine, cocaine, opium, and other drugs and died from a drug overdose at twenty-six (Starks 1982). Alma Reubens, a "great star of the silent film," was arrested for morphine possession, spent time at a sanitar-ium and kicked the drug habit in 1929, but died at a young age in the early 1930s while facing charges of smuggling narcotics from Mexico to San Diego (Silver 1979; Starks 1982). Film star Paula Ives publicly admitted to a four-year drug addiction (Silver 1979). The showgirls Evelyn Nesbit and Helene French also lost their careers to drugs, as French explained in a news story subtitled "Show Girl Falls from Days of Luxury" (Silver 1979). Other addicted show business personalities included the vaudeville actress Mary Haynes, Julia Bruns, once called "America's Most Beautiful Girl," and the "tempestuous actress" Jeanne Eagels, and these were not isolated examples.

The less glamorous levels of show business also provided an entree into the world of drugs, usually through a male contact. The *North-west's Own Magazine* (April 10, 1938) ran "True Story of a Dope Addict," which chronicled how Josephine B. had run away from a comfortable suburban New York home at age fifteen to become a chorus girl in a burlesque show. She became an addict by taking her husband's "lung medicine," which was actually opium, for a cold. The article noted that the two hundred dollar supply of opium Josephine needed would have cost twelve dollars before passage of the Harrison Act (Silver 1979).

Drug addiction and abuse among actresses did not begin only through treatment or social contacts. Recounting the making of the 1939 film *Babes in Toyland* with Mickey Rooney, Judy Garland de-scribed the studio practice of providing the child stars with pep pills to keep them awake for filming, sleeping pills to give them four hours of sleep, and stimulants again for the next seventy-two hours of filming (Starks 1982). In the 1940s, barbiturates, or "goofballs," became popular in Hollywood, and stars like Anne Sterling, Susan Hayward, Judy Garland, Corinne Calvet, and Abigail Adams reportedly overdosed, Adams fatally (Silver 1979).

Marijuana

Narcotics and cocaine were not the only drugs subjected to greater regulation during the Classic Era. Marijuana smoking, first observed in Texas around 1910, spread to the West and Southwest in the 1920s. Although practiced primarily by Mexican immigrants who had crossed into the United States looking for agricultural work, marijuana smoking also spread among Southern blacks (Himmelstein 1983). In addition, Prohibition forced drinkers to seek out substitutes for alcohol, and many turned to marijuana.

Marijuana use increased steadily between 1910 and 1930, yet initially, there was little concern. Neither the Harrison Act of 1914 nor the Narcotic Drug Import and Export Act of 1922 mentioned marijuana (Himmelstein 1983). The few legislative initiatives against it were limited to those parts of the country where marijuana use was most blatant: in Texas, where the city of El Paso passed a municipal ordinance against marijuana in 1914, in Louisiana, which passed similar antimarijuana state laws in 1927, and in Colorado, which followed in 1929.

When Harry Anslinger assumed control of the Federal Bureau of Narcotics in September 1930, he immediately launched a campaign against marijuana. Some have argued that the motivation behind this campaign was his wish to coerce states into adopting antidrug legislation rather than either an expansionistic plan for his own agency or anti-Mexican sentiment per se (Himmelstein 1983). Whatever the rationale, Anslinger's Bureau succeeded in defining society's views about the dangers of marijuana. Although some members of the medical community had the temerity to challenge the Bureau by suggesting that marijuana appeared to be no more harmful than alcohol and was not linked to marked deviance, Anslinger successfully bullied both the Congress and public opinion. As he hoped, the Uniform Narcotics Act passed in 1932 included marijuana, and thus made it possible for individual states to control the drug simply by relabeling it as a "narcotic."

In order to achieve this goal, Anslinger linked marijuana to two major dangers—violence and its harmful impact on America's youth, who might be turned into "dope fiends" (Himmelstein 1983). As a subtext, he released federal propaganda portraying marijuana as an aphrodisiac that increased the threat of attack on young girls, a thought unwelcome to most Americans in view of its racial-ethnic pattern of use. In "Marijuana: Assassin of Youth" (*American Magazine*, July 1937), Anslinger casually blurred the drug's classification in recounting a "typical" tragic story:

> The sprawled body of a young girl lay crushed on the sidewalk the other day after a plunge from the fifth story of a Chicago apartment house. Everyone called it suicide, but actually it was murder. The killer was a narcotic known to America as marijuana, and to history as hashish. It is a narcotic used in the form of cigarettes, comparatively new to the United States and as dangerous as a coiled rattlesnake. (High Times 1994: 30)

In the same article, Anslinger told of a fifteen-year-old girl, a runaway, who was arrested in a Detroit marijuana den supposedly representative of those "frequented by children of high school age . . . from coast to coast," hoping to convince Americans of the ubiquitous dangers of marijuana-associated crime:

> It would be well for law-enforcement officers everywhere to search for marijuana behind cases of criminal and sex assault. During the last year a young male addict was hanged in Baltimore for criminal assault on a ten-year-old girl. His defense was that he was temporarily insane from smoking marijuana. In Alamosa, Colorado, a degenerate brutally attacked a young girl while under the influence of the drug. (p. 32)

In later years, he would cite the case of a marijuana user in West Virginia in 1937 who raped a nine-year-old girl as a further example of how marijuana use led to "debauchery and sexuality" (Anslinger and Tompkins 1953). In the *FBI Law Enforcement Bulletin* for February 1938, Anslinger included rape among the dangers of marijuana use.

The press and the Hollywood film industry continued to sensationalize the drug issue, vastly exaggerating drug use and its danger to society. A 1932 news story under the byline of the journalist Winifred

Black was headlined "New Dope Lure, Marijuana, Has Many Victims." A story in the *Portland Oregonian* (February 23, 1936) displayed the banner headline "Evils of the Mexican Border Hot Spots: 2000 Miles of Trouble." *Murder at the Vanities,* a 1934 film, showed the heroine being splattered with blood as she finished singing "Sweet Marijuana." *Tell Your Children,* the most propagandistic of the antimarijuana films, later became *Doped Youth,* and still later, *Reefer Madness* (Silver 1979).

While marijuana was vilified by the press, it was glamorized by the music and jazz clubs. The singer Janet Clark's experience reflects the heavy use of marijuana among jazz musicians in the 1940s:

> So I must have started even before I was married—smoking pot . . . He kept saying that pot was cool; it wasn't habit-forming. And then I read the *New York State Report on Narcotics,* whatever that was, to make sure before I was going to try. I was very cautious at this point. (Hughes 1961: 71)

Mezz Mezzrow, who told the judge at one of his drug trials that "the only thing you'd ever have to watch out about is its effect as an aphrodisiac," described a scene in one of the jazz clubs:

> She had cut loose from her partner and was throwing herself around like a snake with the hives. The rhythm really had this queen; her eyes almost jumped out of their sockets and the cords in her neck stood out stiff and hard like ropes. What she was doing with the rest of her anatomy isn't discussed in mixed company . . . Then with one flying leap she sailed up on the bandstand, pulled her dress up to her neck, and began to dance. I don't know if dance is the right word for what she did—she didn't move her feet hardly at all, although she moved practically everything else. (1990: 75)

In *The Lonely Trip Back,* Florrie Fisher wrote that her twenty-year career of addiction, prostitution, and criminality had begun with marijuana. In her lectures after her rehabilitation, she frequently admonished young adults about the dangers of drugs, specifically "innocent, nonaddictive Mary Jane, that started me on the hard stuff. I insisted that any kid who started on it was a fool because pot was the most dangerous thing in the world" (1971: 189).

By 1937, in response to federal pressure, forty-six of the forty-eight states had passed antimarijuana legislation. On the federal level, using a mechanism similar to the Harrison Act twenty-three years earlier,

Congress passed the Marijuana Tax Act, which imposed a tax on transactions involving marijuana. Signed into law by President Franklin Roosevelt on August 2, it took effect on October 1 and made the use and sale of marijuana a federal offense punishable by a combination of fines and imprisonment (Himmelstein 1983).

After this success, however, the Federal Bureau of Narcotics faced growing dissent on the issue of the "menace" of marijuana. Medical investigations and reports, such as the influential LaGuardia report of 1945, based on six years of research, challenged Anslinger's dire warnings. But he was able to deflect much of this opposition, and the Bureau, in its own self-interest, propagated a new theory, the "stepping-stone" hypothesis: although not truly "addicting," marijuana was dangerous because it would lead to more dangerous narcotics. This clever tactic allowed the Bureau to retain the same level of funding in its nationwide fight against drugs and at the same time to reduce the number of "addicts," thus attesting to the "success" of its drug-fighting efforts.

The Pure Food, Drug, and Cosmetic Act of 1938 increased the controls that had been partially introduced in the Food and Drug Act of 1906. Signed by President Roosevelt, the Act brought under legal control all drugs used in the diagnosis of disease as well as all drugs that affected "the body's structure or function." All therapeutic devices now became subject to FDA regulation, and new drugs could not enter the consumer market until they had been tested for patient safety under the conditions of use prescribed in their labeling (Young 1967; Jackson 1970).

Approaches to Treatment

Cures for addiction were pursued actively, if less than successfully, during the Classic Era. In March 1921, after the closing of the New York City drug treatment clinic, the Presbyterian Church, under the direction of the Presbyterian Board of Temperance and Moral Welfare, opened a fifteen-room house in Brooklyn to provide treatment and "spiritual salvation" to female drug addicts. As the two women who ran the home declared, "the drug and narcotic habit is ruining hundreds of young girls and women annually. Business women, it would appear, are particularly subject to the habit because of its temporary energizing effect" (*New York Times*, March 10, 1921). One "slender, pretty girl, white faced and trembling," who had obtained a business degree and worked for a large corporation, was paraded around at a press conference by New York City's Special Deputy Police Commissioner in charge of the Narcotic Squad to stress the need for treatment facilities (*New York Times*, February 21, 1921). In her case, addiction followed the prolonged use of narcotics to treat a painful toothache.

Sanitarium treatment remained available to those few women who could afford it. As she tells the story in *No Bed of Roses*, O.W.'s treatment at two private sanitariums, one in Eastport, Connecticut, and the other in North Carolina, was underwritten by a wealthy uncle. A Bellevue physician had earlier warned her about sanitarium treatment programs: "He didn't seem to take kindly to my plan to go to the sanitarium, and seemed to say that Dr. Stanley was crooked" (1930: 216). As she noted about an addicted female friend, Dr. Stanley "took her over for plenty of money, too, on the pretense that he could cure her of using heroin" (p. 200).

In the 1920s, Bellevue Hospital offered three different treatment regimens for addicts: gradual reduction, acute stoppage of drugs ("cold turkey")—O.W. was admitted to Bellevue for rapid detoxification before continuing on to a private sanitarium—which were also offered at many public hospitals and prisons, and a third treatment with narcosan, "a fluid invented and put forth by a chemist . . . from Vienna," which was promoted briefly (*New York Times*, December 18, 1928). Physicians such as M. O. Magid, whose female patients "all had narcosan with good results" (1929: 309), supported its use, as did Alexander Lambert and Frederick Tilney (1926), who claimed good therapeutic results with narcosan in 147 women. But this therapy was soon rejected as ineffectual by the Mayor's Committee on Drug Addiction (*New York Times*, January 12, 1929). Other therapies attracting devotees during these years relied on belladonna, atropine, hyoscine, dionine, strychnine, and bromides.

Gradual weaning from drugs and a three-month recuperation, still another treatment approach, failed to gain wide acceptance because of the amount of time it required. Other suggested cures relied on broadly conceived therapies. They included the administration of sodium rhodanate, "a compound designed to wash the brain and nervous system clean of the 'habit,'" which, it was claimed, thinned brain proteins thickened by prolonged use of narcotics (*New York Times*, January 16, 1932); fifteen to twenty hot water baths a day for the relief of pain, a treatment employed with drug addicts at the State Reformatory for Women in Bedford, New York (*New York Times*, March 9, 1924); and even five days in a refrigerated room to reduce body temperature to seventy-five degrees, which reportedly cured two morphine addicts (November 4, 1939). New ideas also filtered in from abroad, such as phlyctenotherapy, "a method of inoculation with a liquid serum obtained by vesication or blistering from the sufferer himself," from Egypt (*New York Times*, December 11, 1929).

Each proposed "cure," however, soon fell into disrepute, and the unsuccessful search for a workable treatment produced growing frustration. O.W. commented in *No Bed of Roses* that "few dopers really try to be cured. They will go to a sanitarium and swear to the high heavens they will be serious, but before long they are scheming and sneaking to get more than their regular shots" (1930: 288). Bingham Dai's Chicago study devoted a small section to the "effective rehabilitation of drug addicts," which remained the exception rather than the rule. In one case, following numerous failed cures and a suicide attempt, a fifty-six-year-old woman overcame her two-and-a-half-decade morphine addiction in a religious mission, where she was saved by "the blood of Christ" (1937: 180). Even Harry Anslinger admitted that "when the accused was a woman, the State often has no suitable institution in which to care for her" (Anslinger and Tompkins 1953: 158).

Psychiatric treatments for addiction, introduced on a limited basis in the sanitariums, were gradually expanded. A German physician, cured of his own addiction through psychoanalysis, opened a sanitarium in Germany. Here, treatment included medical withdrawal, during which the patient was kept in a trance with a sleep-producing agent to prevent conscious pain, and psychoanalysis, "leading to the disclosure of the patient's inner life back to his childhood with the object of creating in him an entirely new initiative and will power" (*New York Times*, November 10, 1929). According to Dr. Alexander Lambert, a Cornell professor who chaired the mayor's committee on narcotics, addiction was a response to psychological maladjustment. Because of personality deficiencies, most addicts had turned to drugs to escape the "wear and tear of normal daily living" (*New York Times*, April 12, 1930). But O.W. concluded that "the Lambert and hyacine treatments are just added expenses to fill a doctor's purse" (1930: 290). One result of Lambert's proposal, however, was the New

York City Commissioner of Correction's recommendation that addicts be confined in state-sponsored institutions for life (*New York Times,* July 22, 1931).

The Lexington and Fort Worth Treatment Facilities

Throughout the 1920s, frustrated and disillusioned physicians witnessed addiction increase among a population over whom they had less and less control. By the mid-1920s, ambulatory treatment of addicts according to various regimens, as well as treatment in sanitariums, had been discredited, and support for some kind of mandatory institutionalization of addicts intensified. Dr. Thomas Joyce, resident physician at the inpatient drug treatment facility of New York's Riverside Hospital, had concluded as early as 1921 that ambulatory treatment was a failure, and that detoxification within an institution in a "humane and scientific manner" was necessary (*New York Times,* March 6). By the late 1920s, the federal government had reached the same conclusion: addicts could be effectively treated only if confined to a place where access to drugs could be controlled (Courtwright 1982). The situation called for a modern adaptation of Fitzhugh Ludlow's quarantined "Lord's Island" (Day 1868).

Although some physicians tried to retain a sense of humanity in drug treatment programs, the popular characterization of addicts—as compulsive and dangerous criminals—dominated the thinking that led to the establishment of the drug treatment "farms." As U.S. Surgeon General Rupert Blue recommended in 1928, addicts were divided into two general classes. The first class, attesting to the continued presence of iatrogenic addiction, consisted of "legal or medical addicts . . . who habitually use narcotics because of disease, injury, or the infirmities of age, and for whom these drugs may be prescribed by physicians for the relief of pain." The other class consisted of criminals, psychopaths, and those who used narcotics for other than medical reasons—"the real addicts" (*Establishment of Two Federal Farms* 1928). Blue's comments clearly embodied the implicit double standard of the previous half-century: private care for some and confinement for others.

Beginning in 1929 and over the next decade, the Committee on Drug Addiction and Narcotics of the National Research Council focused on developing substitute, nonaddictive opiates (Isbell 1965). In January of the same year, Congress passed PL 672, which outlined the four basic elements of the Public Health Service program for narcotic addiction: (1) treatment and rehabilitation of narcotic drug addicts convicted of federal offenses; (2) prevention of federal narcotics offenses by treatment and rehabilitation of voluntary patients as well as those already convicted of federal offenses; (3) encouragement of states and their constituent communities to provide adequate facilities and methods for the care of their narcotic addicts with the benefit of federal cooperation and experience; and (4) research and training in the causes, diagnosis, treatment, control, and prevention of narcotic drug addiction (Simrell 1970).

As a result of this law, two "federal farms" were established, one at Lexington, Kentucky, in 1935, and the other at Fort Worth, Texas, in 1938. These facilities were intended to house the overflow of convicted addicts from the federal penitentiaries, which were becoming overburdened because of the vigorous pursuit of the new antidrug laws. The "farms," in actuality modified prisons with walls, barred windows, and strict security, were intended to provide supportive treatment for drug withdrawal in a setting removed from the crime-ridden life on the streets. From 1946 on, methadone was used in the drug withdrawal regimen. The facilities also offered individual analysis, group therapy, outdoor work, and job training in an effort to restore addicts' physical and mental health. Women were not admitted to these facilities, however, until 1941 (see Chapter 6).

By the close of the Classic Era, women, once the majority of America's addicts, had become the minority. As female drug use increasingly shifted to the poorer, marginalized segments of society, the plight of female addicts garnered less and less attention on the nation's antidrug agenda. Prostitution, the Hollywood film industry, Jazz Age clubs and music, and the emergence of marijuana as a "new aphrodisiac" reinforced the sense of predatory female sexuality associated with drug use. But following the closure of the early drug maintenance clinics, treatment for women was almost nonexistent except for those who gained access to federal or private facilities. From the mid-1920s to the mid-1940s, therefore, women who were addicts had little hope that national drug policy, dominated by Harry Anslinger, would soon change its hard-line approach.

six

THE SECOND WORLD WAR AND AFTER

The narcotic problem at the close of the 1930s—diminishing supplies, higher prices, and a hard-to-treat population of socially marginalized addicts—became acute with the outbreak of the Second World War. Although intrahemispheric trade routes reportedly flourished (Walker 1981), international trade routes were abruptly, and almost totally, disrupted, as a headline in the *New York Times* announced: "Narcotics Traffic Is Curbed by War" (September 27, 1942). The net effect was a "panic" like the one in 1919 after the Supreme Court cut off the supply of legal opiates to addicts, forcing them to seek drugs by whatever means available.

Law enforcement, emphasizing policing and imprisonment of addicts, continued to dominate United States drug policy. During the peak of the hysteria over drugs in the late 1950s and early 1960s, many states not only mandated substantial minimum terms, they also denied narcotics offenders eligibility for probation, and suspended sentences and sometimes parole (Allen 1965; *Drug Use in America* 1973). In the 1950s, New Jersey law called for penalties of two to fifteen years for a past illegal drug sale or possession offense, and ten years to life for a third offense, with the added provision of two years to life for sale to a minor (Anslinger and Tompkins 1953). By 1957, antidrug sentiment favoring harsh legislation had become so strong in Texas that the state legislature voted unanimously in favor of the death penalty in certain cases involving drug sales to minors.

On the federal level, two major legislative initiatives increased the penalties for addiction: the Boggs Act, passed in 1951, which called for a mandatory minimum sentence of five to twenty years for all second and subsequent narcotics offenses (*Drug Use in America* 1973); and the Narcotic Control Act (Boggs-Daniel Law), passed in 1956, which further increased sentences but also required that anyone ever convicted of a drug violation, as well as anyone who was currently an addict or a drug user, must register and obtain a special certificate to leave and reenter the United States. The resulting prosecution of thousands of offenders clogged the courts. In the interim, President Eisenhower had called for a "new war on narcotic addiction at the local, national, and international level" (*New York Times*, November 28, 1954). Then in 1956, in a crowning blow, the medical use of heroin was prohibited and all existing heroin supplies were ordered surrendered to the government.

How Many Addicts?

Determining the actual number of addicts in America remained as problematic as ever. Researchers expected that once drug supply lines were reestablished after the war, drug use would rise sharply. But they registered little increase until the early 1950s, when a jump in heroin use was reported (Morgan 1981). By then, the withdrawal of the crime syndicate from the heroin market under the pressure of stricter federal controls had created a free market of independent operators, which discouraged tracking of drug distribution.

The three major sources of information during the 1940s and 1950s on the prevalence of drug use in the United States were the New York City Register, the records of the Federal Bureau of Narcotics, and the admissions records of the Lexington and Fort Worth treatment facilities. The Federal Bureau of Narcotics compiled records on those who violated narcotics laws and on other addicts who came to its attention, although the data did not cover drugs such as cocaine and marijuana. In 1931 and again in 1934, the Bureau counted between four and five thousand violations of federal narcotics laws (Winick 1965). Although the number of narcotic addicts had declined during the war, estimated numbers reached forty-eight thousand by 1948 and between fifty-five and sixty thousand by 1955.

Physicians, nurses, and other health care professionals, although representing a small subcategory of addicts, would not generally have been included in surveys unless they had come to the attention of law enforcers or had sought treatment at Lexington or Fort Worth. They were considered "nonthreatening," since they had easy access to drugs and were thus less likely to be engaged in criminal activity. Michael Pescor (1942), who worked at the Fort Worth facility, found that the proportion of physicians there was eight times greater than in the general population. Pescor constructed a composite profile of the "typical" patient: a white, fifty-two-year-old male with a thirteen-year history of morphine addiction, who had suffered a number of cure failures and relapses, tended to have no criminal record other than Harrison Act violations, and was likely to carry a diagnosis of "psychopathic diathesis." His past history was usually unremarkable—native-born, Protestant, normal childhood, middle class, married with two children. Pescor also found that despite obvious economic, social, and educational advantages the prognosis for physicians was comparable to that for other Fort Worth addicts: only half remained drug-free six months after discharge. Writing in the *Journal of the American Medical Association,* Rasor and Crecraft (1955) reported that between 1950 and 1953, 186 of the 457 meperidine (Demerol) addicts admitted to the Lexington treatment facility were physicians, nurses, or ancillary professionals. A *New York Times* article (February 12, 1958) claimed that one out of every one hundred doctors was a drug addict, compared to one in three thousand in the general population. As late as 1962, 1.5 percent of those admitted to Lexington and Fort Worth were physicians (Maddux 1965).

According to the Federal Bureau of Narcotics, women continued to account for a quarter of the nation's addicts (Winick 1965). After the Second World War, it was estimated that half of all female addicts lived in New York City (Cuskey, Premkumar, and Siegel 1972). But epidemiological studies based on criminality undercounted addicted women, since prostitutes were far less likely to be arrested than thieves, who tended to be male (Winick 1965). Rasor and Crecraft (1955) reported that although women made up 25 percent of the total admissions to the Lexington treatment facility in the early 1950s, they comprised over 40 percent of the meperidine (Demerol) addicts. Demerol-addicted women tended to be slightly younger than addicted men: they became addicts at an average age of thirty-four compared to thirty-eight for men (the onset of opiate addiction, in contrast, began in the late teens or twenties). Of the 120 women in Rasor and

Crecraft's study, 79 were registered nurses and the remainder worked in related professions. These women chose meperidine because it was more readily available than other opiates, less toxic, less socially stigmatizing, and less allergenic—and because they could conceal their addiction more easily. The Committee on Drug Addiction and Narcotics of the National Research Council concluded that "all too frequently, a nontransient addict will be a physician or a nurse," and meperidine the most likely drug of addiction (Anslinger and Tompkins 1953).

Drug Sources

Until the end of the 1950s, most narcotic addicts found it extremely difficult to obtain drugs. In *Junky,* William Burroughs noted that heroin had been "virtually cut off" during the early part of the war. In addition, getting narcotics from physicians—or "croakers," as he called them—was becoming increasingly impossible, since "all croakers pack in sooner or later" (1977: 23). Florrie Fisher, who wrote of her twenty years as an addict and a prostitute in *The Lonely Trip Back,* recalled the panic in New York in 1946, when morphine was as "precious as liquid gold" (1971: 100). An addict interviewed in *Addicts Who Survived* noted the change: "Well, once 1950 hit, things with doctors started to become a little difficult . . . You couldn't find that many. It was easy up to that point; after that doctors who would write became scarce. It seemed that there were more addicts coming from nowhere, just popping up . . . When the doctor's office became overcrowded with people looking for narcotics, along with his patients, it became very fearful for him" (Courtwright, Joseph, and Des Jarlais 1989: 139).

Some addicts, however, continued to receive drugs from physicians, who braved considerable penalties out of sympathy—or greed. One female addict told of procuring drugs by traveling across the country from doctor to doctor. Having first become addicted to meperidine while in nursing school in the 1940s, she subsequently became addicted to methadone (Dolophine) through a physician. During the 1950s she and her husband traveled with carnivals as concession stand operators, but they specialized in "making [outsmarting] doctors" in towns throughout the country. Using a direct approach—locating doctors in the phone book and bluntly asking for prescriptions—she was "amazed to find that quite a few did give it to me" (Courtwright, Joseph, and Des Jarlais 1989: 140). Some physicians wrote her prescriptions for large quantities of drugs, provided that she never return. Because small-town physicians were often in need of money, she found that her chances of obtaining prescriptions were better in the small rural towns throughout the country. Some doctors wrote just one prescription and charged appropriate fees, but those who were known to write repeated prescriptions were offered large sums of money to continue to do so. A Chicago physician, who prescribed for anyone who would pay the charge of two dollars per pill, lost his narcotics license in 1955 after repeatedly ignoring warnings from narcotics officers.

Florrie Fisher (1971) was also able to outsmart doctors by faking painful physical illnesses. In one desperate attempt to obtain drugs, Fisher contaminated her urine specimen with her own blood, which got her a prescription for Dilaudid, a proprietary brand of dihydromorphinone hydrochloride, from a urologist who thought she had kidney stones. She also obtained drugs by outright forgery of prescriptions and by giving wrong names and addresses to physicians. During one of her incarcerations in the state prison in Raiford, Florida, Fisher traded sex with a prison physician for drugs.

The dislocation caused by the squeeze on drug supplies during the late 1940s and 1950s led some addicts to switch to whichever drugs were available: opiate addicts, for example, replaced their opiate of choice with another opiate. One longtime female addict, who was eighty-one years old when interviewed for *Addicts Who Survived*, switched to heroin in the 1930s when her supply of opium was cut off. After the war, when she lost her heroin connection on New York's Lower East Side, she switched to Dilaudid: "I got the Dilaudid from doctors. I got my needles from a druggist in the Bronx . . . He must have known I was addicted . . . I used to cash my Dilaudid prescriptions in there, so he knew" (Courtwright, Joseph, and Des Jarlais 1989: 83).

Other addicts told similar stories of coping with a diminishing supply of narcotics. One married couple switched from opium to heroin after the war but encountered high prices and poor quality. Emily, the wife, explained how things changed: "When I became a junkie, I lost my life. There's nothing like a pipie [opium smoker]. They kept themselves immaculate—dresses, furs . . . There was a million times difference between heroin and opium users" (pp. 101–102). A female addict who got her drugs from Spanish and black street peddlers recalled that "buying heroin was the easiest thing in the world" (p. 163). Another, whose source for ten years was a physician who was herself an addict, switched from heroin to Dilaudid. A male addict procured heroin from a woman whose husband stole narcotics from the hospital where he worked. After the woman was arrested, however, he was forced to turn to more expensive, but poorer quality street heroin.

Other opiate addicts turned to illicit nonopiate drugs. Florrie Fisher recognized the value of cocaine when heroin was unavailable: "The other girls were junkies too. They'd know what that cocaine was worth if they saw it" (1971: 121). Desperate addicts consumed large quantities of over-the-counter medicines, which contained small amounts of codeine, paregoric, or alcohol. Some turned to "uppers," such as benzedrine, while others used barbiturate-containing "downers," such as "goofballs," to take the edge off their narcotic withdrawal. As William Burroughs said of one friend, "When he couldn't get junk—which was about half the time—he drank and took goof balls" (1977: 31).

Crime

The combined effects of diminishing drug supplies, limited treatment options, and more aggressive drug control measures strengthened the linkage between drugs and crime that had begun to emerge after the *Webb* and *Doremus* Supreme Court decisions in 1919. Addicts were forced to turn to new sources and new types of drugs or to pay exorbitant prices to street pushers, for whom selling was increasingly risky. Some addicts bought street heroin, which was expensive and increasingly adulterated with fillers like sugar or powdered milk, while others resorted to stealing from warehouses, drugstores, and doctors' offices. As one might expect under these circumstances, the Uniform Crime Reports found that arrests for narcotic drug law violations increased from 2,648 in 1932 to 5,014 in 1940; following the wartime decline, they rose again, to 13,030 by 1950. The Chicago police department reported that the most common drug-related offenses were larceny-theft (59 percent), robbery (16 percent), and burglary (10 percent) (Finestone 1957). Harry Anslinger was quite comfortable with the "strong relationship between crime and drug addiction" and the fact that the underworld was "the principal recruiting ground for new addicts" (Anslinger and Tompkins 1953: 268).

The nation was finding it difficult to accept the new generation of heroin addicts, who tended to be young, ethnic males concentrated in New York, Los Angeles, Detroit, and Chicago. From 1947 to 1951 the heroin market expanded to include more youths and the lower classes. By 1955, Harris Isbell, writing in the *Bulletin of the New York Academy of Medicine,* could characterize the stereotypical addict as male, poor, and black. At the same time, the number of Puerto Rican users increased, from under 2 percent of the drug-using population in 1953 to 10 percent in 1957 and 12 percent in 1962 (Bates and Crowther 1974). Such stereotyping sanctioned the social marginalization of these addicts, as it had opium-smoking "Orientals," cocaine-using "Negroes," and marijuana-smoking "Mexicans."

The growing number of young addicts was noted with no little concern. In New York (Chein et al. 1964) and in Chicago (Finestone 1957), narcotic addiction became closely associated with minority youth, already sidelined from mainstream society, whose drug use involved them in criminal activity. In New York City, increases in the number of adolescent addicts admitted to Bellevue Hospital were recorded in 1950 and 1951 (Winick 1965). In Chicago, where in 1932 young addicts had made up about one-fifth of the addicted population, the proportion had risen to one-third by 1952. What made the rise in drug use more alarming was that it followed on the heels of a decline among that age group between 1920 and 1950 (Kolb 1962).

Women and Crime

After the passage of the Harrison Act, addiction to illicit narcotics, increasingly heroin-based, was considered a "man's disease." Women were less likely to commit crimes to obtain drugs, and those they did commit, such as prostitution and petty theft, were nonviolent and thus of less concern to the general public than the crimes generally committed by male addicts. A late 1950s study of fifty-six primarily black female addicts in the Illinois State Reformatory for Women found that just over half were incarcerated for narcotic-related offenses and about a third for larceny, robbery, or burglary (Robinson 1961). Of this sample, the majority had become addicted to marijuana and progressed to heroin or cocaine. Although on average the women had served three sentences, and some as many as nine, most had committed nonviolent crimes to get money for drugs. The study concluded that in-prison treatment for addiction, combined with emotional and educational guidance, could achieve parole for some and reduce the amount of criminality. Many female addicts, including the singer Billie Holiday, served time at the penitentiary in Alderson, West Virginia, where no treatment for addiction was available.

Personal stories attest to the varied forms of criminality among these addicts. As Howard Becher noted in a postscript to Janet Clark's diary, *The Fantastic Lodge:*

> Eventually, as was inevitable in the kind of life she led, she was arrested again . . . and served a six-month sentence . . . But the experience in jail did not change her course . . . The next time I saw her, several months later, she told me of her adventures in shoplifting. She had taken to stealing, as so many addicts do, in order to raise money to support her habit . . . Shortly after this, she began to "hustle." She worked on her own, picking up men in bars and getting five dollars a "trick" . . . She was turned in to the police by jealous whores whose territory she was encroaching on. She paid bribes to policemen to avoid being arrested. (Hughes 1961: 264)

Clark's criminal activities had actually begun years earlier: "I had been working at this record store where they did not have a cash register, poor fools, and I accumulated quite a sum of money. I'd take five to ten dollars a day and make it up one way or another" (pp. 94–95).

A female addict who had been a prostitute in the 1930s before becoming addicted to opium reported that she made fifty to seventy dollars a day in the late 1950s by stealing and reselling meat (Courtwright, Joseph, and Des Jarlais 1989). She had begun selling heroin in the early 1950s, was arrested once for drug possession, and spent five years in jail, during which time she continued to procure drugs. After her release, she supported her habit by stealing expensive pocketbooks from department stores. She was arrested twice in the 1960s for shoplifting and incurred twenty-eight lifetime arrests for prostitution.

The pattern of multiple arrests for relatively minor charges was typical among female addicts. In *Cookie*, Barbara "Cookie" Goodman Quinn told of a life of heroin addiction, gang involvement, prostitution, and theft until she kicked her habit and became one of the founders of Phoenix House, a drug rehabilitation center (cited in Palmer and Horowitz 1982). Another addict also maintained her drug habit in the 1950s through petty crime. For drug money, she resorted to burglary: "I'll break into people's apartments, and I have given holdups . . . I'll take a radio, a watch, men's suits, ladies' dresses—anything that's good to sell" (Larner 1964: 137). A significant part of Florrie Fisher's *The Lonely Trip Back* deals with her "thirteen years of hustling, shoplifting, conning for money, thirteen years in and out of jail, the House of Detention for thirty-, sixty-, or ninety-day sentences, Bedford for two years, Raiford for four years, Lexington several times" (1971: 121). Fisher was a college graduate but, as she wryly observed, she earned her "real education" in the House of Detention and prisons in New York and Florida. Occasionally, women became large-volume drug dealers. The *New York Times* reported the arrest of a twenty-one-year-old woman, one of Newark's "most vicious" drug dealers (February 28, 1951). A model-dancer was arrested for running a two-hundred-dollar-a-day narcotics business in Times Square (*New York Times,* February 19, 1952).

Many women became trapped in lives of crime and prostitution. Florrie Fisher became a prostitute in order to buy marijuana. As she declared later in her career, "most whores do turn to dope" (1971: 73). Fisher herself turned to heroin, becoming "so dreamy, so detached" that nothing really mattered. A twenty-seven-year-old prostitute with a fifteen-year heroin habit told a story of criminal convictions for prostitution, narcotics possession, and robbery in a never-ending struggle to maintain a two-hundred-dollar-a-day habit (Cortina 1970). Other prostitutes, such as twenty-four-year-old Rosey and forty-four-year-old Hope, spoke of similar criminal involvement once they entered the maze of addiction. Carmen, another prostitute, reported in *The Addict in the Street,* a series of vignettes about dope addicts, that although she had "regular customers," during the 1950s she often became desperate: "I'll give you a good time. So please, I need the six dollars badly. Please, don't let me down. Please" (Larner 1964: 138). A cameo portrait of Lilly in *Portraits from a Shooting Gallery* also illustrates the vicious cycle of taking heroin in order to be able to function as a prostitute and becoming a prostitute to earn money to buy drugs (Fiddle 1967).

Women forced into addiction and prostitution lived demeaning, impoverished lives, often in subservience to men. In *Manchild in the*

Promised Land, Claude Brown depicted the "epidemic" of heroin use in Harlem in the 1950s and male attitudes toward teenage hustlers:

> You could tell if a bitch was a junkie by the way she looked. Their skin just seemed a little faded. Even if they weren't high, they looked dingy. If you saw a young girl up in Harlem, looking like she'd been living down on the Bowery, you'd know that she was strung out. And if she was strung out on shit, there just wasn't much she could do in bed for anybody. (1965: 194)

Billie, a male Puerto Rican addict, expressed a similar sentiment: "I can't see myself going out with a junkie broad. 'Cause I don't like the way they carry on what they have to do . . . I don't want to have nothin' to do with a junkie broad" (Fiddle 1967: 111). A female addict who had been called a "filthy bitch" and a "pig," countered: "these lousy bastards, they have no consideration for a woman like us drug addicts" (Larner 1964: 138). Weighing only seventy-five pounds and aware that she was "murdering [her] body," Florrie Fisher used water from the toilet bowl to prepare her drugs: "I'd flush the toilet, reach in, pull the swirling water up from the commode into my syringe and put it into the spoon" (1971: 87).

An unknown number of female addicts were lesbians, in part because they wished to escape the demeaning role of handmaidens to men. *Portraits from a Shooting Gallery* (Fiddle 1967) includes several stories of lesbianism among addicts. In *The Addict in the Street,* Carmen, who worked as a prostitute, recalled getting along well with the lesbian addicts she met in the hospital and "was the wife of one of them one time" (Larner 1964: 155). Florrie Fisher noted that in jail, she "learned to be a lesbian, both sides of it. How to be a mommy, and how to be a daddy" (1971: 140).

Other Users

Although the American public reacted strongly to the crime-drug subculture, it perceived little threat in the marijuana and cocaine-using bohemians of New York's Greenwich Village and San Francisco's North Beach, or the Hollywood "smart set." But when Lila Leeds and Robert Mitchum were arrested for marijuana possession in 1948 (Silver 1979), the only film offer Leeds received following her conviction later that year was the role of a marijuana smoker in *Wild Weed*

(Starks 1982). Into the mid-1950s, the industry-imposed Code of the Motion Picture Producers Association of America prohibited the production of films depicting any aspect of drug addiction (Anslinger and Tompkins 1953).

Jazz musicians, primarily those in New York City, the jazz hub, and on the East Coast, were drawn to heroin. One study of over four hundred musicians found that 40 percent were either occasional or regular users (Winick 1959–1960). Janet Clark, who traveled with avant-garde jazz artists in the 1940s and 1950s, recalled in her diary that "practically everyone was either a junkie or tried junk" (Hughes 1961: 103). Florrie Fisher (1971) reported being introduced to heroin in an after-hours jazz club in New York City. In *Stroke a Slain Warrior,* one musician noted: "I was surely surrounded by it [heroin] during the summer when I was out on the road with these professional bands . . . I was with the band leader who was himself an addict" (Cortina 1970: 49). In his study of addicts at the Lexington facility in 1951– 1952, John Fort (1954) recorded the story of a pianist who went to work for a "famous dancer" who "herself had had some experience with heroin." When Dr. Marie Nyswander, a pioneer in the treatment of opiate addiction, organized a Musicians Clinic for drug addiction in 1957 with a grant from the Newport Jazz Festival, she had no difficulty in filling available treatment slots (Hentoff 1968).

Treatment

Addicted women of means could always obtain treatment at private sanitariums. Almost half of the patients admitted to the Clifton Springs Sanitarium and Clinic in upstate New York in 1950 were women. "Housewife" was the most common recorded occupation— followed by physician, physician's wife, and nurse, attesting to the continuing problem of drug abuse within the medical community (Brecher 1972).

A major demographic development of the postwar years was the increasing number of young addicts. Throughout the 1950s, the newspapers reflected this shift: for example, a sixteen-year-old Bronx student told of using marijuana, cocaine, and heroin, and of her life of burglary and prostitution to get money for drugs (*New York Times,* June 13, 1951); the director of the Welfare and Health Council in New York pointed out the growing number of female teenage addicts (*New*

York Times, May 9, 1952); and headlines such as "Narcotics in Schools" (*New York Times,* May 14, 1957) warned of student drug use. Despite this obvious trend, few treatment programs for young people existed.

In response to public pressure, treatment was made available to adolescent addicts in New York City beginning in 1952. The Riverside Hospital on North Brother Island in the East River, a 140-bed facility staffed with physicians, psychologists, social workers, and education specialists, provided rehabilitation services to both male and female teenagers under the age of sixteen, some admitted voluntarily and others by court order. There they received inpatient services for a three-month period as well as follow-up care (Trussell 1971). In time, however, the Riverside treatment program encountered a series of problems, including patient pregnancies resulting from contacts with hospital guards. After a study revealed that treatment was unsuccessful and could not justify the cost—ten thousand dollars per patient per year—(Eldridge 1962), the program was terminated in 1963.

Although it lasted hardly more than a decade, the Riverside Hospital program supplied valuable demographic data on young urban female narcotic addicts. A study of twenty mostly teenage women at the Riverside facility in 1955–1956 found that most had been introduced to heroin by experienced users (Chein et al. 1964). They used heroin initially in the company of other women, but once hooked, they tended to share the experience with males or in male-majority mixed groups. Many of them were aware that heroin was illegal, habit-forming, and debilitating, but they had tried it out of curiosity, because of its reputation as "a good way to get high," unconcerned about the long-term perils associated with its use.

The teenagers in the study supported their habits in a variety of ways—by living with addicts or pushers, working, prostitution, theft, or relying on gifts of drugs from user friends. Overall, Isidor Chein and his colleagues found these women to be "seriously maladjusted adolescents prior to addiction" (1964: 309). This judgment was confirmed by another study of the same population, who, it was felt, had begun to use drugs "in the context of serious maladjustment, into which they had limited insight" (p. 318). Most of the girls had come from families with irresponsible, cold, unencouraging parents, usually an absentee father and a dominant mother, who were not consistent or reasonable in disciplinary practices. Chein concluded that "the female adolescent opiate addict developed her difficulties in social adaptation and her psychopathology through immersion—or at least while immersed—in a malignant familial environment" (p. 319).

Earlier in the century, the United States had briefly experimented with drug maintenance clinics, a rather primitive medical approach to addiction at a time when social services were nonexistent. At midcentury, in view of the greater numbers of disadvantaged addicts, alternatives to prosecution and jailing began to gain support. In 1955, the American Bar Association and the American Medical Association established a joint committee, headed by Judge Morris Plowscowe, to reassess the drug problem. The final report, issued in 1961, outlined plans for research in five areas: treatment of drug addicts in an outpatient experimental clinic; causative factors in addiction and rehabilitation; educational and preventive research; legal research; and research in the administration of current laws (Eldridge 1962).

The most controversial aspect of the report was the proposal for the establishment of "an experimental facility for the out-patient treatment of drug addicts, to explore the possibilities of dealing with at least some types of addicted persons in the community rather than in institutions" (Eldridge 1962: 37–38). In opposition to this very tentative proposal, the American Medical Association Council on Mental Health had deliberated the same question and concluded that drug-dispensing clinics were not feasible at that time. In addition, the Federal Bureau of Narcotics, headed by Harry Anslinger since 1930, was quick to issue a sharp attack on the joint committee, its findings, its director, its two parent organizations, and even the writers cited in the report's footnotes (Eldridge 1962).

This national initiative to "medicalize" addiction was not an isolated one. A movement favoring outpatient drug treatment had gained momentum, led by groups such as the Medical Society of Richmond County (Staten Island) in New York and the New York Academy of Medicine. The Academy proposed a six-point program predicated on the underlying principle that an addict was a "sick person, not a criminal" ("Report on Drug Addiction" 1955). It advocated eliminating illicit drug trade profits by setting up federal drug treatment programs that would be open twenty-four hours a day, seven days a week; close medical supervision of addicts with a view toward rehabilitation; education about the adverse effects of drugs aimed at young potential users; and data-gathering about the epidemiology and pathogenesis of addiction. In rejecting the harsh, repressive strategies of the previous forty years, the Academy concluded that its program represented a "reasonable and humane approach to the solution of drug addiction" (p. 607). In 1954 a California citizens' advisory committee to the attorney general on crime prevention proposed that incurable addicts receive narcotics legally. That same year the New York State delegate to the annual American Medical Association convention proposed, unsuccessfully, that the AMA favor the establishment of narcotics clinics (Brecher 1972).

Despite strong opposition from the Federal Bureau of Narcotics, the joint committee report set the stage for a more medically oriented view of addiction in the following decades. The New York City mayor's Commission on Health Services declared in 1961 that, aside from its antisocial manifestations, drug addiction was no different from cancer, heart disease, or any other chronic illness and recommended that the city develop a detoxification program for addicts willing to take advantage of such a service (Trussell 1971).

One of the earliest drug treatment programs in New York City, a detoxification unit using methadone opened in 1961–1962, was a collaborative effort of the Department of Hospitals and Beth Israel Hospital. Another program from about the same time was based at the Metropolitan Hospital and run by its Department of Psychiatry, reinforcing the emerging view of the addict as a patient with specialized medical and psychiatric needs. When it opened, however, the Metropolitan program did not admit women, a further example of the continued invisibility of women. Therapeutic communities (TCs) such as Synanon, another approach to the treatment of addiction, took root in the later 1950s and flourished in subsequent decades (see Chapter 9).

Women at the Lexington Treatment Facility

For those seeking drug detoxification, the major option was admission to one of the federal drug treatment centers, the facility at Lexington, which accepted addicts from 1935 to 1974, or the facility at Fort Worth, which offered treatment from 1938 to 1971. The two facilities expanded rapidly, and by 1965 they provided a combined total of over eighteen hundred beds for treating men and, after 1941, women. Although most patients ended up at Lexington and Fort Worth as a result of convictions for narcotic offenses (the "cons"), others presented themselves voluntarily (the "vols"). The treatment program called for rapid withdrawal, which in the early years was accomplished over a difficult five- to fourteen-day period. In 1946, methadone (amidone) was introduced as a more gradual approach to eventual drug abstinence.

During almost four decades, the federal facilities at Lexington and Fort Worth treated over 82,000 patients. Between 1941 and 1965, they admitted a total of 14,866 female patients—18 percent of all admissions at the two hospitals during that period (Chambers, Hinseley, and Moldestad 1970). Women, with the exception of the 109 treated at Fort Worth between 1947 and 1952, received treatment at Lexington (Cuskey, Moffett, and Clifford 1971). Between 1967, when the treatment focus at Lexington became more research-oriented, and 1971, 934 women (21 percent of addicted patients) were admitted (Maurer and Vogel 1973).

But as drug use in the general population changed over those years, the prototypical female addict also changed. According to Michael Pescor (1944), the first one hundred women to arrive at Lexington in 1941 were not unlike most female addicts prior to enactment of the Harrison Act. They were typically white, native-born, rural Protestant housewives, with limited education, whose average age was forty-three. The cause of their long-standing morphine addiction (an average of fourteen years) was usually iatrogenic: they had become addicted through treatment "for the relief of some painful or distressing physical condition" (p. 772).

Over the next twenty-five years, however, the composition of this population shifted markedly. In a study of one hundred addicts admitted to Lexington in 1964–1965, men outnumbered women, who came primarily from the north central states, by four to one (Ellinwood, Smith, and Vaillant 1966). Iatrogenic addiction became much less common, about 20 percent of female admissions, and occurred more frequently among white (41 percent) than among black (15 percent) women (O'Donnell 1974). By the 1960s, as many as two-thirds of women addicts reported that they had started using drugs either out of curiosity, to belong to a gang, or for kicks. Heroin displaced morphine and was usually procurable from other addicts, although in order to buy drugs women were likely to engage in prostitution, and one-third of them had narcotic convictions. The women in the study sample tended to be high school dropouts with a high rate of truancy; 70 percent had not held a job in the previous year and 33 percent had not had a regular job in the previous six years (Ellinwood, Smith, and Vaillant 1966).

The racial composition of addicts was also shifting: the percentage of black females admitted to Lexington increased sharply between 1941 and 1966 (Chambers and Moffett 1970). Before 1950, about 10 percent of the black addicts at Lexington were female. By 1953, this figure had more than doubled; in 1955 it peaked at about 25 percent and then declined slightly over the next six years to about 23 percent. A survey of the 172 women admitted to Lexington from June to December 1965 revealed that although blacks comprised about 11 percent of the female population of the country, they constituted one-third of the female admissions to Lexington (Chambers, Hinseley, and Moldestad 1970; Williams and Bates 1970). By 1967, approximately half of the women admitted were black (Cuskey, Moffett, and Clifford 1971).

During the 1960s the two racial groups presented significant social and demographic differences. Most of the white women were from the South, whereas the majority of the black women were from the north central states. All the black women and three-quarters of the white women had been raised in metropolitan areas. The white women tended to be older, with a mean age of thirty-seven years compared to thirty years for black women. Both black and white women had an average of only ten years of education, and most had not finished high school. Of the total female addict population, under 20 percent had recently held legal jobs, while over 40 percent had pursued illegal activities to support themselves, and just under 40 percent were dependent on spouses, family, or social welfare programs. Black patients more frequently reported intact marriages, but these were more often common-law than legal (Chambers, Hinseley, and Moldestad 1970).

Race also largely determined the pattern of narcotic use. Black women began using drugs at a mean age of twenty-one, six years earlier than their white counterparts, and tried heroin first more often than white women. Of the 60 percent who were primarily heroin users, more black women had first tried heroin with a friend out of curiosity or for "kicks." Almost 50 percent of the total female population at the federal facilities reported using marijuana, but white women, whose addiction was more often iatrogenic, used less than black women; many more white women, however, used sedative and hypnotic drugs such as barbiturates (Chambers, Hinesley, and Moldestad 1970).

Approximately one-third of the women, mainly white, were initially exposed to addictive drugs in a medical or quasi-medical context, and usually obtained medicinal morphine or opium through pharmacists or physicians. The smallest group, mainly black women, began with illegally procured narcotics obtained from an addicted family member, usually their husbands (Chambers, Hinseley, and Moldestad 1970). Almost two-fifths of the women—most commonly white women from the nonurban South—had been able to continue obtaining drugs through legal or quasi-legal routes.

Both groups used distinctive methods of drug administration: heroin addicts took their drugs intravenously; those addicted to narcotics like codeine and paregoric, mainly white, took them orally; and those who took Demerol, Dilaudid, or morphine did so intramuscularly or subcutaneously (Chambers, Hinseley, Moldestad 1970). In keeping with these patterns, most white women got their drugs from legitimate sources, while black women got theirs from "pushers."

In contrast to the 1941 cohort, women at the Lexington facility in the mid-1960s were seeking treatment earlier, perhaps because of the difficulties they faced in obtaining drugs. Although these women had been addicted for an average of nine years—compared to nineteen years in 1941—about 40 percent were seeking treatment for the first time (Chambers, Hinseley, and Moldestad 1970). Almost all the white women and 70 percent of the black women were admitted voluntarily, the remainder having reached the facilities through court and prison referrals.

About one-quarter of the women, more commonly black women, reported selling drugs as a primary means of support. Almost half of the women, more blacks than whites, admitted to being prostitutes, and half of these women had been arrested for prostitution. Almost one-third of the women had never been arrested, but of those arrested, blacks outnumbered whites. Of those with an arrest history, almost one-third had been arrested prior to first drug use. Over half of the women had medically diagnosed "psychiatric deviances" ranging from personality disorders to psychotic and psychoneurotic disorders.

In 1971, Walter Cuskey and his colleagues compared two groups of female opiate addicts, one admitted to the federal facility in 1961 and the other in 1967. Their analysis identified three major socio-demographic groups: (1) white female heroin addicts who were characteristically young, had used marijuana at an early age, currently used intravenous heroin obtained through pushers, had an addicted spouse, had one or more broken marriages, and supported their habit by illegal means; (2) white female medical addicts who generally obtained drugs other than heroin from a physician, had not used marijuana, did not have addicted spouses, and worked or were dependent on others; (3) black female heroin addicts, a younger, more homogeneous population, who had used marijuana and obtained intravenous heroin from a pusher and had high rates of broken marriages and arrests, usually for prostitution.

One Chinese female was discharged from Lexington during the years 1957–1962, and Mexican women comprised a small ethnic group at the Lexington and Fort Worth facilities. Only 14 of the 102 Mexicans admitted in 1961 were women; only 10 Mexican women were admitted in 1967 (Chambers, Cuskey, and Moffet 1970). Mexican-American women came primarily from the states of California, Texas, Illinois, Colorado, Arizona, and New Mexico. They were generally Catholic, poorly educated, unemployed, and supported their drug habits through illegal means.

Living conditions at Lexington were primitive and hardly seemed conducive to recovery from addiction. When Marie Nyswander, a young physician, arrived at Lexington in 1945, she encountered women who had not been out of their building for four years except to attend a weekly movie. To remedy the lack of recreational facilities for women addicts, she tried—unsuccessfully—to convert a fenced-in, weed-filled yard into a recreation area (Hentoff 1968). In *The Fantastic Lodge,* Janet Clark gave a first-hand account of trying to kick her drug habit at Lexington under difficult, even cruel conditions. She likened it to Mary Jane Ward's *The Snake Pit* (1946), an exposé of the primitive conditions in asylums treating mental disease: "You never get over that first shock. After a while, they all start looking like people to you, and everything, and you get used to it. You get used to looking at the sores, at women that are so thin that it just shouldn't be" (Hughes 1961: 213). Clark described the "narrow, uncomfortable metal beds" and the "bareness, and the bars at the window, the misery in everyone's face" (p. 214). She also detailed the daily dilute shots—

of opiates, perhaps morphine, and sedatives—that painfully prolonged withdrawal, the prohibition of books in the withdrawal ward, and the lack of any kind of diversion: "There's nothing to do—nothing—except talk about junk" (p. 216).

Clark's observations also confirmed the marked differences among the women confined at Lexington:

> The first thing that amazed me, more than anything else, was the high number of what I call medical junkies that were there. These would be people who had something legitimately wrong with them, at one time or another, and went to a doctor for a prescription, and he prescribed morphine or dilaudid or some of the other various kinds of narcotics, pantopon [methadone] or something of that sort. And then, without even knowing that they were drawn up in the drug fascination, and before they knew it, they were hooked. (pp. 217–218)

Clark blamed the physicians who had so liberally prescribed narcotics for these women. Most of these "medical junkies" were Southerners, she noted, and played "the sickwoman act," insisting that there was something medically wrong with them. The "illicit junkie," in contrast, "thinks of himself or herself as a member of the underworld" (p. 219). On the positive side, Clark admitted that the Lexington medical facilities were "pretty fair" and that "they had a regular dentist office and so forth" (p. 224).

Women discharged from the Lexington facility exhibited a high recidivism rate. In *Addicts Who Survived* (Courtwright, Joseph, and Des Jarlais 1989), one addict related that she entered the Lexington federal treatment facility in 1953, after meeting a physician who had himself gone through detoxification there. Addicted to Dilaudid at the time of her admission, she withdrew on liquid methadone. Only two days after her release, however, she started using drugs again. She tried to detoxify at Lexington several more times and was sent there once on a possessions conviction, but she became readdicted to Dilaudid following each release. Florrie Fisher, a periodic "vol" at Lexington, experienced the same lack of success, her longest stay lasting one week. Lexington never helped her at all, she wrote, and all the Lexington women "ended up the same way, back on the drugs" as soon as they were released (1971: 124).

It was certainly the case for Janet Clark. She described the powerful pull of drugs, which readdicted so many of those who left treatment facilities, when she signed herself out of Lexington against medical advice: "Since I got on the bus, I *knew* that I would be making it [taking drugs] as soon as I got back into town. In fact, I felt that that would be the first thing I would do" (Hughes 1961: 231). Her relapse was accompanied by the self-loathing and despair many female addicts felt at being unable to control their own lives and a desire for self-anesthesia to dull unhappiness:

> But I just felt that there was no reason at all to be doing this, that I was with my own kind down there, and I saw how things were with them, and that's what I would be in another fifteen or twenty years. And time in joints across the nation, being locked up for years, didn't seem to make any difference to them. Why should I expect that it would make any difference with me? I stayed in bed most of the time and cried, and felt miserable. So, naturally, I made it again. (p. 233)

Authorities were aware of the high failure rate of the Lexington program, since such personal anecdotes were borne out statistically. The New York Demonstration Center, established by the National Institute of Mental Health in 1957 to continue community-based habilitation of addicts discharged from Lexington, immediately encountered difficulty in providing ongoing service to the first 912 enrollees, requiring changes in the traditional casework approach (Brill 1965). Of the first hundred female patients admitted to Lexington in 1941, Michael Pescor had recorded that each "would be given a guarded prognosis for continued abstinence from drugs which is a vague way of stating that she will probably relapse" (1944: 773). In a study of 1,881 patients, 344 of whom were women, who were discharged from Lexington between July 1952 and December 1955 and resided in the New York City area, 90 percent of both the total and the female group became readdicted, the majority within six months of discharge (Hunt and Odoroff 1962). A five-year follow-up study of the same population found that about half of the 170 women studied became readdicted, black females having the highest recidivism rate of 74 percent (Duvall, Locke, and Brill 1963). Females as a group, however, had a lower rate of arrest (57 percent) than males (73 percent), and received shorter prison sentences. Rates of drug-related arrests were lowest among older white women (41 percent), highest among younger white women (73 percent), and intermediate among black women.

These high relapse rates apparently continued into the 1960s. Cuskey's study of female addicts at Lexington revealed that approximately 40 percent of the women who were discharged were readmitted for retreatment (Cuskey, Moffett, and Clifford 1971). Vaillant (1966) also found high rates of recidivism. These patients, who became known as "winders," spent much of their lives in and out of Lexington seeking a cure that would continue to elude them.

The Lexington and Fort Worth facilities thus proved as unsuccessful as previous treatments in "curing" opiate addiction as long as "cure" was defined as abstinence. In 1967, the National Institute of Mental Health, which assisted the Public Health Service in developing treatment programs for addicts incarcerated by the Federal Bureau of Prisons, converted them into addiction research centers (Simrell 1970).

Prescription Drugs

Just as treatment for addiction seemed to offer a glimmering of hope, the development of tranquilizers and stimulants in prescription form produced new patterns of addiction that would disproportionately affect the lives of women in the ensuing years. Beginning in the 1950s, drug manufacturers marketed these products aggressively, doctors prescribed them, and patients, many of them women, began to use—and abuse—them. The World Health Organization had enlarged its definition of drug abuse to include the use of tranquilizers, antidepressants, diet pills, and other psychoactive drugs. Suddenly, a large number of women in postwar America were officially considered addicts.

Contemporary newspapers and magazines hailed the arrival of these new "miracle" drugs. Industry advertisements in medical journals claimed, falsely, that they were safe and nonaddicting. One advertisement, for example, advised physicians that their slightly overweight women patients would be able to refuse rich desserts if they prescribed Methedrine (methamphetamine), an appetite suppressant. Other drugs, such as Preludin (phenmetrazine) and Tenuate (diethylproprion), which also dulled appetite but had fewer stimulant properties, became widely popular. In addition, supposedly safe and effective drugs for the relief of stress were promoted in superlatives—"Wonder Drug of 1954," "Don't-Give-A-Damn Pills," "Happiness Pills," "Mental Laxatives," "Pacifier for the Frustrated and Frenetic," and

"Peace of Mind Drugs"—and became an accepted part of contemporary American life (Smith 1991).

Like their nineteenth-century counterparts, who had recommended opiate-laden "soothing syrups" and related compounds for patients suffering from psychic stress, overzealous physicians began to prescribe these medications with little sense of control, once again reaching for the prescription pad to treat women's neuroses and maladjustments. As in the past, most physicians were male: women, who might be expected to be more sensitive to the needs of other women, had comprised 4.5 percent of medical school classes in 1941 and 10 percent in 1945, but declined to 5 percent in the years 1950–1965.

The barbiturates, the first of these "modern" drugs, had been available since 1903, but after the introduction of phenobarbital in 1912 their use markedly increased. Barbiturates replaced non-narcotic sedatives such as potassium bromide, chloral hydrate, and paraldehyde, which had been common in the late nineteenth century. Other barbiturates were developed for medical uses such as sedation and short-acting anesthesia—amylobarbitone in 1923, hexobarbitone in 1932, thiopentone in 1934, and thiobarbitone in 1935 (Dundee and McIlroy 1982). By the end of the 1930s, doctors were writing prescriptions for more than a billion grains of barbiturates annually, but their potential abuse attracted scant attention.

The 1950s were nothing less than a "boom time" for the American pharmaceutical industry. Doriden, a sedative-hypnotic introduced in 1954, was soon prescribed almost as often as phenobarbital, and the manufacturer reported sales of over one billion tablets and capsules in the first year (Fort 1969). Tranquilizers,[1] which differed from depressants and sedative-hypnotics in providing patients with a sense of equilibrium and balance, offered physicians a quick and easy treatment for nonspecific complaints, with little reported risk of addiction. By 1957, doctors were writing 48 million prescriptions for tranquilizers annually.

Thorazine (chlorpromazine) was first used in 1952; by the end of the 1960s, tens of millions of patients had been treated with this drug or one of its first-cousin phenothiazines (Fort 1969). Miltown (meprobamate), another type of tranquilizer, appeared in 1955, followed shortly by Librium (chlordiazepoxide) and Valium, a related benzodiazepine. The antidepressants, another group of mind-altering drugs introduced during this decade and promoted as safe pharmacological remedies for mild depressive states featured trade names such as Marsilid, Nardil, Parnate, Tofranil, and Elavil.

Amphetamines, synthesized in 1887, were introduced in the 1930s as mild stimulants and appetite suppressants, and within a few years had become widely available. Benzedrine was apparently well known to nurses, who could supply this stimulant to friends. A student at the University of Chicago recalled: "Man, I have to cram for an exam and I'm exhausted—and someone would know someone who was a nurse with knowledge of this new thing Benzedrine—Hey, why don't you get a few Bennies" (Huncke 1990: 57).

To assist them in meeting the demands of postwar American life— long days at work or school, the responsibilities of work and children, and even body image ideals of weight reduction and control—women increasingly turned to psychoactive drugs. In some cases, prescription drugs were used to readapt women who had gained job satisfaction during the war to roles as housewives once again. One woman remembers her doctor prescribing "diet pills for the weight . . . Miltown for the restlessness (Darling 1995: 199). By 1958, concern about both the safety of these drugs and the prescribing practices of many physicians led to Congressional hearings. In a study of nonhospitalized patients in New York, Sam Shapiro and Seymour Baron (1961) found that during an average one-week period, 12 percent of all prescriptions were for psychotropic drugs. Twice as many prescriptions were written for women as for men, and this discrepancy persisted among patients between the ages of fifteen and sixty-four. The researchers also noted that women aged fifteen to forty-four had a high concentration of prescriptions for antidepressive medications, 40 percent of which were for obesity. A study of a Washington, D.C., population (Baron and Fisher 1962) produced similar findings: women received prescriptions for psychotropic drugs one and a half times more frequently than men. In fact, women were prescribed every class of psychotropic agent, except those used for high blood pressure, more frequently than men. This pattern was most striking for amphetamines, which were used for obesity, since their usage peaked in the summer bathing-suit season.

For drug-addicted women in the postwar years, much remained the same as before the war. Opiate-addicted women continued to represent a significant minority of America's population of addicts, and they tended to cluster in the lower socioeconomic classes, perpetuating the trends that followed the passage of the Harrison Act. In the 1950s, as the American pharmaceutical industry entered a period of explosive growth, physicians increasingly prescribed psychoactive drugs, which they perceived as "safer," to their middle- and upper-class female patients. The impact of addictive drugs on pregnant women had not yet become a major issue, although it would soon play an important role in the national debate on drugs.

The late 1950s witnessed the emergence of a range of therapeutic options for treating drug addiction. In general, the nation showed signs of putting aside its repressive approach to drug use, which, according to Francis Allen, a law professor at the University of Chicago, had been "overwhelmingly in the direction of increased severity of criminal sanctions" (1965: 24), for a more humane and medically oriented approach to drug addiction.

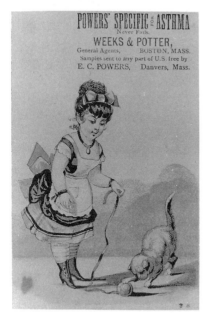

Examples of patent medicine advertising cards, probably turn of the century, showing the manufacturers' appeal to mothers in treating their children's ailments. The card without a label is for St. Jacob's Oil, "the great remedy for pain," and proclaims on the back: "Every ache or pain succumbs . . . Millions of bottles sold and in every one a cure."

AN HONEST DRUGGIST,

An undated illustration (probably from the 1890s) showing an affluent woman purchasing Dr. Pierce's Golden Medical Discovery, a widely used patent medicine. Despite Pierce's denials, Thomas Faulkner and J. H. Carmichael reported in *The Cottage Physician* (1892) that the preparation contained tincture of opium.

The prototypical image of the nineteenth-century morphine addict—
a white, middle- or upper-class woman who became addicted after
treatment by a physician following a painful physical or emotional
injury. From Maria Weed's novel *A Voice in the Wilderness* (1895).

The interior of a New York City opium den (photo dated April 12, 1926). Each woman occupies a separate couch or compartment, and the woman at top left is holding an opium pipe.

Cleo Howard, a blonde film dancer, in a Los Angeles lockup following her arrest on April 11, 1936. She and her husband, Willard Howard, a nightclub master of ceremonies, were suspected of being the primary source of "loco weed" (marijuana) in Hollywood.

Undated photograph of a seventeen-year-old New York girl in drug detoxification at the federal treatment facility in Lexington, Kentucky. Between 1941 and 1965, approximately fifteen thousand women underwent similar treatment.

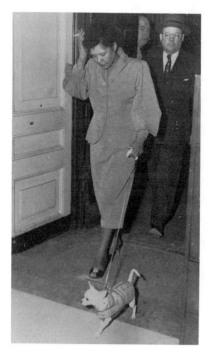

Singer Billie Holiday leaving a Philadelphia jail in 1956. Arrested on narcotics charges at her hotel in an early morning raid, she was released on bail.

First class postage stamp issued by the United States Postal Service on July 31, 1971.

Rosemary, a twenty-two-year-old welfare client, mother, and heroin addict in her apartment on the Lower East Side of New York, 1972.

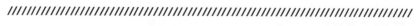

A clinic nurse handing out the daily dosage of methadone mixed with Tang (March 1973). The mixture must be consumed on the spot in view of the nurse, who then destroys the plastic bottle to prevent the drug from getting out onto the street.

National Organization for the Reform of Marijuana Laws (NORML) billboard (May 1977) for a film recalling the "reefer madness" craze of the 1930s.

Cover of a March of Dimes brochure (1994).

seven

THE 1960s

As the decade of the 1960s opened, fear continued to fuel public opinion in favor of more punitive and repressive social policies toward addicts. Against the background noise of increasing "hard" drug use, higher crime rates, reports of drug abuse by American soldiers in Vietnam and returning Vietnam veterans, and a new generation of young Americans experimenting with old—and new—drugs, neither a "medical model" of addiction nor the medical needs of addicts attracted public attention.

During the decade, the federal government expanded its control, not only over narcotics but over other drugs as well, and many Americans supported the hard-line approach. Until the day he retired from the Federal Bureau of Narcotics in 1962, Harry Anslinger kept the national level of concern simmering by claiming that Communist China was undermining the national will and financing its plans for global domination through heroin exports to the United States (Anslinger and Tompkins 1953). Congress added the Drug Abuse Control Amendments of 1965, designed to curb the black market in amphetamines, barbiturates, and other psychoactive drugs, to the Federal Food, Drug and Cosmetic Act, which went into effect in February 1966. Among other provisions, the new laws declared that prescriptions would be valid for no more than six months and that they could not be filled more than five times without the reauthorization of the prescribing physician (Brill 1973). These amendments made it more difficult to divert legally manufactured amphetamines to the black market, but they also stimulated the illegal manufacture of these drugs (Brecher 1972). In 1968 the Federal Bureau of Narcotics merged with the Bureau of Drug Abuse Control to form a more centralized drug-fighting agency, the Bureau of Narcotics and Dangerous Drugs, under the Department of the Treasury.

Other developments, however, were pushing the national dialogue over drugs in new directions. The election of John F. Kennedy to the presidency in 1960, an important Supreme Court decision in 1962, and increased awareness of the etiology and biochemistry of addiction inspired attempts to find concrete and effective long-term ways to combat the drug problem. As Lawrence Kolb, a renowned expert on addiction, noted sadly in 1962, "Our approach so far has produced tragedy, disease, and crime" (1962: 169). In seeking alternatives to the harsh policies of the Classic Era, and looking back at its half-century of failure, the nation was prepared to confront the drug problem in radical new ways.

The Numbers Game

In 1962 William Eldridge, a spokesman for the American Bar Foundation, called "the lack of accurate, complete, and fully-revealing statistics and data on the administration and effect of drug control policies in the United States . . . at one time understandable and astonishing" (p. 66). Isidor Chein, a professor of psychology at New York University, also questioned the accuracy of the "numbers game" and concluded that "there is a serious problem of addiction, but it is not nearly of the magnitude we have come to take for granted" (1965: 108). One reason for the confusion was the spread of drug use into urban ghettoes and its diffusion among a growing minority population. In New York City, for example, the number of Puerto Ricans swelled from 70,000 in 1940 to over 600,000 in 1960. Although as a group Puerto Ricans had no discernible problem with heroin before the mid-1950s, they represented almost 14 percent of the patients treated at the Lexington and Fort Worth facilities by 1966, when they comprised only 1.5 percent of the U.S. population. Addiction also increased among blacks who migrated to Northern urban centers, such as New York City, where the black population increased from 450,000 in 1940 to about one million in 1960 (Bates and Crowther 1974).

Most of the newer epidemiological data were based on the calculations of the Federal Bureau of Narcotics, which had begun compiling statistics in 1953. The Bureau reported slightly over 45,000 opiate addicts at the end of 1961 and almost 47,000 addicts in September 1962 (Chein 1965). One estimate placed the number of opiate addicts at 61,000 (Winick 1965). Another, by Harris Isbell (1965), a professor of medicine at the University of Kentucky, concluded that a total of about 60,000 addicts, limited largely to cities such as New York, Chicago, and Los Angeles, were living in the United States in the mid-1960s. Although admitting that "the number of persons addicted to narcotics or using them with some regularity . . . is not known," other researchers concluded that the "most reasonable" estimate of the number of opiate addicts in mid-decade was somewhere between 60,000 and 100,000 (O'Donnell and Ball 1966). In contrast, during the same period, the New York City Narcotics Register listed almost 95,000 addicts within the metropolitan area alone (Kiev 1975). By the late 1960s, it was clear from a variety of sources that the number of illicit narcotics users had escalated to somewhere between 100,000 (Fort 1969) and well over a million (Hunt and Chambers 1976). Added to this number were an estimated six to twelve million users of marijuana, twenty to twenty-five million regular users of prescribed sedatives, and hundreds of thousands of users of LSD and related compounds (Fort 1969).

William Eldridge (1962) called attention to one of the few bright spots in the increasingly complex drug scene of the early 1960s: cocaine use had diminished "to the point of near extinction." Another noted that even in the late 1960s, the use of cocaine, "the most potent stimulant drug," was still "negligible in the United States" (Fort 1969). The decrease in cocaine use, however, did not extend to all populations under study. Among a group of 422 heroin-addicted men interviewed in New York in the late 1960s, two-thirds, most of them black, reported using cocaine: it was second only to marijuana, which was used by 92 percent of respondents (Langrod 1977). In a Philadelphia study, almost one-third of the heroin addicts also reported cocaine abuse (Chambers and Taylor 1973).

As the decade drew to a close, drug use, according to public perceptions, had reached crisis levels. In 1971, a national poll ranked drug addiction as the third most important national problem (Glasscote et al. 1972). For many Americans, the prototypical "addict" was a young minority urban male involved in crime either prior to addiction or in order to support his addiction. Yet this prototypical picture obscured a critical fact: during the 1960s the total number of addicts was rising but the percentage of addicted women was relatively fixed; thus, the total number of female addicts must certainly have been increasing.

Using what they called a representative sample of addicts in treatment at Lexington in 1962, John Ball and William Bates (1970) found that 22 percent of their 925 patients were women. According to another study, 18 percent of the methadone addicts discharged from Lexington in 1962 were female (Sapira, Ball, and Cotrell 1973). In the late 1960s, between 8 percent and 12.5 percent of the hard-core heroin addicts admitted for methadone treatment in a Philadelphia program were women (Wieland and Chambers 1973; Chambers and Taylor 1973). These figures were slightly lower than Federal Bureau of Narcotics and New York City Health Register estimates of 16 percent to 21 percent (Ball and Chambers 1970) and the Texas Christian University study figure of 17 percent (Hunt 1977). A 1968 survey of over 1,300 high school girls in Portland, Oregon, published in the *American Journal of Public Health,* showed that about 10 percent had used marijuana, about 12 percent had used amphetamines, more than 25 percent had used sedatives and tranquilizers, less than 10 percent had used any type of narcotic, and only 1 percent or so had used cocaine (Johnson et al. 1971). Since all of these surveys dealt with specific populations, however, none can be considered complete or fully representative.

Newspapers reported the growing involvement of teenagers in the drug scene. In affluent Westchester County, just north of New York City, "boys and girls gathered in private homes to smoke marijuana cigarettes and use cocaine, heroin and opium derivatives in pills, by inhalation and by hypodermic injection" (*New York Times,* March 18, 1960). Two of the girls in this group were reportedly driven to prostitution to support their drug habit (April 2, 1960). An eighteen-year-old Westchester female addict was reported missing for two weeks, and two female heroin pushers, aged twenty-two and twenty-three, were arrested in the disappearance (*New York Times,* August 20, 1964). Following publicity surrounding the fatal heroin overdose of a twelve-year-old boy, the *Times* reported that the twelve-year-old daughter of a "wealthy East Side psychiatrist" had been found after a three-day spree on hashish, marijuana, LSD, heroin, and amphetamines (January 29, 1970). Also becoming commonplace were reports of thirteen- to fifteen-year-old white, black, and Hispanic girls who supported their addiction by selling drugs, stealing, and prostitution (Fixx 1971: 245–246; 332–341).

One continuing subpopulation of female addicts was that of medical professionals. As Alfred Lindesmith (1965), a sociology professor at Indiana University, commented, "the most persistent ecological feature of addiction rates in the Western world has been the high prevalence of addiction in the medical profession and its ancillary professions." According to the American Nursing Association, seventy-four nurses lost their licenses in 1961 for illegal use of opiates (Winick 1965). A survey of thirteen state health departments in 1965 found that the reported incidence of Demerol (meperidine) addiction among nurses was high; according to a number of respondents, reports underestimated the true extent of the problem (Garb 1965).

The overrepresentation of nurses in the addicted population was reflected at the Lexington treatment facility. William Bates and Betty Crowther (1974) concluded from a sociological study at Lexington that there were three general types of female addicts: heroin users, nonheroin users, and nurses. At one point in 1965, seven of the eleven college-educated female addicts admitted to Lexington were nurses (Chambers, Hinseley, and Moldestad 1970). Between 1962 and 1967, ninety nurses were treated at the facility for addiction to narcotics, which they had obtained from physician and hospital supplies, drugstores, and family as well as through forged prescriptions (Poplar 1969). Many of these women said they used drugs because of physical illness, emotional problems, and work pressures.

They came from thirty states and one territory, and were generally around forty-two years old, twelve years older than the average Lexington patient. Demerol, to which they had ready access, was the drug of choice, followed by morphine, paregoric, codeine, Darvon, and barbiturates. Other less frequently used drugs included elixir of terpin hydrate with codeine, Dilaudid, Doriden, amphetamines, heroin, Pentothol, methadone, and Percodan. The nurses differed from other women at Lexington in several ways: the relatively late onset of their addiction; their solitary rather than shared drug experiences; their stable, conventional home backgrounds and supportive family structures; their higher levels of education; and their sense of optimism. Although these patients were reportedly "doing well," two died from medication overdoses after discharge, thirty-nine left the hospital against medical advice, and eight were readmitted for retreatment (Poplar 1969).

A similar study, based on interviews with twelve nurses who were admitted to Lexington in 1973, found an average age of forty and a primary addiction to "medicinal" opiates (Demerol and morphine), followed by sedative-hypnotics (barbiturates, glutethimide, and methaqualone). Researchers noted that these women displayed an "extensive lifelong use of medical services," characterized by frequent past surgery, outpatient and inpatient psychiatric treatment, and over two hundred hospital admissions for the group (Levine, Preston, and Lipscomb 1974).

In *Narco Priest,* Father Roland Melody tells of a nurse-addict who became hooked on amphetamines while facing the pressures of nursing school:

> Whenever I was on duty and it was time to give the patients their pain pills or sleeping pills, I took my keys, opened the cabinet, and prepared the tray of pills—each patient's dosage in a small paper cup. I recorded each dose under the patient's name and distributed the individual cups. Then, contrary to nursing procedure, I left each patient alone . . . I knew many of them wouldn't take their pills if I wasn't there. Later, when I made the rounds, it was easy to collect all the unused pills. It wasn't long before I acquired a dangerously high tolerance level for sedatives and tranquilizers. (1971: 123)

This nurse progressed to codeine and then compromised her patients' care by stealing their morphine: "I gave them their money's worth—a shot of distilled water . . . and stockpiled the morphine for myself" (pp. 124–125).

Crime

Proponents of "hard line" policies toward drug users based their position on the continuing connection between drug use and criminality. For many Americans, the vast amounts of money stolen to buy narcotics, estimated at millions of dollars a day, the growing number of drug-related deaths and drug-related arrests, the increasing prevalence of younger users, and reports of drug use by American soldiers in Vietnam called for repressive strategies.

Among the states, penalties for narcotics violations—for addiction itself, possession, possession for sale, and sale to a minor by an adult—varied considerably. In Louisiana, possession of narcotics alone could bring a sentence of five to fifteen years, and sale of narcotics ten to fifty years. In some states a minor transmitting marijuana to another minor could receive a five- to fifteen-year sentence; in Missouri it could result in the death penalty (Fort 1969). In Michigan, some judges felt that mandatory state penalties were too harsh and refused to convict many people under such rigid sentencing guidelines. By 1969, thirty-one states required a minimum sentence of two years in prison for a first conviction for marijuana possession; forty-four states had maximum penalties of five years to life for the same offense (Fort 1969). In addition, more aggressive police work and prosecution produced a substantial increase in arrests. In California between 1960 and 1967, drug-related arrests of adults rose by 200 percent, and of juveniles by 900 percent (Fort 1969).

Personal testimonials and press coverage of addicts' experience eventually inspired public concern about the link between women addicts and crime. Prostitutes provided the most obvious example of law-breaking women. On a narcotic raid in the late 1960s, Father Roland Melody met an addict named Annie, an "agitated scarecrow figure, barely recognizable now as a woman." Annie typified the down-and-out female addict of the time: she had a history of ten arrests for soliciting and two convictions for heroin possession. At forty-five she looked seventy and "on the brink of physical death" (1971: 4–5).

Father Melody described the physical condition of these addict-prostitutes:

> During the search all three girls, dressed only in torn and stained underpants, wandered aimlessly around the room . . . Just skin and bone, they looked more like leprous zombies than anything human. Their flanks were stringy and shriveled; their pathetic breasts, flat and pendulous. The backs of their arms, hips, and legs were covered with "track marks" (needle punctures), some were reddened, swelling, and ulcerated from using tincture of opium (when heroin was not available). Their hair was matted like old birds' nests and they stank. (p. 8)

Stroke a Slain Warrior related horrific stories of the descent into prostitution and crime. As one recovering addict who ran a rehabilitation center recalled: "Oh, yes, I was skin and bone, my teeth were bad . . . I was always breaking out with sores . . . Physically, I was in poor condition . . . I certainly wasn't eager to look at myself in the mirror . . . looking at the face frightened me" (Cortina 1970: 191).

In previous decades, women were usually arrested for nonviolent and property crimes, such as selling drugs, prostitution, theft, and shoplifting. During the 1960s, however, the number of crimes committed by women increased sharply, a trend that continued into the 1970s, when arrest rates rose faster for women than for men (Silverman 1982). By 1969, 60 percent of the women in New York City prisons were addicts (New York Times, September 23, 1969). At the same time, according to the Uniform Crime Reports, between 1960 and 1965 female involvement in a broader range of criminal offenses, especially burglary, auto theft, fraud, embezzlement, and larceny/theft, also increased (Silverman 1982). Narcotics violations by women climbed from thirteenth to seventh on the "rank list," a numerical ranking of crimes committed, while the rate of such arrests rose from 18 per 100,000 population in 1965 to 102 per 100,000 in 1977. During the same period, arrests of women for narcotics violations rose from just over 1 percent to almost 6 percent of all female arrests. Even more striking was the increase in arrests of female juveniles for narcotics violations, from under 7 per 100,000 to slightly over 150 per 100,000. Although the percentage of arrests for prostitution contributing to total female arrests dropped slightly, actual numbers of arrests for prostitution rose from 84 per 100,000 women in 1965 to 96 per 100,000 women in 1977 (Silverman 1982).

The newspapers translated these statistics into anecdotes understandable to the lay public. In 1964 a prostitute was arrested for smuggling three to five million dollars' worth of cocaine from South America (New York Times, December 8, 1964). A seventy-seven-year-old woman was given a five-year prison sentence in 1969 for selling drugs, including heroin, to children (New York Times, December 20, 1969). Women were often used as "mules," carrying drugs into the United States in their brassieres, panties, and stockings. Even high school girls were arrested as pushers, and in the late 1960s a Phi Beta Kappa Barnard College student was arrested as a major supplier of drugs at Columbia University (New York Times, May 22 and 23, 1970).

Carl Chambers and Arthur Moffett (1970) offer informative data on crime in a sample of fifty-seven black female addicts admitted to Lexington in 1965. They found that 91 percent of the women had a previous history of arrests, two-thirds of which were for narcotics-related offenses, and 75 percent had a history of actual incarceration. Approximately one-third of the women had been admitted as federal prisoners or probationers, often for the sale of narcotics, but none had been admitted for a violent crime.

During the 1960s and early 1970s, younger women were increasingly involved in drug-related crime. Narcotics violations among juvenile females rose tenfold, from seventeen on the rank list in 1965 to six in 1977. Although juvenile arrests for drug violations rose faster between 1965 and 1973 than those in any other category, they dropped off in the late 1970s with the decriminalization of marijuana. Juvenile arrests for prostitution also increased during the late 1960s and early 1970s but constituted a relatively small part of all juvenile female offenses (Silverman 1982).

Civil Commitment

In response to escalating concern over drugs and crime, several states pioneered a new approach to the drug problem: civil commitment. Under the direction of Governor Edmund Brown, California launched a large-scale civil commitment program in 1961 for narcotic addicts or those "in imminent danger of becoming addicted." This program, based on the 1935 Lexington model, was the outcome of a 1957 meeting of the State Board of Corrections and a 1959 report based on the board's recommendations. The legislation went into effect in September 1961, and although it provided harsher penalties for repeat offenders, it also offered addicts the option of civil commitment for drug treatment, created the California Rehabilitation Center, and set up a mandatory follow-up program. In addition, it required chemical testing to determine narcotic use and stepped up rehabilitation research efforts (McGee 1965). Offenders were committed to the rehabilitation center for an indeterminate period not to exceed seven years, after which criminal charges could be reduced or dropped if the addict was drug-free for three years.

During the first decade of its operation, almost eighteen thousand people passed through the California program. Some studies found that civil commitment, especially in combination with methadone maintenance treatment, not only reduced drug use and criminal activity but increased postconfinement employment in males (McGlothlin, Anglin, and Wilson 1977; Anglin and McGlothlin 1984). Critics who defined "success" as total drug abstinence, however, pointed out that only 16 percent of addicts remained drug-free after three years in the California program (Meyer 1972).

Some female addicts were fortunate in finding their way into civil commitment programs rather than the criminal justice system. Under the California program, women were initially housed at the California Institution for Women in Corona, about fifty miles from Los Angeles. In 1969 the women's unit, with three hundred patients, was moved to Patton State Hospital. This facility was among the first to tailor programs to the specific needs of addicted women. Individual programs were based on a woman's past drug use, criminal activity, desire to change her lifestyle, and past performance in treatment programs (Glasscote et al. 1972).

In December 1965, 268 women were receiving active treatment at the California Rehabilitation Center. An additional 665 women had been released, and although 263 of those women had returned for additional treatment, their need for retreatment did not constitute "failure." Only 4 percent had incurred criminal charges after discharge (Wood 1966). One hundred women had been returned to the community, some for as long as three years, and of those women, only sixteen had been recommitted. The California Civil Commitment program treated a racially diverse group of women (60 percent white, 20 percent black, and 20 percent Mexican) with an average age of twenty-six and an average IQ of 111. These women were well educated and in general had no record of prior arrests (Glasscote et al. 1972), which helped to explain the relatively high success rates.

New York State initiated a civil commitment program in 1966 under the auspices of the Narcotic Addiction Control Commission. For many years the epicenter of the drug epidemic, the state had been particularly hard-hit by an acute heroin shortage in late 1961, which set off a "panic" among addicts. The Metcalf-Volcker Act, passed in 1962, acknowledged the human and economic costs of addiction. It mandated that the Commissioner of Mental Hygiene develop a comprehensive, long-range plan, based on a mental health model, to prevent and control drug addiction within the state (Meiselas 1965). Under this legislation, following an arrest an addict could be admitted to a mental hygiene facility as a condition of probation, by court certification, or voluntarily. This public-health-oriented approach to the problem of addiction included treatment and rehabilitation, research, prevention and education, and contractual relationships with agencies to supply services. The Department of Mental Hygiene received an allocation of sixty-five million dollars to encourage local governments in designing and implementing drug treatment programs, and an additional two hundred million dollars to build, acquire, and rehabilitate drug treatment facilities. The implementation plan included the creation of units for male and female adolescents along with a separate facility for adult females. By 1973 a total of thirty-four states had established similar civil commitment programs; seventeen left the period of confinement indefinite, and the remainder provided commitment for periods from thirty days to as much as ten years. Ultimately, however, the success and the value of these civil commitment programs were never clearly documented, and some condemned them, finding no justification for the "legal and personal abuses" they inflicted (Ashley 1972). By 1974 they had lost their support, and by 1979 all had been closed down.

New Approaches

In contrast to state actions, on the federal level a less punitive approach was developing, which advocates hoped would prove more effective in combating drug use. The Kennedy administration initiated a fresh look at mental health issues and recruited health professionals, lawyers, and social scientists interested in aiding the country's addicts. The new team in Washington focused on alternative ways to approach the drug problem, including a system of clinics and medical maintenance programs, medical help for addicts, and research on addiction, to replace the harsh law enforcement approach of previous decades.

The planning did not always proceed smoothly. A number of government departments—Housing and Urban Development (family life centers), Justice (Safe Streets Act), and Defense (which joined with the Veterans Administration to offer services for returning veterans)—initiated drug treatment programs simultaneously, creating a bureaucratic tangle of scattered and incoherent policies.

President Kennedy demonstrated his personal commitment to the drug issue by establishing the White House Conference on Drug Use and Abuse. As the conference's ad hoc panel stated, it welcomed "careful, rigorous, and well-monitored research" designed to learn whether "certain addicts who cannot be weaned permanently from drugs . . . can be maintained in a socially acceptable state on an ambulatory basis" (*White House Conference on Narcotic and Drug Abuse* 1962). Kennedy's Advisory Commission on Narcotic and Drug Abuse endorsed the proposal the following year, and the government began investigating drug maintenance as a possible treatment for certain addicts. The Commission recommended "that the definition of legitimate medical use of narcotic drugs and legitimate medical treatment of a narcotic addict are primarily to be determined by the medical profession" (*President's Advisory Commission on Narcotic and Drug Abuse* 1963). This important and radical departure from popular thinking, coupled with the timely retirement of "narcotics czar" Harry Anslinger in 1962, nurtured a new federal drug policy, one that increasingly featured treatment among its goals.

The new federal approach to addiction gained support in *Robinson v. California,* an important 1962 Supreme Court case. In its ruling, the Court stated that drug addiction was a disease, and that it was thus unconstitutional to punish addiction as a crime. The decision overturned a California statute defining the "status" of addiction as a criminal offense and making it a misdemeanor for a person "to be addicted to the use of narcotics." At the same time, however, the *Robinson* decision also provided support for civil commitment programs: "In the interest of discouraging violation of such laws, or in the interest of the general health or welfare of its inhabitants, a State might establish a program of compulsory treatment for those addicted to narcotics . . . [and] might require periods of involuntary confinement" (Allen 1965: 30–31). Mr. Justice Stewart, questioning whether being mentally ill or a leper or carrying a venereal disease was a criminal offense, stressed the decision's major point: "in the light of contemporary human knowledge, a law which made a criminal offense of such a disease would doubtless be universally thought to be an infliction of cruel and unusual punishment in violation of the Eighth and Fourteenth Amendments."

The *Robinson* decision was similar to that in a 1925 case, *U.S. v. Linder,* which found that a physician was not in violation of the Harrison Act for dispensing a small amount of morphine to a known addict for personal use. In *Linder,* the Court ruled that the intent of the Harrison Act was to tax and regulate narcotics, not to redefine the status of addiction as criminal or to limit the activities of physicians. Although the *Linder* ruling failed to stop the harassment and prosecution of physicians and addicts, the *Robinson* ruling was much more conducive to new approaches to an old problem.

Formal treatment for drug addiction in the early 1960s was limited to the federal facilities at Lexington and Fort Worth, civil commitment programs, some detoxification programs in New York City, and the beginnings of therapeutic communities. In the early 1960s, Dr. Lawrence Kolb proposed that with certain safeguards in place, narcotics should be prescribed for addicts by their personal physicians. Kolb also suggested an increase in treatment facilities and the recognition that some opiate addicts "should be given opiates for their own as well as the public welfare" (1962: 174). William Eldridge also concluded that repressive policies were not working, and that "concern over the causes of addiction and the plight of the addict find very little place in the criminal sanction approach." Advocating the "medical approach," Eldridge felt that "the medical profession is the only body capable of making decisions as to the therapeutic efficacy and desirability of treatment procedures" (1962: 121). Isidor Chein advocated providing addicts with "quality controlled drugs at inexpensive prices" (1965: 113). In 1965, the Committee on Public Health of the New York Academy of Medicine issued a policy statement calling for all addicts to be brought "under medical supervision because they are all sick people." In recognizing the need for medical supervision, the Committee noted that "because of the high psychological element in addiction and the high frequency of recurrence, the addict should not be removed from narcotics until another salutary crutch is provided" (Brill 1973: 21).

Some believed that such a crutch was already available in the form of methadone, another addictive narcotic. Under the leadership of Vincent Dole and Marie Nyswander at the Rockefeller Institute and Beth Israel Hospital in New York, trials with methadone were begun as part of a regimen of maintenance treatment and successfully demonstrated that methadone could be highly effective in restructuring the lives of heroin addicts. Maintenance contrasted sharply with forced abstinence, which had for many years characterized the policies of the Federal Bureau of Narcotics. The work of Dole and Nyswander, it has been claimed, "applied the coup de grace to the anti-maintenance policy and brought the classic era of narcotic control to a close" (Courtwright, Joseph, and Des Jarlais 1989: 276).

In at least one state, drug maintenance therapy continued throughout the interwar years and after. A study of 266 addicts in Kentucky revealed that from 1914 on, 87 percent of addicted women and 67 percent of addicted men had obtained narcotics from a physician (O'Donnell 1969). About one-quarter of the men and over half of the women reported being maintained throughout their drug-using careers. Addicts tended to frequent different physicians and pharmacists to arouse less suspicion, but it was also understood that drug enforcement officials tended to ignore physicians who were writing prescriptions for small quantities of drugs. As the study reported, "Of the older men and the women who had been addicted before 1940, and who were obtaining drugs from a physician, most were tacitly allowed to continue their addiction" (O'Donnell 1974: 37).

In 1965, the Advisory Council of Judges of the National Council on Crime and Delinquency advocated that narcotic addicts be treated as sick people rather than as criminals. The Council recommended more research in the field of addiction and downplayed civil commitment programs. The Council also stated that the policies of the Federal Bureau of Narcotics, which prohibited physicians from prescribing narcotic drugs to addicts, were inconsistent with the aims of the Harrison Act and should be changed (Ashbrook and Solley 1979). Perhaps due partly to these recommendations, the Bureau issued a pamphlet to "generate interest in treating and curing addiction and to make clear that the policy of the U.S. Government does not restrict physicians who desire to treat narcotic addicts in the course of ethical practice of medicine" (*Prescribing and Dispensing of Narcotics under the Harrison Narcotic Law* 1966).

The Narcotic Addict Rehabilitation Act (NARA), passed in 1966, was a widely heralded federal attempt to provide a civil commitment treatment alternative for addicts in lieu of prosecution (Title I), as an alternative to jail time (Title II), or voluntarily, without criminal charges (Title III). When fully implemented, NARA authorized grants (90 percent federal, 10 percent state supported) to states and to private organizations and institutions to develop and evaluate programs and cooperative arrangements for treatment centers and facilities (Simrell 1970). NARA also encouraged states and municipalities to develop new treatment programs (Title IV). By July 1971, twenty-three community-based granted programs were in operation and an additional twenty-five had been funded (Besteman 1978). By 1974, the number of programs had reached two hundred.

Federal policy also called for the establishment of mental health centers, which recognized narcotic abuse as a specific health problem for the community as well as the individual addict. Representative of the widening of treatment opportunities in the 1960s, the Economic Opportunity Amendments of 1966 provided approximately twelve million dollars for community addiction programs and for legal service programs intended to advise addicts and their families on alternatives to prosecution (Simrell 1970). By 1968–1969, a national study (Glasscote et al. 1972) identified 183 drug treatment programs, most of them located in New York, New Jersey, Connecticut, Massachusetts, Illinois, and California. From 1969 to 1972 the federal government operated Matrix House, a self-help residential community on the grounds of the renamed National Institute of Mental Health Clinical Research Center (Addiction Research Center) at Lexington, Kentucky. Modeled after Synanon, Matrix House also incorporated psychological, physiological, and social psychology evaluation of the addicts (Cancellaro 1972).

New Users

Despite the substantial numbers of female opiate addicts in federal facilities and the many others who were still on the street, addicted women continued to go largely unnoticed. "Unnoticed" easily became "nonexistent," and these women languished in the federal facilities, with small chance of effective treatment or eventual recovery. What preoccupied the press instead were the middle-aged housewives who were using psychoactive prescription drugs, and the students and younger women who were "turning on" to marijuana and LSD. Barbara Kerr's *Strong at the Broken Places* presents case histories of six addicted women drawn from an interview sample of forty addicted women of "intelligence, willfulness, creativity, taste, physical attractiveness, good health, educational opportunities, and middle-class backgrounds" (1974: 13). They lived in New York City, Oakland, Boston, Chicago, the Georgetown section of the District of Columbia, and an unnamed Midwestern college town.

During the turbulent 1960s, women experienced more personal

freedom, achieved higher levels of education, and enjoyed expanding economic and social opportunities. These dramatic changes were associated with changes in drug use patterns. The counterculture of the 1960s fostered an atmosphere that encouraged women to experiment with "non-traditional lifestyles," including legal and illegal drugs. As one commentator noted: "The 1960s 'love' culture encouraged both men and women to explore new lifestyles. The social disapproval of open drug use by women gave way to social approval of experimentation with drugs, at least among young middle-class women" (Worth 1991: 6). In her autobiography, *Take the Long Way Home,* Susan Lydon comments that her craving for "sexual adventure and excitement," coupled with "boredom and restlessness," was largely responsible for her experimentation with LSD (1993: 85–86). Cross-addiction and poly-addiction were publicly acknowledged for the first time, since many middle-class women used some combination of alcohol, psychoactive prescription drugs, stimulants, hallucinogens, and antidepressants.

Once the use and abuse of marijuana, hallucinogens, and psychoactive prescription drugs moved into mainstream society, one segment sought to distance itself from the problem by claiming a "generation gap" and labeling all who used drugs as "deviant." Those who stereotyped drug users as the "fringe elements" of society considered marijuana not simply a symbolic but an actual threat to American social values. As Susanna Kaysen recalled in *Girl, Interrupted:* "It was 1967 . . . there was a strange undertow, a tug from the other world—the drifting, drugged-out, no-last-name youth universe—that knocked people off balance. One could call it threatening" (1993: 39–40). This feeling was also expressed by Myra, a rich girl with a two-hundred-dollar-a-day heroin habit, during her fifth treatment attempt in a sanitarium: "Do you know why the public wants us destroyed? Because we are the gross realization of themselves. We are all of those traits in themselves they most fear, loathe, and conceal . . . We have completely copped out . . . we've crashed . . . while the public is in torment about their daily near-misses . . . their averted crashes" (Cortina 1970: 58).

During the decade of the 1960s, as drug use became more mainstream, treatment became more possible. Some adults sympathized with the rebellious, disenchanted young. They realized that on the other side of the "generation gap" stood their own children. Middle-class youths challenged each other to "turn on, tune in, and drop out" and coopted mainstream commercial slogans, such as "Better Living through Chemistry." Young people expressed their dissatisfaction and discontent in a variety of ways, from the activism of the New Left, Students for a Democratic Society (SDS), antiwar and antidraft groups, hippies, Yippies, and the Black Panthers and Brown Berets to involvement in the campaigns of Eugene McCarthy and Robert Kennedy or the Peace Corps, to rock music, psychedelic light shows, and freer forms of artistic expression. Hovering over all was the fatalistic threat of nuclear devastation.

The baby-boomers experimented with a wider range of drugs than any previous generation. In *Trips*, Ellen Sander, a journalist, wrote of her first-hand experience in the drug culture of New York's Greenwich Village, where grass, hashish, acid, uppers and downers, and cocaine were widely available: "We were getting turned on in so many ways, lit up to new experiences, discoveries, adventures, music, all of which had something very tangibly related to the drugs available" (1973: 20). One highly publicized segment of the nation's youth wandered in search of the next drug experience. When grass wasn't available, amphetamines and hard narcotics served as substitutes. Sander described one dirty, underage runaway, who was tolerated only because she had a ready supply of amphetamines, morphine, and Seconals. Another woman started using heroin in place of Methedrine with friends in Haight-Ashbury who considered heroin a "civilized drug": "I thought it would be better for me, less dangerous to my health" (Kerr 1974: 69).

Father Melody noted the destruction of one young, middle-class girl once she was hooked on drugs:

> Not too long ago she was going to football games as a member of the cheerleading squad. Not too long ago she was boy crazy. Her whole pattern of life and dress was dictated by the latest male singing star or movie hero. Now her personality and interests had changed. She had to make seventy-five dollars a day to keep her in dope. Now men were animals, and she felt they deserved to be treated as such. She took sadistic delight in shaming or embarrassing the men who paid for her sexual favors. (1971: 89)

The thousands of young people who flooded into San Francisco and Berkeley encountered drugs everywhere (Gay and Gay 1972). "The two years I spent in San Francisco in both Haight-Ashbury and North Beach," one woman recalled, "were as psychotic as any I ever want to experience. The pathetic young kids who lined the streets were homeless, broke, hungry, and so high they enjoyed it. So did I" (Kerr 1974: 58). In *Slouching towards Bethlehem*, Joan Didion commented on the disintegration of a society in which "the center was not holding." Drugs were at the center of this "atomization":

> When I was in San Francisco a tab, or a cap, of LSD-25 sold for three to five dollars . . . LSD was . . . sold by pushers of hard drugs, e.g. heroin, or "smack." A great deal of acid was being cut with Methedrine . . . Grass was running ten dollars a lid, five dollars a matchbox. Hash was considered a "luxury item." All the amphetamines, or "speed"—Benzedrine, Dexedrine, and particularly Methedrine—were in far more common use . . . Where Methedrine is in wide use, heroin tends to be available, because, I was told, "You can get awful damn high shooting crystal, and smack can be used to bring you down." (1961: 108)

Didion noted the sexual exploitation of naive young girls in one of the communiques posted in a Haight-Ashbury window:

> Pretty little 16-year-old middle-class chick comes to the Haight to see what it's all about & gets picked up by a 17-year-old street dealer who spends all day shooting her full of speed again & again, then feeds her 3,000 mikes & raffles off her temporarily unemployed body for the biggest Haight Street gangbang since the night before last. The politics and ethics of ecstasy. Rape is as common as bullshit on Haight Street. (p. 101)

At the Haight-Ashbury Free Medical Clinic in San Francisco, women made up one-third of new heroin junkies and about 15 percent of those who had used heroin before 1964 (Gay, Newmeyer, and Winkler 1972). The risky practice of needle sharing, even among those who had already contracted hepatitis, was common in the Haight by the mid-1960s (Howard and Borges 1972).

Even Middle America was experimenting with drugs. In *White Rabbit*, Martha Morrison recalled growing up in the early 1960s in Fayetteville, Arkansas: "Drugs—particularly pot and LSD—were everywhere. If you wanted them, they were easy to get from the college kids who brought them in from out of town" (1989: 34). By the end of the decade, "Fayetteville was like a candy store for junkies—every sort of narcotic, barbiturate, and amphetamine was available for the taking" (p. 66).

The mass media focused on the popular entertainment favored by the young. As Terry Southern remarked, "Music was the message, and it was heavy" (Sander 1973: viii). Influential rock groups turned songs with drug themes into hits. The Beatles recorded "Lucy in the Sky with Diamonds," "I Am the Walrus," and "A Little Help from My Friends." The Rolling Stones scored with "Mother's Little Helper." Jefferson Airplane's "White Rabbit" told listeners to "feed your head, feed your head," while another, "Runnin' Round the World," with its explicit reference to "trips," was banned from one of the group's albums. The Doors did "Crystal Ship," Canned Heat sang of "Amphetamine Annie," and Donovan added "Sunshine Superman" and "The Trip." The Byrds made Bob Dylan's "Mr. Tambourine Man" into a huge hit, although their own "Eight Miles High" was banned from significant air exposure because it dealt with drug themes (Sander 1973). Bob Dylan himself contributed "Rainy Day Women No. 12 & 35" to the acid-rock movement. Jimi Hendrix composed "Purple Haze," "Stone Free" ("Stone Free to do what I please"), and "Are You Experienced?" Ivy League audiences cheered Tom Lehrer's wry approval of "the old dope peddler" with his "powdered happiness." Huge outdoor love-ins at Newport, Rhode Island, Woodstock, New York, and Monterey and Altamont, California, became era-defining celebrations of music, sex, and drugs. The last of these, Altamont, added a violent metaphor to the contemporary lexicon. As Ellen Sander noted, "Bad wine spiked with bad acid" led to "bad vibes" (1973: 160). The deaths of Jimi Hendrix and Janis Joplin from drug overdoses also cast a pall over the drug scene.

The media focus on the youth drug scene introduced large numbers of teenagers and young adults to drugs. Yet, while romantic glorifications of drug use in popular music attracted young people, moralistic preaching about the dangers of drugs by adults also had a similar effect. As one commentator noted, "Recently, many persons, especially young ones, have wanted to use these drugs primarily because society threatens . . . punishments" (Weil 1972: 189). Antidrug propaganda also contributed to increased drug use among disillusioned and mistrustful youth. Once these new users had tried LSD, marijuana, and other psychoactive drugs, they discovered an incongruity between their own "mind-expanding" experiences and the warnings they had received. As Joan Didion described it, "the signals between the generations" were "irrevocably jammed" (1961: 122). The antidrug campaign was out of touch with the reality experienced by America's youth and thus lacked credibility among this new, drug-using generation. Through raids, busts, and the ensuing press coverage, law enforcement officials inadvertently provided free advertising for "happenings" in hippie locales such as Greenwich Village and Haight-Ashbury. Abbie Hoffman and Paul Krassner formed the antisociety Youth International Party in 1968 and recruited thousands of "Yippies."

New Drugs

Marijuana. Used historically among Native Americans, Mexican immigrants, blacks, and the working class, in the 1960s marijuana found its way into mainstream American life and "turned on" a generation. Its advocates, especially students, found the drug relatively safe, cheap, easy to grow or obtain, and enjoyable; it provided a "high" without "hard drugs." "Teeny boppers," young girls eager to ingratiate themselves into the free and easy world of sex, drugs, and rock and roll accepted marijuana as a "normal enough" part of the new "lifestyle" (*New York Times,* May 28, 1967). Teenage deaths associated with "hard drugs" seemed to confirm their dangers and, by implication, the relative safety of marijuana. A May 1969 Gallup poll found that 22 percent of students had smoked marijuana, 10 percent had used barbiturates, and 4 percent had tried LSD. Later that year, Gallup estimated that ten million Americans, half of them under the age of twenty-one, smoked marijuana. That same year, Stanley Yolles, the director of the National Institute of Mental Health, testified before a Senate subcommittee hearing that between eight and twelve million Americans had tried marijuana at least once. A researcher at the University of Maryland found that marijuana use had doubled, from 15 percent in 1967 to over 35 percent in 1969, the most dramatic increase occurring among women students (Brecher 1972). A 1967–1968 study of San Francisco residents aged eighteen to twenty-four found that about one-third of the women and one-half of the men had tried marijuana (Manheimer, Mellinger, and Balter 1970). According to a poll in December 1970, an estimated 42 percent of all college students had experimented with marijuana (Brecher 1972).

Marijuana use was not restricted to the young. That it was a naturally grown product made it seem less dangerous than chemical substances, and because smoking it was similar to cigarette smoking, it was more acceptable to the middle class. One survey showed that one-fifth of those who used marijuana were over thirty-five (Manheimer, Mellinger, and Balter 1970). Marijuana use was common among women in America's "elite," including executive secretaries, entertainers, doctors' wives, businesswomen, and one woman who had served on a presidential commission (*New York Times,* January 10, 1968). In a *New York Times Magazine* article, a housewife in her mid-thirties reported:

> Marijuana was a godsend. It's much milder than liquor and much pleasanter, so I carry my own. When everyone else drinks, I open my cigarette case, pull out a joint, and everyone is very impressed . . . But I just smoke enough to get a slight high. I don't really like the super-boo that takes the top of your head off. I just want to feel more relaxed, more in the mood for a party. I love it. (Blum 1970)

The bohemian communities of the East and West Coasts became strongholds of marijuana use in the 1960s, and the drug's association with rebels and intellectuals only enhanced its attractiveness. Alice B. Toklas, friend and companion to the expatriate American writer Gertrude Stein and an excellent cook, became a counterculture heroine for her marijuana brownie recipe, which was deleted from her 1955 *Cook Book* but reappeared in the 1960 edition. Although she denied knowledge of the recipe, which she had received from a friend, her contribution to the drug scene was memorialized in a popular 1968 film, *I Love You, Alice B. Toklas,* starring Peter Sellers.

Critics concerned about the increase in marijuana smoking argued that it would serve as a "gateway drug" to heroin, and that the combined effects of alcohol and marijuana would be particularly devastating. A follow-up study of New York drug law offenders who used marijuana found that 40 percent went on to use heroin (*New York Times,* September 17, 1968). Although disclaiming that their data substantiated a "stepping stone" theory of addiction, Jeffrey Freeland and Richard Campbell (1973) showed significant co-use of marijuana and narcotics in a sample of over eight hundred addicts in treatment during 1968–1969. About one-quarter were female, and most of them had been introduced to marijuana through associations with male marijuana users.

Anecdotes appeared to offer substantiation. One of the prostitutes quoted by Father Roland Melody in *Narco Priest* described her entry into the drug world: "Greta gave me a few puffs of a special cigarette. It made me giggle and feel so strange . . . Greta said it was time I really learned about the sweet life. 'Time to torch up and turn on' . . . Greta said the magic word was cocaine! She taught me to snort and later to joy-pop for a quicker high . . . One day she told me she had a new 'connection' who wanted her to let him give a works party at her apartment. That's where I learned to mainline heroin" (1961: 11–12). Three of the six women in Barbara Kerr's *Strong at the Broken Places* (1974) explicitly talk of marijuana use, one describing a "gradual process" of reentry into the drug world, a second telling of initial use in high school and a third of being introduced to it during her involvement in the Civil Rights movement.

Many middle-class youth totally rejected the "stepping-stone" hypothesis, finding marijuana enjoyable, accessible, and not at all like the fearful picture being painted by adults and "straight society." As Susan Lydon recalled, "Grownups said that smoking marijuana would lead to shooting heroin, but we knew that was a lie promoted by the Establishment to keep all us kids from having fun" (1993: 37).

In an effort to limit marijuana use, American and Mexican agents launched Operation Intercept, a twenty-day exercise intended to shut off the flow of marijuana from Mexico, in September 1969 (Brecher 1972; Fixx 1971). Even before the Operation began, however, some narcotics officials were already apprehensive that pot smokers might switch to other, more dangerous drugs. Contemporary surveys proved them correct: many marijuana users turned to hallucinogens, such as mescaline and LSD and the stimulant "speed," during a marijuana shortage. A Los Angeles survey conducted from May to October 1969 showed that, although half of the marijuana users had decreased their use during Operation Intercept, the other half continued to use marijuana in spite of higher prices. The survey also found increased use of other drugs, such as alcohol, hashish, hallucinogens, sedatives, and cocaine (McGlothlin, Jamison, and Rosenblatt 1970). As a Radcliffe senior told a *Wall Street Journal* reporter, "I really didn't want to try acid before. But there's no grass around, so when someone offered me some [LSD], I figured, 'What the hell.' I didn't freak out or anything, so I've been tripping ever since" (cited in Brecher 1972: 435).

The strong antimarijuana laws passed throughout the 1960s reinstated the repressive thinking of Harry Anslinger's Bureau of Narcotics (Himmelstein 1983). As late as 1970, harsh penalties for marijuana sale or possession remained in place in states such as Alabama, Colorado, Georgia, Illinois, Louisiana, Massachusetts, Missouri, Rhode Island, Texas, and Utah. In Georgia, a first offense for selling marijuana to a minor was punishable by life imprisonment, a second by the death penalty (Brecher 1972). In other ways, however, laws against marijuana were softening. Increasing marijuana use among the middle class and the realization that youthful users were "someone's children" (Himmelstein 1983) reframed the marijuana debate. Reducing simple possession from a felony to a misdemeanor began at the state level in the mid-1960s and at the federal level at the end of the decade, a trend that would grow into a significant movement in favor of decriminalization.

LSD. Psychedelic drugs were long known and used among Native American peoples. James Mooney of the U.S. Bureau of Ethnology produced the first account of peyote use by the Kiowa Indians of Oklahoma in 1896 (see Strasbaugh and Blaise 1991). Throughout the twentieth century, others experimented with psychedelics. Mabel Dodge Luhan, a bohemian aesthete and New York salon hostess who lived out her days in Taos, New Mexico, described her own peyote-induced visual hallucinations in 1914, during an "another-world night." The writer Anaïs Nin recorded a similar experience in her multivolume diary but with LSD (cited in Strasbaugh and Blaise 1991; Palmer and Horowitz 1982). Before the 1950s, LSD, which had been discovered in 1938 but not actively studied until 1943, was a little-known, little-used, and relatively unavailable hallucinogen. In addition to the increasing nontherapeutic use of LSD through the 1950s and 1960s, a number of women documented extensive psychiatric use of the drug—including Anaïs Nin, Constance Newland (in *My/Self and I*), and Adelle Davis (under the pseudonym Jane Dunlap in *Exploring Inner Space*) (cited in Palmer and Horowitz 1982).

Following the thalidomide tragedy in 1962, when malformed babies were born to mothers who took the drug during pregnancy, the FDA and the Congress tightened regulations on LSD and on other drugs under investigation. LSD was banned in many states in 1965, and the manufacturer, Sandoz Laboratories, limited its distribution. Despite these restrictions, LSD quickly became popular among the counter-culture and was increasingly used by young, educated, middle-class women willing to challenge cultural norms and societal conventions. To them, LSD was as cheap, accessible, and enjoyable as marijuana. A newspaper headline of the time proclaimed "LSD Spread in U.S. Alarms Doctors and Police" (*New York Times,* February 23, 1967). As Susan Lydon, who first tried LSD in Berkeley in the late 1960s, commented: "I liked this drug. It opened my mind to different possibilities. It didn't feel nearly so dangerous as people had warned me it was" (1993: 91). Another young woman spoke of the "beautiful ecstatic, glorious feeling" that came with LSD use and the sensation of being able to "react with feelings more than you could with pot" (Kiev 1975: 70). Most of the women Barbara Kerr interviewed had taken LSD during the 1960s. All found the first few trips exciting in a positive way.

A Gallup poll revealed that the percentage of college students who had ever tried LSD rose from 1 percent in 1967 to about 4 percent in 1969 and to 14 percent by the end of 1970 (Goode 1972). Another report noted that by 1970, between one and two million Americans had tried LSD (McGlothlin and Arnold 1971). Horrific reports of "bad trips" and psychotic episodes, however, soon put a more negative spin on the drug, and its use declined in the mid-1970s. Disillusionment with LSD was predictable. One woman reported that it took her "two days to come down" (Kerr 1974: 186); another found that LSD mixed with speed or strychnine was both terrifying and dangerous: "My heart felt like it was going to burst . . . I don't ever want to take that kind of acid again" (p. 281).

In *Narco Priest* Father Melody portrayed a girl caught in a bad LSD trip: "She was sitting motionless in a chair with the barrel of a pistol clenched tightly between her teeth . . . her eyes stared right past me. What was going on in her mind? She made no sign to acknowledge my presence" (1971: 66). Susan Lydon also recalled a bad trip: "I became frightened. I could no longer remember my name, my home, or other details of who I was. I saw rattlesnake skins discarded in the gullies and sensed the presence of terrible danger. Panic struck me" (1993: 94). The newspapers reported further tragedies linked to LSD: a "tall, slender 19-year-old brunette" who drowned in her bathtub after an LSD trip (*New York Times*, November 26, 1968), and the daughter of the well-known television entertainer Art Linkletter, who had jumped to her death from a sixth-floor window while under the influence of LSD (*New York Times*, October 6, 1969).

Another factor also contributed to the decline in LSD use: its implication in genetic damage. Early anecdotal and equivocal data were translated into the "fact" that LSD use during pregnancy irreversibly damaged the fetus. The press concluded, on very little scientific evidence, that one dose of LSD might cause malformations or retardation in offspring. "Acid Burned a Hole in My Genes" and other, similar articles appeared in *East Village Other*, a countercultural publication (Goode 116). The National Foundation–March of Dimes distributed a leaflet acknowledging the lack of basic data but nevertheless warning of serious LSD-associated birth defects, which included graphic illustrations, although these were actually more typical of thalidomide-affected infants. At a time when concern about the effects of these drugs on fetal development was more frequently expressed, such national campaigns helped to reduce the "acceptability" of LSD use among some women. On April 26, 1970, the *New York Times* reported that "many youths are abandoning psychedelic drugs."

Psychoactive Prescription Drugs. Psychoactive drug use mushroomed during the 1950s and early 1960s. As the chief of the Psychopharmacology Research Branch at the National Institute of Mental Health testified before a U.S. Senate subcommittee, the number of new prescriptions for psychotropic drugs filled in the United States rose 65 percent between 1958 and 1967, from almost forty-three million to over seventy million. The most common were for minor tranquilizers, followed by hypnotics, stimulants, sedatives, major tranquilizers, and antidepressants (Balter and Levine 1969).

Not surprisingly, the growth in the psychotropic drug industry disproportionately affected women. Through the decade of the 1960s the number of women using psychotropic agents rose from 27 percent to 38 percent (Mellinger, Balter, and Manheimer 1971). A Connecticut state panel was told that excessive use of barbiturates and tranquilizers by women had resulted in the term "housewives' disease" (*New York Times*, March 18, 1964). A federal Department of Health, Education and Welfare panel heard testimony from an Equanil-addicted Missouri housewife that her addiction had led her to neglect her housework and five children (*New York Times*, July 16, 1966). A California study carried out in 1967 showed that women were twice as likely to be using stimulants, sedatives, or tranquilizers as men (Manheimer, Mellinger, and Balter 1968). A national study in the mid-1960s found that 31 percent of women and 15 percent of men used psychotropic agents, and that among the women, sedatives and tranquilizers were more common than stimulants. Although the study found no imbalance in the geographic representation of women, those termed "downwardly mobile" exhibited high prevalence rates (Parry 1968). Anecdotal personal histories confirmed what the statistics were saying. One woman, for example, found that "downers, Seconal and Doriden particularly" were effective ways to decelerate from amphetamines' speeding effects (Kerr 1974: 278).

By the late 1960s, about two-thirds of all psychoactive prescription drug users were women, and women also made up three-quarters of antidepressant users (Balter and Levine 1969). A more limited study (Linn and Davis 1971) of ninety-nine white, married Los Angeles women found that 46 percent were taking a prescription drug for at least one of six common symptoms. Among these women, drug-taking was associated with perceptions of chronic health problems, social and psychological stress, and frequent visits to physicians; 84 percent reported that a physician had first recommended a particular drug. Other studies revealed that a woman's age was a major determinant of patterns of psychotropic drug use: amphetamines, minor tranquilizers, and antidepressants earlier in life, sedatives and barbiturates in the middle and later years (Balter and Levine 1969).

Women accounted for 82 percent of amphetamine use (Balter and Levine 1969). Although most were between twenty and forty-nine, younger students were also heavy users. Susan Lydon recalled her experiences with amphetamines at Vassar: "I loved those little magic pills. They made me feel brilliant and motivated, and—icing on the cake—also killed my appetite" (1993: 45). One woman told Barbara Kerr (1974) that she received from home "sixty pills every two months" (p. 183), while another remembered that stimulants were not only sanctioned, they were promoted: "The pills were legal, the doctors would prescribe them, and the infirmary practically shoved them down your throat" (p. 95).

By the mid-1960s, four major sources supplied the national market for amphetamines and related stimulants: physicians' prescriptions, primarily to women; domestic supplies of legal stimulants that had been diverted to the black market; legal stimulants exported to Mexico and smuggled back; and illicit drug supplies manufactured by "speed labs." A federal agent testified before the Senate Antitrust and Monopoly Subcommittee in 1968 that "weight control doctors" were making fortunes by prescribing "pep pills" at huge price mark-ups (*New York Times*, January 31, 1968). By the end of the decade, however, all four were facing government pressure as hearings and press coverage revealed their workings. But when the dangers of amphetamines became apparent, as in the "Speed Kills" campaign launched by the Food and Drug Administration, many women switched to a "safer" stimulant—cocaine.

The prescribing practices of physicians largely determined patterns of psychotropic drug use. General ignorance about addiction and a lack of training continued to plague the medical profession. According to Andrew Weil (1972), despite an acknowledged drug problem among Harvard (and other) undergraduates, his Harvard Medical School training in the 1960s "included not one word" on the subject of addiction, prompting a student petition for an extracurricular lecture on the subject. In many cases, addiction to prescription pills such as barbiturates and amphetamines could be extremely dangerous. Yet neither patient nor physician equated this dependency with "real addiction" to drugs like heroin, and thus such abuse often went unrecognized and untreated. In other cases, pill-popping was linked to the glamour of Hollywood, as in Jacqueline Susann's 1966 novel, *Valley of the Dolls*, masking its danger.

Some claimed that sexism played a major role in shaping physicians' attitudes toward their female patients, that physicians tended to reach for the prescription pad simply to "shut them up." During these years, women made almost 60 percent of all visits to physicians—and received 60 percent of all prescriptions (Brecher 1972). Studies of American and Canadian women found that they were likely to receive prescription drugs if they described their problems in social or psychological terms, if they decribed physical complaints but were felt to be experiencing "problems of living," or if they reappeared with chronic somatic complaints (Cooperstock and Lennard 1979). The "depressed housewife" was a common feature of lists of amphetamine users (Goode 1972). Following the delivery of a stillborn baby, Susan Lydon's physician prescribed sleeping pills and "a kind of long-acting tranquilizer that in time would alter my brain chemistry and stop the depression" (1993: 63). Like the chloral hydrate and bromides given to women in the previous century, these new psychotropic drugs provided relief to middle-aged, middle-class women for anxiety, mild depression, and a general sense of dissatisfaction that had no known organic basis.

Ruth Cooperstock, a sociologist who wrote extensively on the subject (1978), proposed three reasons for women's high rate of prescription drug use: culturally, it was more acceptable for women than for men to be ill or to report illness; because women were at home, the sick role was more compatible with women's responsibilities than with men's; and women's assigned roles were considered more stressful and anxiety-provoking. Addicted women acknowledged that these drugs could be abused, but they tended not to identify themselves as addicts. In coping with stress and anxiety, many women who abused medications felt, as one psychologist said, that "if your life is unhappy and unsatisfying, anything pleasurable you become addicted to is hard to give up" (Borgman 1973: 532). As critics made clear, these drugs did not "cure" anything. Physicians, encouraged by drug companies, had "medicalized" basic human problems that were best treated in other ways, and women, victims of stereotyping in both diagnosis and treatment, were being overmedicated (Smith 1991). Irresponsible prescribing could produce a dependent population of women just when they were needed in the home and in the workplace.

Advertising had a major impact on physicians' prescribing practices. In marketing its products, the pharmaceutical industry defined normative and appropriate uses for these drugs and thus greatly influenced diagnosis and treatment. Drug companies expanded the indicated applications of these drugs by redefining ordinary life stresses as psychopathological conditions. Drug advertisements perpetuated society's prejudices about women, who were "almost always portrayed unfavorably" as weaker, as less able to cope, as helpless (Seidenberg 1971: 29). Information provided by drug companies promoted these agents as the "treatment of choice," before psychotherapy or other forms of social intervention. By 1970 the Federal Trade Commission had begun a study of the detrimental impact of "massive advertising" of prescription drugs. One senator called for a study of the practice of giving "sleeping tablets to ease the burden of the nights . . . benzedrine tablets to get through the day . . . tranquilizers to ease the tension" (*New York Times,* July 26, 1970). The Food and Drug Administration was moved to curb the widespread use of "pep pills" (*New York Times,* August 9, 1970).

Women as Childbearers

Awareness of the possible adverse impact of drug use during pregnancy became increasingly sophisticated among the general public as well as physicians during the 1960s. The concepts of the "placental barrier" and "fetal invulnerability" were shattered by the congenital rubella (German measles) epidemic and the thalidomide tragedy. Every drug now became suspect as a possible teratogen, a substance that produces a physical defect in newborn infants when taken during pregnancy, and the activities, behavior, and diet of pregnant women came under close scrutiny.

As the *New York Times* reported on October 11, 1967, researchers had linked three hallucinogenic drugs to birth defects in hamsters. A few weeks later, on November 24, the newspaper ran a piece on LSD, which researchers had found produced chromosomal damage and fetal defects (Cohen, Hirschhorn, and Frosch 1967). The May 5, 1968, issue of the paper reported on study findings that LSD caused breaks and other abnormalities in the chromosomes of approximately three-quarters of LSD users and in about one-half of the babies born to mothers who had used LSD during pregnancy. Another study found that women who used LSD during pregnancy suffered spontaneous abortions at twice the rate of the general population and gave birth to babies with an eighteenfold risk of serious congenital malformations (*New York Times,* May 10, 1970). Although some contradictory findings were published in the medical literature (for example, Tjio, Pahnke, and Kurland 1969; Dishotsky et al. 1971), the press highlighted the possible, but still unproven, negative effects of LSD, further igniting public concern about the drug.

Concern also focused on the effects of maternal heroin use on the fetus and newborn infant. The *New York Times* reported a 15 percent to 20 percent increase in the number of babies "born with narcotic addiction" in New York City (March 18, 1966). Medical researchers, having previously published only anecdotal reports and studies of a small number of babies, which lacked the full scientific credibility of large series, now began to publish articles describing larger numbers of heroin-exposed infants.[1] They found that mothers who used heroin during pregnancy were afflicted by a wide range of medical problems, including tuberculosis and sexually transmitted diseases such as syphilis. In addition, the social and economic conditions of their lives often resulted in nutritional deprivation and little or no prenatal care.

Infants exposed to heroin often suffered deficient growth during the intrauterine period and were small at birth (Kandall et al. 1976). After birth, the infants usually experienced an uncomfortable withdrawal characterized by agitation, excessive crying, jitteriness, fever, diarrhea, and vomiting (Kandall et al. 1977). Some early reports, published before effective treatment was developed, noted extremely high mortality rates in heroin-exposed infants. Television and newspaper portrayals of these infants stigmatized them as "junkie babies" and "babies with a habit." This kind of publicity, coupled with the fact that heroin-exposed babies were born primarily to disadvantaged black women, made it easy for society to regard these infants as "innocent victims" of their mothers' "wanton" drug use. Drug-addicted women were increasingly portrayed as dangers to their children. At a conference on the dangers of addiction in New York City, for example, a deputy medical examiner told the audience about one "woman addict" under the influence of drugs who had inadvertently suffocated her young baby (*New York Times,* October 20, 1969).

Despite the obvious impact of heroin on pregnant women and their children, services for female addicts were rarely available. To confront this deficiency, Ray E. Trussell, the commissioner of hospitals for New York City, presented a plan that would provide services for pregnant addicts to the administrators of fifteen of his municipal hospitals:

> "You know, ladies and gentleman, you've got 16,000 beds between you. Let's find twenty-five beds for pregnant addicts." To my utter amazement I was flatly told where I could go by people who were on my payroll! Furthermore, they formed a committee and sent me a letter saying, "Drug addiction is not a medical problem, it's a social and criminal problem, and keep it away from us." (1971: 4)

The percentage of female addicts classified as "hard addicts" remained relatively stable throughout the 1960s; at the same time, however, total numbers swelled and became more diverse as a result of widespread prescription drug use and the recruitment of new counterculture users of marijuana, LSD, and other psychedelics. These new users ensured that drugs would cross ethnic as well as socioeconomic borders. The impact of "hard drug" use among women on crime statistics was becoming apparent, while drug use during pregnancy reemerged as an area of public concern.

More women were using drugs, but relatively little specific information on women and drugs was available, and even at the end of the decade, treatment opportunities were only beginning to be discussed. Edward Brecher's comprehensive *Licit and Illicit Drugs* (1972) made few specific references to women. But he outlined four major contemporary problems: the increased availability of all drugs; the increased drug use among young people; the heavy reliance on penalties, which resulted in more criminalization; and the inappropriateness, even counterproductivity, of existing programs designed to reduce drug use, which insured that America's drug problem would continue to receive a great deal of attention in the political arena.

eight

THE 1970s

In 1970 President Richard Nixon signed the Comprehensive Drug Abuse Prevention and Control Act. It included the Controlled Substances Act, which ranked drugs in five categories, or "schedules," according to their reputed potential for addiction and medical utility. The rankings reflected a social agenda rather than sound medical science: cannabis (marijuana and hashish), psychedelics (LSD, mescaline, peyote), and heroin were lumped together in a "Schedule I" designation as the most dangerous drugs, with no medical utility, while cocaine and other narcotics, such as opium, morphine, and codeine, were designated as the less dangerous "Schedule II" drugs.

Federal efforts toward further regulation of illicit drugs were fueled by concern that drug use by troops in Vietnam was affecting the war effort and that returning veterans would exacerbate the nation's perceived drug problem. In April 1971, two members of Congress who had visited Vietnam claimed that as many as 30 percent of GIs were addicted to heroin (Jaffe 1978). The influential National Commission on Marihuana and Drug Abuse estimated that approximately 10 percent of American soldiers in Vietnam were involved in significant drug use (*Drug Use in America* 1973).

Paralleling the hard government line was a growing recognition that the drug-fighting policies of the past had been ineffectual, and that creative new approaches were needed. In its report to the president, the Commission bluntly summarized the nation's failed policy: "increased use of disapproved drugs precipitates more spending, more programs, more arrests and more penalties, all with little positive effect in reducing use of these drugs" (1973: 25). The Commission also criticized the blanket condemnation of all drugs, regardless of risk: "The government has often weakened its moral authority by threats which it cannot enforce and raised undue expectations by promises which it cannot keep" (p. 278). The report of the Consumers Union, *Licit and Illicit Drugs,* similarly concluded that "the relentless campaign to suppress heroin" had failed (Brecher 1972: xi).

Fear of crime among the general populace dominated the drug-control agenda into the early 1970s. According to estimates of the Hudson Institute in New York, heroin addicts were responsible for as much as 1.7 billion dollars in crime nationwide. The National Commission also acknowledged public concern about crime and drugs, especially heroin, and devoted twenty-seven pages to the problem in its final report. The Commission questioned whether law enforcement was "winning the war on drugs" and whether it would ever be possible to cut off the supply of illicit drugs completely, noting that there was a 300 percent increase in drug seizures from 1970 to 1971, despite a 400 percent increase in drug arrests from 1967 to 1971 (*Drug Use in America* 1973). While cautioning that more information was needed, the report tentatively endorsed methadone treatment programs: "the data available strongly suggest a reduction in the criminal behavior of patients in treatment" (p. 177).

The nation was also alerted to the impact of illicit drugs on U.S. industry. Newspaper headlines such as "Startling Abuse of Drugs Is Found in the Business World" (*New York Times,* June 17 and July 6, 1970) and "Business Finds Drugs a Problem" (*New York Times,* March 12, 1971) continued to drive home the point that heroin and other drugs were by no means confined to urban ghettoes.

Political pressure, responding to widespread fear of drugs and crime, produced an upsurge in federal appropriations to combat the use of illicit drugs. The federal budget grew from 86 million dollars in 1969 to 102 million dollars in 1970, 212 million dollars in 1971, and 418 million dollars by 1972. Although this rapid growth slowed with President Nixon's proclamation in 1973 that the nation was winning the drug battle, by 1978 expenditures had increased further, to 884 million dollars (Goldberg 1980). From 1970 to 1975, under President Nixon, almost two-thirds of the total drug budget was allocated to prevention, education, and treatment programs.

In addition, as the National Commission noted, by 1973 the federal government had earmarked seventy-four million dollars of the annual budget for drug-related research, a 400 percent increase from 1969 (*Drug Use in America* 1973). Between 1976 and 1981, however, the percentage of money going toward these "demand reduction" efforts dropped, to slightly over 40 percent of the drug budget. The Commission pointed out the "rapid growth in bureaucracy, with an almost compulsive spending on drug projects without benefit of evaluation or goal setting" (1973: 3) and the fragmentation of the drug-fighting effort: "there is still no coherent direction of the governmental response or coordination of its disparate elements" (p. 289).

Although the White House had created the Special Action Office for Drug Abuse Policy (SAODAP), directed by Jerome H. Jaffe, in 1971, the Commission found that coordination between the National Institute of Mental Health, the Department of Justice, and the Social and Rehabilitation Service was poor: over thirty separate grant programs were spread out among various agencies and subagencies. The Commission strongly urged that "all primarily drug-related federal functions be housed in a Single Agency" similar to the Atomic Energy Commission. This recommendation resulted in the establishment of the Drug Enforcement Administration in 1973, which merged the Bureau of Narcotics and Dangerous Drugs, the Office of National Narcotic Intelligence, the Office of Drug Abuse Law Enforcement, and the drug investigatory wing of the United States Customs Services. In addition, the National Institute on Drug Abuse (NIDA), created as part of the Department of Health, Education and Welfare, became a critical player in the antidrug effort and in the early 1970s developed specific programs for female addicts. After a century of obscurity, addicted women began to move out of the shadows.

Even without a coordinated federal approach, SAODAP began to develop overall federal strategies for prevention, education, treatment, rehabilitation, training, and research (Jaffe 1978). The Drug Abuse Prevention and Treatment Act of 1972 indirectly assisted methadone programs and encouraged the development of over fourteen hundred community-based drug treatment programs. The Narcotic Addict Treatment Act of 1974 further promoted narcotic maintenance and detoxification, inspired by the Commission's significant redefinition of "success" in drug treatment: it "does not necessarily require the removal of physical dependence . . . [the] goal is restoration of normal social functioning and the redirection of the patient's life away from drug-using and drug-seeking behavior" (1973: 322). And in a compromise measure, the Act required physicians who dispensed narcotics for maintenance or detoxification to register, thus allowing the federal government to retain control over the distribution and use of legal narcotics (Cooper 1988).

Society's ambivalence toward drug use was also evident in the confused approach to marijuana legislation. State penalties varied widely—from very lenient in Nebraska to extremely harsh in Texas, where simple possession could result in life imprisonment (Goode 1972)—and state laws continued to account for most arrests. Marijuana-related arrests rose sharply, from almost 19,000 in 1965 to over 440,000 in 1976 (Federal Bureau of Investigation 1965–1976).

On the federal level, however, a clear tendency toward relaxing antimarijuana laws was evident. The Court's ruling in 1969 *Leary v. United States* declared the Marijuana Tax Act of 1937 largely unconstitutional. In 1970 the Comprehensive Drug Abuse Prevention and Control Act reduced simple possession and distribution of small amounts of marijuana to misdemeanors and relaxed penalties for first offenses (Himmelstein 1983). The Consumers Union report on drugs (Brecher 1972) took a strong position against the repressive tactics aimed at marijuana, which had been classified as a Schedule I drug in 1970. The report urged the repeal of all federal laws pertaining to marijuana, the passage of state laws that would legalize aspects of marijuana production under appropriate regulations, an end to imprisonment for marijuana possession, and the release of those currently in prison for sharing or possessing marijuana.

The Commission downplayed the harmful effects of marijuana, noting that "the only crimes which can be directly attributed to marihuana-using behavior are those resulting from the use, possession, or transfer of an illegal substance" (*Drug Use in America* 1973: 159). Although the "availability of this drug should not be institutionalized at this time" (p. 224), the Commission recommended that "the unauthorized possession of any controlled substance *except marijuana* for personal use remain a prohibited act" (p. 273; emphasis added). Decriminalization of marijuana appeared to be a negotiated compromise between the basic wish to prohibit the drug and the recognition that such widespread use made the law unenforceable. Following Oregon's lead in 1973, eleven states, home to over one-third of the country's population, had passed decriminalization statutes by 1978; no additional statutes have been passed in subsequent years.

The "Numbers Game" Continues

In the "war on drugs," despite the optimistic assessment of President Nixon and the National Commission's claim that "the United States is comparatively fortunate . . . to have a surplus of national resources to devote to its resolution" (*Drug Use in America* 1973: 38), the nation seemed to be losing to an ill-defined enemy. Not quite sure where to place their resources, Americans watched as the drug epidemic spread. Often, preventive planning seemed impossible, since new drugs materialized overnight. Among the counterculture in Berkeley, Susan Lydon recalled, "heroin appeared all of a sudden, out of nowhere, and quickly became ubiquitous" (1993: 111).

In spite of liberalizing recommendations, the legacy of the repressive Classic Era, an underground, underworld culture of drug users, lingered. As the National Commission noted, "We simply do not know the number of persons who can be characterized as . . . pre-dependent . . . or even the number who are already incapacitated by drug dependence" although "chemically induced mood alteration is taken for granted . . . in contemporary America" (*Drug Use in America* 1973: 197–198, 42). The director of the National Institute of Mental Health estimated in 1970 that there were 125,000 "active narcotic users" and 250,000 to 500,000 users of dangerous drugs (*New York Times* editorial, May 12, 1970). The Bureau of Narcotics and Dangerous Drugs, however, set the number of active addicts at about 560,000 (NIDA 1976: 173). In the mid-1970s, the National Institute on Drug Abuse estimated that there were about 500,000 opiate (largely taken as a synonym for heroin but not carefully defined) addicts, a number based only on treatment figures and certainly an underestimate (NIDA 1976). Combined with the National White Paper estimate of about 400,000 to 500,000 daily chronic heroin users not in treatment in 1975 (Ashbrook and Solley 1979), a reasonable estimate for the total number of heroin users would be about one million. An even more pessimistic estimate of over four million active heroin users could also be found (Hunt 1977).

A mid-1970s study drawing on thirty thousand face-to-face interviews found that women were proportionately represented among the

4.5 million regular users of barbiturates and 350,000 regular users of nonbarbiturate sedatives, and overrepresented among the 5 million regular users of minor tranquilizers, 500,000 regular users of anti-depressants, 750,000 regular users of amphetamines, and almost 4 million regular users of non-narcotic analgesics (Chambers and Griffey 1975). According to the National Commission report, in 1970 physicians wrote 214 million prescriptions for barbiturates and related compounds, which accounted for 972 million dollars in retail sales (*Drug Use in America* 1973). By 1972, they were writing about 260 million prescriptions for psychoactive drugs annually (Brecher 1972). Physicians' own narcotic use persisted, as it had during the previous century: according to one estimate, about 1 percent of physicians were addicted to narcotics, primarily Demerol, methadone, Dilaudid, and morphine (Goode 1972). A report from the Lexington federal facility in the early 1970s confirmed that nurses continued to be overrepresented in the sample of female addicts and that Demerol (meperidine) and Talwin (pentazocine) were the most frequently abused drugs. Interviews with addicted nurses revealed that taking "medicine" was considered more acceptable than "illicit drugs," although both resulted in debilitating dependency (Levine, Preston, and Lipscomb 1974).

Many of the major epidemiological studies of addiction overlooked women. One 1970 study of drug use in 2,200 male youths found that 21 percent had used marijuana in the past, compared to 7 percent for hallucinogens and under 2 percent for heroin (Richards 1981). *Young Men and Drugs—A Nationwide Survey,* John O'Donnell's landmark 1976 report based on 1974 and 1975 data, found that more than one million men aged twenty to thirty had used heroin, between two and three million had used cocaine, and more than ten million had used marijuana (Richards 1981). But according to Barbara Kerr, "there are enormous numbers of middle-class women who depend on drugs for their day-to-day living. There are junkies, drunks, pillheads, and potheads in every nook and cranny of middle-class life. They are in the beauty salons, the supermarkets, the department stores, the dress shops, the tea rooms, and the country clubs of all the big cities, small towns, and rural areas that make up middle America" (1974: 294).

Although the National Commission expressed pessimism about defining the scope of addiction, in the 1970s researchers finally developed epidemiologic tracking surveys of drug use. The National Household Survey was begun by the Commission in 1971–1972 and continued after 1974 under the sponsorship of NIDA (*National Household Survey on Drug Abuse* 1988). The data gathered in these studies highlighted the emergence of unmistakable and ominous trends between 1972 and 1979 (Fishburne, Abelson, and Cisin 1980). Among twelve- to seventeen-year-olds, lifetime prevalence use of marijuana doubled, from 14 percent to over 30 percent. The use of hallucinogens rose 48 percent, to 7 percent of the population, and cocaine use soared over 250 percent, to about 5 percent of the population. The nonmedical use of stimulants, sedatives, and tranquilizers remained relatively constant at about 3 percent to 4 percent of the population, and heroin use was reported by about 0.5 percent of the survey sample.

Data from young adults aged eighteen to twenty-five revealed the same trends. Although heroin use fell slightly, cocaine use tripled, from 9 percent to over 27 percent, and smaller increases were seen in marijuana use. Nonmedical use of stimulants rose by 50 percent, of sedatives by 70 percent, and of tranquilizers by more than 100 percent. Among those over age twenty-six, lifetime prevalence figures tripled for marijuana, hallucinogens, and cocaine, and doubled for heroin. While nonmedical use of stimulants and sedatives almost doubled, the use of tranquilizers decreased by about 40 percent. Although eye-opening, these figures were almost certainly gross underestimates of national figures, since the survey did not look at those populations in which the number of users would be large—prisoners, the homeless, hospitalized patients, and students.

As part of the Monitoring the Future study, a special subpopulation of young users, high school seniors, was studied longitudinally during the 1970s (Johnston, Bachman, and O'Malley 1979). From 1975 to 1979, lifetime prevalence use of marijuana/hashish rose from 47 percent to 60 percent of the surveyed population, and cocaine use from 9 percent to over 15 percent, while hallucinogen and heroin use declined. The use of sedatives and tranquilizers also declined, but that of stimulants increased (Johnston, O'Malley, and Bachman 1987). By 1977, illicit drug use among these high school seniors had reached an alarming level, almost 62 percent of the surveyed population, and it continued to rise, to 65 percent by 1979. Marijuana was the most widely used drug, rising from 47 percent of the population in 1975 to 60 percent in 1979; heroin use remained at slightly over 1 percent of this population in the late 1970s. Overall, drug use remained more common in young men than in young women, but in 1979 the survey found that, excluding marijuana, female drug use had reached approximate parity with male drug use (Richards 1981). A study in New York State in 1971 and 1972 showed that about one-third of more than seven thousand high school students had used illegal drugs, the most common being marijuana (29 percent), followed by hashish, LSD, cocaine, and heroin. There was little difference between boys and girls in drug use patterns, signaling a national trend toward gender parity, which would become evident in the 1979 national study (Kandel, Single, and Kessler 1976).

Heroin

Peter Bourne, working in the SAODAP, noted that although women made up about one-quarter of heroin addicts, "relatively little attention has been paid to the use patterns of women as opposed to men" (1974: 9). Of the total population of heroin addicts, female addicts were always underrepresented, but during the 1970s the gender gap narrowed considerably. Drug Enforcement Agency studies, based on police reports, found that the percentage of female opiate addicts (that is, those on heroin and related drugs) remained constant, at 15 percent, between 1970 and 1974 (Hunt and Chambers 1976), while earlier studies put the number of women addicts at approximately one-fifth to one-quarter of all heroin addicts (Hamburger 1969). According to another study, by 1973 women addicts comprised 28 percent (Hunt 1977). A Johns Hopkins study published in 1974 found that women represented 17 percent of methadone maintenance patients, 24 percent of those in treatment centers, 19 percent of those in inpatient and outpatient programs, and 22 percent of patients in ambulatory abstinence programs (Hunt 1977). In certain areas, such as Bedford-Stuyvesant in Brooklyn, high female prevalence (30 percent of a random population of heroin addicts) was already apparent in 1971 (Walter, Sheridan, and Chambers 1973).

Walter Cuskey and Richard Wathey (1982) rather conservatively estimated that the number of female heroin addicts grew from 22,000 in 1968 to 50,000 in 1971 and 83,000 in 1973, before declining to 78,000 in 1975. In the mid-1970s, 30 percent of the slightly more than 16,000 heroin addicts admitted for treatment in California were women (State of California 1975). National data on populations of women entering drug treatment found heroin to be the most widely used drug, which is not surprising, since they were receiving methadone treatment. Of over 14,000 female clients entering approximately 1,400 federally funded treatment programs in 1976, one national study found that heroin was the most prevalent drug used, crossing lines of both age and race (Tyler and Thompson 1980). Of more than 51,000 women voluntarily seeking treatment in federally funded programs, heroin accounted for almost 60 percent of admissions, about five times that for marijuana, barbiturates, or amphetamines, and more than ten times that for sedatives or tranquilizers (Tyler and Frith 1981).

During the 1970s, for the first time, gender-specific sociological studies delineated the broad range of medical, emotional, and social problems faced by addicted women and the support services these women required. Clearly, the life experiences of women addicts were radically different from those of men. They came from fragmented, violence-prone families or had no family, which rendered treatment extremely difficult (Vandor, Juliana, and Leone 1991). Those who used heroin frequently had histories of delinquency, divorce, and criminal association, and rarely much education or vocational training. Self-loathing, suicidal tendencies, immature behavior, low self-esteem, and hostility toward men were not uncommon (Binion 1982; Colten 1979). As one woman related, "I didn't feel anything . . . I didn't feel hurt, I didn't feel bad, I didn't feel loneliness, I didn't feel guilty about the things I did" (Kiev 1975: 87). Unfortunately, using drugs to anesthetize feelings of victimization left these women vulnerable to the effects of the drugs themselves and the lack of available treatment options. As researchers discovered, women often turned to drugs to relieve stress and depression; to deal with traumatic events such as childhood sexual abuse, family alcoholism or drug use, and abusive relationships with dominant males; and to reduce inhibitions and provide a feeling of independence, excitement, and peer acceptance (Vandor, Juliana, and Leone 1991). A study of thirty-five black female addicts from Washington, D.C., found that about half had begun using heroin because of the influence of friends, about 40 percent out of curiosity, and about 20 percent for relief of personal distress (Brown et al. 1971). One reason for the desperation felt by female addicts was their lack of supportive male relationships. A woman living with a heroin addict might use drugs out of curiosity, to share her partner's mood, to support them both through prostitution, or to dull depression, anger, or low self-esteem (Rosenbaum 1981a).

In her study of a population of heroin-using women in the San Francisco area, Marsha Rosenbaum (1981a) found that they tended to come from disturbed social backgrounds and disrupted homes, to have experienced sexual and physical violence in their lives, and to be involved in relationships with men who used heroin. They were initiated into a heroin-dominated world through a "hippie trip," the "outlaw world" of high school gangs, or the "fast life" out of poverty by way of quickly obtained attention and material goods. In all three, women sought to escape what they perceived to be lives of limited social, economic, and educational options. As one addict commented: "I had a Cadillac . . . I was dressing right . . . goin' out to nice clubs, and things like that. We traveled a lot . . . That kind of made me up in the life—up with the *big time* people" (pp. 42–43). According to another, "taking a shot of heroin is like putting on an expensive mink coat" (Maurer and Vogel 1973: 36).

Ironically, women who at first seemed to have wider options rapidly sank into lives of "risk, chaos and inundation" dominated by their heroin habit (Rosenbaum 1981a). Many were able to support their early drug use through legal employment, but eventually, the financial demands of an increasing drug habit forced them into illegal activities, such as drug dealing, check forging, shoplifting, "boosting" (selling stolen goods back to a store), auto theft, burglary, conning, and pickpocketing. Female heroin addicts also drifted toward sex-related careers such as pimping and prostitution, and their modern-day extensions in massage parlors, topless bars, and the pornography industry.

For addicted women, particularly black women, debasement and degradation were often intrinsic to their relationships with men, making their prospects for treatment and recovery bleak. As bell hooks (1981) observed in *Ain't I a Woman: Black Women and Feminism,* the devaluation of black womanhood made it extremely difficult, if not impossible, for black women to develop a positive self-concept. Another social commentator suggested that black female addicts were "thrice oppressed"—by race, by gender, and by their habit (Rutlin 1975: 136). Describing black ghetto life in the mid-1970s, Julia Hillsman, the project administrator of Central City BRICKS/KICKS, a comprehensive treatment and rehabilitation program in South Central Los Angeles, commented:

> This environment makes treatment extremely difficult, and even more so for the black woman. Her needs are extremely unique and her learning processes difficult. For the most part, the black female addict has not been afforded the luxury of having been a kept woman. The ghetto drug subculture is very rough. Unlike any other ethnic group, the wounds are deeper, means of survival more severe. Goals are confusing and far more difficult to reach. Obstacles are insurmountable in many instances. (Nellis 1975: 122)

Marsha Rosenbaum also found that women were disproportionately stigmatized for drug use, most notably in interpersonal and sexual relations, where they were viewed as "damaged goods" (1981a: 132). Disparagement had several sources. An obvious one was the addict's physically wasted, unattractive appearance; another, the disparity between society's view of "being" a good mother, a good wife, a good girl, and "doing" drugs (p. 50). As one young addict told Judianne Densen-Gerber (1973), founder of Odyssey House in New York, she had done "terrible things" and could not escape her feeling of being unclean. Drug-using women could also be an unwelcome economic drain on their partners:

> Once a male is on drugs he doesn't want to go with a girl on drugs because then she cannot easily support his habit. Instead, the only ways that she finances her boyfriend's habit, if she too is on drugs, is to go into something else, such as prostitution or stealing . . . there is a special stigma to the female taking drugs. She's avoided by the population in general. (Rayburn 1975)

Although the emerging stereotype of the female heroin addict was of a minority urban dweller living in poverty, the social spectrum was much broader. In a study of seventy-three addicted women in Detroit, Victoria Binion (1979) found that the family structure of these women was generally more stable than it had been portrayed. Compared to nonaddicted women of similar socioeconomic class, addicted women were just as likely to describe their family lives as happy, to come from stable economic environments and intact family networks, and to regard both their fathers and mothers as supportive parents. These findings were replicated in Binion's (1982) study of 170 heroin-addicted women enrolled in treatment facilities in Detroit, Los Angeles, and Miami.

Susan Lydon, who had grown up in a middle-class suburban New York home and received a Vassar education, progressed through alcohol, marijuana, and LSD before becoming a twenty-year hard-core heroin addict in 1972. She became addicted quite rapidly and underwent dramatic physical changes in just a few months: her weight plunged to ninety pounds and she looked "like a skeleton" (1993: 129). Lydon continued on her downward spiral through addiction, despair, crime, physical battering, and depression. By 1979 she realized that she was "so demoralized and beaten down by the drugs," she was "striking out blindly in a futile attempt to stave off certain death" (p. 173). The theme of seeking help only after reaching "rock bottom" is a common one among women addicts. An attractive thirty-five-year-old black woman who lived in the Bronx "felt that her mind was going" when the police identified her as an addict, which made it impossible for her to raise her six children (Brill, Nash, and Langrod 1977: 57). Another woman in the same survey, a Puerto Rican addict, had been badly beaten, had no money, and was pregnant and suffering from toxic elevation of her blood pressure (p. 58).

Like Susan Lydon, Martha Morrison did not seem a candidate for addiction: she was born in Fayetteville, Arkansas, in 1952 to middle-class Southern Baptist parents. Yet in *White Rabbit* she tells the story of her seventeen-year battle with addiction. Her case is particularly noteworthy here because it represents the convergence of two important themes: women and addiction and addicted physicians. Morrison, a doctor, detailed her tortuous odyssey through multiple substance abuse, including Darvon, tobacco, alcohol, marijuana, nonprescribed cough medicines, hashish, LSD, mescaline, Preludin, crystal, Dilaudid, amphetamines, Seconal, peyote, Talwin, Demerol, codeine, barbiturates, Valium, Contac, morphine, cocaine, MDA, STP, Tofranil, Mellaril, methadone, heroin, Quaaludes, Mepergan, Elavil, Ritalin, Percodan, Fastin, Cogentin, Artane, and Ativan (1989: 167–168). Interwoven with her drug use were sexual promiscuity, crimes such as forgery and burglary, three hospitalizations and one rehabilitation admission by the age of nineteen, two divorces, and several close brushes with death. She ends her story on a note of optimism, however, having completed medical school and a psychiatric training program.

Women, Drugs, and Crime

Women's involvement in crime to support a drug habit increased markedly in the 1970s. Between 1960 and 1973, drug-related arrests of women under the age of eighteen rose by 6,045 percent.[1] FBI figures indicated that 11 percent of the indexed crimes in 1972 were committed by women, an increase from 6 percent in the previous year. In 1972, 30 percent of all persons arrested for larceny, fraud, and embezzlement, and 25 percent of all persons arrested for forgery were women (Shearn 1975). A study of over forty-two thousand drug abusers who were admitted to fifty treatment programs in the early 1970s found that although women were less likely to have been arrested before they entered treatment and to have had repeat arrests, convictions, and incarcerations than men, 30 percent of those surveyed had served time in jail (Ball et al. 1975). In 1976 narcotics offenses made up approximately 6 percent of all female arrests. Overall, female crime accounted for 14 percent to 16 percent of all reported crime during the decade (Bowker 1978).

At the end of the 1970s, the U.S. Bureau of the Census conducted a survey of 2,255 female state prison inmates (Miller 1984). Between one-third and two-fifths of these women had been active heroin or cocaine users, about 10 percent had been involved with methadone, close to 30 percent had used "prescription medication" barbiturates or amphetamines, about 20 percent had used LSD, and 13 percent had used PCP (phencyclidine). The drug with the highest reported usage was marijuana, which had been used by over 60 percent of the women. Almost 30 percent of the women had been under the influence of drugs at the time of their current incarceration, and 10 percent had been convicted of drug-related offenses.

Offering another perspective on women and crime, James Inciardi and Anne Pottieger (1986) studied 153 female narcotic addicts on the streets of Miami during 1977 and 1978. This group, of mixed ethnicity, were regular users of heroin (98.7 percent) and marijuana (93.5 percent), and lesser users of cocaine, sedatives, and other drugs. Inciardi found that these 153 women had commmitted a total of 54,548 offenses in the previous twelve months, an average of 357 per respondent. Almost 90 percent had been arrested, but these arrests had resulted from less than 1 percent of the actual offenses. Very few of the offenses were crimes of violence, such as robbery and assault, and most were nonviolent, such as shoplifting (36 percent) and prostitution (15 percent). Among a group of 63 black female heroin users in Miami in 1978 (Inciardi, Pottieger, and Faupell 1982), all reported past criminal activity, most commonly shoplifting (35 percent), theft and larceny (22 percent), and prostitution (11 percent). Current criminal activity remained at a high level: the women reported a total of over 32,000 offenses, although only 0.4 percent of the offenses resulted in arrest. Inciardi also found that, contrary to the often advanced hypothesis that drug use leads to criminality, the first arrest preceded the use of heroin by almost two years.

Barry Brown and his colleagues (1971) reported that a third of the black female addicts they surveyed in Washington, D.C., committed their first illegal act in order to obtain drugs, roughly twice the percentage of a comparable male population. Overall, 40 percent of the women, about half that of a comparable male population, committed illegal acts prior to their first use of heroin, and far fewer women (20 percent) than men (53 percent) had been arrested before beginning to use heroin. In a population of women in detention at the Philadelphia House of Corrections in 1976–1977, Brenda Miller (1981) found that self-reported "high drug use" was associated with early-age juvenile delinquency in conjunction with incarceration. These women also tended to be arrested for property and drug offenses, while women in the "low drug use" group tended to be arrested for less serious offenses. Some analysts concluded that judges tended to be more lenient toward women because of their protected place in society and because of the judicial system's paternalistic regard for women as child rearers. Conversely, other researchers felt that some judges acted in a more punitive manner toward female drug offenders because of the disparity between their behavior and society's expectations (Shearn 1975).

The major female criminal activity associated with drug abuse continued to be prostitution. Overall, it was estimated that between 30 percent and 70 percent of female drug users were prostitutes (Goldstein 1979). In San Francisco in 1975, about 98 percent of women under the age of seventeen who were involved with hard drugs were supporting their habits through prostitution (Flohr 1975).

Another mid-1970s study of sixty women from New York, Massachusetts, and Florida, forty-three of whom were prostitutes, found that 96 percent of the "low-class" prostitutes used heroin and 64 percent used cocaine (Goldstein, Ouellet, and Fendrich 1992). The researchers found that prostitutes tended to use heroin to relieve physical pain or blunt the reality of prostitution. In their study, Jennifer James and her colleagues (1979) found that addict-prostitutes were generally involved in crimes that provided a satisfactory monetary return and were relatively safe, such as larceny, shoplifting, and forgery.

Cocaine

Cocaine never entirely disappeared from the American drug scene, but it had faded from view for several decades. In the 1970s, however, cocaine experienced a revival. It was glamorized by rock stars at a time when the dangers of amphetamines were becoming apparent and federal pressure discouraged importation of opiates. The children of the 1960s, who had experimented with marijuana and other hallucinogens, embraced it like an old friend. As one female freebaser commented in *Cocaine Changes:* "I'm a product of the late sixties and drugs were an identity and it was part of who we were. So that made me open to it. There was nothing wrong with drugs in my mind" (Waldorf, Reinarman, and Murphy 1991: 109)

According to the National Commission on Marihuana and Drug Abuse, the National Household Survey found that 1.5 percent of youths and 3.2 percent of adults had used cocaine at least once (*Drug Use in America* 1973: 63). A survey by the New York State Division of Substance Abuse Services in 1976 found that 135,000 adults had used cocaine in the previous six months; this number rose to 437,000 by 1981 (Stone, Fromme, and Kagan 1984). The National Institute on Drug Abuse reported that cocaine-related admissions to federal treatment programs rose from just over 2,000 in 1975 to over 11,000 in 1980. Cocaine-related visits to hospital emergency rooms in New York rose 158 percent between 1979 and 1980, from 771 to 1,991 (Stone, Fromme, and Kagan 1984). The Drug Abuse Warning Network (DAWN) reported that cocaine-associated deaths increased markedly in Miami and New York between 1977 and 1980. At a press conference in March 1981, the Drug Enforcement Agency reported that the amount of illicit cocaine entering the United States had increased from nineteen metric tons in 1977 to fifty-one metric tons in 1980.

The new cocaine epidemic was different from that of the recent past. Now college students, intellectuals, and young professionals were experimenting with the drug. Cocaine was used on college campuses and in discotheques by those seeking new "highs" of sexual release and mind-expansion. Easily administered by sniffing, cocaine made its devotees feel confident, creative, sexually turned on, and invincible. A twenty-nine-year-old woman who freebased recalled: "When I first started listening to people talk about cocaine, they would always call it the rich man's drug. You know, we're not rich, but when we have coke, we kind of feel, 'Hey, we're rich!'" (Waldorf, Reinarman, and Murphy 1991: 95).

Cocaine was used by the "jet set," by athletes, and by rock stars, and thus represented money, power, and success. The rock icon Eric Clapton performed the song "Cocaine" for the nation's youth: "If you got bad news, you wanna kick them blues, cocaine . . . When your day is done, and you wanna run, cocaine." The Grateful Dead added "Casey Jones" ("Ridin' that train high on cocaine") and "Truckin'" ("livin' on reds, vitamin C and cocaine"). Steppenwolf sought ecstasy on an "airline made of snow."

Cocaine found a very receptive audience among women. A 1975–1976 survey found that 39 percent of cocaine users were women (Stone, Fromme, and Kagan 1984). Lifetime prevalence use of cocaine among female high school seniors increased from about 7 percent in 1975 to almost 10 percent in 1978 (Johnston, Bachman, and O'Malley 1979). Cocaine became popular in social settings, such as beach parties and weekend concerts (Waldorf, Reinarman, and Murphy 1991). A female executive entertained her clients with the drug: "Later in the evening I would do it like partying with clients because in my business cocaine is expected. You are expected to treat your clients with dinner, cocaine, champagne, and booze" (p. 43).

Other women used cocaine to release their inhibitions and enhance sexual experience. Susan Lydon described her introduction to the drug in Berkeley in 1970 as "snorting cocaine and having sex," feeling a sense of "exhilaration and joy" (1993: 110–111). One female user, recalling that she developed a weekly cocaine habit of ten to twenty-five dollars yet functioned responsibly as a student and part-time mail clerk, commented: "It's a very sensual drug. This makes your body feel good" (Waldorf, Reinarman, and Murphy 1991: 255). Other interviewees found that cocaine allowed them to perform sexual acts they "would never have dreamed about" and "increased their feelings of sexual communication" (pp. 47, 52).

Expanding business and social opportunities exposed more women to cocaine, and they found it a convenient energy booster. A waitress at a rock-and-roll bar interviewed in *Cocaine Changes* claimed that cocaine helped her focus on her job; she got better tips because she was more outgoing. Another interviewee found that cocaine was useful in coping with fourteen- and fifteen-hour days as she tried to open a new restaurant, while still another woman took cocaine to survive her seventy- to eighty-hour work weeks as a store window designer and restaurant waitress (Waldorf, Reinarman, and Murphy 1991).

Women also used cocaine as an appetite suppressant; it helped them feel thin, young, and energetic. Nancy, also interviewed in *Cocaine Changes,* reported that she would "snort a line" before dinner to reduce her appetite and keep her weight under control, thus maintaining a slim figure (Waldorf, Reinarman, and Murphy 1991). But the negative side of cocaine and body image is starkly revealed in Gelsey Kirkland's *Dancing on My Grave* (1986). A celebrated dancer in the glamorous ballet world of the 1970s, Kirkland turned to cocaine for excitement, artistic affectation, relief from pain and depression, and erotic stimulation, and ended up in her own version of hell.

The ability of cocaine to suppress appetite was clearly linked to Kirkland's earlier bodily mutilation as she sought to achieve the ballerina's Balanchine-defined "perfect body." It "turned my preoccupation with my looks into a nightmarish obsession. In my fanatical pursuit of beauty, I was at war with myself, driven by vanity and mortified by my appearance" (1986: 35). Along with a friend, she became increasingly anorexic and drug-driven: "The bonds linking us were compulsory starvation, the dreams of food, and the drastic measures required to maintain our diets. We later induced vomiting by downing an emetic intended for babies. The forbidden fruit of the modern ballerina was thus disgorged" (p. 56).

This ultraslender body image not only became the standard for classical ballet but, aided by the fashion industry, strongly influenced how ordinary women evaluated their own bodies. Balanchine's "concentration camp aesthetic," his advice to "eat nothing," was intended to produce "an almost skeletal frame," angular and "defeminized." As Kirkland later explained to her cocaine dealer: "I needed the cocaine to work . . . The drug made the work bearable" (p. 289).

Kirkland also described the power cocaine wielded in her sexual life: "Random promiscuity had advantages which I found irresistible. Sex could be exchanged for coke; coke could be exchanged for sex" (p. 332).

Kirkland's well-publicized personal tragedy appears to have mirrored the experience of many others in the worlds of dance, theater, and the arts. In her own "cocaine klatch" there were "other dancers and theater personnel involved with drugs at various times—an ever-increasing number" (p. 284). Although *Dancing on My Grave* is clearly the story of a personal journey, drug abuse permeated the artistic world, affecting possibly "twelve dancers out of ninety, or a hundred" as well as "choreographers, musicians, teachers, stage-hands, and costume people" (pp. 307–308).

Almost half of the patients coming to the attention of the Haight-Ashbury Medical Clinic for treatment of cocaine use in the early 1970s were women (Newmeyer 1978). Even into the late 1970s and early 1980s, among the "street hippie" population of San Francisco's Haight-Ashbury district, 33 percent of those admitted to the Free Medical Clinic for detoxification from cocaine were women (Gay 1981). One chronic cocaine user went on a year-long coke binge when she received a large inheritance in 1973, lived with drug dealers, and spent her way through the money in five years (Waldorf, Reinarman, and Murphy 1991). Another young woman squandered a twenty-five-thousand-dollar inheritance and a fifteen-thousand-dollar insurance payment in a few years through heavy drug use, and still another spent her entire salary and savings on cocaine and began trading sex for drugs. Others courted personal danger by dealing cocaine in a violent drug culture.

Marijuana

According to the *National Survey on Drug Abuse* (Fishburne, Abelson, and Cisin 1980), marijuana was the most commonly used drug in the 1970s, which continued a trend first seen in the previous decade. Almost 70 percent of young adults aged eighteen to twenty-five reported at least some experience with marijuana, and almost 50 percent reported that they were current users. From 1971 to 1979, lifetime prevalence use among young males aged twelve to seventeen increased from 14 percent to 34 percent of the surveyed population, while use of marijuana among young females doubled, from 14 percent to 28 percent. From 1976 to 1979 the use of marijuana by young adults aged eighteen to twenty-five increased more rapidly in females (44 percent to 61 percent) than in males (62 percent to 71 percent). The same trend held true in those over age twenty-six, where marijuana use increased from 19 percent to 26 percent among males, but doubled from 7 percent to 14 percent among females.

Although marijuana could serve as a "gateway drug," most women continued to use it only for recreation. Some viewed marijuana as an integral part of the protest movement against the war in Vietnam. Others agreed with the twenty-year-old female student interviewed at Project R.E.T.U.R.N. in New York, who commented, "I don't think the social problems affected my use of drugs at all. I'd say the environment that I was living in at college—a very hip, liberal school—encouraged my use of drugs more than anything else because everyone around me was getting high off drugs" (Kiev 1975: 15). Still others tried it to escape a feeling of social isolation. One user reported "loneliness, a great deal of social pressure to be hip, to be cool, to take things in stride" (p. 35).

Women users might come from homes in which alcohol and tranquilizers were an integral part of daily life. One study cited the example of two young women who explained that their mothers were constantly "popping pills," so that drug use was accepted and the pills themselves were available in the home (Kiev 1975). One commentator noted that "drug-using children were found to come from families where one or both parents abused alcohol and tranquilizers. The generation gap was defined as merely a difference in tastes, so far as intoxicants are concerned" (Meyer 1972: 7).

Prescription Drugs

Throughout the 1970s women remained the major users of prescription drugs. In 1971 the *New York Times* (March 14) reported that pharmacists had filled 225 million prescriptions for mind-altering drugs in 1970 compared to 166 million in 1965. Data from the long-term "Psychotropic Drug Study," funded by the National Institute of Mental Health, revealed that 29 percent of the women surveyed had used psychoactive prescription drugs during the previous year. Some 20 percent of all American women used sedatives and minor tranquilizers, which had become the leading form of psychoactive prescription drug use in the country (Brecher 1972). The National Institute on Drug Abuse reported that an estimated one to two million women experienced some degree of addiction to prescription drugs. One researcher (Fidell 1973) noted that those most heavily involved in barbiturates, nonbarbiturate hypnotic-sedatives, relaxants, major and minor tranquilizers, antidepressants, pep pills, diet pills, noncontrolled narcotics, and analgesics were women. Reviewing ten studies of patterns of psychotropic drug use in the United States, Ruth Cooperstock and Penny Parnell (1982) found that women consistently used these medically prescribed substances more frequently than men. According to NIDA, 60 percent of all drug-related hospital emergency room visits involved women: two-thirds of these visits were the result of suicide attempts and one-third of drug dependency or adverse drug reactions ("Women and Prescription Drugs" 1978). In 1974 women accounted for three-quarters of the 62,340 hospital emergency room visits involving Valium and three-quarters of the 14,322 visits involving Librium (Blackenheimer 1975), as well as 40 percent of the total of drug-related deaths.

The epidemic of drug use among women did not go unnoticed by the National Commission on Marihuana and Drug Abuse, which openly acknowledged that "large numbers of middle class adults, particularly women, have developed chronic using patterns of orally administered low dose stimulant preparations" (*Drug Use in America* 1973: 146). The Commission further acknowledged that the "use of a variety of new mood-altering drugs to cope with stress is undoubtedly a significant social development, *particularly among women*" (p. 23; emphasis added): 62 percent of women used "any psychoactive," 46 percent used "ethicals," classified by the National Survey as prescription sedatives, tranquilizers, and stimulants, and 36 percent used similar over-the-counter "proprietaries." While recognizing this widespread and dangerous pattern of drug use, the Commission noted that "self-medication by a housewife . . . with amphetamines or tranquilizers . . . is generally viewed as a personal judgment of little concern to the larger community" (p. 42). Roger Meyer's *Guide to Drug Rehabilitation* summed up the problem in a phrase: "the obese, depressed housewife given a prescription for diet pills" (1972: 93). In the early 1970s, however, neither the House and Senate Committee reports on drug abuse nor the report of the Strategy Council on Drug

Abuse mentioned women, and there were no women on the nineteen-member Domestic Council Drug Review Task Force (Lawton 1975).

The attitudes of the medical profession perpetuated women's reliance on psychoactive drugs. Women had historically visited physicians more often than men, and with a greater variety of vague and possibly psychological symptoms that might be managed with mood-altering medications (Fidell 1973). Many physicians refused to believe women capable of tolerating minor ailments without the support of drugs. As a result, in 1974 two-thirds of the almost twenty-two million new prescriptions and thirty-eight million refill prescriptions for Valium were written for women, and 71 percent of the over six million new prescriptions and twelve million refill prescriptions for Librium were for women (Blackenheimer 1975). One user commented that doctors would "give you anything . . . ups I always went to the doctor for, or I got Speed. Downs, you have to hit a few different doctors, and they give them to you pretty easily" (Kiev 1975: 69–70).

As in the 1950s and 1960s, drug advertising also contributed to the perpetuation of sex-role stereotypes: physicians were always active men while their patients were passive women complaining of "diffuse anxiety, tension, and depression" (Fidell 1973: 5). As the pharmaceutical companies produced an increasing array of profitable new drugs, their advertising pointed out to physicians appropriate uses for these products. Critics began to comment on the "sexism" of pharmaceutical advertising, which marketed not only amphetamines but "new improved" combinations of amphetamines and barbiturates in diet pills for women (Kunnes 1973).

These reactions were well founded. Both physicians and the Nixon administration accused the pharmaceutical industry and Madison Avenue "image makers" of "excessively promoting" drugs to control obesity (*New York Times,* November 17 and 24, 1970). Jane Prather and Linda Fidell (1975) found that 60 percent of the advertisements in four major medical and psychiatric journals between 1968 and 1972 were aimed at women with "psychogenic" illnesses. In addition, not one portrayed a female physician, although at the time 7 percent of American physicians were women. Nurses, however, were always female. An even broader survey of 2,675 advertisements in the *American Journal of Psychiatry* between 1959 and 1975 (King 1980) found that a preponderance of them focused on women's "psychological ailments": 81 percent of the antidepressant advertisements, and between 52 percent and 55 percent of those for major and minor tranquilizers and hypnotics, were tailored specifically to women. They depicted women as physically dependent on a male authority figure, more likely than men to be neurotic rather than psychotic, "the problem" even when another family member was being treated, and in need of drug treatment to restore them to their gender-determined roles of wife, mother, and child rearer. Another study found that females were almost never portrayed as therapists, although 15 percent of all psychiatrists were female (Seidenberg 1971).

A five-page spread in the *Journal of the American Medical Association* in May 1971 is representative. An advertisement for methaqualone, an addictive sedative-hypnotic, advised physicians that a middle-aged housewife under stress because of her daughter's upcoming marriage or a young actress preparing for her opening night could be appropriately sedated with this wonderful new medication. In commenting on this marketing strategy, the National Commission on Marihuana and Drug Abuse pointed out that "drug taking, both legal and illegal, is a commonplace activity" in literature, the stage, and television (*Drug Use in America* 1973: 109).

During the 1970s Valium made its mark as the most widely prescribed drug in recorded history. Ironically, it was often given to patients to reduce the effects of hyperactivity and insomnia brought on by the overuse of stimulants. Barbara Gordon, a network television producer, described her abuse of Valium in *I'm Dancing as Fast as I Can*. She depicted her struggle, through frequent hospitalizations and difficult withdrawals, to overcome her addiction, which had followed treatment for a back injury and anxiety attacks. During treatment, Gordon came to recognize the counterproductive role of her therapist, a "treat-the-symptom man," in perpetuating her addiction. "As long as I took the pills," she realized, "I had been incapable of feeling the anger necessary to make changes in my life" (1979: 176).

Gordon also noted that almost every patient she met in the hospital had been given "large amounts of mind-altering drugs, generally on the advice and with the consent of their doctors." She strongly resented the "drug gurus" of the 1960s:

Much later I had only to hear Timothy Leary's name to feel a terrible rage, recalling the tragic advice he had given to a generation of young people. Jim was probably one of thousands of kids who had followed that advice, who had experimented with mind-altering drugs and hadn't made it back to reality. In my months in the hospital, I met other young people, all of whom had bouts of serious mental illness after experimenting with drugs in Vietnam or here at home . . . every one of the patients on Six North had used and abused a drug, generally with the complicity or at least the approbation of their doctors. (p. 211)

The nonmedical use of psychotherapeutics continued at high rates, primarily among eighteen- to twenty-five-year-olds. According to the NIDA Household Survey (Fishburne, Abelson, and Cisin 1980), 16 percent to 18 percent of young people in that age group reported nonmedicinal use of stimulants, sedatives, and tranquilizers. Among women aged eighteen to twenty-five, 9 percent to 15 percent used these classes of drugs as well as analgesics. For younger women (twelve to seventeen) and older women (over twenty-six) the rate remained under 4 percent.

Like the psychiatrist who treated Barbara Gordon (1979), many physicians believed that Valium was nonaddicting. It took the increased scrutiny of physicians' prescribing practices to bring the use of these medications under control. The practice of overprescribing was considered the "natural outgrowth of medical school socialization and the influence of drug advertising" (Smith 1991: 142). But as Gordon told her female therapist, "I have a haunting, almost obsessive picture in my head . . . thousands of women all across the country being given pills by male doctors. Men sedating women, tranquilizing them, helping to rob them of themselves. It's obscene" (1979: 184).

Although the Women's Movement had begun to challenge gender assumptions, the prescription drugs issue would have to wait for a stronger female presence among medical students and faculty.[2] The Association of American Medical Colleges reported that in twenty years the percentage of female medical students had risen from 5 percent (1950–1965) to 10 percent (1970). By 1975 it was 24 percent, and by 1991, 40 percent (Jolly and Hudley 1992). According to an American Medical Association report, in 1970 only 25,000 (8 percent) of the 331,000 physicians in the United States were women. The number of female physicians increased to 9 percent in 1975, 12 percent in 1980, and almost 15 percent in 1985 (AMA 1992). In 1994, 17 percent of all practicing physicians were women and the number was expected to rise to around 30 percent by the year 2010. Despite these impressive gains, women constituted only one-fifth of the faculty members of American medical schools in 1991, and fewer than one-third were associate professors or professors. No U.S. medical school could claim a woman dean, and women held only eighty-seven of two thousand academic chairs (Jolly and Hudley 1992).

New Initiatives

As a direct result of the National Commission on Marihuana and Drug Abuse report, Congress established the National Institute on Drug Abuse. In 1974, PL 94–371 was enacted, which mandated that drug abuse and dependence among women receive special consideration for treatment and prevention. Within the National Institute on Drug Abuse, the Program for Women's Concerns (PWC) was established and charged with "remediat[ing] the paucity and inadequacy of female oriented treatment, prevention, research and education," and providing leadership in serving women to states and local communities (Henderson 1975). The PWC mandate was to collect nationwide data on women's functional health, monitor NIDA-funded female-oriented programs, collect information from programs that attracted and retained large numbers of women, and collect data on drug use during pregnancy. The first director of the PWC found the situation worse than expected. Because women were excluded from most drug-related population studies, a revised estimate of women addicts in the addicted population increased the number from 28 percent to almost 50 percent.

Much important information was derived from an analysis of four drug treatment demonstration projects, designed specifically for women, in New York City, Boston, and Detroit (Reed and Leibson 1981).[3] These projects—two therapeutic communities and two outpatient methadone maintenance programs—were funded by the Services Research Branch of NIDA in 1973–1974. As part of this effort, data gathered by the Women's Drug Research Coordinating Project (WDR) substantiated the existence of racial and ethnic diversity among the patient population. These differences were confirmed in larger studies comparing the white and black women enrolled in twenty-six drug abuse treatment programs, either therapeutic communities (TCs) or methadone-dispensing programs (Reed et al. 1980; Moise et al. 1982). Black women were more often users of heroin alone, or heroin combined with "recreational drugs," and less likely to be users only of nonopiates. They entered outpatient treatment more frequently, were more likely to be welfare recipients, and were less likely to have access to lawyers and physicians. Black women were also less likely to have been married but more likely "to have ongoing responsibility for a larger number of children" (Reed et al. 1980: 837). In contrast, white women seemed to have a higher stress indication level and exhibited a higher number of suicide attempts and drug overdoses. These and other differences solidified the need for race-specific and ethnic-specific interventions in addition to the gender-specific programs coming into existence in the 1970s.

The National Institute on Drug Abuse also initiated a series of educational seminars, including the Conference on Perinatal Addiction and two national conferences on women and drugs in 1974, the National Forum on Drugs, Alcohol and Women in 1975, and the National Conference on Women and Drug Concerns in 1976. The 1975 conference was the first federally funded conference devoted solely to women, drugs, and alcohol. It drew a broad array of professionals from diverse fields, including clinical medicine and nursing, health administration, health education, politics, labor, business, drug treatment, criminal justice, public health, mental health, family therapy, law, career development, social work, biostatistics, and religion. In his opening address, William Simon openly acknowledged that "most of the social problem literature is sexist" (1975: 4). Robert DuPont, director of NIDA, noted that, although women had achieved parity with men in the seriousness of their drug involvement, "this parity is not reflected in the institutionalized activities of the field" (DuPont 1975: 7). In another stark admission of the "triple handicap" of being poor, female, and addicted, DuPont pointed out that NIDA had been "as inattentive to the problem as the rest of the field" (p. 11). This message reached the politicians who attended the conference. Representative Peter Rodino, a Democrat from New Jersey and chair of the House Committee on the Judiciary, responded:

> The frightening truth is that an ever-increasing number of women—homemakers, teachers, sales clerks, secretaries, students and professionals, women from the ghettos and upper class suburbanites—depend on all kinds of drugs—legal and illegal—for their day-to-day living. Despite the alarming increase in alcoholism and drug abuse among women in recent years, little attention has been given to their particular problems. (p. 33)

An important outcome of the 1975 conference was the establishment of five regional coalitions to address the following issues: 1) the lack of attention to female addiction; 2) the need for funding for special gender-based programs; 3) the development of information and communication systems; 4) the removal of sexist barriers to effective therapy for women; and 5) the absence of coordinated services for this specific population (Nellis 1975). In addition, NIDA undertook the task of publishing and disseminating educational materials to health care providers and to the larger community of addiction service providers.

In 1975 NIDA began funding six three-year demonstration projects for drug-dependent women, including methadone maintenance programs for pregnant addicts, therapeutic communities, and one outpatient drug-free program. In 1977 NIDA brought the five regional coalitions resulting from the national conference in 1975 into a single nationwide Alliance of Regional Coalitions on Drugs, Alcohol and Women's Health. The Alliance provided NIDA with national information about the success of existing programs and the need for future programs (Mosher 1975).

The formation of NIDA's Program for Women's Concerns (PWC) provided initial funding, but more important, it also provided the climate and organizational structure necessary to support and advance the study of drug-dependency in women. These efforts were aided in large measure by the Women's Movement, which sought to obtain equal rights and equal access under the law for women. In 1973 the National Organization for Women organized its first local task force on women and addiction in Washington, D.C. Two years later, however, Lois Chatham, representing the National Institute on Alcohol Abuse and Alcoholism, admonished: "Clearly, women aren't coming into treatment programs, not the way they should be. But, until women get together and demand changes, nothing is going to happen" (1975: 27).

With these educational and service initiatives finally in place, seminal studies began, for the first time, to differentiate important disparities in the treatment approaches and options available to men and women. The increasing problem of female adolescent drug abuse was highlighted by George Beschner and Kerry Treasure (1979), who concluded that to succeed, programs must consider both the seriousness of the problem and the uniqueness of this target population. In addition, federal agencies formally acknowledged the complexities of treatment for pregnant women and the need for gender-specific treatment approaches.

Having analyzed studies of 146 addicted females from representative programs throughout the country, Beth Glover Reed and Rebecca Moise (1979) recommended to NIDA that comprehensive programs for women's health care should incorporate self-help groups, regular checkups, and special targeted classes on gender-specific issues. Another study, of 140 female addicts in ten treatment programs, confirmed the need for medical services for addicted women: on admission to drug treatment, 29 percent were found to have dental problems, 36 percent had circulatory problems, and 45 percent had genito-urinary problems (Andersen 1980). Also needed, Reed and Moise (1979) advised, were childcare services; training in homemaking skills; education and employment counseling sessions on self-esteem, confrontational strategies, sex-role issues, and family-oriented strategies; and the development of new sources of support.

By the end of the decade, important changes in approaches to women and drug use were beginning to crystallize. Up to this point, drug treatment programs had focused almost entirely on men and thus based their treatment approach on a confrontational, male-oriented model, one that was soon recognized as counterproductive, and even potentially destructive, for most women. Traditionally, women who used drugs had been regarded as "sicker," more deviant, and more difficult to treat than addicted men, a partial explanation of why treatment options for addicted women were so limited until the mid-1970s. The Women's Movement and other self-help initiatives—among tenants, welfare recipients, and homosexuals, for example—the publication of personal testimonies, and NIDA recognition that drug-using women had very special needs, proved to be important turning points in the nation's attitude toward addiction in women. In 1981, Joyce Lowinson, a pioneer in drug treatment, was able to say that "the women's movement has made those responsible for treating drug abusers more sensitive to women's issues" (Beschner, Reed, and Mondanaro 1981: v).

No longer were addicted women to be treated with benign neglect; they had became the focus of growing concern. Yet greater government and public awareness, along with some increased funding, failed to expand available treatment options for women significantly. The use and abuse of prescription drugs continued to cross racial-ethnic and socioeconomic boundaries, and in the 1980s cocaine would return—in the more ominous form of the street drug "crack."

nine

ENLIGHTENED TREATMENT

The decades of the 1960s and 1970s saw a marked increase in treatment options for drug addicts. New treatment modalities, new funding, and new research into the biochemistry and sociology of addiction offered hope of change. Having emerged from the Classic Era of narcotic control, which had relied almost exclusively on repression, interdiction of drug supplies, and the penal system, the nation appeared ready to push forward the Kennedy administration agenda of innovation and reform: detoxification, therapeutic communities, outpatient nonmaintenance clinics, inpatient treatment, correctional treatment programs, and methadone maintenance.

Detoxification

As a treatment approach, detoxification has the longest history. In the nineteenth century physicians had attempted to detoxify patients (either "cold turkey" or through gradually decreasing doses of morphine) but with little success. For a brief time, between the late 1870s and 1885, many enthusiastically promoted cocaine as a cure for morphinism—that is, until the dangers of cocaine became known. Other remedies for opiate use were also tried in the sanitariums and later the federal clinics, but most treatments proved unsuccessful. It was only in the 1960s that methadone, an effective opiate substitute, was shown to be able to prevent discomfort and alleviate the marked physical signs of withdrawal experienced during the detoxification process.

Beth Israel Hospital in New York opened one of the earliest detoxification facilities in 1961. By 1972, over thirty thousand addicts were receiving care; indeed, in that year alone almost eight thousand addicts were admitted for heroin detoxification (Richman, Feinstein, and Trigg 1972). No detoxification beds were set aside for women until 1972, and then only 76 of a total of 305 were designated as exclusively for women. Detoxification services were in constant demand: of the eight hundred to twelve hundred addicts awaiting admission at any one time in 1970, men faced an average waiting time of six to eight weeks and women, of two weeks. Using a schedule devised by Dr. Harold Trigg, the program director, detoxification proceeded through methadone stabilization and then a gradual dose reduction over fourteen to eighteen days. Early reports from the Beth Israel program claimed success rates of 95 percent (Richman, Feinstein, and Trigg 1972), thus partially offsetting the criticism of methadone programs at the time.

Following Beth Israel's lead, the New York City Department of Health established a network of outpatient detoxification clinics in 1971; at their peak enrollment, these clinics treated over twenty-two thousand patients a year. In the 1960s and 1970s, although many detoxification programs were carefully structured to include supportive and aftercare services, relapse rates remained extremely high, suggesting that this approach might better serve as a prelude to other types of treatment rather than as a treatment in and of itself. In the face of fiscal tightening, these programs closed, one after another, in the mid-1970s; by the late 1980s, virtually no outpatient detoxification was available in the entire city of New York (Newman 1988). Another detoxification program based at St. Luke's Hospital treated 407 patients, approximately 20 percent of whom were women, on an outpatient basis between 1966 and 1973 (Cushman 1978).

In the Connecticut Drug Dependence Unit, only 25 percent of female addicts treated in a day program were still enrolled after nine months, but this was better than the 2.5 percent retained in an outpatient detoxification program (Ramos, Howard, and Forrest 1978). A twenty-one-day outpatient program in San Diego found that one-quarter of the addicts in treatment were female (Kahn and Schramm 1978). An employer-based program in the Midwest (Illinois Bell Telephone Company) found that women made up 30 percent of the eighty-nine employees referred for drug treatment. Of the twenty-seven women in treatment, four were addicted to heroin, three were heavy marijuana users, sixteen were polydrug users, and four were listed as addicted to "other" drugs (Hilker, Asma, and Ross 1978).

Therapeutic Communities

Therapeutic communities (TCs) offered another avenue in the treatment for addiction. Synanon opened its doors in Ocean Park, California, in May 1958. The TC approach was broadly defined by Charles E. Dederich, its lay founder, as "a kind of group psychotherapy . . . [run by] one Synanist who is himself an addictive personality . . . [who] acts as a moderator" using "the weapons of ridicule, cross-examination, [and] hostile attack as it becomes necessary" (Yablonsky and Dederich 1965: 194–195). Other therapeutic communities, usually modeled after either Synanon or the second such residential program, Daytop Village, which was established in 1963, grew in importance during the late 1960s and 1970s. In 1976 the first national assembly of TC programs met in Washington, D.C. By the mid-1980s, "therapeutic community" had become an umbrella term encompassing over five hundred residential programs.

In the beginning, therapeutic communities worked primarily with male opiate addicts. During the 1970s, however, the patient population became more diverse and began to include women and users of other drugs. By 1985 over 60 percent of TC clients were being treated for using drugs other than opiates (De Leon 1985). By treating a variety of addictions, TCs reached a large population of drug users. TC programs regarded the drug abuser as someone with arrested emotional development. Using a system of rewards and punishments, the TCs sought to move the addict to drug abstinence through various stages: "motivation, isolation, deprivation, denunciation, confrontation, participation, elevation, and graduation" (Glasscote et al. 1972: 37). In her testimony before the National Commission on Marihuana and Related Drugs, Dr. Judianne Densen-Gerber, the founder of Odyssey House, derided drug maintenance and advocated drug abstinence: "The simplistic approach of replacing one drug with another makes as much sense as replacing Scotch with Bourbon" (February 24, 1972).

TCs employed intensive psychotherapy in a highly structured, group-centered approach that confronted problems of social adjustment directly. Except for Teen Challenge and similar religious communities, which assumed innate human goodness before God, TCs were generally confrontational and demeaning. Increasingly also, it became apparent that the TC model was inappropriate for female addicts, who were often guilt-ridden, ashamed of their addiction, involved in debasing and abusive relationships, and in great need of supportive intervention. Frank Cortina wrote of one addict, who said that in her search for help she felt "adrift on an ocean with no place to land" (1970: 40). Another expressed her own self-loathing: "We don't need for the public to call us anything . . . because no matter what they call us it can't be anything to match what we call ourselves . . . they can't punish us one half as hard as we punish ourselves . . . they can't do anything to us that's anything near like what we do to ourselves" (p. 153).

Synanon, which by the early 1960s had over four hundred members (Yablonsky and Dederich 1965), included women from its inception. Fourteen of the first fifty-two addicts entering Synanon after July 1958 were women (Volkman and Cressey 1963). Eleven of these women were between twenty-one and thirty years of age, seven had been supplied with drugs or money for drugs by mates or family, and five of the seven had obtained money for drugs illegally, usually through prostitution. Charles Dederich himself described the composition of the ideal synanon, or group structure, as three males, three females, and the Synanist (Yablonsky and Dederich 1965). By the early 1960s, women comprised 27 percent of the addicts actively enrolled in the Synanon movement. Another program, run by New York's Bronx Psychiatric Center, which offered methadone treatment in a TC setting, admitted nineteen women among its first fifty-five patients (Del Rey et al. 1977). In 1975, women made up 25 percent of the patients treated at Su Casa, a methadone-to-abstinence TC on New York's Lower East Side (Kaufmann, Williams, and Broudy 1978). Of those women treated in the New Haven TC program, only 16 percent were retained after twelve months of treatment and only 25 percent of adolescent girls were still in treatment after a nine- to twelve-month program (Ramos, Howard, and Forrest 1978).

Florrie Fisher's *The Lonely Trip Back* provided a window on the early TC movement. Fisher began her road to recovery at Synanon after twenty years of hard-core addiction. Confrontational sessions, she reported, were often composed of a "mixed assortment of ten to twenty people, white, black, men, women" (1971: 173). Between 1964 and 1967 Fisher progressed through "self-understanding" to increasing levels of "trust" and "independence" within the Synanon community. When she was unjustly thrown out because of a false report that she had taken two diet pills, she had already found the inner strength to begin her life over, this time without drugs. As a reformed addict, Fisher achieved a degree of fame as an antidrug crusader, writer, and lecturer.

In 1963, Daytop Village, which was modeled on Synanon, opened in New York as a residential treatment center for convicted male addicts on probation. Daytop overcame initial administrative difficulties and opened three separate facilities in New York. By 1968 it was serving about four hundred addicts (Glasscote et al. 1972). Treatment at Daytop followed the assumption that addiction was the result of a character disorder and poor socialization, which caused "withdrawing into a protective shell, namely drugs" (p. 86). Paternalistic group therapy isolated addicts and focused on their immaturity and irresponsibility, using techniques such as role modeling, behavioral conditioning, and group therapy, to rebuild them into useful, drug-free citizens. In the late 1960s, Daytop residents tended to be younger (only 14 percent were over twenty-eight), more often white (71 percent), and of higher socioeconomic status than the typical addict on the New York City Narcotics Register.

Although the Daytop program was originally designed for men, women were admitted in the late 1960s; by 1969, they made up 13 percent of the residents. Three-quarters of the female residents were between twenty-one and thirty years of age, and all were under forty. Most were addicted to "heroin and other opiates" (34 percent) or "mixed drugs" (58 percent). A much smaller number used marijuana. Residents who remained at Daytop for twelve to eighteen months and made significant progress became eligible for "reentry" into society and eventual "graduation." By the end of the 1960s, although it was extremely hard to assess success, and patient follow-up was difficult and limited, an estimated 10 percent of the more than a thousand Daytop residents had successfully completed detoxification.

Another successful treatment center was Phoenix House. It was established by five detoxified ex-addicts in May 1967 and grew to over a thousand residents by 1970. Phoenix House was actually a series of fifteen individual TCs that relied on group encounter and rehabilitative activities in a therapeutic residential environment. Women made up only 10 percent of the residents of Phoenix House, and preliminary data in the early 1970s found that women residents were as successful as males in achieving "reentry" into the community (Biase 1972). A subsequent 1974 study of young addicts at Phoenix House, slightly over half of whom were opioid users and two-thirds of whom were black, was conducted by George De Leon and Nancy Jainchill (1981–1982). In that study, women (25 percent of the sample) did significantly better. Success, defined by a two-year absence of criminal activity and cessation of opioid or other drug use, was achieved by 38 percent of the men and 42 percent of the women; improvement over pretreatment status was achieved by 60 percent of the men and 66 percent of the women. In addition, four-fifths of the women but less than half of the men experienced overall psychological improvement.

Gateway Houses Foundation, under contract with the multiservice Illinois Drug Abuse Program (IDAP), ran another representative TC. The Foundation, in fact, ran three separate TCs, all modeled after Daytop Village. IDAP also operated Tinley Park, a TC housed on the grounds of a state mental facility near Chicago, which had a patient capacity of a hundred; in 1971–1972, 40 percent of the residents were women (Glasscote et al. 1972). DARTEC, another TC established in Connecticut in 1969 to accommodate thirty-three men and twelve women, offered a twelve- to fifteen-month program stressing education in the areas of social skills, academics, and vocational training. Another component of the Connecticut program was a small branch of Daytop; 20 percent of the residents it served were women (Glasscote et al. 1972).

In January 1966, Metropolitan Hospital in New York City opened Odyssey House. It offered a maintenance program combined with long-term psychiatric intervention under the direction of Dr. Judianne Densen-Gerber. In March 1967, the program was incorporated as a TC, and later that year it expanded to a building on the Lower East Side, which housed forty male and twenty female patients. By 1969, two Odyssey House facilities could house a total of 130 residents. By 1971 Odyssey House had also opened a number of facilities in New York, an out-of-state facility in New Hampshire, and outreach centers in New York, New Jersey, New Hampshire, and Utah. The same year, Odyssey House began a separate residential program for female addicts in their teens. Dr. Densen-Gerber recognized that young female addicts frequently suffered from low self-esteem and poor self-identity, having been "used, sold, beaten, violated, conquered, derided, exploited" (1973: 321). As part of their therapy they confronted issues such as fear, lack of trust, and female sexuality.

Odyssey House was one of the first treatment centers to offer a program for pregnant drug addicts and their children (Densen-Gerber 1973). The Odyssey House Mabon Parents Demonstration Program (MPDP) was funded from 1974 to 1977 under a NIDA grant, and during that time it served 304 women and 158 children. The MPDP program developed from the recognition that addicted women, especially those with children, faced a unique set of problems, which in the past had precluded successful treatment outcomes: a male-model approach to therapy; programs with inadequate knowledge, capacity, and resources to meet the special needs of women; the chronic medical and complex psychosocial problems unique to women; and the presence of dependent children. Program evaluators admitted the degree of the problem early in their study of Odyssey House: "Though the problem of female addiction is one of growing seriousness, relatively little is known concerning its processes and implications. When contrasted with the literature dealing with men, that devoted to women appears sparse, and an increased research effort over the past decade has produced few new insights" (Cuskey and Wathey 1982: 9).

In setting up a new TC model, Odyssey House program founders noted that female addicts tended to react negatively to its founding principles and were unlikely to achieve success through its confrontational, male-oriented treatment models (Cuskey and Wathey 1982: 13). In a study of 641 Odyssey House residents between 1970 to 1973, Janet Sansone (1980) found that retention rates for women were substantially lower than those for men, dropping from 37 percent at twelve weeks (53 percent for men) to only 10 percent at forty-five weeks (34 percent for men). Traditional TC encounter sessions, which sought to "tear away" addicts' pretenses and attack their antisocial behavior, only intensified women's feelings of victimization, and their expectation that they would be hurt and abused by men (Cuskey and Wathey 1982). The MPDP thus became a necessary evaluation project because, as the authors wrote, "TC approaches for female residents do not now appear to be successful" (p. 37).

The Mabon Parents Demonstration Program opened on Ward's

Island in New York City in 1974 with accommodation for forty mothers and forty children. The average age of residents was twenty-three; 50 percent were black, 29 percent were white, and 13 percent were Hispanic. Patients passed through several stages: induction, motivation (two to six weeks), consisting of "inquiry-in" and "candidate-in" status, and a three-level treatment phase lasting eight to twelve months. At the end of in-residential treatment, the difficult reentry phase began and sometimes lasted more than six months. Residents achieved "candidate-out" status when they had completed the program, which took eighteen to twenty-four months.

Follow-up data on women in the MPDP program showed variable results. All graduates were drug-free less than six months after discharge, but one-quarter reported relapses a year after discharge; almost all former residents were arrest-free at first contact, and 84 percent remained so at one year. Employment figures, however, were less encouraging: only 14 percent of the graduates found jobs. Similarly, only 20 percent of the group reported "educational experiences" at the final follow-up contact (Cuskey and Wathey 1982). In client surveys the women said the most positive aspects of the program were their ongoing contact with their children, their association and easy communication with other women, the counseling sessions, and the assistance they received with legal and family problems. Yet, despite the concerted effort to offer personalized treatment and supportive services, "the majority of the Mabon clients did not complete the program" (Cuskey and Wathey 1982: 113).

The MPDP provided an important benchmark for programs in the 1980s and 1990s aimed specifically at addicted women. The entry populations of early TC programs probably typified the "hard-core" female addicts of the 1970s. They shared high levels of depression and low self-esteem; disrupted marital relationships; past histories of criminal activities, arrests, jail terms, and prostitution; and low levels of employment (Cuskey and Wathey 1982: 129). The program demonstrated several important discoveries: that female staff might serve as effective role models, and that supportive interaction between women and keeping mothers and their children together were positive therapeutic strategies. In addition, although on short-term follow-up it was clear that educational and vocational improvement needed further attention, a large number of graduates reduced their use of drugs and alcohol and showed a better appreciation of mothering, less antisocial behavior, and less criminality.

The Odyssey House program was able to use this experience to develop a model of female addiction that would influence subsequent programs: in the young female child, environmental and familial discontinuity, deprivation, and disorganization led to stress, anxiety, conflict, and instability. Circumstances like these encouraged deviant behavior, which in adolescence was expressed in more severe acting out, such as involvement with drugs. Continued drug use and addiction then resulted in further deviancy, antisocial behavior, and more serious medical, psychiatric, and interpersonal problems.

Data from other treatment centers began to become available. William Aron and Douglas Daily (1976) reported on a sample of 286 addicts enrolled in a Camarillo State Hospital TC between 1972 and 1973, where two-thirds of the addicts entered treatment under pressure from the California legal system. Success among female patients, who constituted one-third of the sample, was associated with psychological issues, most specifically a strong self-image. Another pioneering residential TC, Integrity House, was founded in 1968 in Newark, New Jersey. This program, which served about 125 clients, approximately one-quarter of whom were female, tried a variety of approaches in developing special services for women. When a 1974 study found that women at Integrity House faced derogatory and hostile attitudes on the part of the male staff, the center hired ten women in positions of clinical and administrative authority to develop innovative programs, such as special therapy groups and nonstereotyped vocational counseling (Doyle 1977). It also created an all-female house with an all-female staff, but this effort proved unsuccessful and was discontinued.

Other feminist therapy groups, such as the TODAY program in Newtown, Pennsylvania, reported greater success. By encouraging women to be "strong, assured and self-reliant" and providing strong female role models, administrators found that 88 percent of the women who completed the TODAY program were leading drug-free lives on follow-up (Schultz 1975). W.O.M.A.N. (Women's Organization Movement against Alcohol and Narcotics) in Detroit claimed similar success (Carter 1975). This program, one of four projects funded by NIDA in the mid-1970s, provided role models in the form of an all-female board, volunteer corps, staff, and student intern group. Chrysalis, a feminist program in Minneapolis, enlisted female ex-addicts or ex-alcoholics to demonstrate that the cycle of dependency could indeed be broken (Starr 1975).

Another treatment program devoted entirely to women was Women, Inc., in Dorchester, Massachusetts, which began in 1973 as a detoxification project but received NIDA funding the next year as a residential program for drug-free women. Women, Inc., was a tightly controlled and structured program for addicted women involving direct confrontation of feelings in a setting of graded and increasing responsibility and freedom. Susan Lydon successfully completed this program after twenty-five years of drug addiction. As she noted, "At Women, Inc., we had to ask for everything, . . . because as dope fiends we could not distinguish our wants from our needs" (1993: 242). The center's approach was "scary" and "uncomfortable," but it also included "understanding, maybe, or compassion" (p. 245). Lydon viewed her own struggle with addiction through another "self-help" initiative, the civil rights struggle of blacks in America: she called her chapter on entering the program "Walkin' to the Freedom Land," and her final chapter "Free at Last."

In *White Rabbit*, Martha Morrison described her redemption at Ridgeview, a Georgia TC, aided by the tender support of a counselor who could also "be highly confrontational and rigid . . . he was one tough dude who cleaned house for even the slightest infringement" (1989: 195). Dr. Morrison also drew strength from her Southern Baptist roots. In a moment of anguish and hopelessness, she cried out to God for recovery or death:

> Suddenly, I felt as if the weight of the world had been lifted from my shoulders. At first, I figured that I had become irreversibly psychotic; this experience was too incredible. The warmth, the peace of mind, the profound sense of relief, just washed over me . . . That all-powerful, overwhelming urge to use drugs had been lifted from me, and I knew a freedom I had never known before. (pp. 216–217)

Various religious groups offered alternative approaches to treatment for drug addiction based on the power of spirituality (Langrod, Joseph, and Valdes 1977). Within the New York area alone, Protestant-sponsored programs such as Exodus House, Addicts Rehabilitation Center (ARC), Samaritan Halfway Society, and the Salvation Army, the last of which had opened a residence for female addicts in

1968, were established in the 1950s and 1960s. The Quaker Society of Friends opened Baird House, a residential facility for female addicts, in 1967. The Roman Catholic Church operated programs such as Village Haven, a halfway house for women, and St. Dismas Center for Drug Addiction in Paterson, New Jersey. In May 1973 the Methodist Church organized an exploratory conference on Women and Drug concerns in Washington, D.C. (Price 1975). Jewish philanthropic efforts supported drug treatment programs at Beth Israel Hospital in New York City.

In contrast to these efforts, Pentecostal programs used their religious beliefs to try to cure addiction. One program, the Christian Youth Crusade of the Damascus Christian Church, existed from 1963 to 1968 and was followed by a number of others, such as the Hope Christian Mission in the Bronx, Anchor House in Brooklyn, and the Good Samaritan program in New Jersey. The most publicized was the Pentecostal-based Teen Challenge, originally called Teenage Evangelism, whose beginnings are detailed in David Wilkerson's book *The Cross and the Switchblade* (1963). Reverend Wilkerson, a rural Pennsylvania pastor, organized the program in the late 1950s in a dilapidated three-room apartment in Staten Island. Supported by the Assemblies of God, a fundamentalist religion, Teen Challenge sought to reclaim addicted teenagers using a supportive, nonconfrontational approach to their physical, mental, social, and spiritual needs. They were expected to undergo a personal conversion and "give themselves" to Christ (Glasscote et al. 1972).

Wilkerson undertook an intensely personal and direct "street corner" approach to saving troubled boys and girls who were caught in the web of drugs, violence, and crime. Early in his crusade, Wilkerson was particularly moved by the hopelessness of Maria, a young prostitute, who told him, "I'm a mainliner, Davie. There's no hope for me, not even from God" (1963: 32). Through experiences like these, Wilkerson recognized the special needs of young female addicts, referred to as "Debs," who belonged to male-dominated gangs: "The girls, I quickly discovered, were often the cause of trouble on the streets. I know of one rumble that started because a Deb from one gang complained that a boy from a rival gang made a pass at her. Later the girl confessed that she was lying all the time; she made up the story just so there would be a fight. She did it for kicks" (p. 162).

Wilkerson's first Teen Challenge Center specifically addressed the needs of the young girls who sought his help: "There would be women workers: some would specialize in girl gang members, others with girls who had sexual problems, others with addiction" (p. 129). Girls had separate rooming facilities on the second floor of the Center with the women and the married members of the staff. Although young women were allowed into some Teen Challenge programs, they were barred from others because of their "deeper emotional problems." As one administrator observed,

> women have a more righteous restraint than men; they seem to be a little more principled. But when this restraint breaks down, whether through drugs or something else, they go to the bottom so fast that it's difficult for them to recover. Something must happen psychologically that puts them in a state of constant despair that they will ever be able to recover true womanhood. Often they turn to prostitution or become involved in common-law marriage, which is basically against their ideals. (Glasscote et al. 1972: 157–158)

By 1972 Teen Challenge programs had been established in forty cities across the United States, and by 1983 they had grown into a national network of over 150 such centers, including a twenty-one-bed facility for girls in Garrison, New York, induction houses, reentry houses, rural training centers, outreach programs, and a Teen Challenge Institute of Missions (Wilkerson 1963).

Outpatient Nonmaintenance Treatment

Outpatient nonmaintenance treatment involved a wide range of approaches, from crisis intervention (such as drop-in "rap centers") and short-term therapy, both medical and emotional, to a more extensive network of concrete medical, psychiatric, and vocational services. Some programs borrowed the "Twelve Step" approach from alcohol treatment programs and applied it to addiction.[1] Although women constituted a significant portion of the patient population, outpatient nonmaintenance treatment was not gender-specific.

The Illinois Drug Abuse Program (IDAP) began operation in January 1968 in response to the recommendations of the Illinois Narcotics Advisory Council established by the state legislature in 1966. This program, headed by Dr. Jerome Jaffee, grew rapidly, from two facilities serving 108 patients in 1968 to fifteen facilities serving 912 patients in 1970 (Glasscote et al. 1972). Although in the early 1970s three-quarters of the patients were male, IDAP was one of the first programs to offer methadone treatment to pregnant women, despite the lack of research data on its efficacy or an optimal dosing regimen. Pregnant women were kept on a "fairly low dose" and brought down to twenty milligrams a day prior to delivery.

IDAP took a pragmatic approach to drug abuse treatment, realizing that not many patients would be able to become "law-abiding, productive, drug-free, emotionally mature member[s] of society" (Glasscote et al. 1972: 131). Although it maintained a small inpatient detoxification service, IDAP eventually shifted its treatment focus to community-based outpatient treatment with methadone. Other IDAP facilities included Safari House, which provided methadone maintenance, ambulatory withdrawal, ongoing counseling, and crisis intervention; and the 79th Street Clinic, which treated addicts, many of them women, who had failed treatment and had "special problems."

The Connecticut state program also offered a wide array of addiction services. Although Raymond Glasscote claimed that "in the mid-1960s drug abuse had not surfaced as a problem in Connecticut" (Glasscote et al. 1972: 185), some practitioners anticipated an inevitable outbreak. State-funded and operated treatment services were initiated in 1968, and by 1971 a number of separate treatment components were in place. The Hartford Regional Outpatient Clinic, serving a patient population that was one-quarter female, emphasized a group process "self-help model" in conjunction with methadone maintenance, and a "drug line" telephone service for acute intervention. In 1968, with the aid of a National Institute of Mental Health grant, Connecticut opened an outpatient mental health center whose catchment area was New Haven and surround. In 1972, women comprised 20 percent of the total population but about one-third of those on methadone maintenance. Methadone treatment was also used with pregnant women, but they were kept on "considerably lower doses" (Glasscote et al. 1972: 219).

In September 1967, Reality House, an outpatient detoxification program, opened in a drug-ridden area of Harlem. Professionals worked alongside a staff of former addicts, using a less confrontational strategy in its group therapy (Kaufman 1972). By May 1970, approximately thirteen hundred patients, 20 percent of whom were women, had applied to Reality House, but only a relatively small number progressed as far as extensive vocational training.

In one of the first studies to include gender as a significant variable in the assessment of drug treatment outcome, Carolyn Eldred and Mabel Washington (1976) looked at a multiservice program in Washington, D.C., that offered methadone maintenance, detoxification, and counseling to heroin addicts. According to their data, women were more likely than men to be introduced to heroin by a partner of the opposite sex. They were also more likely to be currently using heroin with that partner and to be economically dependent for their habit on that partner. These findings suggested that for women, successful treatment would have to consider the social milieu of drug taking and the potential supportive networks available to them.

Gender-specific analysis, however, was not universally useful. In a study of 13,000 clients, over 3,400 of them female, taken from the almost 147,000 client database of the national Client Oriented Data Acquisition Process (CODAP), gender was not associated with completion of treatment: only 22 percent of males and 24 percent of females achieved that standard of success. But the authors noted that women may actually have benefited more from treatment, since they had to overcome more societal obstacles to gain access to and complete treatment (Rosenthal et al. 1979).

Inpatient Chemical Dependency Treatment

The most expensive treatment option, inpatient treatment for drug addiction, also developed along the lines of alcohol addiction programs. Often privately financed, these highly structured programs included intensive psychiatric evaluation, group education, and individual counseling. Chemical dependency (CD) treatment resembled the therapeutic community (TC) approach in striving for abstinence through graded behavioral change, and its strong emphasis on personal responsibility in a setting of supportive counseling. It was shorter than TC treatment, often confined to twenty-eight days, and stressed the role of education and psychotherapy rather than the housekeeping chores considered integral to the TC process. Some programs adopting the inpatient model recognized the specific needs of female addicts.

Blue Hills Hospital in Connecticut served as an inpatient facility, providing opiate detoxification or methadone stabilization with the eventual aim of detoxification. Twenty-five percent of the patients at the facility were women, primarily between the ages of sixteen and thirty; in 1972 all eleven of the screening counselors were men (Glasscote et al. 1972). Blue Hills offered a range of therapeutic services, including individual and group therapy, "rap sessions," educational training, couples groups, and methadone maintenance. Other inpatient treatment facilities in Connecticut included Norwich Hospital, Fairfield Hills Hospital, with a detoxification unit for twenty men and ten women, and Connecticut Valley Hospital, with ninety beds for men and thirty beds for women.

A small inpatient service in St. Louis, begun in 1968, generally admitted women as 10 percent of its patient population (Glasscote et al. 1972). An inpatient program in New Jersey treated 802 patients between February 1971 and May 1973, approximately 30 percent of whom were women (Sheffet et al. 1978). A short-term twenty-one-day inpatient treatment detoxification program treated twenty-four women and twenty-six men during a six-month period in 1974 (Patch et al. 1978). Most programs, however, found high rates of relapse.

In *Take the Long Way Home*, Susan Lydon offers a female perspective on an inpatient detoxification unit. In 1986 she was admitted to Conifer Park in Schenectady, New York, one of a chain of private treatment centers run by Avon Products. Although women were admitted, men outnumbered them by about twenty to one. One of the more comfortable facilities, Conifer Park offered a pool, a jacuzzi, a steam room, maid service, and "fabulous food." When Lydon arrived, she was "burned out, exhausted, weak, and utterly defeated, in total despair" (1993: 216). The treatment program encouraged self-understanding and paved the way for her transfer to Women, Inc., in Massachusetts.

Correctional Treatment Programs

Prison-based drug treatment programs were intended to provide intensive therapy for incarcerated addicts and aftercare when they were paroled. They included highly structured militaristic approaches as well as therapeutic community models (Gerstein and Harwood 1990). Although the rate of success was quite low, and the rate of criminal recidivism quite high, patients in well-run residential programs with close links to community treatment during follow-up did appear to have a better chance of success. Women comprised a relatively small part of the prison population, however, and treatment was generally male-oriented, as in Oregon's Cornerstone Program (Field 1989), with little thought given to the special needs of women.

New York's Stay'n Out Program for incarcerated addicts, which opened in 1978, ran a separate forty-bed unit for female inmates. It was structured like Phoenix House TC but adapted to a prison setting. Following their release, clients usually entered community-based TCs for follow-up services. Women who completed this program were arrested significantly less than their counterparts who did not take part, and more women from these programs successfully completed parole than nonparticipating women (Gerstein and Harwood 1990).

Under the California civil commitment program, Vinewood Center, a halfway house located in Hollywood, opened its doors in August 1965. It accommodated twenty-five women whose backgrounds were less privileged than those of women treated at the Patton State Hospital. Most of the women stayed at the halfway house for about forty days, and between one-half and three-quarters of them were employed while under treatment (Glasscote et al. 1972).

Methadone Maintenance

During the early 1960s, Drs. Vincent Dole and Marie Nyswander, assisted by Mary-Jeanne Kreek at the Rockefeller University Hospital in New York City, found that methadone, a synthetic opiate developed in Germany in the early 1940s, could block both the euphoriant effects of heroin and the addict's craving for heroin. These pioneers developed a "metabolic theory." They postulated that heroin addiction caused cellular metabolic derangements, which made the addict feel unwell or "incomplete," and that this could be treated with methadone replacement. The physicians interpreted anecdotal stories from addicts, subsequently bolstered by findings of low endorphin[2] levels, in the light of the "metabolic theory" to explain the high rate of treatment failure when abstinence was the therapeutic endpoint. The team advocated replacing abstinence with maintenance treatment: methadone-maintained addicts who were treated with appropriate dosages of methadone, generally more than eighty milligrams per day, could regain control over portions of their lives and productively reenter society.

Following its initial success with a small group of patients, the methadone treatment program was expanded during the mid and late 1960s to Manhattan General Hospital and Beth Israel Hospital in New York City and became a therapeutic mainstay under the leadership of Drs. Harvey Gollance, Marvin Perkins, and Harold Trigg. By the end of 1972 the Beth Israel program was treating 3,800 addicts on an inpatient or outpatient basis: patients progressed from a six-week inpatient phase to a longer outpatient phase stressing personal and vocational stability. The Beth Israel experience attracted national attention, and its programs were soon replicated in cities such as Philadelphia and Chicago.

One of the early programs to develop from the Rockefeller Hospital experience was based at the Bronx State Hospital (Albert Einstein College of Medicine) in New York. Led by Dr. Joyce Lowinson, who had established a pilot project with Dr. Harold Trigg at Beth Israel Hospital in 1965, and aided by Beatrice Berle, John Langrod, Herman Joseph, Ira Marion, and others, this program made major contributions to the knowledge of how to best treat heroin addicts.

The Minneapolis–St. Paul methadone program originated in the office of one local internist, who began dispensing methadone in 1968 (Carlson and Westermeyer 1988). The methadone approach then became institutionalized and was adopted in a number of facilities between 1969 and 1972. Initially, these programs employed "high dosage blockade": maintenance doses averaged 160 to 180 milligrams a day. But as the Minneapolis program, like others around the country, soon found, take-home methadone was being diverted into illicit street sales. New admissions were addicted to street methadone, and in 1970 and 1971 about 60 percent of the deaths from opioid overdose were attributed to methadone. By 1971, in part to reduce the availability of methadone on the street, maintenance doses were lowered to about 55 milligrams a day. In 1975 the Minneapolis–St. Paul programs merged into the Hennepin County Methadone Program.

One of the early programs in the Southwest, the Patrician Movement, began in San Antonio in 1966 (Maddux and Desmond 1988). Within a few years, others—such as TOUCH, the San Antonio Free Clinic, religious programs such as Teen Challenge and Victory Outreach, and programs at the San Antonio State Hospital and the Bexar

County Mental Health–Mental Retardation Center—had been established to provide treatment to the increasing number of drug addicts. By 1969, "hard-core" heroin users numbered approximately twenty-five hundred, an increase attributed in part to the movement of heroin over the border from Mexico. Although inpatient treatment was available in San Antonio in 1969 and 1970, by 1972 almost all treatment was provided on an outpatient basis.

The nation's largest methadone maintenance program originated in New York City. In 1970, under the direction of Dr. Robert Newman, the City Department of Health committed major resources to methadone maintenance. Within two years, 40 methadone clinics, serving over ten thousand opiate-dependent patients, had been established (Newman 1988). By March 1975, New York City was serving over thirty-three thousand patients in 138 clinics (Todd 1975). In addition to dispensing methadone, these programs also offered counseling, social services, vocational rehabilitation, and legal advice. Although private initiatives also attempted to meet the demand, about two-thirds of all patients received treatment through the City Health Department, Beth Israel Hospital, and Bronx State Hospital.

At the beginning of the 1970s, when both the private and government sectors became increasingly involved in drug abuse treatment, the federal government suffered a significant fragmentation of its drug abuse services. These services, originally coordinated through the centralized Public Health Service facilities at Lexington and Fort Worth after the closure of the federal farms, had been divided among the more than thirty separate agencies and subagencies involved in the antidrug effort (Glasscote et al. 1972).

In 1971, therefore, President Nixon declared drugs "Public Enemy Number One," established a special drug office in the White House, and increased his budget request for all antidrug activities. Under pressure because of the known connection between drug use and crime, the need to find an acceptable treatment for opiate addiction, and early reports of the adverse impact of heroin addiction on pregnancy, President Nixon declared that methadone maintenance was the "treatment tool most productive of tangible results" (Todd 1975: 9). He suggested that drug treatment, especially with methadone, be made available to all addicts who requested it. By mid-1971, about twenty-five thousand patients were receiving methadone treatment; the number of heroin-dependent addicts, however, was estimated to be over three hundred thousand, far exceeding available treatment slots (Glasscote et al. 1972).

The Consumers Union report issued in 1972 strongly recommended methadone treatment: "To date, no program other than methadone maintenance has demonstrated its ability to rehabilitate more than a minute portion of addicts." The expert panel advised "that methadone maintenance be promptly made available under medical auspices to every narcotics addict who applies for it" (Brecher 1972: 530). By 1973, the National Commission on Marihuana and Drug Abuse had adopted a more "realistic" view of methadone treatment, acknowledging that methadone "maintenance is not inconsistent with cure" (*Drug Use in America* 1973: 322). This prestigious national body had finally voiced what physicians treating addicts, and addicts themselves, had been claiming for more than a century: *most opiate addicts could not overcome their addiction.* The debate over whether, for the majority of patients, addiction is a medical or a socioenvironmental problem continues; yet by the 1970s it was already obvious that many patients might remain productively dependent on methadone for the rest of their lives.

Undoubtedly, methadone played a pivotal role in reducing crime. Officials in New York City acknowledged that "certainly the potentiality of methadone maintenance for controlling crime was a major factor in the decision of the federal government to promote its use" (Todd 1975: 56). Methadone had proven an effective and inexpensive way to block opiate craving. Methadone-treated addicts showed better outcomes—reduced criminal behavior, improved employability, improved economic status, increased personal freedom, and generally improved health. Society also benefited from the curbing of the heroin black market, a reduction in the recruitment of new addicts, and reduced welfare costs.

By the mid-1970s, methadone had earned a secure place in the arsenal of the "war on drugs." By 1974, 78,000 patients, about 60 percent of the estimated 130,000 opiate addicts in the United States, were enrolled in methadone treatment programs. In 1977, the number of patients in methadone maintenance programs peaked at approximately 80,000. In subsequent years, however, the numbers began to decline, and by the end of the decade, only 70,000 to 74,000 patients were in treatment. By the beginning of the 1980s, the number actively in treatment had fallen further, to 68,000 (Cooper 1988).

Methadone treatment faced strong opposition from individuals and community groups who opposed the establishment of drug treatment facilities in their neighborhoods as well as from medical societies, law enforcement agencies, supporters of abstinence-directed treatment approaches, public and private agencies, and activist groups representing black and Puerto Rican minorities. Many in the anti-methadone camp firmly believed that total abstinence was the only worthwhile treatment goal, the one true measure of "success." To achieve this goal, they claimed, required the institutionalization of addicts during treatment in a drug-free environment to protect the community as a whole.

Representatives of anti-methadone groups also pointed out that merely substituting one addiction for another failed to address either the root causes or the lifestyle issues that placed the addict at medical and social risk. Methadone maintenance was an unimaginative approach that stood in the way of creative efforts to achieve abstinence. Methadone that had been legally obtained from maintenance clinics, critics claimed, would almost certainly be diverted into illicit drug channels on the street. In addition, minority rights groups considered methadone maintenance therapy a manipulation of ethnic minorities by the white majority, a cheap and convenient way to "buy off" a generation of addicts without having to provide them with opportunities to improve their social and economic circumstances.

Some of those objections and concerns were valid, but only if methadone clinics merely dispensed an opiate without providing a coordinated program of supportive social and medical services. In their pioneering research, however, Drs. Dole and Nyswander made it clear that methadone should—and must—be regarded as a medical stabilizer for opiate addiction and that it should be accompanied by exactly those comprehensive services that would allow opiate addicts to restructure their lives. Much of the politically based criticism overlooked several crucial points: addiction is a chronic relapsing condition; and the "neuro-adaptation" caused by methadone, in the context of a stable lifestyle, is radically different from heroin "addiction," which is characterized by preoccupying drug-seeking behavior, criminal activity, and other dangerous and possibly fatal actions such as unprotected sexual contact and self-injection with contaminated needles.

Despite moral, political, legal, and philosophical opposition, methadone treatment expanded in the early 1970s. Once it was accepted that some addicts could not attain a "drug-free" state, maintenance goals shifted to improving physical health, economic status, social status, self-image, and employability as a "legal," medically supplied drug user.

Methadone maintenance provided a major therapeutic alternative for opiate addicts who could not, or did not wish to, become drug-free by enabling them to achieve medical and social stability. Methadone was inexpensive, and because it was taken orally, it weaned addicts from their needle habit. Needle sharing had become increasingly dangerous in the wake of blood-borne infections such as hepatitis B, and it would assume a far more deadly role in the 1980s with the spread of HIV-associated diseases, including AIDS.

Reflecting on the opposition to methadone maintenance, which to many professionals was a rational and effective treatment for opiate addiction, Dr. Robert Newman commented:

> It's a lot of things: it's race and class; it's fear, the realization that addicts have to commit crimes to support their habits; and it's resentment that people are feeling that good three, four, five times a day. It's hard to express this hostility because there's nothing to focus against. But a methadone clinic brought all these problems together. It was a *building*, in front of which you could picket, or wheel your baby carriages, or go to the press about. I think people really wanted to express their hostility against a problem that was so evanescent that they couldn't do it any other way. (Courtwright, Joseph, and Des Jarlais 1989: 347)

Women in Methadone Programs

Women derived specific benefits from methadone maintenance. Obtaining narcotics legally recalled the clinic years of the early 1920s: women were able to free themselves from their quest for illegal drugs and their dependence on men as pimps, protectors, or sexual partners. In addition, eliminating needles offered women protection against blood-borne diseases and needle-related medical complications, such as abscesses, pneumonia, infections of the heart valves, and tetanus.

The original Dole-Nyswander-Kreek methadone trials had excluded women because medical information on safety and appropriate dosing was still so limited. As Dr. Dole explained, "I didn't want a woman to get pregnant and present a danger of damaging the fetus. And I didn't want to get into the hormonal variables of menstrual cycles" (Courtwright, Joseph, and Des Jarlais 1989: 335). A small group of four women soon entered the program, however, and appeared to benefit significantly from methadone treatment. A reporter commented favorably on the first sixty-five women who had been treated with methadone maintenance. These women, ranging in age from twenty-one to fifty-two, had stayed out of jail and had begun to restructure their lives. While driving by Needle Park, her old neighborhood, one woman, a former prostitute and heroin addict, remarked, "God, I'm glad I'm not out there" (*New York Times,* October 15, 1967).

From 1964 to 1968, 80 percent of the women who entered treatment stayed for at least two years, although rates of success among women with previous criminal records, multidrug abuse, and alcohol abuse were low (Chambers, Babst, and Warner 1973). A 1969 study at the Morris J. Bernstein Institute of Beth Israel Hospital and Harlem Hospital found that for women who remained in the program for twenty-four months, the rate of employment rose from 14 percent to 57 percent. In addition, the number of women on welfare dropped from 49 percent to 14 percent over an eighteen-month period, and some were able to return to school to continue their education (Gearing 1971). A later ten-year assessment of methadone maintenance by Frances Gearing and her colleagues found high patient retention rates and increases in "social productivity" as defined by employment, vocational training, or school attendance (Gearing et al. 1978). Women showed greater increases in social productivity, although success was limited by reduced employment opportunities for women. A decline in antisocial criminal behavior was also noted in the group but was not broken down by gender.

Other methadone treatment programs also began to include women. An innovative methadone maintenance treatment program for incarcerated female addicts was initiated in New Orleans in the early 1970s. Every day a police van transported the female prisoners to the treatment program for their dose of methadone and then returned them to jail. When the women were released from jail, they were stabilized on methadone and could entertain the possibility of breaking their heroin habit. In the Hennepin County Methadone Program (Minneapolis–St. Paul), female representation increased from 18 percent in 1969 to 25 percent in 1983 (Carlson and Westermeyer 1988). In San Antonio, only 12 percent of the patients admitted to the Bexar County drug facility in 1970 were women, but this number grew to 27 percent in 1980 and to 31 percent in 1984 (Maddux and Desmond 1988). The Drug Abuse Council, which assessed four methadone treatment programs in four geographically and socially diverse areas in the early 1970s found that women made up 24 percent of the enrollees in a New York program for adolescents, 16 percent of those at the New Orleans clinic, and 14 percent of registrants in both East Boston and Albuquerque (Danaceau 1973).

During the years 1969 to 1973, women made up almost ten thousand of the forty thousand patients treated in federally funded drug treatment programs, which had grown in number from 16 to 926. The proportion of women in methadone treatment programs during those years varied from 22 percent (Drug Abuse Reporting Program) to 32 percent (Treatment Outcomes Prospective Studies) to 39 percent (Drug Abuse Treatment Outcome Studies). Women in treatment were generally between the ages of twenty-one and twenty-five, and equally divided between black and white; often they also had prior arrests (Hindelang et al. 1977). During the first four years of its operation, the New York City program enrolled almost 21,000 patients, 25 percent of whom were women (Newman 1988). In 1971, in two Bronx programs, women made up 20 percent of methadone patients (Ruiz et al. 1977). By 1972, 28 percent of the New York City client population was female, and by 1973 the number of women in the program had increased from the one in six recorded earlier to one in three (Todd 1975).

During the latter part of the decade, women continued to represent between 20 percent and 30 percent of all patients seeking treatment: in California, for example, women made up 25 percent of the heroin-addicted patients in treatment in 1976–1977 (Ashbrook and Solley 1979) and 37 percent of those in treatment in 1981 (Anglin and McGlothlin 1985). In 1980, 30 percent of the almost 22,600 new patients admitted to methadone programs across the country were women (Cooper 1988).

Although the number of female enrollees in methadone treatment programs increased, their specific needs usually remained unaddressed. Early programs were male-oriented and male-dominated. They functioned in limited space with inadequate facilities, lacked gender-specific programs such as childcare and vocational training, and tolerated overt sexism (Rosenbaum 1981a). Women in these programs felt pressured to conform to sexual stereotypes, and endured exploitation, voyeurism, and psychological abuse (Peak and Glankoff 1975; Ashbrook and Solley 1979). It was as if the administrative personnel making treatment decisions had bought Professor Henry Higgins's line in *My Fair Lady:* "Why can't a woman be more like a man?" Despite increased female enrollment in the New York City program during the early 1970s, female retention rates began to decline (Todd 1975), which suggested a real need for specific gender-directed services within a maintenance context. A review of four geographically diverse methadone programs conducted by the Drug Abuse Council in 1973 barely mentioned women, although they comprised between 14 percent and 24 percent of patients. A review of outcomes in New York City methadone programs over a ten-year span, which was based on over 50,000 patient treatment years, did not mention gender differences at all, although women made up 25 percent of the total (Cushman et al. 1976).

At the time, it was not widely recognized that women sought drug treatment for any number of different reasons: to find temporary refuge from the street; as a result of an order from a judge or child protection agency; pregnancy; to escape from abusive relationships; poor health and the need for acute care; the advice and support of a partner; or for legal or counseling services. Some entered a treatment program simply to reduce their heroin dependence: "I'd take the pills and do dope to get my habit down—to taper off so I didn't have to do so much" (Rosenbaum 1981a: 122).

Although methadone programs often did not provide needed services for women, women reported the benefits of methadone itself. In *Addicts Who Survived,* an eighty-one-year-old woman who had used heroin and Dilaudid for sixty years commented:

> I entered the methadone program because I couldn't get Dilaudid. The doctor got a call from an agent who told him not to give it to me anymore. So he stopped. That was in 1976. I heard people talking about the methadone program, so I figured I'd go and check in. I want to stay on methadone. At my age, if I got off I'd die. I'd never make it. (Courtwright, Joseph, and Des Jarlais 1989: 81)

A married couple switched unsuccessfully from opium and heroin to Dilaudid before entering methadone treatment, which was a "lifesaver" for them (pp. 89–102).

Other female addicts found methadone less satisfactory. Lotty, a heroin and Dilaudid addict who had been on methadone for six years, found that, although she preferred heroin, at least "methadone does keep me from getting sick" (Courtwright, Joseph, Des Jarlais 1989: 176). A San Francisco addict admitted that becoming drug-free, or even stopping heroin use, was out of the question: "Almost everybody that went there didn't really have the intention of cleaning up. They came there just mostly to get the pills when they couldn't score or just to have them" (Rosenbaum 1981a: 123). Susan Lydon offered a more critical view of methadone maintenance: "Getting on methadone to cure a heroin habit is like pulling yourself up on quicksand to keep from drowning in water" (1993: 156). Even while she was in the methadone program, Lydon continued to abuse other drugs, especially heroin, and developed what she called a "double habit" (p. 157). Marsha Rosenbaum also found that female heroin addicts frequently used a variety of drugs. During the late 1970s, Lydon became a drug dealer—an "occupational addict"—despite her admitted awareness that "in New York the Rockefeller laws made it mandatory life for anyone caught dealing smack or coke" (1981a: 158).

Child-Rearing and Child-Bearing

The issue of addicted women as mothers and child rearers received little attention during the early 1970s. For most women, dependent children ruled out any chance of residential treatment, since facilities for families were almost never provided. Even most outpatient settings did not offer daycare for mothers with small children. What these women needed were comprehensive services provided in a supportive, nurturing environment that fostered self-confidence and self-esteem. Addicts who were prostitutes required additional services—outreach and street work, crisis intervention, and family reunification.

Motherhood offered one opportunity for enlisting female addicts into treatment. Addicted women lived in constant fear that their children would be removed from their custody by child protective agencies, thus stripping them of one of the most important validations of their womanhood (Rosenbaum 1981a). In interviews, they consistently expressed guilt about taking drugs when they needed to provide for the well-being of their children. One woman reacted badly to the court-ordered removal of her child: "That's when I went downhill all the way. I tried at first, but they wouldn't let me see the baby for two months and I couldn't handle that . . . I just started using heavy and heavy and heavy" (Rosenbaum 1981a: 100). In order to protect her custody rights, Susan Lydon avoided her ex-husband while copping drugs: "I was afraid if he found out I was a junkie, he'd try to take Shuna away from me, and I couldn't bear that; I'd already lost too much" (1993: 168).

During their pregnancy, as researchers began to realize, women could be directed into both the health care system in general and addiction treatment in particular. It was known that methadone restored women's normal menstrual function, sexual function, and fertility (Wallach, Jerez, and Blinick 1969), thus countering criticism that methadone treatment was being used to control the reproductive capacity of women, especially minority women.

Scientific data on the perinatal effects of drug use began to appear in the medical literature during these years, but the medical community remained uncertain about how to manage such patients. Leaving a pregnant woman on street drugs was considered unreasonable and unacceptable, but it was unclear whether pregnant women should be detoxified rapidly, stabilized with methadone, and then slowly detoxified or kept on low-dose methadone or higher-dose methadone. Those in favor of high-dose methadone argued that a "blockade" dose would block a woman's drug-craving, stabilize her life, and satisfy the higher medication doses necessary to achieve clinical stability during pregnancy, when a woman's blood volume expanded. Those who advocated low-dose methadone were concerned about possible but unsubstantiated effects on the fetus and newborn infant, reasoning that "the lower the dose, the better." Those who, given the lack of information on methadone's safety, advocated reducing dosage to achieve a drug-free state extended the argument to "better no fetal exposure at all."

These treatment options were being weighed in a national setting of increasing litigation. Physicians expressed concern that such "high-risk" pregnancies, which might result in compromised or damaged infants, would render them liable to malpractice suits. Having received little or no training in Addiction Medicine, physicians often viewed these pregnant patients as difficult and noncompliant. But when women seeking medical and prenatal care encountered judgmental, negative attitudes, they avoided getting the help that would have improved the outcome of their pregnancies (Rosenbaum 1981a).

Initially, methadone was regulated by the Food and Drug Administration and the Drug Enforcement Administration (formerly the Bureau of Narcotics and Dangerous Drugs). In June 1970, the Justice Department promulgated new guidelines for methadone use that called for the exclusion of pregnant addicts (Brill 1973). Upon the recommendation of the medical community, however, the government finally classified pregnant women as "patients requiring special consideration" (p. 26). The new guidelines represented what the government assumed to be a cautious but medically responsible position:

> Safe use of methadone in pregnancy has not been established. There is limited documented clinical experience with pregnant patients treated with methadone, and animal reproduction studies have not been done. It is therefore preferable that pregnant patients be hospitalized and withdrawn from narcotics. If such a course is not feasible, pregnant patients may be included provided the patient is informed of the possible hazard. To minimize the risk of physiological dependence of the new born, or other complications, pregnant women should be maintained on minimal dosage. (p. 31)

Pregnant women were thus enrolled in methadone treatment with little data on the safety of the drug during pregnancy and no studies of its possible impact on the fetus, newborn infant, or growing child. Confusion over dosing during pregnancy was evident in a Drug Abuse Council report. In New Orleans, although most patients were maintained on eighty milligrams of methadone a day, pregnant patients were kept "relatively low" (Danaceau 1973: 33). In East Boston, although a baby born to a mother on seventy milligrams a day "was not addicted at birth," the medical director of the clinic decided that in future, he would maintain pregnant women on thirty or forty milligrams of methadone (p. 62). In Albuquerque, thirty-three pregnant women were treated by reducing their methadone dose to thirty or forty milligrams a day. A case review of the infants, however, indicated significant problems, and the medical director of the clinic considered making drug-free therapy the treatment of choice for pregnant opiate-addicted women. Commenting on the lack of information on methadone and pregnancy outcome, the director admitted that he had no knowledge "about what has happened to these children since birth and whether there is any indication that methadone may have some lasting effects" (p. 92). The New Haven methadone program maintained pregnant women on low doses of forty to sixty milligrams a day until delivery, after which they were detoxified and referred for aftercare (Kleber 1971).

The idea of "comprehensive care for women" was taking shape, but not without some resistance. Comprehensive care was difficult to implement for a number of reasons: addiction was viewed as an individual illness without wide family repercussions; female addicts were generally bypassed in favor of young criminal males, who were perceived to have a greater need for services; methadone treatment lent itself to a "bare bones" approach of dispensing medication but failing to provide the accompanying supportive services; pregnant addicts were considered difficult, noncompliant, irresponsible, and a liability risk; and the development and funding of expensive comprehensive programs remained problematic (Suffet, Hutson, and Brotman 1984).

Program development was also slow because many addicted women failed to seek treatment. For many women, this failure was a direct result of their guilt and shame as pregnant drug users. Even within the community of addicts, pregnant addicts were at the bottom. Female addicts who were not pregnant at the time agreed on only a single issue: their contempt for pregnant addicts. Many women, therefore, avoided seeking prenatal care because they were unwilling to confront their own self-hatred or to face the negative attitudes of hospital staff (Rosenbaum 1981a).

Despite these obstacles, the National Institute on Drug Abuse initiated funding in 1975 for a series of comprehensive drug treatment demonstration grants for women in Detroit, Houston, New York, Philadelphia, Washington, D.C., and San Rafael, California, using pregnancy as the entry point. The grants demonstrated that the issue of drug use during pregnancy had reached the national policy agenda. They represented "a commitment by our country's highest level of government to the idea that pregnant addicts were as worthy of good care as anyone else, and that the effort to develop the best methods of care for them was a worthwhile expenditure of public funds" (Brotman, Hutson, and Suffet 1984: 20).

As late as 1977, however, even after the FDA had reclassified methadone as a New Drug approved for general treatment use, its availability remained limited (Todd 1975). The revised guidelines in the *Federal Register* (October 28, 1977) on methadone use during pregnancy now read:

> Caution shall be taken in the maintenance treatment of pregnant patients. Dosage levels shall be maintained as low as possible if continued treatment is deemed necessary. It is the responsibility of the program to assure that each female patient is fully informed concerning the possible risks to a pregnant woman or her unborn child from the use of methadone, e.g., safe use in pregnancy has not been established in relation to possible adverse effects on fetal development. (p. 56902)

Data on the adverse effects of heroin had been available since the 1950s, and now the publication of studies on the impact of methadone treatment on heroin addicts during pregnancy encouraged the development of new programs. Opiate addiction during pregnancy remained a matter of considerable concern, but beginning in the mid-1980s funding streams were diverted to cocaine, which slowed or even stopped much of the research into the perinatal effects of opiates. Reassuring data on the safety of methadone administration during pregnancy, however, accumulated. It became obvious that pregnant women gained enormous benefit from entering comprehensive treatment, commonly building on methadone maintenance as a base. Once medical treatment for drug addiction and prenatal care had replaced "street life," women's general health improved significantly (Iennarella, Chisum, and Bianchi 1986).

One program with a "multivariable approach" was the Family Center program in Philadelphia begun by Dr. Loretta Finnegan and her colleagues, including James Connaughton and Ronald Wapner (Connaughton et al. 1975; Finnegan et al. 1972; Kaltenbach and Finnegan 1992). One of the earliest comprehensive programs and thus a historically unique undertaking, Family Center provided outpatient medical—primarily methadone—treatment and psychosocial services to drug-dependent pregnant women. Obstetricians and pediatricians who were also experts in the field of addiction supplied comprehensive perinatal medical services; other personnel trained in mother-child interaction and early childhood development subsequently joined the staff. Research at the Family Center, led by Dr. Karol Kaltenbach, provided valuable data to the pediatric literature on outcomes of infants of addicted mothers.

In its early days, the program focused on a wide range of psychosocial services addressing education and treatment. Since Family Center staff also recognized that social problems—lack of food, clothing, and shelter—required attention before they could effectively address psychological and behavioral problems, they established a clothing bank and a small food bank for registrants. Convinced that gender-specific approaches would yield the best results, Family Center women-only groups and parent education groups were organized to build on programs fostering mother-child attachment.

The Pregnant Addicts and Addicted Mothers Program (PAAM) also capitalized on pregnancy as an entry point for providing health services to addicted women. PAAM was officially launched in upper Manhattan, where its offices were located and services provided, in February 1975 (Brotman, Hutson, and Suffet 1984), but it had actually been initiated at the Center for Comprehensive Health Practice of New York Medical College in 1969 as a pilot project offering obstetrical, pediatric, and psychological services to East Harlem mothers and their children. At first the project was funded by a grant from New York Medical College and the New York Junior League, but it eventually received two successive three-year NIDA grants (1975–1981) and began operating under contract to the New York State Division of Substance Abuse Services. PAAM was open to all pregnant addicts and to addicted women who had given birth within the past three months. It served a maximum of 120 families at any one time, and the turnover rate, four cases per month, was low. Most of the women remained in the program until they delivered their babies, and over 50 percent stayed in it until their children were at least a year old.

When PAAM opened officially as a government-funded program in 1975, it emphasized comprehensive care, providing on-site addiction treatment, a wide range of medical services, individual and group counseling, child development services, parent education classes, a preschool nursery, and developmental assessments of infants. Infant assessment was a key component, since medical data on the outcome of methadone-treated pregnancies was still fragmentary. Women were required to attend scheduled examinations, to visit five days a week for their methadone dosage if prescribed, and to attend parent education classes and at least one counseling session every week. What made the PAAM program different from many others was the fact that all services were housed on the same floor of one facility, providing easy communication between providers and convenient patient access to services—the "one stop shopping model" that increased in popularity in subsequent years.

When PAAM opened in 1975, 110 women enrolled. By August 1977, 170 women had taken part in the program and by 1980, 278 women. The program served an ethnically diverse population: 42 percent black, 42 percent Hispanic, and 16 percent white. Ninety percent of the women were pregnant when they entered the program and the remainder had just given birth, 75 percent had never been married, and most were young and relatively uneducated.

Other programs, such as the Kings County Program in Brooklyn (Harper et al. 1974) and the Hutzel Hospital program (Strauss et al. 1974), which began in the basement of the Hutzel Hospital in Detroit, also demonstrated the benefits of engaging addicted women in gender-specific programs during pregnancy.

If methadone treatment offered significant benefits to women during pregnancy, it was also beneficial to their fetuses and infants. The fetus was found to be more clinically stable under the influence of daily methadone than when exposed to street drugs in different dosages and at uncontrolled intervals. Researchers also noted improvement in the intrauterine growth of the fetal body and brain, which suggested that the developing fetus was receiving a more normal level of nutrition (Kandall et al. 1976; Doberczak et al. 1987). The incidence of congenital malformations, always a concern when unproven medications are administered during pregnancy, did not increase following methadone exposure. In addition, although methadone-exposed infants went through withdrawal after birth much like heroin-exposed infants, the problem could be easily managed with medication and supportive care. It was—and remains—difficult to separate the benefits of methadone itself from the positive lifestyle changes effected in the context of a methadone treatment program; at the same time, it became indisputable that methadone administration during pregnancy was safe and advantageous for both the mother and her infant (Finnegan and Kandall 1992).

During the 1980s, when funding was diverted to studies of cocaine, researchers lost an extremely valuable opportunity to track the long-term effects of methadone use during pregnancy on exposed infants. Short-term studies, however, provided data that proved to be, if not comprehensive, at least reassuring in failing to identify any specific neurobehavioral abnormality attributable to intrauterine methadone exposure (Finnegan and Kandall 1992). Today, after twenty-five years of continuing methadone treatment during pregnancy, there are still no long-term data on exposed children to fully assure us of methadone's safety. Basic management questions—such as the "optimal" dose of methadone during pregnancy, the safety of reducing or increasing dosages during respective trimesters of pregnancy, and the relationship of maternal dosing regimens to neonatal health, severity of withdrawal, or ultimate neurobehavioral outcome—remain unanswered.

The Treatment "Glass"

By the late 1970s, the treatment "glass" for addicted women could be considered both half-full and half-empty. On the positive side, some women were finding their way into treatment. While heroin use remained a greater problem for men than for women (who comprised 20 percent to 30 percent of users), in federally funded programs women made up about one-half of all patients being treated for tranquilizer abuse and about one-third of those being treated for abuse of other sedatives, amphetamines, barbiturates, and nonheroin opiates (Glynn, Pearson, and Sayers 1983). To show how far the United States had come in beginning to address the concerns of addicted women, NIDA's Program for Women's Concerns published *Women's Drug Abuse Treatment Programs* (1980), a directory representing the various treatment strategies that were available to women across the country.

On the negative side, the need for services greatly outstripped the small number of treatment slots, and many female drug users were still having difficulty gaining access to drug treatment. In addition, most drug treatment programs were based on male treatment models and did not accept pregnant addicts. Debra Ashbrook and Linda Solley (1979) found that, in California, men held twice the number of administrative positions in the drug treatment field that women held, only one-third of the treatment programs for heroin addiction offered single-sex groups, and only 6 percent of the programs provided childcare. Reviewing the decade, Jane Prather and Linda Fidell (1978) noted the general inadequacy of treatment programs for

heroin-addicted women: most lacked health care, childcare, job training, career counseling, and job placement, and subjected women to
sexual abuse by almost exclusively male staffs.

In an influential survey for NIDA in 1979, George Beschner and
Peggy Thompson (1981) assessed the impact of the legislation (PL
94–371) passed a few years earlier to provide increased funding and
treatment opportunities for drug-dependent women. Of the forty-four
programs they initially identified, only twenty-five met all the inclusion criteria for provision of services and cooperated in the data-gathering process. Interviews with personnel in these twenty-five programs
(twenty-one drug-free clinics and four methadone programs), which
served 547 women, revealed that although most women were receiving basic drug-related services and 82 percent had received routine
medical care, 54 percent had not received gynecological examinations,
74 percent were not counseled about birth control, and 83 percent
had not received dental care. In addition, 67 percent of the women
had not received vocational training, and 82 percent had not received
either job placement or educational training. Only a small number of
dependent children received services in the form of daycare, medical
examinations, recreation, and education. Services varied widely between one program and another, often because of inadequate financial
and staff resources.

In an important publication accompanying the 1979 survey for
NIDA, George Beschner, Beth Reed, and Josette Mondanaro (1981)
concluded that, although a great deal of information about women
and drugs had been gathered in the 1970s, female addicts remained
underserved. By gathering gender-specific essays into a single reference
source, they hoped to provide important "how to" information on
the intake process, counseling, community linkages, health and medical services, vocational training needs, and issues related to family
therapy and relationships between female addicts and their children.

If specific treatment programs for women were being developed,
however slowly, the evaluation process seldom considered the role of
gender in outcome. The first large-scale assessment instrument, the
Drug Abuse Reporting Program (DARP) based at Texas Christian
University, evaluated treatment outcomes for almost forty-four thousand patients in fifty-two programs in the United States and Puerto
Rico between 1969 and 1973. Although approximately one-third of
the patients were female—and gender was entered as a demographic

variable—many of the summary articles from the study did not touch on male-female differences. Sells et al. (1978), for example, presented data that dealt almost exclusively with a subject population of just over two thousand males. A subsequent study of over 4,600 DARP patients also focused on males (Simpson and Sells 1982). The Treatment Outcome Prospective Study (TOPS), the second large national study assessing outcomes of over 4,200 treated patients from an inital cohort of almost 10,000 patients, was published in 1989. Although TOPS reported that women made up about one-third of methadone-treated patients and drug-free outpatients, and about one-fifth of patients in residential programs, the study did not examine gender differences (Hubbard et al. 1989). Other general review articles assessing a range of treatments (Allison and Hubbard 1985) and specific approaches, such as treatment centers (De Leon 1985), also failed to deal with gender as a treatment outcome variable.

All in all, the professional community and the public became more aware of women and addiction, and increased attention encouraged at least the beginning of available, accessible treatment. Yet the dramatic changes in qualitative forms of treatment were not matched by a quantitative increase in available treatment slots, although the number of addicted women was growing. In addition, a new federal administration with a less sympathetic social agenda, compounded by the appearance of "crack" cocaine, a devastating social catastrophe-in-waiting, further jeopardized the lives and children of drug-using women.

ten

OPPORTUNITIES AND PROSECUTION

Following the passage of the Harrison Act in 1914, drug control policy in the United States was shaped by one basic assumption: that enforcement and expansion of antidrug laws could control or even eliminate drug use. The Reagan administration not only embraced the idea, it made drug policy almost entirely a law enforcement issue. From 1981 to 1986 funding for drug law enforcement increased, and much of it was directed at drug interdiction on the nation's borders. At the same time, federal control of drug policy, through the National Institute on Drug Abuse, was weakened by the transfer of much of the money for prevention and treatment efforts to the individual states through block grant programs.

President Reagan's "zero tolerance" approach did not overlook marijuana. Although the 1970s had seen movement toward the decriminalization of marijuana, the Comprehensive Crime Control Act of 1984, the Anti-Drug Abuse Act of 1986, and the Anti-Drug Abuse Amendment Act of 1988 all increased the penalties for the possession, cultivation, and selling of marijuana. State laws were also unevenly toughened in the 1980s, leading to irrational differences in penalties across individual state lines. In 1983 more than 400,000 people were arrested for marijuana violations (Himmelstein 1983). In 1992 more than 340,000 people were arrested for violating marijuana laws and now faced penalties ranging from fines to life imprisonment. By the middle of 1994 approximately four million arrests for marijuana violations had been recorded since the early 1980s (Schlosser 1994).

Estimates of the number of people imprisoned for marijuana offenses in federal, state, and local facilities exceeded 40,000 in 1994, despite the fact that medicinal use of marijuana was legal in thirty-six states (Schlosser 1994). More generally, the number of state and local arrests for drug violations between 1982 and 1991 increased almost 50 percent, from 676,000 to over one million (*Drugs and Crime Facts* 1992).

The increase in federal crime-fighting dollars was accompanied by a reciprocal decrease in funding for prevention, education, and treatment. These funds declined by about 65 million dollars between 1981 and 1985, representing an inflation-adjusted drop of about 40 percent, thus reversing many of the efforts of the Nixon and Carter administrations. The federal prevention campaign rapidly decelerated to First Lady Nancy Reagan's slogan, "Just Say No," which emerged as the media centerpiece of the administration's antidrug campaign. Increases in state drug expenditures compensated for some of the decrease in federal funding for drug treatment, as did a shift from "public tier" financing to "private tier" financing (Gerstein and Harwood 1990).

By 1986, top administration officials were admitting that their policies were not working. General Accounting Office studies in 1983 and 1985 found that interdiction efforts had failed, but this did little to prevent significant funds from flowing into this effort. Noting these failures, Congress passed a bill in 1983 to consolidate the fragmented drug-fighting effort under one cabinet-level post, but President Reagan vetoed it. In 1986 Congress passed a comprehensive Anti-Drug Abuse Act, which authorized more than 1.7 billion dollars in new funds, bringing the total federal antidrug expenditure to almost four billion dollars. Under the Act, money available for "demand reduction" more than doubled, to a total of 950 million dollars. Funds were appropriated for prevention and education initiatives, but more than 75 percent of federal antidrug money continued to be funneled to activities aimed at "supply reduction."

Toward the end of the 1980s, following the acknowledged failure of past efforts, the emergence of "crack" cocaine, and the onslaught of AIDS, new initiatives began to emerge. Prevention efforts included school- and community-based programs as well as media campaigns. Although some funding was directed toward treatment programs hard hit by funding cutbacks, by the end of the decade public programs could provide treatment slots for only 148,000 of the nation's estimated 1.3 million intravenous drug users. Data collected by the National Drug and Alcoholism Treatment Utilization Survey (NDATUS) revealed that the number of individuals in drug treatment had increased by a relatively small amount, from 229,000 in 1976 to 263,000 in 1987. The latter, however, was the largest number of patients in treatment yet recorded, as were the 5,100 programs reporting to NDATUS (Gerstein and Harwood 1990). In addition, the weakening of the prevention and treatment infrastructure cost valuable time when "crack" took hold in mid-decade, a drug epidemic rooted in poverty and homelessness and thus extremely difficult to contain. Without an effective pharmacological treatment, like methadone for heroin addiction, the "crack" epidemic spread.

The Numbers Again

Even though the United States considered drug use a "problem" as early as the 1850s, in the 1980s the nation was still grappling with its true quantitative dimensions. Reflecting both the level of national concern and an attempt to establish a sound epidemiologic footing, government-funded agencies developed or improved major drug-use indicators. These included the National Household Survey on Drug Abuse (NHSDA) begun in 1972; the High School Senior Survey (NHSS) begun in 1975; the National Ambulatory Medical Care Survey (NAMCS); the National Hospital Discharge Survey (NHDS); the Drug Abuse Warning Network (DAWN) begun in 1972; the National Vital Statistics System; the Uniform Crime Reports (UCR) initiated in 1930 but later refined; Drug Use Forecasting (DUF) begun in Washington and New York City in 1987; NIDA's Client-Oriented Data Acquisition Process (CODAP); and the Drug Enforcement Administration's System to Retrieve Drug Evidence (STRIDE) initiated in 1971. The National Institute on Drug Abuse also conducted the National Drug and Alcoholism Treatment Unit Survey (NDATUS) and the Drug Services Research Survey (DSRS), and provided supplementary funding to the National Maternal and Infant Health Survey, the National Survey on Family Growth, and the National Longitudinal Survey of Labor Market Experience of Youth. Each of these indicators demonstrated distinct strengths and weaknesses. The National Household Survey, for example, used self-report, with its inherent risk of underreporting, carried a refusal-to-answer rate of 16 percent to 23 percent, and failed to include groups in which drug use would be expected to be higher, such as the homeless, the incarcerated, the hospitalized, and students on college campuses.[1]

Nevertheless, the consistency of sampling techniques over time highlighted broader trends. In 1982, when the seventh sequential household survey, which looked at 5,624 Americans over the age of twelve drawn from a total U.S. population of 182,481,000, was conducted (Miller 1983), heroin use, not broken down by gender, remained relatively low—recent use, within the previous month, was reported by less than 0.5 percent of adolescents (over age twelve), young adults, and older adults. Past use of cocaine, however, was reported by 35 percent of males and 22 percent of females, and recent use by 9 percent of males and 5 percent of females. From 1979 to 1982, lifetime prevalence use of cocaine had increased slightly in adolescents from 5.4 percent to 6.5 percent and in young adults from 27.5 percent to 28.3 percent, but in older adults it had doubled, from 4.3 percent to 8.5 percent.

The 1982 survey also showed that the number of Americans who had ever tried marijuana had dropped slightly, from 31 percent in 1979 to 27 percent. Recent use of marijuana had fallen in the twelve- to seventeen-year age group from 17 percent in 1979 to 12 percent currently, and from 35 percent to 27 percent in young adults aged eighteen to twenty-five. Although marijuana use continued to be more prevalent in males than in females across all three age subdivisions, 25 percent of young women, 60 percent of young adult women, and 17 percent of older adult women reported using it. Across the three age subdivisions, the incidence of marijuana smoking in women showed little change from 1979 to 1982. The survey did not break down the use of LSD, PCP, and similar hallucinogens by gender, but recent use was reported by about 1 percent to 2 percent of those surveyed.

The survey also showed that males used prescription-type psycho-therapeutic drugs (stimulants, sedatives, tranquilizers, and analgesics) nonmedicinally more commonly than women. The findings related to gender were reversed, however, for the medical use of prescription psychotherapeutic drugs; just as in the 1950s and 1960s, physicians prescribed stimulants, sedatives, tranquilizers, and analgesics much more frequently to women than to men. According to the survey, these drugs had been medicinally used in the recent past by 7 percent of girls and 4 percent of boys, by 8 percent of young adult females and 6 percent of young adult males, and by 16 percent of older women and 10 percent of older men. Women in the two age groups over twenty-six used every category of prescription drug more than men. The large majority of women, 68 percent of those aged eighteen to twenty-five and 80 percent of those over twenty-six, had used these drugs by prescription.

In 1981, in an effort to introduce some degree of rationality into drug-policy planning, NIDA published a monograph using demographic modeling to project the amount of nonmedicinal drug use in the United States for the years 1985, 1990, and 1995 (Richards 1981). Drawing on data from six sources,[2] drug use trends from the 1970s, and population forecasts, this study projected that overall drug use in America would fall during the next fifteen years: recent use of heroin in the eighteen- to twenty-five-year-old female group from 254,000 in 1985 to 213,000 in 1995, and in males from 918,000 to 771,000 over the same period; use of other opiates in young women from 127,000 to 106,000, and in young men from 225,000 to 189,000; and recent cocaine use in young women from 254,000 to 213,000, and in young men from 950,000 to 798,000.

The study also projected that active marijuana use in young males would fall from 5,652,000 in 1985 to 4,747,000 in 1995, and in young females from 3,308,000 to 2,766,000 during the same period. Decreases would also be seen in hallucinogen use, in young females from 223,000 to 186,000, and in young males from 483,000 to 406,000. The study warned, however, that these projections could be radically altered by changes in the minority population, immigration patterns, fertility rates, mortality rates, geographical mobility, changing family structure, and job opportunities. Indeed, the commission experts could hardly have anticipated economic recession, a rise in urban violence and homelessness, AIDS, and new drugs such as "crack" cocaine, smokable heroin, methamphetamines, and "designer drugs," all of which certainly rattled "expert" projections during the next ten to fifteen years.

A survey conducted by the National Association of State Alcohol and Drug Abuse Directors (NASADAD) in 1988 recorded almost 519,000 drug treatment admissions during that year, approximately one-third of which were female. Between 1985 and 1988, total heroin admissions to treatment programs rose 28 percent, but admissions for cocaine abuse rose 239 percent. Total expenditures for these state-supported programs in 1988 exceeded 2.1 billion dollars, over three-quarters of which went to treatment (Butynski 1991). According to another national survey, in 1988 women made up one-third of out-patient drug-treatment clients, with little variation between mental health center, hospital, and other organizational contexts, or between methadone treatment or drug-free treatment modalities (Price et al. 1991). Despite the long history of women's involvement with drugs and the recent documented increase in the severity of the problem, an influential Institute of Medicine panel, convened in 1988, published a national report on drug treatment that hardly mentioned women, and noted that "no conclusion could be drawn" regarding treatment of addicted women with children (Gerstein and Harwood 1990).

By the early 1990s, twenty-three million Americans admitted to having used cocaine, and almost three million to having used heroin; one million heroin users were reportedly still active. Of the over fifty-nine million women of child-bearing age (fifteen to forty-four years), it was estimated that almost five million were active users of illicit drugs. Of particular note was the finding that slightly over six hundred thousand women in the child-bearing age group alone were actively using cocaine, a far higher number than the 1981 commission had predicted (*Maternal Drug Abuse and Drug Exposed Children* 1992).

The NIDA Monitoring the Future Study (Johnston, O'Malley, and Bachman 1994), covering the years 1975 to 1993, found that despite appreciable declines in illicit drug use during the previous decade, favorable trends had stalled in the mid-1980s. By 1992, "alarm bells" were sounding. Drug use among college students and young adults was increasing, and eighth-graders were using more marijuana, cocaine, LSD, and other hallucinogens. One-quarter of women between the ages of nineteen and thirty-two reported using an illicit drug during the previous year: the highest prevalence rate was 21 percent for marijuana, far ahead of the 4.5 percent for cocaine, 3.5 percent for both stimulants and tranquilizers, 2.5 percent for hallucinogens, and 0.1 percent for heroin. Although "recent" drug use—defined as use within the past twelve months—had declined from 1986 to 1992, almost two-thirds of all female respondents had tried an illicit drug, most commonly (excluding marijuana) cocaine and "crack," stimulants, tranquilizers, and LSD, in that order, at some point during their lives. As NIDA's analysis concluded, "despite the improvements in recent years, it is still true that this nation's secondary school students and young adults show a level of involvement with illicit drugs which is greater than has been documented in any other industrialized nation in the world" (p. 20).

The alarm sounded again with the publication of the 1993 data. Although among college students and young adults, marijuana use leveled out, it rose sharply among eighth-, tenth-, and twelfth-graders. The proportion of high school seniors using any illegal drug other than marijuana rose from almost 15 percent to just over 17 percent. The use of cocaine, which had declined between 1986 and 1987, remained low but leveled off. Use of "crack" cocaine, however, continued to decline, a change attributed to "intense media coverage of the hazards" (Johnston, O'Malley, and Bachman 1994: 13). As expected, heroin use among the student population remained quite low, about 0.5 percent, and the use of other opiates continued to decline to less than 3 percent. Tranquilizer use, however, rose significantly, as did use of stimulants, and the gradual two-decade decline in barbiturate use came to a halt. Adolescent males were more likely to use marijuana and other illicit drugs, but adolescent females used somewhat more stimulants. Among the college and young adult populations, both sexes showed similar patterns of stimulant, tranquilizer, barbiturate, heroin, and other opiate use.

In the late 1980s and early 1990s, the NIDA National Household Survey found that about 9.3 million women aged fifteen to thirty-five had used an illicit drug within the past year, of whom 4.9 million were very recent users. Almost 1.5 million of the 4.6 million drug users felt to require treatment were women (Gerstein and Harwood 1990). By 1991 the number of women who were recent drug users fell slightly, to 4.3 million, and 75 percent of them used marijuana ("Women and Drug Abuse" 1994). A Massachusetts study from 1988 to 1990 found that women constituted one-third of the population applying for drug detoxification (McKusker et al. 1995). A mid-1990s study from Washington, D.C., found that 30 percent of heroin users and 35 percent of cocaine users were women (Flynn et al. 1995). A Georgia study of addiction found that women comprised 21 percent of those studied (Kingree 1995).

Recognizing that the prevalence of drug use during pregnancy had never been addressed as a primary question, NIDA conducted the National Pregnancy and Health Survey between October 1992 and August 1993, and released its preliminary findings on September 12, 1994. Of the estimated four million women who had given birth during that period, approximately 221,000 (5.5 percent) used some illicit drug during pregnancy, most frequently marijuana (118,700, or 2.9 percent), amphetamines, sedatives, tranquilizers, and analgesics in a nonmedical context (61,200, or 1.5 percent), and cocaine (45,100, or 1.1 percent). Fewer than 0.5 percent of the women had used methamphetamine, heroin, methadone, inhalants, or hallucinogens. As Dr. Alan Leshner, the director of NIDA, reported, illicit drug use was more commonly seen in women who were not married, who had less than sixteen years of formal education, who were not working, and who relied on public funding to pay for their hospital stay.[3]

Metropolitan centers were also generating better data. New York City, historically the epicenter of the national drug problem, reported that annual treatment admissions for heroin dependency remained relatively constant, between 10,600 and 12,600, during the years 1986 and 1992 ("Current Drug Use Trends in New York City" 1993). Although total treatment admissions for heroin increased only slightly, and "heroin arrests" not at all, from 1990 to 1992, the number of "heroin or morphine emergency room episodes" soared, from under four thousand in 1991 to over eight thousand in 1992. This increase most likely reflected the increasing purity of "street" heroin, which jumped from 37 percent in 1990 to 72 percent in early 1992 (Frank and Galea 1992). Hospital emergency room visits caused by cocaine- and opiate-related emergencies also increased in Atlanta, Baltimore, Boston, Chicago, Detroit, and Los Angeles between 1991 and 1992 (*New York Times,* October 5, 1993).

Another troubling trend was the increase in intranasal use of heroin, which comprised 25 percent of heroin admissions in 1988 and 44 percent in 1992 (Frank and Galea 1992). Although the decline in injected heroin use during that same time period, from 71 percent of heroin admissions to 58 percent, represented good news—potentially reducing needle-related complications such as HIV and hepatitis B—increasing use of noninjected heroin also meant that women were more likely to be recruited into the pool of heroin users. Between 1990 and 1993, women consistently made up 31 percent to 32 percent of the heroin users (26 percent of injectors and 33 percent of inhalers) seeking treatment in city-funded programs ("Current Drug Use Trends in New York City" 1993). Heroin-related emergency room visits by female patients rose slightly, from 26 percent in 1988 to 28 percent in 1991 (Frank and Galea 1992). Ethnographers working on the streets of New York in the early 1990s were also reporting increasing numbers of female heroin dealers.

New York City data on cocaine use revealed contradictory trends. Emergency room visits attributed to cocaine increased about 20 percent between 1988 and 1992, but during the same period the number of cocaine-related arrests declined by about 31 percent. At the same time, although women represented a stable 38 percent to 41 percent of patients seeking admission for treatment of cocaine dependency (42 percent of "crack" users and 31 percent of users of other forms of cocaine), the number of babies identified as being born to cocaine-using mothers fell from 3,168 in 1989 to 1,786 in 1992 (Frank and Galea 1992; "Current Drug Use Trends in New York City" 1993). Data from the entire state in the mid-1980s indicated that women comprised about 30 percent to 40 percent of the "crack"-addicted population (Kaestner et al. 1986).

Treatment center admission figures for marijuana were only a tenth of those for heroin and cocaine (Frank and Galea 1992). Yet, consistent with national reporting data, primary marijuana admissions to treatment programs rose by 23 percent from the second half of 1991 to the first quarter of 1992. Women made up between 28 percent and 33 percent of marijuana smokers seeking treatment.

One major factor limiting the accuracy of epidemiologic surveys of drug use was the growing number of homeless Americans. Determining how many people were homeless at any one time was itself highly problematic; recent estimates range between half a million and close to two million (Jahiel 1992). The 1990 Institute of Medicine report on drug treatment speculated that 20 percent of homeless individuals had drug-related disorders and that women with children made up 25 percent of the homeless (Gerstein and Harwood 1990). In late 1993 in New York City, city shelters, churches, and synagogues were housing approximately 25,000 people every night. Although city officials did not know how much substance abuse there was among the homeless population, they did acknowledge that it was "pervasive" in these settings (*Reforming New York City's Response to Homelessness* 1993). In one small study of twenty-nine homeless pregnant women in Ohio, 35 percent reported taking prescription drugs, and 10 percent reported using drugs illegally (Wagner, Menke, and Ciccone 1993).

At the other end of the socioeconomic spectrum, drug abuse by physicians remained problematic, as it had been in the past. According to contemporary surveys, approximately 8 percent of physicians experienced substance abuse problems (Schaumburg 1993). In 1993, state medical societies, as well as programs designed to treat physicians for substance abuse, revealed that between 1 percent and 3 percent of physicians were formally reported for violations of chemical abuse policies (Schaumburg 1993). A 1992 study found that one out of nine physicians had used benzodiazepines, and one out of six had used minor opiates without medical supervision during the previous year (Hughes et al. 1992). Overall, compared to the general population, physicians ran a fivefold risk of substance abuse. Recognizing the extent of substance use, each state formed a "physician health committee" to identify physicians at risk for substance abuse. Some of these committees were coercive, but most were not—as long as a physician participated in treatment. Each state also enacted medical practice acts, often local versions of the American Medical Association's Model Impaired Physician Treatment Act.

While studies of nurses continued to indicate a high prevalence of drug use, as in the past, it was not until 1982 that the American Nurses Association passed a resolution addressing chemical dependency in the nursing profession. The First National Symposium on the Impaired Nurse was held in 1982, and two years later the American Nurses' Association released *Addictions and Psychological Dysfunctions in Nursing: The Profession's Response to the Problem,* its first official publication on drugs. Although as late as 1985, little information on the incidence of drug dependency among the nation's 1.7 million registered nurses was available, in 1981 thirty-five of thirty-seven state boards of nursing already regarded substance abuse as a serious problem. A study examining addiction as the primary cause of disciplinary action against nurses in 1980 found that 32 percent of 139 chemically dependent nurses were dependent on narcotics and alcohol and 23 percent were addicted to narcotics alone (Sullivan 1987). In 1987, an estimated 6 percent to 8 percent (120,000 to 160,000) of nurses reportedly had either alcohol- or drug-related problems (Haack and Hughes 1989). In a group of 300 nurses (257 females) who were recovering from alcohol or drug dependency, Eleanor Sullivan and her colleagues (1990) found that 43 percent had been dependent on strong narcotics, 32 percent on milder narcotics, 28 percent on amphetamines, and 22 percent on marijuana.

Some researchers concluded that drug use among nurses was a result of life stressors inherent in a female-dominated profession: reduced autonomy, subservience to physicians, low pay, the need to learn new technologies, and the constant pressure of dealing with serious illness, often in the noisy, crowded settings of intensive or emergency care. Although Marsha Rosenbaum did not comment on the number of nurses in her San Francisco survey, one of the nurse-addicts described working and maintaining a habit: "It was pretty easy to go to work and do that sort of thing [heroin]" (1981a: 64). A home health care nurse found it easy to divert medications from her patients and became so dependent on tranquilizers that she could hardly wait for her patients to die in order to steal their remaining pills. Her pill-taking was related to an unhappy marriage, excessive eating and drinking, the stresses and anxieties associated with attending nursing school at age thirty-nine, and being a single-parent of three teenagers. To deal with her despair, she moved from taking sedatives to Demerol and morphine. When an alert pharmacist noticed discrepancies in some prescriptions, her problem was discovered and she sought professional help (Thobaben, Anderson, and Campbell 1994).

The perception that addiction among nurses warranted specific attention inspired innovative treatment programs (Haack and Hughes 1989; Sullivan, Bissell, and Williams 1988). In 1981 two San Francisco nurses founded the Bay Area Task Force for Impaired Nurses (BATFIN). A similar program, DISCOVERY, was established in Los Angeles in 1983, and shortly thereafter, in Florida, the Intervention Project for Nurses. The Employee Assistance Programs, group therapy such as Nurses Assisting Nurses (NAN) in Lexington, Kentucky, and self-help models were also developed.

"Crack" Cocaine

Earlier epidemics of cocaine use, at the turn of the century and more recently in the 1970s, had for the most part involved male users. But the outbreak of "base" or "crack" use in the mid-1980s drew in large numbers of female users. Between 1983 and 1989, women comprised one-third to two-fifths of all callers to the National Helpline (Gold 1992). For middle-class and upwardly mobile women, cocaine was a new way to meet their own expectations and those imposed by society.

As one woman commented, she used coke "as a way to shape myself, to make me into a particular idea of what a woman should be: thinner, smarter, more articulate, more glamorous" (Darling 1995: 230). She also dated doctors to gain access to pharmaceutical cocaine and to downers such as Valium. Data from the Drug Use Forecasting Program, which tracked drug use among those arrested for serious crimes, showed that in 1990 more women than men tested positive for cocaine in thirteen of the twenty-one monitored cities (National Institute of Justice, August 1991; cited in Inciardi, Lockwood, and Pottieger 1993: 13). Terry Williams, an ethnographer working on the streets of New York from 1982 to 1986, confirmed anecdotally in his novel *Crackhouse* what statistics were showing—that more than 40 percent of the crackhouse regulars were young women, most of them Latina and African American, some of them in their teens (1992: 12).

During the 1960s and 1970s cocaine was usually taken by inhaling or "snorting," but a small number of users were experimenting with "base" or "freebase," the basic alkaloidal (plant derivative) form of cocaine. "Base" was first incorporated into marijuana joints and cigarettes, but later it was smoked directly in pipes or devices made from laboratory pipettes (Williams 1989: 5–6). "Base" was peddled and even given away in the late 1970s because rising production resulted in large stockpiles that needed to be sold. Another glut of cocaine in 1983 led to the production of "crack," or freebase cocaine, which was packaged in amounts costing five dollars or less and marketed to a new population of users (p. 7).

This new smokable form of cocaine was attractive because it delivered an intensely pleasurable "high,"[4] it was easy to administer, and it bypassed the dangers of intravenous needle use. Young girls associated with the "crack" trade as users became involved at the retail level: in New York City, as Terry Williams reported, "the distribution and sale of cocaine . . . involves mostly African-American and Latino boys and girls under eighteen" (1989: 8). In Miami, James Inciardi and his colleagues (1993) found that early initiation into drug use was associated with "crack" dealing. Money and drugs were obvious rewards, but another strong motivating force was "the desire to show family and friends that they can succeed at something" (Williams 1989: 10). Using cocaine temporarily increased self-esteem, as did the sense of "belonging" to a clique or a gang, even when men showed little loyalty to women (p. 85).

Most of the women who became "crack" addicts, however, were afforded no status as gang members. Confined to urban ghettoes, these women were down-and-outs, often homeless prostitutes who put their lives in jeopardy either through direct "crack"-related violence or through exposure to sexually transmitted diseases. As Terry Williams reported,

> crack . . . also quite frequently leads female users to unprotected sexual behavior with intravenous drug users, as crack reduces inhibitions while creating a desire for more drugs, and male users often barter drugs for sex. This puts these women at increased risk of acquiring sexually-transmitted diseases, including HIV infection. In short, crack use can indirectly put teenage girls at risk of acquiring AIDS. (1989: 111)

A large multisite study of 774 young "crack" smokers, of whom 348 were women, in New York, Miami, and San Francisco in 1992 confirmed the extent of this risky behavior. "Crack" smokers reported sexual behavior that put them at increased risk for HIV acquisition, and these behavior patterns were often stronger among women than among men. Almost three-quarters of female "crack" smokers, for example, had at some time exchanged sex for money or drugs, compared to less than 5 percent of women who did not smoke "crack." Female "crack" smokers were also more likely to have more male sex partners, frequently more than one hundred, in comparison to non-smokers. In addition, female "crack" smokers only infrequently used condoms during sex, which increased the risk of acquiring sexually transmitted diseases for both male and female "crack" users (Edlin et al. 1992; Inciardi, Lockwood, and Pottieger 1993).

Many of the "crack" addicts who were trading drugs for sex or were engaged in prostitution recognized the risk, but as one Miami "crack" addict acknowledged, "I try not to think about it. I just try to be safe. It's scary, I'm out there scared all the time" (Inciardi, Lockwood, and Pottieger 1993: 101). In New York, when Paul Goldstein and his colleagues interviewed "bag brides" and "skeezers," these women said things like "I never exchanged sex for drugs. I'm not getting no VD" and "I've turned down offers of sex from men because of fear of AIDS" (Goldstein, Oulette, and Fendrich 1992: 357). Other women, however, would not pass up unprotected sex if the money was right: "I used to use them [condoms]. But not always . . . once you get this rock in your system, a person might almost do anything" (p. 358).

Other life-threatening conditions, such as tuberculosis, also compromised the lives and health of these women. Between 1982 and 1991, reported cases of tuberculosis, which had been in steady decline during the twentieth century, leveled off at between twenty-two thousand and just over twenty-six thousand annually ("Morbidity and Mortality Weekly Report" 1992). Many of these infections were antibiotic resistant, further increasing the risk of death from this disease.

In the 1980s "crackhouses," a degraded contemporary version of earlier opium dens and heroin "shooting galleries," became common in American cities (Inciardi, Lockwood, and Pottieger 1993). These establishments, widely discussed in the media, represented the dark intersection of much of what had gone wrong in American society— "crack" cocaine, poverty, homelessness, unprotected promiscuous sex, and AIDS. One Miami crackhouse owner, or "kingrat," philosophized: "It is that mystic place beyond the edge of the world where dreams are really nightmares and where nightmares are always real. And more, it is home—home to the wretched, the depraved, and the perverted" (p. 59). A hardened New York "crack" addict considered crackhouses "the worst of places" (p. 63). Typically, according to Terry Williams,

> the establishment is desolate, uninviting, dank and smoky. The carpet in the room is shit-brown and heavily stained, pockmarked by so many smoke burns that it looks like an abstract design. In the dim light, all the people on the scene seem to be in repose, almost inanimate, for a moment . . . As my eyes adjust to the smoke, several bodies emerge. I see jaws moving, hear voices barking hoarsely into walkie-talkies— something about money; their talk is jagged, nasal and female. One woman takes out an aluminum foil packet, snorts some of its contents, passes it to her partner, then disappears into another room. In a corner near the window, a shadowy figure moans. One woman sits with her skirt over her head, while a bobbing head writhes underneath her. In an adjacent alcove, I see another couple copulating. Somewhere in the corridor a man and woman argue loudly in Spanish. Staccato rap music sneaks over the grunts and hollers. (1989: 107)

Young adolescent girls, often from poor urban areas, also found their way into the "crack" world. Williams described one fourteen-year-old: "She is tiny, with dirty fingernails and pockmarked arms.

Her jeans are dark, discolored, unwashed, and raggedy . . . There is desperation in her eyes. If there was any dignity before she started using crack, [there] is no sign of it now" (1993: 67).

In an ethnographic study of thirty-seven adolescent "crack" addicts in Miami, James Inciardi and his colleagues (1993) found that two-thirds were involved in the business of dealing. All were involved in high-volume criminal activity such as theft, prostitution, and robbery. This was especially true of young female "crack" dealers, whose criminal offenses in the previous twelve months totaled over forty thousand.

In a drug-infested world that afflicted both men and women, it was "crack"-addicted women who faced disapproval and disgrace, who were more likely to be condemned by those around them: "Certainly the women are more likely to be viewed as 'bad.' Once a woman ventures into the crack culture, she is oftentimes cast out by her family and friends as a 'whore' and it is difficult for her to restore her reputation" (Williams 1992: 105). Epithets such as "junkie broad," "junkie chick," and "bag bride" reflect the "throwaway" attitude toward "crack"-using women. Ethnographic studies from New York and Chicago in the mid-1980s provided anecdotal evidence from women who were trading sex for drugs: "I blocked it out. I don't want to remember. It made me sick"; "I felt dirty about it . . . The woman who does that is not worth anything"; "Sex-for-drugs degrades me" (Goldstein, Ouellet, and Fendrich 1992: 356).

In spite of this publicity, the decreasing role played by the federal government in addressing both "crack" addiction and its root causes, such as poverty and limited life expectation, allowed the most recent epidemic to get a head start. It took some time for the government to acknowledge that "crack" was spreading from urban areas into the suburbs and to develop funding sources to counter it (*New York Times*, October 1, 1989 and October 1, 1991; Massing 1989). The fact that "crack"-using women were stereotyped as economically deprived women of color did not help their cause in a country that was swinging right politically and toward fiscal conservatism in a downsized government. Accordingly, an Institute of Medicine study at the end of the 1980s noted with regret the "scarcity of research data since the onset of the crack-cocaine era for drug dependence in women who are pregnant or mothers of young children" (Gerstein and Harwood 1990: vii).

Heroin

Media attention to "crack" in the 1980s obscured the fact that heroin remained a significant problem for women. Although women were believed to represent about 30 percent of the heroin-using population, female heroin addicts continued to be underrepresented in treatment programs. By 1992, however, women made up one-third of patients in methadone programs in New York and 43 percent of patients in treatment in California. In 1994, women made up 30 percent of the 120,000 patients in federal methadone programs. In 1995 women made up 32 percent of the 42,300 patients in treatment in New York State.

Many of the reasons for this imbalance are already familiar: society's ongoing preoccupation with drug-associated male crime; the relegation of drug use among women to the shadowy sidelines of American life; and the shortage of gender-specific programs offering needed services for women, such as domestic counseling and childcare. More general issues, such as the exclusion of women from clinical trials of new medications and the unwillingness of medical professionals to care for pregnant addicts for fear of malpractice suits, also helped to insure women's underrepresentation in treatment programs. The reluctance of professionals to treat female addicts, and addicts' own unwillingness to seek treatment, also found expression in the feminist literature on substance abuse. Elizabeth Ettore (1992) emphasized the sense of defilement and bodily pollution experienced by female addicts.

> If women are seen to 'abuse' in any way their already abused bodies, they are seen to be worse than their male counterparts. This is because these women are seen to defile and indeed to desecrate the sacred symbol of their female essence: their bodies which house their wombs or reproductive power. While the female body is the embodiment of women's reproductive nature, substance abuse is seen as an attack on women's nature. A substance-abusing woman is the quintessence of a wicked woman defiling her body with harmful substances. (p. 10)

Feminist writers of the 1980s railed against the harmful impact of society's view that female addicts had "failed as women" (Ettore 1992) and were "polluted women," who were "potentially sexless, bad mothers, uncaring for their children or irresponsible wives, not considering the needs of their husbands." A female "junkie," or still worse, a female "pusher," was viewed as having passively lost or actively rejected her femininity and become a "non-woman" in her all-consuming association with a "masculine drug," heroin. This attack on the maternal instincts of women was played out in the press in stories such as "Crack Babies: The Worst Threat Is Mom Herself" (Douglas Besharov, *Washington Post,* August 6, 1989) and "The Instincts of Parenthood Become Part of Crack's Toll" (Michael de-Courcy Hinds, *New York Times,* March 17, 1990). To advance his case that "neither punishment *nor treatment* for mothers is likely to improve things" (emphasis added), and that more forced adoptions and child-removal were needed, Douglas Besharov made the unsubstantiated claim that drug-using women often do not get prenatal care because "crack addicts typically show little or no interest in prenatal care."

Accusatory judgments such as these, which obscured the true reasons for female addicts' poor medical care and ignored the paucity of and lack of agreement among studies of mother-infant interaction in the context of substance abuse, fueled the campaign to limit the reproductive options of drug-using women and to remove drug-exposed children from their biological mothers, regardless of the circumstances of these women's lives or the quality of the parenting they could provide. My own discussions with drug-using mothers suggest a more typical picture of maternal guilt and shame at not being able to stop using drugs, an extremely well-developed maternal instinct (which only compounded their guilty feelings), and frustration at being unable to find nonjudgmental, supportive medical and prenatal care.

A female addict interviewed in *The Addict in the Street,* who desperately wanted her children back after their removal by court authorities, cried "I miss them, I miss them, please help me, please" (Larner 1964: 151). A heroin addict in San Francisco spoke of her inability to find treatment: "Oh, if I can get clean, I hope to go back to work, get my kids back. That's what my goal is. That's why I'm trying to get on the program" (Wenger and Rosenbaum 1994: 3). A "crack" addict recently separated from her daughter said:

> I feel terrible, I feel horrible not being with her. I'm really torn apart. I try not to think about her, because she and I are very close. I talk to her on the phone, but I can't take that either. I have to see her, I *have* to. The only thing is, I don't have the money to go. It's not that I haven't had the money, I have . . . but I spent it on something else. Okay? But

the next time I get the money, I'm going to leave New York City and
go to my daughter and I'm not coming back. (Williams 1992: 136)

As an added measure of guilt and shame, society blamed prostitutes
and female drug users for spreading AIDS into the heterosexual community. Although HIV transmission was much more likely to occur
from males to females, women, especially prostitutes, bore the burden
of society's anger. In the 1980s, "thrice oppressed" became "quadru-
ply oppressed": female, black, addicted, *and* HIV-positive.

Women, Drugs, and Crime

During the 1980s and 1990s an increasing number of women entered
the criminal justice system (Immarigeon and Chesney-Lind 1992).[5]
Indeed, between 1980 and 1992 the number of women in prison in
the United States tripled, to a total of seventy-five thousand. (Viewed
in historical perspective, in 1929 the rate of women's imprisonment
was six per hundred thousand; by 1989 it was twenty-nine per hundred thousand, a fivefold increase.) Between 1984 and 1989, the
average daily population of women in local jails rose by 95 percent.
By the end of 1989, 12 percent of the more than four million adults
in the care or custody of corrections agencies were women. By the
early 1990s women comprised the fastest growing segment of the
American population involved with the criminal justice system. Most
of these arrests and confinements were not due to an increase in the
severity of the crimes women committed but to changes in the legislative response to the "war on drugs" and in law enforcement practices. From 1982 to 1991 the number of women arrested for drug
offenses increased by 89 percent (Federal Bureau of Investigation
1992).

Incarcerated women often had a history of drug use. In 1986,
almost three-quarters of female state prison inmates reported that they
had used drugs at some previous time in their lives (*Drugs and Crime
Facts* 1992). In 1989, 63 percent of the women in national arrestee
populations were illicit drug users (National Institute on Justice 1990).
A survey conducted by the American Correctional Association in 1990
found that half of the women in prison used cocaine; another 20
percent admitted to daily heroin use (Immarigeon and Chesney-Lind
1992). Data gathered by the Drug Use Forecasting Program in 1990

showed that the percentage of women arrestees in different cities who tested positive for at least one illicit drug, excluding marijuana, ranged between 26 percent and 70 percent, and that despite considerable intercity variation, cocaine was generally more widely used than opiates (Wellisch, Anglin, and Prendergast 1993). Among jail inmates in 1989, females (one-third of women) were more likely than males (one-fourth of men) to be arrested for drug charges; convicted women were twice as likely as convicted men to give a recent history of major drug use (Snell 1992). A 1992 survey at the Cleveland House of Correction revealed that over 80 percent of the women inmates had significant drug abuse problems (Singer et al. 1995).

A survey of women in state prisons, published by the U.S. Department of Justice, brought the issue of women, drugs, and criminality into sharp relief: nearly one in three female inmates in 1991, compared to one in eight in 1986, was serving a drug-related sentence (Snell 1994). This change accounted for 55 percent of the increase in the female prison population between 1986 and 1991. Drug use by female inmates exceeded that by male inmates, and over half of the women had used drugs in the month before their current offense. Nearly one in four female inmates had committed a crime to get money for drugs. Although use of heroin and other opiates had remained relatively constant between 1986 and 1991, use of cocaine had doubled, from 12 percent to 23 percent.

Jose Sanchez and Bruce Johnson (1987) found that 175 female drug-using inmates in a New York prison facility had committed 36,373 individual offenses during the preceding six months, most commonly property crimes and drug sales. In a study of 197 female "crack" addicts between 1988 and 1990, James Inciardi and his colleagues (1993) found that 60 percent of "heavy" and "typical" users were involved in criminal activity. "Heavy" "crack" users committed an average of nearly 1,000 offenses each during that time period, and "typical" users committed even more, an average of 2,700 offenses (p. 119). "Crack"-using women were more likely to engage in petty property crimes (77 percent) and drug-business crimes (76 percent) than in violent crimes (24 percent) or major property crimes (6 percent).

Studies also showed that female drug-using inmates were more likely than males to engage in behavior that increased the risk of acquiring HIV infection (*Implications of the Drug Use Forecasting*

Data for TASC Programs 1991). Tracy Snell (1994) found that about one-third of the women reported using needles, and that 18 percent, with the highest rates among Hispanic and white women, reported needle-sharing while using drugs. Snell also found that about half of the women had never participated in a drug treatment or drug education program, and that only 38 percent of the women entered drug treatment while in prison. Of the women who were active drug users, 12 percent were in treatment at the time of their arrest.

Female drug addicts, more often involved in property offenses and vice crimes, including drug sales, committed relatively few violent crimes. In fact, although the total number of women incarcerated in state prisons increased during the 1980s, the number of women incarcerated for violent offenses actually fell while the number of women incarcerated for property offenses rose (Immarigeon and Chesney-Lind 1992). In a sample of 133 active female narcotic addicts, although total offenses had increased markedly in 1983 and 1984, from an average of 357 per respondent during one year to 461 per respondent during a six-month period, violent criminal activity remained low, constituting under 1 percent of offenses (Inciardi and Pottieger 1986). A 1991 national survey found that female drug-users were less likely to have committed a violent offense compared to nonusers, and that female inmates who committed offenses to buy drugs were more likely to be serving sentences for robbery, burglary, larceny, or fraud (Immarigeon and Chesney-Lind 1992).

This pattern of offenses suggested that treatment services for women who are not violent could prove useful in reducing rates of recidivism for both crime and drug use. Some women sought treatment to escape a growing involvement with crime: "I don't want to go back to prison. I don't want to pick up a gun again 'cause if my money's funny, I'll do a robbery" (Wenger and Rosenbaum 1994: 4). But if drug treatment seemed to offer women a way of controlling or terminating drug use altogether, substantiating data were hard to find in selected populations. Surveys of women in state prisons in 1979 and 1986 found that one-third had been in drug treatment at some point, and half of them had entered treatment more than once. A national survey of incarcerated women in 1990 found that about one-quarter had been in drug treatment at some time (Wellisch, Anglin, and Prendergast 1993).

Although drug treatment services have in general been regarded as beneficial to female addicts, services provided to incarcerated female drug users have always been inadequate. Approximately 5 percent of all incarcerated addicts were receiving drug treatment in 1979 (National Institute on Drug Abuse 1981); a decade later this figure had increased to about 11 percent (Chaiken 1989). Current figures on the number of incarcerated women who are receiving drug treatment have not been published, but one researcher has estimated the number to be "fewer than 11%" (Wellisch 1993: 9). Of more general concern was a 1990 survey by the American Correctional Association of the jails and prisons in all fifty states. According to this study, only one-third of the prisons had separate reception and diagnostic facilities for women; most of the institutions had been built for men and were run by male administrators; gynecological-obstetrical care was available in only half of the jails but in about four-fifths of the prisons; most of the facilities neither permitted extended visits with children nor offered on-site childcare during visits; and only one-quarter of the jails but more than four-fifths of the prisons had vocational programs for women (cited in Wellisch 1993: 13).

Prostitution was prominent in the drugs-crime-sex triangle of the 1980s and 1990s. From 1984 through 1987, an ethnographic study called FEMDRIVE was conducted on New York's Lower East Side to examine the relationship between drug use, especially "crack," and sexual bartering (Goldstein, Ouellet, and Fendrich 1992). Of the 133 female drug users and distributors interviewed, 37 reported prostitution without sex-for-drugs bartering, while an additional 15 reported that they did both to support their drug habit. In this study, the most commonly used drugs were cocaine, heroin, and marijuana; three-quarters of the women who traded sex for drugs used heroin and cocaine compared to only half of the prostitutes. A 1989–1990 study in South Florida found that, compared to female arrestees who were not prostitutes, arrested prostitutes were statistically more likely to have tried "crack," other forms of cocaine, amphetamines, heroin, heroin mixed with cocaine, hallucinogens, and other combinations of drugs (Kuhns, Heide, and Silverman 1992). James Inciardi and colleagues (1993), however, noted a dramatic fall in street prostitution in Miami between the mid-1980s (heroin) and the late 1980s ("crack"), which they attributed to two factors: "crack"-using women were finding the economics of selling "crack" far preferable to prostitution, and women were afraid that "crack"-addicted customers would be violent and thus a more dangerous physical threat.

Because of mandatory sentencing, jails and prisons were becoming overcrowded with nonviolent drug offenders while more violent offenders were being released. In New York City, many drug treatment facilities, including Samaritan Village, Daytop Village, Odyssey House, Project Return, PROMESA, Inward House, Resurrection, El Regreso, New Hope Manor, and Veritas introduced a new approach, Drug Treatment Alternatives to Prison (DTAP) ("Charting New Directions" 1994).

One alternative program, designed for drug users considered likely to become increasingly involved with the criminal justice system, was Treatment Alternatives to Street Crime (TASC). This program, initiated in 1972, was functional at over one hundred sites in twenty-five states by 1993. It offered deferred prosecution, creative community sentencing, and pretrial intervention to suitable nonviolent offenders (Wellisch, Anglin, and Prendergast 1993). In the years 1990 to 1991, almost one-fifth of TASC clients were women. In both Illinois and New York, most of the women enrolled in the program were in their twenties and thirties: about three-quarters had one or more prior arrests and used cocaine as their drug of choice, although heroin and marijuana were also reported. Unfortunately, neither program tracked rates of recidivism and both used only "time in treatment" or "status at discharge" as an outcome measure to gauge success.

The innovative Key Extended Entry Program (KEEP), introduced at the Rikers Island prison facility in New York in 1987, provided methadone maintenance to incarcerated heroin addicts who volunteered for treatment (Magura, Rosenblum, and Joseph 1992). Between 1988 and 1990, women comprised one-third of the heroin addicts in the program. Although women injected drugs less frequently than men, they engaged in high-risk behavior that made them more susceptible to HIV infection. Women also reported a high level of criminal activity, averaging twenty-seven lifetime arrests for, most commonly, drug possession or shoplifting. Following discharge, 79 percent of the women reported to a community methadone program, yet attrition rates were high, and less than half were still attending the program after five months.

Another program that provided drug treatment to women referred by the criminal justice system was the California Drug Abuse Data System (CAL-DADS). During 1989–1990, CAL-DADS recorded the admission of almost 45,000 women to California treatment programs (Wellisch, Anglin, and Prendergast 1993). Cocaine use was reported by 40 percent of the women, heroin or amphetamine use by about 20 percent, and a smaller percentage had used marijuana/hashish and PCP (phencyclidine). Almost three-quarters of the CAL-DADS women entered outpatient drug-free programs, while less than 4 percent chose methadone maintenance. Assessing the value of the program was difficult because only 29 percent of the women "completed treatment successfully" (p. 13). A third such program, the Cornerstone program, introduced at the Oregon State Hospital in Salem in 1974, demonstrated that prerelease treatment for substance abuse had a positive effect on the postdischarge criminal activity of participants. Unfortunately, in 1989 only 5 percent of program enrollees were women (Field 1989).

Mothers and Children

The possible impact of maternal drug use on children once again became a convenient way to catch public attention. As in the early years of the century, women were blamed for children's perceived involvement in drugs. The press now implied—and even stated outright—that mothers who used drugs were incapable of exercising supervision over their young children. A series of high-profile newspaper articles and television news stories detailed the breakup of families because of drugs, and claimed that young children were now supporting multigenerational families by selling cocaine. The press seemed to be competing to see which newspaper would come up with the youngest offender in articles like "Family Court Judge Finds 10-Year-Old Did Sell Crack" (*New York Times,* February 2, 1989).

Drug-using women have come under virulent attack in their role as childbearers. Ira Chasnoff (1989) surveyed thirty-six mainly urban hospitals and reported that the prevalence of illicit drug use among pregnant women was about 11 percent, which would result in approximately 375,000 drug-exposed infants every year. Although other surveys (for example, Dicker and Leighton 1991) found much lower prevalence rates, from 37,000 to 100,000 drug-exposed infants, press coverage of the issue almost always quoted Chasnoff's higher figure. A NIDA report acknowledged, however, that "there are no accurate epidemiologic data to indicate if the numbers of pregnant, drug-abusing women are increasing or if the apparent upswing is caused by increased reporting and awareness of the problem" (Selden 1992: 194).

Other studies of individual cities revealed the same alarming increase in drug-exposed infant births. A Boston hospital reported that 17 percent of the women who gave birth at the hospital had used an illicit drug during pregnancy (Frank et al. 1988). A later survey (Zuckerman et al. 1989) at the same hospital found that 31 percent of pregnant women had used marijuana and 18 percent had used cocaine. In Philadelphia, an inner-city hospital found that 18 percent of the delivering mothers were using cocaine, and in Rhode Island, 7.5 percent of the mothers were using an illicit drug during pregnancy (*Maternal Drug Abuse and Drug Exposed Children: Understanding the Problem* 1992). The rate of births in New York City to mothers who reported drug use rose from about seven per thousand births in 1981 to just over thirty per thousand births in 1988 ("Maternal Drug Abuse-New York City" 1989). The startling increase was due in large part to cocaine. During the 1980s, the number of birth certificates reporting cocaine exposure rose twentyfold. In 1991 birth certificates in New York City alone listed illicit maternal drug use in 2.4 percent of all births ("Charting New Directions" 1994).

Whatever the true dimensions of the problem, clearly drug use during pregnancy was exacting a significant toll on women and children. In New York City, for example, maternal drug use during pregnancy was associated with a nearly threefold increase in infant mortality rates (deaths within the first year of life), from 13.1 per 1,000 births to 34 per 1,000 births. Much of this increase was due to the drug-associated increase in low birthweight rates (under five pounds, eight ounces), which quadrupled from 9 percent to 34 percent ("Maternal Drug Abuse—New York City" 1989). Other causes of drug-associated mortality, such as AIDS and Sudden Infant Death Syndrome (SIDS) contributed to increased death rates early in life (Kandall et al. 1993). In addition, drug-associated venereal diseases, such as congenital syphilis, which had almost been eradicated in the 1970s and early 1980s, began to be reported in exponentially increasing numbers ("Maternal Drug Abuse-New York City" 1989; Ricci, Fojaco, and O'Sullivan 1989).

Governmental Response

In 1992, the U.S. Department of Health and Human Services (HHS) articulated the federal government's major areas of concern about drugs and pregnancy: first, maternal drug use during pregnancy posed not only biological risks, such as low birthweight and prematurity, but also social risks, such as child abuse and neglect; second, it was difficult to bring drug-using mothers and their families into medical and social care systems; and third, the nation lacked both appropriate family-oriented policies and adequate facilities to provide effective services to these women and their children (*Maternal Drug Abuse and Drug Exposed Children: Understanding the Problem* 1992).

In response, HHS set forth a strategy that would guide federal efforts into the twenty-first century.

1. Research would continue on the nature and extent of maternal drug use, its biological and neurodevelopmental impact on the fetus, infant, and growing child, and effective intervention strategies. Federally funded NIDA clinical projects on the effects of intrauterine exposure to cocaine were being carried out in several locations, including Chicago, Miami, Philadelphia, and Seattle. Longitudinal studies on the impact of marijuana and marijuana-cigarette smoke were being funded in Pittsburgh and Ottawa, Canada. The National Institute on Child Health and Human Development (NICHD), in collaboration with NIDA, the Office for Treatment Improvement (OTI), and the Administration on Children, Youth and Families (ACYF), was sponsoring projects on licit drugs. In addition, the government set aside two million dollars in Fiscal Year 1991 for the NICHD to analyze these studies. NIDA was also supporting basic research intended to guide the clinical management of drug-using mothers and their children. Studies, frequently carried out in animals, looked at the role of naturally produced opioids (endorphins), endocrine function and sex-related behavior, fetal organ development, drug pharmacokinetics in pregnancy, cardiovascular effects, and the effects of drugs on sperm count and function.

2. A strong emphasis on prevention, intervention, and treatment for women and children would be put into place. Throughout the 1980s and into the 1990s, there was growing recognition that drug abuse among women was a complicated, multidimensional problem. But the appropriation of adequate funding for these women, strongly affected by the surge in "crack" cocaine use, disintegrating family structures, homelessness, and HIV-associated disease, was hampered in large measure by societal indifference, hostility, and criminal prosecution.

Recognition of the special needs of addicted women produced specific set-aside requirements in federally funded programs. Through the Alcohol, Drug Abuse and Mental Health Services (ADMS) block grant—funds passed to the states to serve target populations—Congress designated a 5 percent set-aside in Fiscal Year 1986 for women's alcohol and drug abuse services. In Fiscal Year 1989 this set-aside was raised to 10 percent for women's services, especially those for pregnant women and women with dependent children (*Maternal Drug Abuse and Drug Exposed Children: A Compendium of HHS Activities* 1992).

During the 1990s, addiction services were better integrated into the more general area of women's health, thus making it easier to capture funding dollars. In 1990 the Office of Research on Women's Health, under the acting directorship of Dr. Ruth Kirshstein and then Dr. Vivian Pinn, was opened as part of the National Institutes of Health. The mandate of the new office was to codify what was known about women's health, to indicate major gaps in knowledge, and to develop research priorities (for example, including women in clinical trials and promoting more women to leadership roles in women's health). In 1991 Dr. Loretta Finnegan, a pioneer in advocating treatment for drug-using women, became the Senior Advisor on Women's Issues for NIDA. In September 1994, a NIDA-sponsored conference in Virginia, "Drug Addiction Research and the Health of Women," dealt with women's addictions in the context of history, epidemiology, basic science, biology and behavior, etiology, treatment, prevention, intervention, legal issues, and the interests of defined groups, such as African American women, Hispanic women, Native American women, and lesbians.

In 1990, NIDA established a new program to stimulate basic and clinical research in medications development. Demonstration programs, such as the Emergency Child Abuse and Neglect Prevention Program and the Abandoned Infants Assistance Program, were also supported by the Administration for Children and Families (ACF). In a related effort, the assistant secretary for Planning and Evaluation in the Department of Health and Human Services studied the social needs of drug-using families, Medicaid expenditures, and the development of teacher training materials on substance abuse (*Maternal Drug Abuse and Drug Exposed Children: Understanding the Problem* 1992). NIDA also scheduled two technical reviews in the summer of 1990 to convene leading researchers and plot the direction of future research. In 1990, the Office of Substance Abuse Prevention (OSAP) sponsored the Conference on Alcohol and Drug Dependent Women and Their Children; the Forum on Issues Relating to Mandatory Treatment of Alcohol- and Drug-Dependent Women; two conferences for family court judges; the National Conference on Healthy Women, Pregnancies and Infants; the Issues Forum on Drug-Exposed Children; and conferences with the National Association on Perinatal Addiction Research and Education (*Maternal Drug Abuse and Drug Exposed Children: A Compendium of HHS Activities* 1992). In 1991 OSAP established the National Resource Center for the Prevention of Perinatal Alcohol and Other Drug Abuse.

By June 1994, the NIDA *Publications Catalog* ran to twenty-seven pages and included newsletters, community alert bulletins, capsules, technology transfer packages and videotapes, research monographs, clinical reports, service research monographs, and public education materials. Only a relatively small number of these publications focused entirely or even specifically on women, but these included four books entitled "Maternal Drug Abuse and Prenatal Effects"; two monographs, *Women and Drugs: A New Era for Research* and *Prenatal Drug Exposure: Kinetics and Dynamics;* a video, "Treatment Issues for Women"; and a pamphlet, *Women and Drug Abuse: You and Your Community Can Help.*

3. Monies would continue to flow to the states to fund prevention and treatment services for pregnant and parenting drug-using women. These efforts were carried out in a variety of ways within the Alcohol, Drug Abuse, and Mental Health Administration (ADAMHA). Since 1987, OSAP had administered a series of demonstration programs, including support for innovative approaches to drug prevention, treatment, and education; technical and evaluation assistance; community project support; and a national perinatal addiction prevention resource center. The Office for Treatment Improvement (OTI) had also operated demonstration projects, giving preferential treatment to pregnant and postpartum women under the Waiting Period Reduction Grants Program, which was funded in Fiscal Year 1989 but not in Fiscal Year 1992 (*Maternal Drug Abuse and Drug Exposed Children: A Compendium of HHS Activities* 1992). In addition, OTI and NIDA developed a series of treatment improvement protocols for drug-using mothers and their infants. Dr. Janet Mitchell (1993) chaired one consensus panel and I chaired the other (Kandall 1993).

The last fifteen years have brought considerable enlightenment about the needs of drug-using women who are pregnant or parenting or both. In 1993, Vivian Smith, the acting director for the Center for Substance Abuse Prevention, prefaced the Center's publication on the prevention of perinatal substance use with the compelling statement: "I do not believe there is any more important subject on our national agenda than the prevention of perinatal use and abuse of alcohol, tobacco, and other drugs" ("Toward Preventing Perinatal Abuse" 1993: v). It was clear that primary prevention programs should focus not simply on high-risk individuals but also on their social relationships and their environment. Because women were considered more relationship-oriented than men, those who did not enjoy the reinforcing benefits of being daughters, parents, partners, or friends were most vulnerable to beginning and continuing to use drugs. Primary prevention programs offered a way to break the intergenerational cycle of substance use within families.

Successful prevention incorporated a number of elements. Since pregnancy and birth offer a unique window into particular cultural, family, and religious rituals, prevention programs and evaluation methodologies had to reflect "cultural competence" (*Maternal Drug Abuse and Drug Exposed Children: Understanding the Problem* 1992). Prevention required expert professional training in emerging technical information and, more basically, in sensitivity to the potential barriers of culture and understanding between treatment personnel and patients. It also required improved management practices, an enlargement of system capacity, and better coordination between agencies.

When the delivery of services was tailored to specific populations, program retention and success rates improved. The Department of Health and Human Services strongly reiterated the need to provide "a comprehensive array of treatment services that address each woman's medical, psychological, emotional and practical needs." HHS focused on five areas: biological-physiological, psychological-behavioral-cognitive, sociocultural-demographic, mother-infant development, and early childhood development. Treatment providers could address these areas in a variety of settings: outpatient methadone maintenance clinics, outpatient drug-free clinics, inpatient comorbidity units, short-term or long-term residential facilities, or self-help groups. Recognizing the chronic relapsing nature of addiction and the probable need for more than one treatment modality, HHS stated that "whatever the setting(s), treatment for this population must be put into the context of a woman's reality" (p. 34).

In October 1988, Congress passed the Anti-Drug Abuse Act, which mandated a 20 percent set-aside for women's drug issues. Sections 509F and 509G authorized grants to public and private, and profit and nonprofit entities to fund demonstration model service delivery projects for substance-abusing pregnant and postpartum women and their infants. The Pregnant and Postpartum Women and Their Infants (PPWI) Demonstration Grant Program began funding in 1989. Through the end of 1993, with a budget totaling over 177 million dollars, the program awarded 147 grants in thirty-seven states and the District of Columbia, with the collaboration of the Alcohol, Drug Abuse and Mental Health Administration's (ADAMHA) Office of Substance Abuse Prevention (OSAP) and the Maternal and Child Health Bureau of the Health Resources and Service Administration (HRSA) ("Prevention of Perinatal Substance Use" 1993). It is ironic that, although the history of women and drug abuse stretched back a good century and a half, funders still sought only "demonstration projects," because "not enough is known about the approaches to warrant full-blown scientific testing."[6] Even in the late 1980s, the report acknowledged, most drug treatment programs "were not designed for women, especially pregnant women and mothers" (p. 2).

Although the PPWI executive summary released little data, it did acknowledge a measure of success in treating the target population. Evaluators determined that grantees had been highly successful in improving the coordination and accessibility of services to women. At least one-third of the women had reduced their substance use; babies born to mothers in PPWI programs tended to be healthy, especially if the mothers received prenatal care; and most of the babies who were assessed on follow-up showed normal development (p. 3). Recognizing the inherent value in coordinating comprehensive and easily accessible services, evaluators attributed the general success of the program to several factors: the culturally appropriate provision of child-care and parenting training; individual and group single-sex therapy to help women cope with abuse, low self-esteem, and depression; physical and social supports, such as home visits and transportation aid; educational and vocational guidance; and family services such as family counseling. In addition, women benefited from prenatal care, obstetrical care, labor and delivery services, postpartum care, and general medical services. The programs were somewhat less successful in providing infants with developmental screening, medical assessment, sensory stimulation, infant massage therapy, and routine neonatal medical care. At the same time, reflecting the frustrations and failures that had come to characterize decades of less-than-comprehensive treatment efforts, the PPWI program acknowledged that almost two-thirds of the grantees had experienced client drop-out, relapse, arrest, and homelessness; more than half had reported that women were still overwhelmed by the day-to-day struggles of life and frequently missed appointments; and 40 percent still lacked adequate resources to meet their clients' needs.

Another major NIDA initiative in the area of perinatal addiction was the creation of the "Perinatal 20" sponsored by the Research Demonstration Program under authorization by the 1988 Anti-Drug Abuse Act, which funded ten centers in 1989 and the remaining ten in 1990. The organizers of the initiative recognized that merely establishing a program did not guarantee that women would use it. To evaluate the effectiveness of various strategies for improving enrollment, retention, and outcome in treating pregnant women and mothers with children, the initiative awarded treatment research demonstration grants. These programs, either comprehensive in nature or targeted to assess the effectiveness of a specific, well-defined therapeutic intervention, were designed to assess various short-term and long-term treatment modalities, including drug detoxification and methadone maintenance. The preliminary results of the "Perinatal 20" study, which had cost about a hundred million dollars, were presented at the July 1994 Resourcelink 3 Conference sponsored by the Center for Substance Abuse Prevention. According to study findings, funded programs were treating primarily cocaine abuse (55 percent) in women who were largely African American (about 75 percent), had no jobs (over 75 percent), had not graduated from high school (over

65 percent), and were single (over 85 percent) (*Maternal Drug Abuse and Drug Exposed Children: Understanding the Problem* 1992).

4. *The child welfare system would be improved to better serve the needs of drug-using women and their children.* Reports of child abuse and neglect had increased dramatically, from 60,000 cases in 1974 to 1.1 million in 1980 to 2.4 million in 1990. These reports had a signficant impact on foster care placements in the United States, which rose by roughly 50,000 in two years, from about 282,000 in 1986 to about 330,000 in 1988 (*Maternal Drug Abuse and Drug Exposed Children: Understanding the Problem* 1992). Both trends were closely tied to the "crack" cocaine epidemic, which began in the mid-1980s. Two of the states hardest hit by the increase in drug usage, California and New York, also were the hardest hit by the increasing demand for foster care. From 1986 to 1989, the foster care population rose by 41 percent in California and by 98 percent in New York. Other states, such as Georgia, found that substance abuse was associated with 50 percent to 60 percent of all referrals of children to protective services (Neims 1990). This development had occurred despite the passage of the Adoption Assistance and Child Welfare Act in 1980, which emphasized the importance of keeping families together both prior to placement and through early reunification.

In 1991 the Administration for Children and Families (ACF) undertook a renewed initiative: to put children first, to build and preserve families, to construct "communities of concern" around children and families, and to insure early steps toward termination of parental rights and adoption when family unification proved impossible (*Maternal Drug Abuse and Drug Exposed Children: Understanding the Problem* 1992: 49). These goals were carried out through model projects, cross-disciplinary training programs, resource development projects, early intervention programs, and Pediatric AIDS Demonstration Centers. Specific services targeting drug-exposed children included the Emergency Child Abuse and Neglect Prevention Program, which awarded ninety-four grants in Fiscal Year 1991, and the Temporary Child Care for Children with Disabilities and Crisis Nurseries Program, which awarded 122 grants in forty-six states between 1988 and 1992. Monies also became available through the Social Services Block Grant, Child Welfare State Grants, Child Abuse and Neglect State Grants, the Criminal Justice Grant Program, Campus Treatment Projects, the Target Cities Programs, the Critical Populations Grants Program, and Family Violence State Grants. In addition, ACF provided foster care and adoption assistance and supported drug abuse prevention efforts among runaway and homeless youth, youth gangs, and Head Start families, funding forty centers in Fiscal Year 1990 and Fiscal Year 1991.

As in other areas, these projects yielded a number of useful initiatives. States applying for federal dollars were required to develop effective screening programs in order to respond quickly to reports of child abuse. Many states explored and supported expedited or "fast-track" adoption. Throughout the country state agencies developed and adopted risk assessment models for children. Case management, although not a new concept, became more widely used in meeting the complex needs of drug-using mothers and their children. Other important developments included the provision of comprehensive or colocated services in a "one-stop shopping" model; programs allowing mother and child to remain together in residential treatment settings; specialized foster care capabilities, with differential payment schedules; family preservation services, with home-based service provisions; and respite services for stress reduction.

5. *Medical insurance and disability income would be provided for eligible women and their children.* Building on the basic services provided by Medicaid, a federal Title IX Program of the Social Security Act, the Health Care Financing Administration sponsored a series of waiver demonstrations (Improving Access to Care for Pregnant Substance Abusers) in 1992, which allowed five states to offer services for pregnant women. In addition, payment under the Social Security Disability Insurance (SSDI) Title II Program, or under the Supplemental Security Income (SSI) Title XVI Program, would be available to substance-using mothers and their children.

AIDS-related service grants were another source of services for substance-using women. By September 1993, women constituted slightly over 40,000 (12 percent) of the approximately 333,000 diagnosed cases of AIDS in the United States. By mid-1994, AIDS had become the fourth leading cause of death among women of childbearing age. More than 28,000 (70 percent) of the over 40,000 AIDS cases among women were drug-related: nearly 37 percent were related to heterosexual contact and 55 percent were acquired through sexual contact with an intravenous drug user ("Women and Drug Abuse" 1994). Studies in Chicago in the late 1980s revealed that female intravenous drug use led to an 8 percent seroconversion rate for every year of continued use (Weibel et al. 1990). Women's use of "crack" cocaine increased their risk of acquiring HIV by a factor of 10.6, and prostitution by a factor of more than 12; a "crack"-using prostitute had a fourteenfold chance of being HIV-positive (Chiasson et al. 1991). At the same time, studies also showed that HIV-positive women were less able to get access to care (Rich 1992), and that men were three times more likely than women to be offered AZT treatment (Stein et al. 1991). Reduced access to care as well as fear of disclosure of HIV status (Rich 1992) and other lifestyle factors may have contributed to the finding that drug-using women from minority groups tended to have courses of HIV infection that were shorter and more rapidly fatal (Rothenberg et al. 1987). Ironically, in New York State African American women made up 52 percent and Hispanic women 31 percent of AIDS cases according to New York State AIDS Institute data.

The Office of Research on Women's Health (ORWH) realized that women were being excluded from clinical trials of useful, even potentially life-saving drugs. The reasons given ranged from claims that female hormonal changes might confound research results, study populations would be less homogeneous, study costs would be higher if sex-specific differences had to be analyzed separately, and recruitment of women would be more difficult, to fears that treatment of pregnant women would invoke the issue of fetal safety and the potentially competing interests of mother and child. In response it created a task force to insure that women would be fairly represented in clinical trials and that barriers to reasonable participation would be removed. In March 1993 the ORWH held a public hearing to focus attention on barriers to women's inclusion in clinical studies and in July convened a conference in Bethesda, Maryland, to address the issue. The prestigious Institute of Medicine recommended that women, especially those of child-bearing age, be included in clinical trials of new medications and therapies, a recommendation that moved from policy into public law. In the early 1990s, at one of their technical reviews, NIDA also addressed the question of inclusion of drug-using women in research trials.[7]

This last point became critically important in 1994, when the findings of the NIH-sponsored clinical trial of the antiviral agent zidovudine (AZT) with HIV-positive pregnant women—and subsequently their newborns—were released. Once the nation's blood supply had become "cleaner" and essentially free of HIV contamination, mother-to-infant transmission was cited to explain increases in pediatric AIDS. By 1993, 88 percent of all pediatric HIV transmission was linked to mothers, either during pregnancy, at the time of birth, or through breast-feeding after birth (National Institute on Drug Abuse 1994). By the end of 1994, 95 percent of all cases of pediatric AIDS in New York State were being attributed to perinatal HIV transmission from an infected mother (*Clinical Guidelines for the Use of Zidovudine Therapy in Pregnancy to Reduce Perinatal Transmission of HIV* 1994). The major contributing factors were the mother's intravenous drug use with contaminated needles or "works" (44 percent) or unprotected sex with an intravenous drug user (20 percent). The large clinical trial showed that treating the women with zidovudine from the fourteenth to the thirty-fourth week of pregnancy and continuing zidovudine treatment in their infants for six weeks after birth reduced the rate of HIV transmission from about 25 percent to about 8 percent, a 67.5 percent relative reduction in transmission risk (Centers for Disease Control and Prevention 1994).

In addition to a number of specific projects dealing with the AIDS risk to children of intravenous drug users or their sexual partners, NIDA supported two large projects that dealt specifically with pregnant women and their children (Breitbart et al. 1994). By Fiscal Year 1990, the Maternal and Child Health Bureau of the Health Resources and Services Administration (HRSA), and the Children's Bureau of the Administration for Children and Families through its Pediatric AIDS Health Care Demonstration Grant Program, were providing financial support to thirty-three programs studying how to prevent HIV acquisition and provide specialized services. Organizers of a 1993 conference on those "model" programs taking on the issue of perinatal HIV transmission identified twenty-three nationwide. The directors of the eight programs selected to participate[8] identified some of the difficulties they encountered in attempting to provide comprehensive services to mothers (usually drug-addicted) and their children, including problems in funding; institutional prejudice against caring for HIV-positive women; negative, judgmental attitudes among health professionals; regulatory constraints imposed by the criminal justice or child protective systems; and patient advocacy efforts, which consumed valuable clinical service time.

Thus, during the 1980s and into the early 1990s there was an impressive increase in federal programs geared specifically to substance-using mothers. Within the Public Health Service, branches of the Alcohol, Drug Abuse and Mental Health Administration (National Institute on Drug Abuse, National Institute on Alcohol Abuse and Alcoholism, Office of Substance Abuse Prevention, Office for Treatment Improvement), the National Institute on Child Health and Human Development, and the Health Resources and Service Administration all initiated and supported specific programs for this population. These efforts were bolstered by programs run by the Office of the Assistant Secretary for Health and by the Administration on Children and Families (Administration on Children, Families, and Youth, Administration for Native Americans, and Administration on Developmental Disabilities) and elsewhere in the Department of Health and Human Services (Health Care Financing Administration, Social Security Administration). Other related programs included the Office of Substance Abuse Prevention's Communication Grants, the National Clearinghouse for Alcohol and Drug Information, and the Community Partnership, as well as three migrant worker health programs run by Health Resources and Service Administration. At last women's long struggle with drugs was the focus of public attention.

But despite the expansion of treatment opportunities, need always exceeded available resources, and many drug-using women remained in desperate straits. They faced obstacles in locating drug treatment programs as well as in entering and remaining in treatment. As Beth Glover Reed (1985) pointed out in the *International Journal of Addictions,* although women comprised more than half of the general population, and by some estimates would have constituted more than half of the patients in drug treatment if barriers to access did not exist, they were still considered a "special population" when the issue was drug policy. Somehow overlooking the rise of the Women's Movement, supported by many other self-help initiatives of the 1970s—such as the Black Power movement, the Civil Rights movement, and Gay Liberation, as well as the antipoverty, homeless, and youth movements—American society still tended to view addiction as a male problem.

As a result, only a small fraction of drug treatment programs in the mid-1980s had female directors, and most of them were in charge of programs designed specifically for women. This gender imbalance—

the underrepresentation of women in treatment and the relative absence of women in leadership positions—served to perpetuate a male-focused treatment agenda. Yet research was better defining core services for women, including health services, vocational training, legal aid, childcare services, family services, training in basic coping skills, drug education, and counseling options, which led to the development of programs and funding (Reed 1985).

That programs for women existed, however, did not guarantee that addicted women would be able to overcome their sense of shame and guilt, both self and societally imposed, to avail themselves of treatment services. Many could have echoed one woman's comment: "I mean I just don't care. I feel worthless so I look like I feel . . . I feel ugly. I feel skinny. I mean, you know, worthless" (Wenger and Rosenbaum 1994: 3). Likewise, women continued to find themselves in male-dominated, sexist "therapeutic settings," where voyeurism, ridicule, or unwanted sexual advances, quite clearly counterproductive to treatment goals, occurred. Recognizing this fact, Reed (1985) recommended that treatment programs develop "explicit" sexual harassment policies in order to protect female addicts. In addition, the classic model of "addiction as disease" promoted addicts' dependency on caregivers and healers, gave a great deal of authority to professionals, and deflected attention from women's multidimensional needs to the more limited issue of disease treatment.

Although Reed argued for all-female as well as mixed-gender programs, she also noted the need for an awareness of cross-gender ethnic interactions and of how the status of women (compared to that of men) affected the treatment dynamic. Other researchers singled out age as an important variable in designing appropriate treatment strategies. In a study of 1,776 adult, predominantly white Midwestern women, Patricia Harrison and Carol Belille (1987) found that women under thirty who were in treatment were more likely to be members of a racial minority, unemployed, undereducated, dependent on public welfare programs, and restless and depressed.

Many feminist activists felt that positive developments were occurring too slowly. As Elizabeth Ettore wrote, "the situations and needs of women were largely unacknowledged and unrecognized within both the treatment and the research world" (1992: 17). In fact, Ettore viewed the study of female addiction as a "non-field." Treatment programs for women with special needs—black women, lesbians, medical professionals, incarcerated women, and those serving in the military—were rudimentary or nonexistent.

When women tried to find help, many could not gain access to treatment programs. One researcher found that of seventy-eight treatment programs surveyed in New York City in the late 1980s, 54 percent excluded pregnant women, 67 percent denied care to pregnant women on Medicaid, and 87 percent refused to treat pregnant Medicaid patients who were using "crack" cocaine (Chavkin 1990). New York City, the epicenter of the drug problem in America, did not establish the Parent and Child Enrichment Program (PACE), its first comprehensive, community-based program for pregnant substance abusers, until 1990 (*New York Times,* December 17, 1990). One of the ironies of the Jennifer Johnson case in Florida was that Johnson had unsuccessfully sought drug treatment during her pregnancy. In the early 1990s, only four of forty-seven non-hospital-based treatment programs accepted women, and Boston had only fifteen residential treatment beds for drug-dependent women (Brown 1992).

In interviews with seventy San Francisco heroin addicts unable to find drug treatment, one-third of whom were women, Lynn Wenger and Marsha Rosenbaum (1994) found that lack of money was the major hindrance to getting into methadone treatment programs. Such financial barriers were the result of the Reagan administration's decision to transfer federal dollars to the states in the form of block grants. Because of this realignment in funding, overall spending on drug treatment was reduced, and private fee-for-service methadone treatment programs replaced federally funded programs. As several of the female interviewees commented, "If you're poor and you're a junkie, forget it," and "They want you to come out with a couple hundred bucks in a couple weeks or something. That amount is just too much." In addition, the waiting-list process was found to be "time-consuming, cumbersome, complicated, and at times demeaning." One woman seeking treatment found that the wait for treatment in the San Francisco area ranged from sixteen to eighteen months, and Wenger and Rosenbaum confirmed this information in conversations with the Community Substance Abuse Services of San Francisco and five methadone clinics. In summarizing the national situation in 1992, Ellen Weber concluded that "appropriate drug and alcohol prevention and treatment services for all women, particularly pregnant women, have been grossly inadequate" (1992: 349). As late as 1995, inadequate financial resources, social isolation, and medical illness continued to keep drug-using women from entering treatment (Nelson-Zlupko, Kauffman, and Dore 1995).

Prescription Drugs

The emerging female drug problem of the 1950s, women's overuse of prescription drugs, continued unabated into the 1990s. According to the National Institute on Drug Abuse, in 1992 more than 1.3 million women had taken prescription drugs (sedatives, tranquilizers, stimulants, or analgesics) for a nonmedical purpose during the previous month ("Women and Drug Abuse" 1994). In 1994, NIDA reported that 3.7 million women had taken prescription drugs nonmedically during the previous year. Large numbers of women were functioning productively in the workforce, but some took medication in order to deal with work-related pressures and others turned to psychotropic medications to cope with the depression associated with their domestic role, limited economic opportunities, financial pressures, or double workload as homemaker and employee. As studies showed, women sought treatment for emotional problems more frequently than men, and they received psychiatric diagnoses between 1.5 and 3.6 times more frequently than men. Women continued to be overrepresented among patients diagnosed with depression, anxiety, and panic attacks. Elderly women, for example, comprised 11 percent of the population but 25 percent of those who used prescription drugs. Nonetheless, the use of these medications retained a "legal" imprimatur, and the pharmaceutical industry pursued its active marketing strategy, which had afforded historically high profits to stockholders.

An underlying assumption of the prescribing practices of many physicians was the belief that women were innately "neurotic." Tranquilizers and sedatives were considered appropriate for "her" while heroin retained its image as a man's drug (Ettore 1992). From a feminist standpoint, women's use of tranquilizers was consistent with society's dual expectation that they be "good girls" *and* "follow the doctor's orders." Women using these drugs were thus "dependent" in a socially acceptable way on "women's drugs" and on male doctors. Unlike female heroin users, these women could maintain their feminine identity without "defiling" or "polluting" their bodies.

Prosecution of Pregnant Addicts

During the Reagan-Bush "war on drugs" of the 1980s, someone came up with a new strategy toward pregnant substance users (Paltrow 1990; Daniels 1993). This unprecedented strategy called for the prosecution of pregnant addicts under state criminal statutes involving child endangerment, assault with a deadly weapon, and the delivery of a controlled substance to a minor. Although these statutes had never been intended to apply in this particular situation, by September 1994 over two hundred women in twenty-four states had been prosecuted for drug-related behavior during pregnancy. This new "punitive" approach arose at a time when two highly controversial issues—the proper focus of the "war on drugs" (reducing supply, reducing demand, or both) and women's reproductive options—were being hotly debated. The prosecutorial attack on pregnant women went forward despite many forceful arguments against the validity and social usefulness of this kind of adversarial strategy. At issue (and many of these topics have already been discussed in these chapters in various contexts) were the involuntary nature of drug addiction; Supreme Court precedents condemning the criminalization of addiction; the unique characteristics of addiction in women; the lack of reasonable access to drug rehabilitation for pregnant women; the discriminatory impact of this policy on minority women of lower socioeconomic status because of biased testing and reporting policies; the acknowledged futility of jailing pregnant addicts for either treatment or deterrence; and the failure to acknowledge and address the complex social matrix, including poverty, physical and sexual abuse, and incest, that was known to influence addictive behavior.

Many major public health organizations in fact condemned these prosecutions, including the American Medical Association, the American Public Health Association, the American Academy of Pediatrics, the American Nurses Association, the American Society of Addiction Medicine, the Center for the Future of Children, the Coalition on Alcohol and Drug Dependent Women and Their Children, the March of Dimes, the National Association of Public Child Welfare Administrators, the National Council on Alcoholism and Drug Dependence, and the Association of Family and Conciliation Courts. Yet a number of states still chose to prosecute women for drug use during pregnancy.

These prosecutions were aided by court officials sympathetic to a conservative social agenda. When President Clinton took office, 70 percent of the sitting federal judges and five of the nine Supreme Court justices were Reagan or Bush appointees (*Newsweek*, March 29, 1993). Although some aggressive prosecutors claimed that they wanted to "scare women into treatment" rather than actually send them to jail, the nationwide publicity only fueled hostility toward these women.

The issue of fetal rights had first surfaced in 1954 in Wyoming in *State v. Osmus:* a woman whose infant was found dead a few days after birth was convicted of manslaughter. In that case, the Wyoming Supreme Court overturned the conviction, ruling that the state's criminal neglect statute could not be applied to a woman's prenatal conduct (276 P.2d 469 [Wyo. 1954]). In 1977 Margaret Velasquez Reyes, a Latina, was prosecuted under California's child endangerment statute for allegedly using heroin and giving birth to allegedly addicted twin boys. As in *Osmus*, the higher Appeals Court dismissed the action on the grounds that the statute was not intended to encompass prenatal behavior (75 Cal. App. 3d 214, 219 [1977]). All subsequent prosecutions occurred after 1987. The cases were widely distributed across the states, including New York, Massachusetts, Connecticut, Virginia, South Carolina, Kentucky, Florida, Texas, Michigan, Nevada, and California, but a disproportionate number of prosecutions occurred in either Florida or South Carolina.

Prosecutors had suffered judicial rebuffs in both *Osmus* and *Reyes*, but in the mid-1980s the public mood began to change and some concluded that a prosecutorial approach might succeed. In 1985, following the delivery of a severely brain-damaged son who died within six weeks of birth, Pamela Rae Stewart, a white drug user, was arrested and charged under a California criminal child support statute. Ms. Stewart was cited for "failure to follow her doctor's advice to stay off her feet, to refrain from sexual intercourse, refrain from taking street drugs, and to seek immediate attention, if she experienced difficulties with pregnancy." With the exception of street drug use, none of the other cited behavior was illegal in itself, and in 1987 the San Diego Municipal Court dismissed all charges against Ms. Stewart, because, it concluded, California's criminal child support statute was not intended to apply to the actions of a pregnant woman (*People v. Stewart*, No. M508197, slip op. Cal. Mun. Ct., Feb. 26, 1987).

Ignoring these judicial setbacks, prosecutors continued to bring similar suits, usually against cocaine-addicted minority women. Many of these women—Geraldyne Grubbs in a 1989 Alaska case, Roberta Christenson in a 1990 South Dakota case, and Oneaver Hart in a 1991 Mississippi case—chose to plea bargain and were incarcerated under lesser charges. As prosecutions increased nationally, at least one woman resorted to another means of escaping criminal prosecution, namely, abortion. In a 1992 case in North Dakota, *State v. Greywind,* Martina Greywind was charged with endangering her fetus through paint sniffing. She obtained an abortion twelve days later, and charges against her were dropped since, as the prosecutor noted, it was "no longer worth the time or expense to prosecute her." In virtually every case in which a woman and her attorney challenged the legal basis for her prosecution, such as the 1991 Michigan case *People v. Hardy* (469 N.W.2d 50, 52–53 [Mich. App. 1991]) and the 1992 Ohio case *State v. Gray* (584 N.E.2d 710, 713 [Ohio 1992]), all or most of the charges were dropped.

The most dramatic and highly publicized of these state prosecutions was the 1989 Florida action brought against Jennifer Johnson. Judge O. H. Eaton, Jr., issued the country's first criminal conviction of a mother under a drug trafficking statute. In finding that Ms. Johnson had "delivered drugs" to her newborn infant through the umbilical cord in the approximately ninety seconds between delivery and the clamping of the cord, Judge Eaton skirted a 1984 Florida precedent, which held that a fetus is not a person for purposes of the battery statute. In July 1989, Ms. Johnson was convicted and sentenced to one year in a treatment program (which she had requested during her pregnancy and had begun after her delivery) and fourteen years of probation. Ms. Johnson was also ordered to perform two hundred hours of community service, was to be placed under court-supervised prenatal care if she became pregnant again, and was forbidden to go to bars, use drugs or alcohol, or associate with people who used drugs or alcohol. On appeal, the Florida Appellate Court upheld the lower court finding, the two male judges voting to uphold and the one female judge voting to overturn the judgment. In 1992, however, the Florida Supreme Court unanimously overturned Ms. Johnson's conviction on the grounds that the legislature had never intended the drug delivery statute to be used in this situation. In its ruling, the court strongly condemned the practice of "creatively" using existing statutes to criminalize behavior not plainly addressed by the law: "The Court declines the State's invitation to walk down a path that the law, public policy, and common sense forbid it to tread" (602 So. 2d 1288, 1297 [Fla. 1992]).

Despite four state supreme court cases, *Hardy, Gray, Johnson,* and the 1993 Kentucky case *Welch v. Commonwealth* (No. 92-SC-490-DG, slip op. Ky. [Sept. 30, 1993]), which rejected the prosecution of pregnant substance-using women, harassment continued. The most recent activity occurred in South Carolina, where by September 1994, over 250 women had faced various charges related to drug use during pregnancy. The identification of a positive toxicology in the infant of a drug-using mother led to the "Sophie's choice" of mandatory drug treatment (little of which existed) or jail. Although the state Department of Health and Human Services had begun an investigation of potential discrimination in policies governing the reporting of drug-exposed infants at the Medical University of South Carolina, on April 21, 1994, the South Carolina House Ways and Means Committee approved SB 155, a bill that would allow the criminal prosecution of a woman for child abuse based on her newborn infant's positive urine toxicology. In September, however, the hospital, which served disadvantaged minority women, the police, and the public prosecutor agreed to abandon prejudicial reporting of urine toxicologies. A bill pending in the state Senate Finance Committee in February 1995, however, would allow physicians to test newborns' urine without consent and would mandate reporting of positive urine toxicologies.[9]

Similar prosecutorial activity has continued in other states as well. In June 1993, the Center for Reproductive Law and Policy filed an *amicus* brief in defense of a California woman charged with murder for the premature birth and subsequent death of her baby because she allegedly used drugs during pregnancy. In February 1994, an Indiana Superior Court judge dismissed charges of reckless homicide against a woman who allegedly took drugs during pregnancy. The judge was persuaded to proceed with possession charges, however, and the state indicated that it would appeal the homicide decision. Also in February, the Pittsburgh District of the Superior Court of Pennsylvania dismissed charges of delivery of a controlled substance, reckless endangerment, and child endangerment brought against a woman who allegedly used drugs during pregnancy.

In March 1994, the Judiciary Committee of the Nebraska legislature defeated LB 1148, which would have amended "abuse" or "ne-glect" to include prenatal exposure to a controlled substance. In 1994, the Nebraska legislature rejected an attempt to extend an existing law permitting civil actions for wrongful deaths to include a viable fetus (LB 921). In Washington state, the deadline for full senate considera-tion of SB 6181, permitting criminal prosecution for the murder of a viable fetus, passed without action in March 1994. In June 1994 in Rhode Island, the house judiciary committee rejected SB 2253, already adopted by the senate, which would have amended child protection laws to make a positive blood or urine test in a newborn for a schedule I controlled substance prima facie evidence of child abuse and ne-glect.[10] In September 1994, a California woman was convicted of child endangerment and narrowly escaped a murder conviction when her two-month-old child died, allegedly from a methamphetamine over-dose delivered through her breast milk. Despite expert testimony that the amount of the drug passed through the milk was minuscule and incapable of causing the death, and that the infant likely died of Sudden Infant Death Syndrome, the mother is now serving a six-year prison term (*New York Times*, September 11, 1994). In December 1994, a Texas Court of Appeals overturned a woman's lower court conviction for reckless injury to a child caused by cocaine use during pregnancy. As of February 1995, similar prosecutions were proceeding in Arizona and Mississippi. In October 1995 the Wisconsin Court of Appeals ruled by two to one that a pregnant woman could be invol-untarily detained for inpatient substance abuse treatment.[11]

In a policy paper, the National Women's Law Center also expressed concern about the "informal practice of judges increasing a criminal penalty in unrelated criminal charges because the female defendant is pregnant and has a drug history" (Smith 1991: 3). The Center pointed to the District of Columbia case of Brenda Vaughan, who was incar-cerated rather than placed on probation for a first-offense theft charge because she was pregnant and tested positive for cocaine. The Center also noted that the judge in the Vaughan case "routinely sentences pregnant adult and juvenile women to periods of incarceration if they test positive for drugs" (p. 4).

Although the issue of prosecution of pregnant substance users im-pinges on a number of constitutional issues, it evoked the most protest from women's groups, especially those seeking to protect the rights of minority women. Over 80 percent of the cases brought to prosecution involved women of color, specifically African American women. Poor and minority women frequently depended on public hospitals and clinics for their medical and reproductive care, and these were subject to a greater degree of governmental surveillance. Drug use crosses all racial, ethnic, and socioeconomic lines, but women of color are disproportionately subjected to testing for possible drug use and reporting of positive results. The prejudicial nature of this practice was made clear in a study from Pinellas County, Florida (Chasnoff, Landress, and Barrett 1990). The study found no difference between private and clinic populations, or between black and white women, in the prevalence of drug use, but black women were approximately ten times more likely than white women to be reported to health authorities.

Along with criminal prosecution, pregnant addicts also faced civil sanctions, most commonly loss of custody of their children. As of September 1994, nine states mandated the reporting of positive urine toxicologies. In fact, when prosecutorial attacks on pregnant substance-using women are beaten back, punitive efforts in many states have been rechanneled into attempts to remove their children using mechanisms established by Child Protective Services. This penalty is devastating to these women, who often have suffered and continue to suffer physical and sexual abuse, and for whom having and raising children is their most important source of affirmation and their sole source of self-esteem. The removal of children from a woman who has used cocaine or heroin has been viewed as peremptory and arbitrary, since arguably, prenatal exposure to alcohol and cigarette smoke poses equal or greater risks to the child. Fear of criminal sanctions can drive pregnant women away from the health care system and thus further compromise pregnancy outcome. Mandated reporting of drug use imposes barriers between women and health professionals and makes the free exchange of important medical information less likely. In addition, placement in foster care has been shown to be an inadequate and often disastrous response to the problem. Foster care, which can involve serial placements within the first few years of a child's life, does not offer the stability children need. They might be better nurtured within a biological family.

The punitive approach to the pregnant addict has deterred many women from seeking prenatal care (Chavkin 1990). Fifteen of eighteen programs receiving federal grant money to support demonstration projects for pregnant drug-dependent women and their children concluded that the threat of punitive action was preventing women from seeking needed services (Weber 1992).

Although the social agenda of the 1980s and early 1990s came to be written largely by conservative administrations intent on reducing the size of government, redistributing wealth to those already more fortunate than most, and restricting women's reproductive options, a great deal was accomplished for drug-addicted women. In the face of budgetary restrictions, which stripped down drug treatment programs, simplistic slogans suggesting that it is easy to "say no" to drugs, legal prosecution of drug-using women of color, and bellicose pronouncements that the "war on drugs" could be won by applying "supply-side economics," many diverse, if inadequate, programs were initiated to help addicted women.

Perhaps these efforts developed from the residual substrate of liberalism, the Great Society of the 1960s, which gave evidence of a more collective sense of responsibility for the plight of fellow citizens. Harking back to the nineteenth century, certainly "helpless women" and "innocent children" would appear to qualify for this modest show of support. Some might say that agencies such as the National Institute on Drug Abuse had recognized this need since their inception in the early 1970s, and speaking now with the voice of full maturity and reason, infused with a note of passion drawn from the Women's Movement, were making themselves heard. The more cynical would say that these initiatives were strictly self-serving, emanating from the feared and actual horror of AIDS and drugs spreading from drug-infested city ghettoes into middle America.

Whatever the reason, drug-using women found themselves in the middle of the ideological battleground, demeaned, vilified, prosecuted, and incarcerated on the one hand and supported and comprehensively treated on the other. Meanwhile, the drug epidemic spread.

eleven

TODAY AND TOMORROW

The use—and abuse—of addictive drugs in American society is a problem as old as the Republic. For the most part unaware of their long-term dangers, nineteenth-century physicians and pharmacists freely dispensed opium, laudanum, and morphine in many forms, and Americans came to rely on these opiates as the "miracle drugs" of their age in treating ills of the body and the mind. Patent medicine manufacturers, mass circulation magazines, and mail-order catalogues brought opiate-laden "cures" to the most remote towns and farmsteads. As long as drug users, whether opiate addicts or "cocainists," were "acceptable" members of mainstream American society, their drug habit was tolerated. When the number of addicted users grew, however, and, more important, when the idealized image of Victorian womanhood was threatened as drugs spread into "socially unacceptable" ethnoracial groups, national drug policy changed. Despite notable exceptions—the drug maintenance clinics (1919–1923), the "federal farms" at Lexington and Fort Worth (1935–early 1970s), methadone maintenance programs (introduced in the 1960s), and the more recent treatment initiatives of the 1980s and 1990s—restrictive legislative approaches aimed at controlling and eliminating drug use have held sway. Over the decades, these control measures have included anti-opium legislation (1875), anti-cocaine legislation (beginning in Oregon in 1887), a ban on imports of smoking opium (1909), the Harrison Act (1914) and subsequent Supreme Court decisions (1919), the Narcotic Drugs Import and Export Act (1922), the Uniform Narcotics Act (1932), the Marijuana Tax Act (1937), the Boggs Act (1951), the Narcotic Control Act (1956), the Drug Abuse Control Amendments (1965), the Comprehensive Drug Abuse Prevention and Control Act (1970), and the Anti-Drug Abuse Act (1988). The last of these initiatives, playing to a public audience, stated somewhat grandiosely: "It is the declared policy of the United States Government to create a Drug-Free America by 1995."

Other contemporary societies, including some European countries and Australia, have accepted the inevitability of drug use and planned public policy accordingly. The United States, however, ignoring or denying its past history, turned up the volume on "zero tolerance" rhetoric. A "drug czar" and a catchy slogan ("Just Say No") on banners, on media posters, and in public pronouncements, formed the centerpiece of the "war on drugs." About 70 percent of the federal drug-fighting budget continued to flow into efforts to reduce the incoming supply of illegal drugs. Privately, however, the administration acknowledged that the enforcement strategy, operative for sixty years, had failed. The growing demand for drugs created by urbanization and economic dislocation could easily be supplied by international cartels using modern transportation methods. Despite sensational newspaper headlines announcing drug seizures, traffickers could simply develop new transport lines and transfer centers when established ones were closed down or disrupted. Thus, they shifted to Nigeria for heroin and to Brazil, Vancouver, and Mexico for cocaine. In a move reminiscent of Operation Intercept in 1969, the federal government was recently reported to be planning another antidrug campaign on the Mexican border (*New York Times*, February 24, 1995). Yet public figures such as William F. Buckley, Jr., former Secretary of State George Schultz, Baltimore Mayor Kurt Schmoke, federal court judges, and columnists such as Max Frankel (see *New York Times Magazine*, December 18, 1994) whose political leanings range from right to left, have concluded that the "war on drugs" is "unwinnable." As the historian Howard Zinn has written, what is needed is nothing short of "a transformation of national priorities" (1980: 577).

To analyze what has become an issue of immense and complex dimensions, I propose a simple but concrete analogy. Let us suppose that the problem of drugs in America is like an inflating balloon. As the balloon has filled up, society's approach has been to squeeze the balloon forcibly in an attempt to deflate it. But without a coherent or effective strategy for reducing the flow of air into the balloon, this tactic has only succeeded in redistributing the air under increasing pressure: squeezing one part of the balloon has simply forced air into another part of the balloon. In terms of drug policy, "squeezing" opium led to more dangerous opiates like morphine and heroin in the early years of the century and to barbiturate use during the Second World War; "squeezing" amphetamines led to cocaine; "squeezing" marijuana led to LSD, and so on. It is a pyrrhic victory at best if the arrest of a Colombian cocaine baron causes a rise in the price of cocaine in New York City and thus a shift to more heroin use (*New York Times,* September 15, 1995).

For what they are worth, government statistics indicate that some progress may have been made in the 1980s in reducing the total consumption of illicit drugs in America. If this decrease is real, however, its impact has been almost nonexistent in the socially marginalized subpopulation of "hard-core" addicts. Although the government has claimed success for its continued pressure on imports and its punitive response to drug use, the reduction was more likely due to the gradual education of the middle class, since declining demand was most apparent in the "reachable" parts of the population. Government hubris should also be tempered by the yearly rise in drug use among teenagers between 1991 and 1994. Marijuana (of a more potent kind) showed the major increase, but cocaine, LSD, and other hallucinogens were also increasingly used by eighth-graders, augmented by higher rates of general drug use among twelfth-graders (Johnston, O'Malley, and Bachman 1994). At the close of 1995, the *New York Times* (December 17) could report: "Drug and Alcohol Use Rising among Teen-agers, Study Finds."

Drug interdiction efforts have failed to prevent the introduction of new drugs or the reintroduction of old drugs, nor have the lessons of the past been well learned. According to one current trend, some are experimenting with opium tea drinking to recapture the "romance" of the Victorian Age. As one artist has remarked: "The whole mystique of it is to be in a visually interesting place, to sit and drink it, and get all degenerate and poetic" (*Newsweek,* August 29, 1994). The U.S. Naval Academy has been the scene of a widening scandal involving the use and sale of LSD and marijuana (*New York Times,* November 7, 1995). LSD and an extrapotent marijuana have also reappeared on the American drug scene (*Parade Magazine*, August 21, 1994; *New York Times*, February 6, 1994). *Newsweek* noted a surge in nitrous oxide inhalation and LSD use at Grateful Dead concerts (August 21, 1995). Fentanyl, a synthetic narcotic painkiller, has become popular among medical professionals, such as the female medical student in Brooklyn who died from an overdose, and among street addicts, seventeen of whom died in 1988 when the drug was sold as heroin (*New York Times*, November 7, 1995). A new sedative drug, Rohypnol, known as "roofies," "roach," or "rope," has made an appearance in Florida, Louisiana, and Texas and is popular among teenagers (*New York Times*, December 9, 1995). And in December 1995 the ABC Network show "20/20" aired a segment on the resurgence of methamphetamine use among girls aged twelve to fourteen in Tarzana, California.

After decades of decline, heroin has also reappeared (*Newsweek*, November 1, 1993). As *New York Times* reporter Joseph Treaster concludes, "heroin is no longer so predominantly the poison of the poor and the avant-garde, but rather is increasingly making inroads among the working and middle classes as well" (September 4, 1994). The accessibility of snortable heroin, and the consequent reduced risk of HIV acquisition, has made the drug increasingly popular among affluent professionals (*New York Times*, August 14, 1995). The use of smokable high-purity, low-cost heroin has also been glamorized by Hollywood celebrities. Trip Gabriel, a young club-hopper, has commented that "at just about every party I've been to in the last six months, whether public or private, whether early or late, there is a definite almond smell" (*New York Times*, September 4, 1994).

Unmindful—or unheeding—of history's lessons, women continue to be swept into the contemporary drug culture. One woman commented to a reporter that her heroin habit, which had rapidly progressed from smoking to intravenous use, had devoured her savings: "All of a sudden all the money you've saved and worked hard for is gone." A new heroin addict interviewed in a popular women's magazine said that "it was one of the few drugs that you can't actually manage . . . it was the first one that made me miserable." As addicted women have known for more than a hundred years, however, before the misery sets in the allure of heroin is irresistible: "on heroin, all your dreams have already come true" (Darling 1995: 234).

Middle-class culture has witnessed a resurgence of films portraying heroin use. Although the board of directors of the Motion Picture Association voted in 1951 to ban all films dealing with narcotics, Otto Preminger's *Man with the Golden Arm* in 1955 was the first in a steady stream of movies that touched on the same subject: *Bird* (1968), *Panic in Needle Park* (1971), *The French Connection* (1971), *Lady Sings the Blues* (1972), *Serpico* (1973), *Lenny* (1974), *Who'll Stop the Rain* (1978), *Prince of the City* (1981), *Liquid Sky* (1983), *Sid and Nancy* (1986), *Drugstore Cowboy* (1989), and *Rush* (1991). The pace clearly accelerated in 1994 with *Killing Zoe, Pulp Fiction, Fresh,* and *L.627* (*New York Times,* August 14, 1994).

The empiric fact that the use of mind-altering drugs persists has no simple explanation. Some may choose to accept the extreme position of Leslie Farber, who as chairman of the Association of Existential Psychology and Psychiatry wrote, "ours is the Addicted Society" (*New York Times Magazine,* December 11, 1966), or that of Andrew Weil, who has argued that "the ubiquity of drug use is so striking that it must represent a basic human appetite" and that this drive is "an innate, normal drive analogous to hunger or the sexual drive" (1972: 17, 19). Others may find a compelling argument in Ivan Illich's assertion that "professionally organized medicine" has transformed pain from "an inevitable part of the subjective reality of one's own body" to a sensation that gives rise to "a snowballing demand on the part of anesthesia consumers for artificially induced insensibility, unawareness and even unconsciousness" (1976: 127, 134–135). Still others may take a narrower view: drugs are prevalent among those who see only poverty, despair, and hopelessness ahead and seek self-induced anesthesia or respect within their own society or the potential of short-term economic rewards offered by a drug-centered world. Whatever the circumstances, the American entrepreneurial spirit has turned the drug scene into a source of huge profit through licit activities such as movies, videos, songs, apparel (*Newsweek,* November 1, 1993), and prescription medications, and through illicit activities such as manufacturing, dealing, and transporting drugs.

The public view of women who use drugs has varied according to the mores of the era and how American society has chosen to define "the drug problem." From the mid-nineteenth century to the early years of the twentieth, whether genteel lady or madame on the streets, harassed housewife or overburdened mother, drug-using women comprised the majority of opiate addicts and a significant segment of those who used other drugs. Although their relative numbers declined after 1914, women represented about 20 percent of the total number of drug users and addicts throughout the Classic Era (1920s–1950s). The percentage jumped during the "crack" cocaine outbreak of the 1980s; in the mid-1990s, women constituted 25 percent to 30 percent of "hard drug" users, more if chronic users of prescription drugs are included.

Throughout the decades, drug-using and addicted women have suffered a range of indignities, from benign neglect during the Victorian period to victimization and repression during the Classic Era. Many, dependent on manipulative, abusive men, found themselves living shadowy lives of deception, degradation, prostitution, and crime. When women admitted that they used drugs and sought help, they were subjected to blame and societal rage; drug-related behavior during pregnancy has even elicited criminal prosecution (Young 1994). The perpetuation of the myth that drug users are "them" and not "us," that the female "drug problem" refers only to black "crack mothers," who are allegedly ripping off the system as "welfare queens" and doing drugs to satisfy their cravings at the expense of their "innocent fetuses," has done little to encourage clear thinking about these women and how to serve them.[1] False stereotypes promote social marginalization, and it is always easier to refuse or restrict funding to promising programs intended for those living on the margins of society.

The reality of the female "drug problem," however, is this: women of all socioeconomic classes and racial-ethnic groups, women who even by conservative standards would be considered mainstream, use and are addicted to opiates, cocaine, and prescription drugs. The sensationalistic coverage and negative language of the press too often play into the hands of legislators more willing to "allocate funds" to the defense budget than to "throw more money" at "futile" social programs. Simplistic or scientifically inaccurate news stories portray hopeless "junkie babies" and "crack kids," and their drug-addicted mothers, who have "lost their maternal instinct" and unfeelingly abandoned or harmed their children. This approach sells newspapers but it does little to clarify public understanding of the tangled roots of addiction. As Andrew Weil (1972) has acknowledged, during his years as a reporter covering the "drug scene" he selected, perhaps unconsciously, illustrative examples that would "whet the emotional appetite" of his readers. In an era of "sound bites," television reports have also failed to explore the historical origins and social complexities of women's addiction, creating false and misleading caricatures of women addicts.

It was the Women's Movement of the early 1970s that brought the issue of women and addiction out of the shadows and into the public forum. The resulting momentum has encouraged a number of creative initiatives over the last twenty-five years and expanded funding for programs to help addicted women. Federal and state governments have established specific offices addressing the issues of women's health and women's drug use, for example, the National Institutes of Health Office of Research on Women's Health (ORWH), the post of Senior Advisor on Women's Issues in the National Institute of Drug Abuse, and the Women's Health Initiative (part of the National Institutes of Health). Women are increasingly included in therapeutic trials—although for 1995 NIDA has considered an "enhanced methadone study" restricted to ninety-two opiate-dependent *males* (National Institute on Drug Abuse 1994). Federal and municipal government agencies, medical schools, and public health organizations and foundations have sponsored conferences on basic science and clinical applications, and these have focused national attention on drug use in women. Treatment opportunities for addicted women have been—and remain—inadequate in quantity and in quality to meet the demand, but at last comprehensive new therapeutic models have begun to consider together drug-related violence against women, parenting needs, and racial and cultural issues that affect drug use—all of which has, of course, required new funding. One innovative program addressing the needs of substance-using women who are victims of domestic violence was initiated by Dr. Machelle Harris-Allen at Bellevue Medical Center in New York City in 1994, under a grant from the New York chapter of the March of Dimes. Despite the high prevalence of women in the drug-using population, women's programs have generally received only a small percentage of the national drug budget. The 1995 NIDA budget, however, includes an appropriation of 88.2 million dollars for "women's health."

The need to help women who are struggling with addiction has taken on added urgency, and the stakes are much higher now than they were in the past. In the last century, opiate addiction undoubtedly took its toll on women, but many lived in secure, intact families and did not need to resort to crime to support their habit. During this century, and especially over the last decade, however, "hard drugs" and crime have come together in a web of poverty and disintegrating family structures, while the nation has become more conservative politically and less willing to view these social changes sympathetically. Addicted women are at increased risk for serious health impairment and even death on the street or in "shooting galleries" or "crack-houses." This risk is starkest in terms of HIV infection and AIDS, which are increasing faster among women than among men and are directly linked to intravenous drug use (Chu, Buehler, and Berkelman 1990; Centers for Disease Control and Prevention 1993).

Drugs have always been with us and will continue to be with us for the foreseeable future. As Andrew Weil concludes, "the fantasy that drugs can be made to go away, the idea that people that want drugs can be discouraged from using them is an impossible dream that gets us nowhere except in worse trouble" (1972: 189). We need to proceed with the urgent business of examining the metaphoric drug "balloon" from all sides in order to devise the best ways to reduce it. Given our long history of failure and our relative inflexibility in dealing with a "drug scene" that is protean by nature, this is obviously a gargantuan task. Squeezing the drug "balloon," even with increasing force, has failed to deflate it. The best strategy would appear to be controlling or slowly reducing the air already inside and directing our major efforts at letting in as little new air as possible. What this means is that drug treatment in the context of "harm reduction" and a massive campaign of education and prevention will be needed. In the contemporary health care environment of cost accountability and industry-controlled "managed care," the benefits of treatment must be demonstrated: we will need to define what *really* works.

Unfortunately, history provides few specific answers to questions about whether treating addiction really works. Past attempts at "treatment," either by private physicians or in a sanitarium setting, and later in the short-lived drug maintenance clinics and the Lexington facility, were limited in scope and duration. They lacked a firm scientific foundation and were never properly assessed. Relapse rates were extremely high, although today the reason for these failures would be obvious, considering what we now know about the complex nature of addiction and the simplistic treatment regimens these early programs offered. Providing services may not always work, but *not* providing services will certainly never work.

Whether early treatment failures were the result of charlatanism, greed, or well-intentioned ignorance may seem irrelevant today. Yet even now, significant treatment approaches are misunderstood and unfairly maligned. Methadone maintenance, for example, has proven to be an extremely valuable treatment for heroin dependence. As the treatment was originally conceived by Dr. Vincent Dole and Dr. Marie Nyswander, methadone could be given in a dosage sufficient to block euphoria and drug craving and could thus be used to bring heroin addicts into comprehensive rehabilitation programs to restructure their lives. Almost immediately, however, political forces reduced methadone to an inexpensive, stripped-down way to "control" a generation of addicts without having to provide essential rehabilitative services, thereby lumping an effective, scientifically based treatment together with previous unsuccessful approaches. In addition, methadone became highly politicized as "just another addiction," a shortsighted attitude that totally obscured the difference between a beneficial "neuroadaptation," in which patients are better able to function and do not need to resort to crime for illicit drugs, and a destructive "addiction," in which heroin-dependent addicts exhaust their lives in drug-seeking and criminal activities and often die prematurely from drug overdoses or needle-related diseases.

If it is eventually shown, as Dole and Nyswander posited, that opiate addiction is indeed a "metabolic disease" involving cellular alterations that require life-long replacement with another opiate to enable addicts to "feel right," then the heated "abstinence versus maintenance" debate would become moot. Since experience has demonstrated that relatively few opiate addicts will become permanently abstinent, many advocate "harm reduction" in the form of drug maintenance: physicians do not treat any other permanent metabolic disease, such as diabetes, hypertension, or thyroid insufficiency, by treating acute symptoms and then discontinuing the medication once the disease is clinically controlled. In the same way, discontinuing methadone once a patient is clinically stable makes no medical sense. And the fact that many *nonaddicted* patients being treated for medical conditions are at times "noncompliant" in their medication-taking spection. Between 1985 and 1987, reports of child abuse and neglect in New York City more than tripled, from 2,627 to 8,521, when mothers or both parents were drug users (Falco 1989). Two highly publicized cases in New York offer heart-rending illustrations. Six-year-old Elisa Izquierdo was abused and then killed in November 1995, reportedly by her "crack"-addicted mother, who is currently in jail awaiting trial. A second child, identified only as Marisol, was returned by the Child Welfare Administration to her biological mother, despite evidence of drug dealing, violence, and neglect in the home. Three months later, Marisol was found "starving . . . naked beneath a urine-soaked sheet. Her front teeth had been knocked out, her feet scalded, her body covered by bruises and cigar burns. One leg bone was splintered, large clumps of her hair were missing, and she had been sexually abused" (*New York Times,* December 14, 1995).

Successful programs based on the family unification model should be expanded. Operation PAR (Parental Awareness and Responsibility), run by Shirley Coletti in St. Petersburg, Florida, began providing residential care for substance-abusing women in 1971 and by 1990 was serving a hundred women. Through its long-term residential program, children from infancy to ten years can live with their mother while she is receiving treatment. The Coalition on Addiction, Pregnancy and Parenting (CAPP), run by Norma Finkelstein in Cambridge, Massachusetts, provides technical assistance and evaluation to two residential homes for women and encourages other residential homes to take in substance-abusing women. One such program is New Day, a ten-bed unit that offers residential care to substance-using mothers and their infants for nine to twelve months and provides a continuum of care before, during, and after pregnancy. Shields for Families in Compton, California, and Families First in Lansing, Michigan, are examples of other programs that emphasize family unification in the context of maternal substance use. Cities such as San Francisco, Los Angeles, and New York, which now allow many drug-using mothers to take their babies home from the hospital under social service supervision, have shown that creative programs can be developed (*New York Times,* September 19, 1991).

A panel of experts in New York City recently recommended that the family unification policy be reexamined, especially in those cases "in which family members abused drugs and alcohol" (*New York Times,* February 12, 1995). Although the city administration did not

should place the "difficult, noncompliant" methadone-treated patient in a more rational medical perspective.

Arguments against methadone treatment for women, especially during pregnancy, have been distorted and taken out of context. Although infants do go through withdrawal from methadone, as they do from heroin, this withdrawal is easy to manage medically. In addition, infants born to mothers treated with methadone do not develop congenital malformations, show much better intrauterine body and brain growth, and show no consistent, definable neurobehavioral consequences as they grow up. And what is perhaps most important, women who give up "street life" and enter methadone treatment engage in less illegal behavior and show decreased rates of needle use and HIV acquisition, they experience an improvement in their general health and nutrition and better obstetrical outcomes, and they receive more consistent prenatal care and better preparation for infant care and household tasks, all of which bestow enormous benefit on the developing infant. As one San Francisco addict commented, "with methadone, you don't have to go out and use any other drugs. You have a choice" (Wenger and Rosenbaum 1994: 4). But the word "choice" is a misnomer. Treatment "on demand" is more rhetoric than reality, and the failure of society to provide heroin addicts with methadone treatment "on demand" should be considered a tragic under-utilization of one of the only therapies with proven efficacy.

We must also sharpen our definition of "treatment success." If we define "success" solely as abstinence, we might just as well fold our tents. The statements of experts in addiction—and the impassioned stories of drug addicts struggling to escape the grip of addiction during the past century and a half—should convince us of the essential futility of those attempts for the majority of addicts. The frustration felt by addicted women is ongoing: "I tried kicking out on the street," one woman reported. "I went to my mom's and there's no way on God's green earth I'm going to kick when I know I can get it. I mean I know and I didn't try to fool myself" (Wenger and Rosenbaum 1994: 3). If we accept the fact that addiction is a chronic relapsing condition, however, we would consider leading a relatively stable life, holding a job, and keeping a family intact (with methadone substitution therapy), as opposed to a street life of drug-seeking and crime, a "success." Although a small number of patients will be motivated enough, and receive enough support, to detoxify to abstinence, detoxification may lead far more patients to relapse, and possibly kill themselves, by returning to street drugs.

We must also continue to focus on what exactly constitutes appropriate treatment for addicted women. Although some common principles may underlie addiction, obviously treatment will vary depending on the nature of the addictive drug; whether a woman has or lacks family support; whether she is black, white, Latina, or Asian; and whether she feels that she can become drug-free or not. In a seminal needs-assessment study of "crack"-using mothers, Wendy Chavkin and her colleagues (1993a) found that almost 60 percent of the women in the study had been homeless within the past two years, half had experienced at least one forced sexual encounter, and two-thirds gave family histories of drug or alcohol abuse. Although three-quarters of the women knew that "crack" was considered harmful to the fetus, and an equal number wanted to stop using drugs, the most common reasons for not seeking care were "having felt bad about using drugs" and having "felt guilty or embarrassed about being a drug-using pregnant woman." Although 86 percent of the women had received some prenatal care, less than one-third had received care that could be defined as "adequate" according to the American College of Obstetricians and Gynecologists. Chavkin also found that women were in need of aftercare, services for children, education and training, addiction services, on-site health care, and more concrete services such as housing and food. It is clear that women want and need an array of services never provided to them before—and never even considered until recently.

Other studies have confirmed the negative impact of sexual violence on drug-addiction in women. A 1989 study of 229 clients in two private nonprofit inpatient treatment programs in Maryland found that the women, who comprised 20 percent of the group, were much more likely than the men to report a history of childhood sexual abuse, sexual abuse as an adult, suicide attempts, and acute emotional distress. Because of these findings, the author recommended addressing abuse issues, emotional and family problems, and anger and victimization in a primary way—as a measure of its importance and centrality to treatment success—especially through single-sex groups (Wallen 1992).

The National Victim Center (*Rape in America* 1992) also noted a strong association between sexual violence and drug use. Com to nonvictims, rape victims were more than five times more lik have abused prescription drugs and more than three to ten time likely to have used marijuana, cocaine, or other "hard drugs." findings could mean that sexual trauma led to drug abuse, b could also mean that these factors are associated but not c related, that women who use drugs live in environments in whi is more likely. Treatment must certainly attend to issues of violence, but prevention efforts must be directed at correc societal factors that exacerbate male violence toward women have also stressed the need for general counseling for post-tr stress disorder as a way of confronting past traumas (Herma Since these therapeutic approaches are relatively new, it will t to assess their impact, but it is important to note that they a way from the simplistic solutions to addiction undertaken tl

These and other studies suggest several avenues for improv ment to drug-addicted and drug-using women. Although s argue that a "comprehensive" approach may be overwhe some addicted women, there is an obvious need to incorpora for problems such as sexual violence, post-traumatic stres and victimization, and family addiction; to provide concre such as housing and food stamps; and to offer counseling i ships with children, all in supportive ways that differ f confrontational therapeutic community (TC) and Twelv proaches. It is not yet clear, however, whether first addr issues such as depression, anxiety, and anger, or focusir treatment would be more beneficial to addicted womer et al. 1993b).

Another useful strategy, one to consider cautiously, family unification. Between 1987 and 1989, the number in foster care in the United States rose 30 percent, to 360,(maternal substance use was the major reason for "b status"[2] in New York City hospitals, accounting for m percent of the total of three hundred "boarder babies" ir given day (Driver, Chavkin, and Higginson 1987). Th State Council on Children reported that the parents of the children in foster care were substance abusers (H Agency 1994). When the home is a setting for drug us bringing family members together must be approached

feel the need to change its policy, the experts recommended that a positive urine toxicology in the infant should once again be considered evidence for child maltreatment and thus grounds for possible foster care placement. Family reunification is considered even when mothers have been incarcerated on drug charges. In 1994, a crime bill was passed in Congress that included a provision allocating 40 million dollars over five years so that nonviolent offenders could serve their sentences in supervised settings where their children could live with them (*New York Times,* July 18, 1994). By the end of 1995, however, sustaining the program was in doubt, since it was not included in Department of Justice appropriations for 1996.

Another "harm reduction" strategy needing further public discussion is needle exchange programs for intravenous drug users. Despite vehement opposition, New York City initiated an experimental needle exchange program in November 1988. The program ran until January 1990, when it was closed by a new municipal administration. In June 1992, in response to an HIV "health emergency," waivers were granted for five needle exchange programs; in October 1994 an estimated twenty-five thousand intravenous drug users were involved. Although these programs provide some supportive services, such as community outreach, holiday meals, and training in safe injection techniques, their major rationale in a city where half of the two hundred thousand needle-using addicts are HIV-positive is to limit the spread of HIV-associated disease. Only blood transfusions are more "efficient" in spreading HIV.

Sharing contaminated "works" in "shooting galleries" and other common meeting places, along with prostitution and trading sex for drugs, markedly increases women's risk of becoming HIV-positive. In one cross-sectional analysis of five needle exchange programs, 30 percent of the 2,525 intravenous drug users were women (Paone et al. 1995a, 1995b). Enrollment in needle exchange programs considerably reduced high-risk behavior. Borrowing used "works" fell from 25 percent to 10 percent, renting used "works" fell from 17 percent to 5 percent, passing on of syringes declined by half, from 18 percent to 9 percent, using bleach to disinfect needles increased from 38 percent to 48 percent, and using alcohol pads to cleanse the skin rose from 38 percent to 82 percent. This positive experience was confirmed in a Connecticut study of needle availability through commercial pharmacies (*New York Times,* August 30, 1995). After finding that needle exchanges reduced HIV transmission in seventy-five programs in fifty-five cities, a prestigious panel of the National Academy of Sciences recommended federal financing of such programs (*New York Times,* September 20, 1995).

Even without needle exchange programs, enrolling female intravenous drug users in methadone treatment has a positive impact on the spread of HIV. Over half of the women with AIDS who were reported to the Centers for Disease Control by 1993 (*HIV/AIDS Surveillance Report* 1993) had acquired HIV by injecting drugs. Methadone maintenance treatment has been shown to reduce the acquisition and spread of HIV. In 1984, when 50 percent to 60 percent of street addicts were already HIV-positive, only 9 percent of the patients who had been in methadone treatment since 1978 were positive and most of them had used cocaine by needle (Novick, Khan, and Kreek 1986). In San Francisco, women's failure to find treatment for heroin addiction was associated with continued high-risk behavior for acquiring HIV (Wenger and Rosenbaum 1994). The 1995 Budget Estimate of the National Institute on Drug Abuse (1994) agreed that putting drug users into treatment would reduce the spread of HIV and save money in HIV treatment: the estimated cost of lifetime medical care for a person with AIDS is seventy-five thousand dollars; the estimated cost per slot for drug treatment is about four thousand dollars (Hellinger 1990). Convinced of the value of treatment geared specifically to women, NIDA also advocated further AIDS intervention programs for women.

At the present time, lacking the requisite funding, "drug treatment" is little more than a slogan. Mainstream America, content in its belief that "it can't happen here," in middle-class neighborhoods, fights allocating money to socially marginalized groups it neither likes nor particularly wishes to help. Expansion of programs like the methadone maintenance and residential facilities, which neither judge nor punish women but rather encourage their efforts to seek help for their drug problem, is badly needed. A summary of a NIDA conference in the early 1990s decried the "lack of thoughtful, organized approaches to developing programs for rehabilitating chemically dependent pregnant women or women with young children, and a lack of existing treatment resources overall" (Howard 1992: 386).

On the other hand, *mandatory* treatment has never been shown to work effectively (Chavkin 1991). The issue of individual human rights notwithstanding, addicted women must be ready to enter treatment: they must have come to the realization that they need to change their current life and they must have a sense that they can make choices about their future. Many professionals regard pregnancy as a unique opportunity to bring women into treatment, yet mandatory drug treatment may actually drive a woman away from the health care system, with dire consequences for her and for her baby. Feelings of guilt and shame may keep a mother from seeking prenatal care or visiting her baby in the hospital after delivery.

Even if treatment does work to reduce the problem of drug addiction, prevention must form the cornerstone of any permanent approach to women and addiction. But preventing drug use and abuse has never been the nation's strong suit. In the fight against drugs, as in other areas, the United States can be characterized as a "downstream society": although we continue to pull dead fish from the river, we are reluctant to venture upstream to find out why the fish are dying. Prevention, unfortunately, is a difficult strategy to implement in a society in which progress is measured in quarterly corporate reports and "long term" means a four-year administration in Washington.

The "downstream" approach is also evident in the nation's decision to build more prisons to combat crime in women.[3] During the 1930s, 1940s, and 1950s, two or three prisons for women were built per decade. But the pace has accelerated: the federal government built seven prisons in the 1960s, seventeen in the 1970s, and thirty-four in the 1980s (Immarigeon and Chesney-Lind 1992). According to an Illinois study, however, 43 percent of these incarcerated women were in minimum-security prisons and 83 percent were single-parent heads-of-household (Citizens' Council on Women, annual reports 1986 and 1987; cited in Immarigeon and Chesney-Lind 1992). Given the non-violent nature of their crimes, the limited drug treatment facilities available to them in prison, and the disruption of their families, exploring strategies other than incarceration would seem a more enlightened idea.

Until recently, prevention efforts and the attendant funding commitment have been paltry. From 1993 to 1994 the NIDA budget rose from 404 million dollars to 425 million dollars. The projected 1995 budget is 579 million dollars, yet only 81 million dollars, or 14 percent of the total, is intended for prevention (National Institute on Drug Abuse 1994).

Ideally, prevention should begin early to capitalize on the unique opportunity to shape children's thinking through age-appropriate messages.[4] One prevention program, a six-year school-based program funded by NIDA in 1985, was recently expanded to include more minority students (Mathias 1994). Another, Project Healthy Choices, was developed at the Bank Street College of Education in New York City with funding from the New York City Board of Education and the U.S. Department of Education. From 1990 to 1994 Project Healthy Choices offered a substance abuse education and prevention program to young children in kindergarten through second grade. The program created a drug education curriculum for schools and families who wanted to educate children about the dangers of substance abuse before they were exposed to peer pressure. The curriculum included an illustrated children's book with handpuppets and a videotape, and radio discussion shows. Project DARE (Drug Abuse Resistance Education), a prevention program for children in fifth, sixth, and seventh grades, is based on a curriculum designed to foster coping skills that was developed and jointly implemented by the Los Angeles Police Department and the Los Angeles Unified School District.

Prevention during the perinatal period has also been addressed, at least conceptually, on the federal level ("Toward Preventing Perinatal Abuse of Alcohol, Tobacco, and Other Drugs" 1992). The federal government report suggests that prevention efforts aimed at women of child-bearing age should include education about family planning, sexuality, and the prenatal effects of drugs; community networks, prenatal care, case management, and drug abuse treatment during pregnancy; and self- and childcare education after delivery. Drug-exposed infants should be properly identified for diagnosis, treatment, appropriate educational opportunities, and comprehensive family services. Families should receive training in parenting skills, drug abuse, sexuality, and values promotion, as well as health care services and outreach initiatives. For young people and adolescents, the report recommends education about drugs, comprehensive school health programs, and community-based prevention services. Education and awareness campaigns along with community-based programs should be developed to inform the general public about drug addiction. Health and social service providers should be trained in the nature and extent of drug problems, maternal-child issues related to drugs, risk assessment, effective client communication, interagency collaboration, and cultural competency. More generally, social and environmental issues—for example, laws and regulations related to drugs, drug-free schools and workplaces, and employee assistance programs—deserve more public discussion.

Prevention efforts should also be directed at physicians. Because physicians have played a central role in the history of female addiction and are in a pivotal position to provide supportive, nonjudgmental care to addicted women, physician education programs need support. Inspired by Brown University's Project Adept and the J. M. Foundation's Medical Student Program, among others, the Greater New York March of Dimes developed a Residency Project in 1992. The program was founded on two basic premises: women view obstetricians as influential primary care physicians; and substance use and abuse crosses all societal boundaries and will be encountered in the majority of obstetric practices. Through lectures, workshops, and site visits this project, in which I have served as a planner and lecturer, provides an educational forum for physicians-in-training and their more senior supervisors. It is intended to help them become more sensitive to the unique needs of pregnant substance abusers and their children and to receive training from a faculty of experts in the diagnosis, treatment, and referral of these problems.

In economic terms, there is evidence that expenditure up front saves huge expenditure later, even without taking into account the human lives saved. A Delaware study (cited in Immarigeon and Chesney-Lind 1992) showed that the availability of more residential treatment beds for women would eliminate the need for at least sixteen prison beds, and pointed to a number of community-based programs, such as Community Services for Women and the Neil J. Houston House in Boston, the Elizabeth Fry Center in San Francisco, and Our New Beginnings in Portland, Oregon, which offer services specifically for addicted female offenders. Excluding court and police expenditures, the current annual cost of incarcerating an offender in New York City is close to 60,000 dollars (Rothman 1994). According to a recent NIDA report, an untreated drug abuser costs society 21,500 dollars over a six-month period; methadone maintenance treatment over the same period costs 1,750 dollars.[5]

A Department of Health and Human Services report for the Pennsylvania, Delaware, Maryland, Virginia, and West Virginia area (Hutchins and Alexander 1990) noted with concern that the cost of caring for a drug-exposed baby is rapidly increasing: in 1993 it was estimated to be about thirty-six thousand dollars (Stockwell 1993). Yet an outlay of one dollar on prenatal care can save a thousand dollars on premature infant care, which may increase to a saving of two thousand dollars when substance abuse is involved. San Francisco General Hospital estimated that caring for 250 cocaine-exposed infants in 1988 cost them three-and-a-half million dollars in excess of Medi-Cal reimbursement (*San Francisco Chronicle*, February 22, 1989). A New York study showed that neonatal hospital costs following intrauterine exposure to cocaine exceeded those for unexposed babies by over five thousand dollars, and that exposure to "crack" cocaine and multiple substances further increased the cost differential (Phibbs, Bateman, and Schwartz 1991). Another New York study found that exposure to cocaine and other drugs increased neonatal costs by almost eight thousand dollars per infant, and that, based on discharge data for 1991–1992, maternal drug use during pregnancy added almost nine hundred million dollars to neonatal medical costs (Joyce et al. 1995).

It is not my intention to debate the merits and shortcomings of drug legalization (see, for example, Nadelmann 1989); the current political climate precludes the possibility that legalization will receive serious consideration. Ultimately, we must acknowledge that women use drugs in large part in response to the stresses they face in their lives—minority status; reduced economic, social, and political expectations; a disproportionate experience of physical and sexual abuse. Some women make the newspaper headlines because they lack even the most basic social supports and abandon or sell their babies on the street in a desperate attempt to find money or save the child's life. We still read too often of the "neediest cases," like that of Celestine B., who was trying to overcome a "twenty-year nightmare" of drug addiction grounded in sexual abuse, homelessness, loss of her children, and joblessness (*New York Times*, February 22, 1995). This stereotypical characterization, however, portrays only those women who, as New York Representative Charles Rangel wrote in a less-than-hopeful op-ed letter, are battling "homelessness, unemployment, lack of education, lack of healthcare, lack of family and, above all, poverty" (*New York Times*, December 26, 1989). For other women, drug abuse is the result of manipulation by the media, inappropriate overmedication by physicians, or their own attempts to cope with the social barriers to achieving equality and self-fulfillment. Although women with economic and family support can mask their addiction, however tragic their circumstances, substance-abusing women are united in a punishing sisterhood whose human costs are inestimable.

NOTES

1. A Historical Perspective

1. Racial and ethnic terminology has changed over the century and a half covered by this history. Some chapters will reflect terms used during the period under discussion.

2. Jane Brody, "Cocaine: Litany of Fetal Risks Grows," *New York Times*, September 6, 1988, p. C1.

3. Sara Blakeslee, "Crack's Toll among Babies: A Joyless View, Even of Toys," *New York Times*, September 17, 1989, p. 1; Barbara Kantrowitz, "The Crack Children," *Newsweek*, February 12, 1990, pp. 62–63.

4. Michael deCourcy Hinds, "The Instincts of Parenthood Become Part of Crack's Toll," *New York Times*, March 17, 1990, p. A8; Kathy A. Fackelmann, "The Maternal Cocaine Connection," *Science News*, September 7, 1991, pp. 152–153.

5. Charles Krauthammer, "Crack Babies: Genetic Inferiors," *New York Daily News*, July 31, 1989, p. 24; Andrew Revkin, "Crack in the Cradle," *Discovery*, September 1989, pp. 62–69; Clara Hemphill, "A Tormented Cry," *New York Newsday*, September 28, 1990; Anna Quindlen, "Hearing the Cries of Crack," *New York Times*, October 7, 1990; Suzanne Daley, "Born on Crack and Coping with Kindergarten," *New York Times*, February 7, 1991, p. A1; Ellen Goodman, "Beyond the 'Crack Baby' Horror Lies the Pain of Troubled Kids," *Miami Herald*, January 16, 1992, p. 23A.

6. Douglas Besharov, "Crack Babies: The Worst Threat Is Mom Herself," *Washington Post*, August 6, 1989, p. B1; Deirdre Anne Roney, "Imprison Addicts, for the Children's Sake," *New York Times*, December 15, 1989 (letter to the editor).

7. A number of excellent books on the general history of addiction in America

are available to the interested reader. Included in this list are, among others, C. E. Terry and Mildred Pellens, *The Opium Problem* (1928); David Musto, *The American Disease* (1973); H. Wayne Morgan, *Drugs in America* (1981); and David Courtwright, *Dark Paradise* (1982). Although these books provide excellent discussions of the history of addiction in America and the development of U.S. drug policy, they do not cover the experience of female addicts in much detail. The reader might also find useful Cynthia Palmer and Michael Horowitz, eds., *Shaman Woman, Mainline Lady* (1982), a compilation of women's writings on drugs; and David Courtwright, Herman Joseph, and Don Des Jarlais, *Addicts Who Survived* (1989), narrative recollections of male and female addicts in the middle of this century. Marsha Rosenbaum, *Women on Heroin* (1981), and James Inciardi, Dorothy Lockwood, and Anne Pottieger, *Women and Crack-Cocaine* (1993), offer focused ethnographic and sociological insights on women's drug use in the modern era. Elizabeth Ettore, *Women and Substance Use* (1992), does not provide a broad historical focus, but its feminist viewpoint is extremely useful for understanding current issues.

8. *Allopathic* ("conventional") medicine, derived from the Greek word *alloin*, meaning "different," uses remedies whose properties are opposite to the symptoms of the disease. *Homeopathic* ("complementary" or "alternative") medicine, derived from the Greek word *homoion*, meaning "similar," uses remedies that produce symptoms resembling the disease in question. See Kremers and Urdang's *History of Pharmacy* (1976), p. 176.

2. The Drug Problem

1. A *narcotic* is any drug that produces sleep or stupor while at the same time relieving pain. An *opiate* is a remedy that contains or is derived from opium; it usually has narcotic properties.

2. For individual treatment recommendations for specific illnesses, see A. W. Chase, *Dr. Chase's Family Physician, Farrier, Bee-Keeper and Second Receipt Book* (1873), Thomas Faulkner and J. H. Carmichael, *The Cottage Physician* (1892), and William K. David, *Secrets of Wise Men, Chemists and Great Physicians* (1896).

3. See James Harvey Young, *The Toadstool Millionaires* (1961) and *The Medical Messiahs* (1967).

4. For a fuller listing, see Faulkner and Carmichael, *The Cottage Physician* (1892), pp. 531–536.

5. See *1897 Sears Roebuck Catalogue*, ed. Fred L. Israel (New York: Chelsea House, 1968).

6. Pierce ran the Invalids' Hotel and Surgical Institute, which supported eighteen physicians and a total staff of hundreds, served as president of the World's Dispensary Medical Association, ran a home consultation service requiring the "payment of monthly fees, in advance," and reportedly sold over 1.2 million copies of his book.

7. See Joseph F. Spillane, "Modern Drug, Modern Menace: The Legal Use and Distribution of Cocaine in the United States, 1880–1920" (1994), p. 61.

8. Dr. William Stewart Halsted (1852–1922) was born into a refined New York family, served as captain of the Yale football team, and entered surgical practice in New York in the 1870s. He subsequently became famous as the leading surgeon at the Johns Hopkins School of Medicine. Halsted developed nerve block anesthesia using cocaine but became an addict himself. He was unsuccessful in curing his cocaine addiction with morphine, and his career went into decline.

3. America's Response

1. Cited in *Cincinnati Lancet-Clinic,* 63 (April 26, 1890): 528.
2. For a history of the Keeley chain, see H. Wayne Morgan, *Drugs in America: A Social History 1800–1980* (1981).
3. For an extended discussion of the movie industry, see Michael Starks, *Cocaine Fiends and Reefer Madness: An Illustrated History of Drugs in the Movies* (1982), and Kevin Brownlow, *Behind the Mask of Innocence* (1990).
4. For a review, see William O. Walker III, *Drug Control in the Americas* (1981).

4. The Harrison Anti-Narcotic Act

1. For a history of the New York City Clinic, see the writings of S. Dana Hubbard listed in the References.
2. Unpublished data, memorandum to Levi Nutt, April 30, 1921 (cited in Courtwright 1982a: 166).
3. Excerpts from report of H. H. Wouters, Special Narcotic Agent, to Levi Nutt, October 6, 1922, and to W. S. Blanchard, Acting Prohibition Commissioner, September 29, 1922 (cited in Musto 1973: 171–172).

5. The Classic Era

1. The text of the Uniform Narcotics Act of 1932 is reprinted in William Butler Eldridge, *Narcotics and the Law* (1962), pp. 133–147.
2. Bingham Dai's sources included the Federal Bureau of Narcotics, the Narcotic Division of the Chicago Police Department, the Cook County Psychopathic Hospital, the Women's Reformatory at Dwight, Illinois, and the Keeley Institute in the Chicago area.
3. See Michael Starks, *Cocaine Fiends and Reefer Madness: An Illustrated History of Drugs in the Movies* (1982); Kevin Brownlow, *Behind the Mask of Innocence* (1990).

6. The Second World War and After

1. The term *tranquilizer* was first applied in 1954 to rauwolfia, a compound derived from a plant root belonging to the dogbane family, whose medicinal applications date back thousands of years.

7. The 1960s

1. For a general review of the perinatal aspects of maternal drug use during pregnancy, see Loretta P. Finnegan and Stephen R. Kandall (1992).

8. The 1970s

1. Letter from U.S. Senator Birch Bayh to NIDA Conference on "Drugs, Alcohol and Women," Miami Beach, Florida, October 24–26, 1975; see Muriel Nellis 1975: 274–276.
2. Women had long been underrepresented among the ranks of America's physicians. Although seventeen medical colleges for women had been established in the second half of the nineteenth century and women had slowly gained acceptance to coeducational medical schools, the percentage of physicians who were women rose only slightly, from less than 3 percent to 5.6 percent, between 1880 and 1900. Female medical students were limited to about 5 percent of the entering classes between 1910 and 1960 except for the wartime years (Starr 1982).
3. The New York City programs were Pregnant Addicts and Addicted Mothers (PAAM), and the Odyssey House Parents Program; the Boston program was Women, Inc.; the Detroit program was W.O.M.A.N. Center.

9. Enlightened Treatment

1. For a description of the "Twelve Step" approach to the treatment of addiction, see *Twelve Steps and Twelve Traditions* (1952).
2. Endorphins are substances produced naturally by the body; they act like opiates.

10. Opportunities and Prosecution

1. For a discussion of epidemiologic methodologies, see "Planning and Changes in Customer Populations: Needs Assessment, Clinical Planning and Special Populations." Center for Substance Abuse Treatment Second Annual State Systems Development Programs Conference, Hot Springs, Arkansas, April 21–23, 1993.
2. Sources were 1) The Drug Abuse Warning Network, a joint project of the DEA and NIDA since 1972, which monitored emergency room visits and deaths; 2) Drug Watch, which surveyed emergency rooms and medical examiners' offices; 3) Client Oriented Data Acquisition, a NIDA-required reporting system for federal grantees; 4) the Drug Enforcement Statistical Report published by the DEA; 5) the Regional Drug Situational Analysis, another DEA compilation; and 6) the National Drug Abuse Treatment Utilization Survey.
3. Statement released by NIDA at Conference on "Drug Addiction Research and the Health of Women," Tysons Corner, Virginia, September 12–14, 1994.

4. When "crack" is smoked it reaches the brain very rapidly, just as it does when injected intravenously. The pharmacokinetics are different from those following the application of cocaine to mucous membranes, which causes blood vessels to constrict and delays the absorption of the drug.

5. See U.S. Department of Justice pamphlet "Women, Drugs, and Crime: Selected Bibliography," June 1994.

6. Draft of executive summary of CSAP PPWI Demonstration Program Findings, July 1994, p. 1.

7. See Wendy Chavkin, "Women and Clinical Trials" (1994). See also papers by Peter Fried, Ann Pytkowicz, Judy Howard, Kenneth Rich, and Emmalee S. Bandstra in "Methodologic Issues in Epidemiological, Prevention, and Treatment Research on Drug-Exposed Women and Their Children" (Washington, D.C.: NIDA Research Monograph Series, DHHS Pub. No. (ADM) 92–1881, 1992).

8. The programs selected were from Wichita, Kansas; New York City; Cobb County, Georgia; Chicago; Bernalillo County, New Mexico; Albuquerque; and Seattle.

9. See Center for Reproductive Law & Policy, *Reproductive Freedom News,* February 10, 1995.

10. *Reproductive Freedom News,* July 8, 1994.

11. *Reproductive Freedom News,* January 13, 1995; February 10, 1995; and October 13, 1995.

11. Today and Tomorrow

1. See A. M. Rosenthal, "The Poisoned Babies," *New York Times,* January 16, 1996.

2. "Boarder baby" was the term applied to babies who remained in nurseries and neonatal intensive care units for social reasons after their medical problems had resolved. See also Cathy Trost, "Babies of Crack Users Crowd Hospitals, Break Everybody's Heart," *Wall Street Journal,* July 18, 1989, pp. A1, A6.

3. D. Rothman, "The Crime of Punishment," *New York Review,* February 17, 1994, pp. 34–38.

4. Robert Mathias, "School-based Drug Abuse Prevention Program Shows Long-lasting Results," *NIDA Notes* 9 (1994): 8.

5. Neil Swan, "Research Demonstrates Long-term Benefits of Methadone Treatment," *NIDA Notes* 9 (1994): 1.

REFERENCES

"Abuse of chloral hydrate." 1880. *Quarterly Journal of Inebriety* 4: 53–54.

Adams, Samuel Hopkins. 1907. *The Great American Fraud.* 4th ed. Chicago: American Medical Association Press.

Adler, Freda. 1979. "The newest and oldest profession." In *Criminology of Deviant Women,* ed. Freda Adler and Rita James Simon, 213–222. Boston: Houghton Mifflin.

Albright, J. D. 1900. *The General Practitioner as a Specialist.* Pottsville, Pa.: Press of the Daily Republican.

Allbutt, Thomas Clifford. 1895. *A System of Medicine by Many Writers.* New York: Macmillan.

Allbutt, Thomas Clifford, and W. S. Playfair. 1897. *A System of Gynaecology.* New York: Macmillan.

Allen, Francis A. 1965. "Current tendencies in American narcotics legislation." In *Narcotics,* ed. Daniel M. Wilner and Gene G. Kassebaum, 19–35. New York: McGraw-Hill.

Allison, Margaret, and Robert L. Hubbard. 1985. "Drug abuse treatment process: A review of the literature." *International Journal of the Addictions* 20: 1321–1345.

American Correctional Association. 1990. *The Female Offender: What Does the Future Hold?* Washington, D.C.: St. Mary's Press.

American Medical Association. 1921. *Report of the Committee on Narcotic Drugs of the Council on Health and Public Instruction: Appendix B.* Minutes of the House of Delegates. *Journal of the American Medical Association* 76: 1669–1671.

———. 1992. *Physician Characteristics and Distribution in the United States.* Chicago: American Medical Association.

American Medicine. 1915. n.s. 10: 799–801.

American Medicine. 1920. 15: 13–14.

Anders, James M. 1899. *A Text-Book of the Practice of Medicine.* 3d ed. Philadelphia: W. B. Saunders.

Andersen, Marcia DeCann. 1980. "Health needs of drug dependent clients: Focus on women." *Women & Health* 5: 23–33.

Anglin, M. Douglas, and William H. McGlothlin. 1984. "Outcome of narcotic addict treatment in California." In *Drug Abuse Treatment Evaluation: Strategies, Progress, and Prospects,* ed. Frank M. Tims, and J. P. Ludford, 106–128. NIDA Research Monograph 51. DHHS Pub. No. (ADM) 86–1329.

———. 1985. "Methadone maintenance in California: A decade's experience." In *The Year Book of Substance Use and Abuse,* vol. 3, ed. Leon Brill and Charles Winick. New York: Human Sciences Press.

Anslinger, H. J., and William F. Tompkins. 1953. *The Traffic in Narcotics.* New York: Funk and Wagnalls.

Arif, Awni, and Joseph Westermeyer. 1988. *Methadone in the Management of Opioid Dependence: Programs and Policies around the World.* Geneva: World Health Organization.

Aron, William Stern, and Douglas W. Daily. 1976. "Graduates and splitees from therapeutic community drug treatment programs: A comparison." *International Journal of the Addictions* 11: 1–18.

Ashbrook, Debra L., and Linda C. Solley. 1979. *Women and Heroin Abuse: A Survey of Sexism in Drug Abuse Administration.* Palo Alto: R & E Research Associates.

Ashley, Richard. 1972. *Heroin: The Myths and the Facts.* New York: St. Martin's Press.

Atwood, Charles E. 1905. "A case of the heroin habit." *Medical Record* 67: 856–857.

Bailey, Pearce. 1916. "The heroin habit." *New Republic* 6: 314–316. Repr. in Morgan 1974: 171–176.

Baker, Jeffrey P. 1994. "Women and the invention of well child care." *Pediatrics* 94: 4.

Baldy, J. M. 1898. *An American Text-Book of Gynecology.* Philadelphia: W. B. Saunders.

Ball, John C., and William M. Bates. 1970. "Nativity, parentage, and mobility of opiate addicts." In *The Epidemiology of Opiate Addiction in the United States,* ed. John C. Ball and Carl D. Chambers, 95–111. Springfield, Ill.: Charles C. Thomas.

Ball, John C., and Carl D. Chambers, eds. 1970a. *The Epidemiology of Opiate Addiction in the United States.* Springfield, Ill.: Charles C. Thomas.

———. 1970b. "Overview of the problem." In *The Epidemiology of Opiate Addiction in the United States,* ed. John C. Ball and Carl D. Chambers, 5-21. Springfield, Ill.: Charles C. Thomas.

Ball, John C., B. K. Levine, R. G. Demaree, and J. F. Neman. 1975. "Pretreatment criminality of male and female drug abuse patients in the United States." *Addictive Diseases: An International Journal* 1: 481–489.

Balter, Mitchell B., and Jerome Levine. 1969. "The nature and extent of psychotropic drug usage in the United States." *Psychopharmacology Bulletin* 5, no. 4: 3–13.

Banner, Lois W. 1974. *Women in Modern America*. New York: Harcourt Brace Jovanovich.

Baron, Seymour H., and Seymour Fisher. 1962. "Use of psychotropic drug prescriptions in a prepaid group practice plan." *Public Health Reports* 77: 871–881.

Bates, William, and Betty Crowther. 1974. *Towards a Typology of Opiate Users*. Cambridge, Mass.: Schenkman.

Beard, George M. 1871. *Stimulants and Narcotics*. New York: G. P. Putnam's Sons.

———. 1878. "Certain symptoms of nervous exhaustion." *Virginia Medical Monthly*. Repr. in New York Academy of Medicine, Pamphlet no. 1280.

———. 1879. "American nervousness: Its philosophy and treatment." *Virginia Medical Monthly* 6: 253–276.

———. 1881. *American Nervousness: Its Causes and Consequences*. New York: G. P. Putnam's Sons.

Beck, John Broadhead. 1884. "On the effect of opium in the infant subject." *New York Journal of Medicine* 2: 7–13.

Bentley, W. H. 1880. "Erythroxylon Coca in the opium and alcohol habits." *Detroit Therapeutic Gazette* 1: 253–254.

Beschner, George M., Beth G. Reed, and Josette Mondanaro. 1981. *Treatment Services for Drug Dependent Women*. Vol. 1. Washington, D.C.: National Institute on Drug Abuse. DHHS Pub. No. (ADM) 81–1177.

Beschner, George M., and P. Thompson. 1981. *Women and Drug Abuse Treatment: Needs and Services*. Washington, D.C.: U.S. Department of Health and Human Services, National Institute on Drug Abuse, DHHS Pub. No. (ADM) 81–1057.

Beschner, George M., and Kerry G. Treasure. 1979. "Female adolescent drug use." In *Youth Drug Abuse: Problems, Issues, and Treatment*, ed. George M. Beschner and Alfred S. Friedman, 169–212. Lexington, Mass.: Lexington Books.

Besteman, Karst J. 1978. "The NARA Program." In *Drug Addiction and the U. S. Public Health Service*, ed. William R. Martin, and Harris Isbell, 274–280. Washington, D.C.: U.S. Department of Health, Education and Welfare. DHEW Pub. No. (ADM) 77–434.

Biase, D. Vincent. 1972. "Phoenix Houses: Therapeutic communities for drug addicts. A comparative study of residents in treatment." In *Drug Abuse*, ed. Wolfram Keup, 375–380. Springfield, Ill.: Charles C. Thomas.

Binion, Victoria J. 1979. "A descriptive comparison of the families of origin of women heroin users and nonusers." In *Addicted Women: Family Dynamics, Self Perceptions, and Support Systems*, 77–113. NIDA Services Research Monograph Series. DHEW No. (ADM) 80–762.

———. 1982. "Sex differences in socialization and family dynamics of female and male heroin users." *Journal of Social Issues* 38: 43–57.

Blackenheimer, Michael. 1975. "Use and misuse of tranquilizers." In *Drugs,*

Alcohol and Women, ed. Muriel Nellis, 157–161. Washington, D.C.: National Research and Communications Associates.

Blair, T. S. 1919. "The relation of drug addiction to industry." *Journal of Industrial Hygiene* 1: 284–296.

Blum, Richard H. 1969. *Society and Drugs.* San Francisco: Jossey-Bass.

Blum, Sam. 1970. "Marijuana clouds the generation gap." *New York Times Magazine,* August 23: 28–30ff.

Bonnie, Richard J., and Charles H. Whitebread II. 1974. *The Marihuana Conviction: A History of Marihuana Prohibition in the United States.* Charlottesville: University Press of Virginia.

Borgman, Robert D. 1973. "Medication abuse by middle-aged women." *Social Casework* 54: 526–532.

Bourne, Peter G. 1974. *Addiction.* New York: Academic Press.

Bowker, Lee H. 1978. *Women, Crime, and the Criminal Justice System.* Lexington, Mass.: Lexington Books.

Boyle, T. Coraghessan. 1993. *The Road to Wellville.* New York: Penguin Books.

Brecher, Edward M., and the Editors of Consumer Reports. 1972. *Licit and Illicit Drugs.* Boston: Little, Brown.

Breitbart, Vicki, et al. 1994. "Model programs addressing perinatal drug exposure and human immunodeficiency virus infection: Integrating women's and children's needs." *Bulletin of the New York Academy of Medicine* 71: 236–251.

Brill, Leon. 1965. "Rehabilitation in drug addiction: A report of the New York Demonstration Center." In *Narcotics,* ed. Daniel M. Wilner and Gene G. Kassebaum, 217–225. New York: McGraw-Hill.

———. 1973. "Introductory overview—Historic background." In *Methadone: Experience and Issues,* ed. Carl D. Chambers and Leon Brill, 5–40. New York: Behavioral Publications.

Brill, Leon, George Nash, and John Langrod. 1977. "The dynamics of de-addiction—A pilot study." In *Drug Detoxification: A Comprehensive Examination,* ed. Joyce Lowinson and John Langrod, 48–64. Oceanside, N.Y.: Dabor Science Publications.

Brotman, Richard, David Hutson, and Frederic Suffet, eds. 1985. *Pregnant Addicts and Their Children.* New York: Center for Comprehensive Health Practice, New York Medical College.

Brown, Barry S., et al. 1971. "In their own words: Addicts' reasons for initiating and withdrawing from heroin." *International Journal of the Addictions* 6: 635–645.

Brown, Claude. 1965. *Manchild in the Promised Land.* New York: Signet Books.

Brown, Elizabeth R. 1992. "Program and staff characteristics in successful treatment." In *Methodological Issues in Epidemiological, Prevention, and Treatment Research on Drug-Exposed Women and Their Children,* ed. M. Marlyne Kilbey and Khursheed Ashgar, 305–313. Rockville, Md.: National Institute on Drug Abuse. DHHS Pub. No. (ADM) 92–1881.

Brown, Lucius P. 1915. "Enforcement of the Tennessee Anti-Narcotics Law." *American Journal of Public Health* 5: 323–333.

Brownlow, Kevin. 1990. *Behind the Mask of Innocence*. Berkeley and Los Angeles: University of California Press.

Bryce, C. A. 1880. "A case of opium poisoning with Dr. Bull's Cough Syrup." *Southern Clinic: A Monthly Journal of Medicine, Surgery and New Remedies* 2: 400.

The Budget of the United States Government, 1923–1945. Washington, D.C.: U.S. Bureau of the Budget.

Burroughs, William S. 1977. *Junky*. New York: Penguin Books.

Butynski, William. 1991. "Drug treatment services: Funding and admissions." In *Improving Drug Abuse Treatment*, ed. Roy W. Pickens, Carl G. Leukefeld, and Charles R. Schuster, 20–52. Rockville, Md.: National Institute on Drug Abuse. DHHS Pub. No. (ADM) 91–1754.

Byck, Robert, ed. 1974. *Cocaine Papers by Sigmund Freud*. New York: Stonehill.

Byford, William H. 1865. *The Practice of Medicine and Surgery Applied to the Diseases and Accidents Incident to Women*. Philadelphia: Lindsay and Blakiston.

———. 1885a. "Cocaine in cracked nipples." *Medical and Surgical Reporter* 53, no. 18. October 31.

———. 1885b. "Cocaine used in the vomiting of pregnancy." *Therapeutic Gazette*, 3d ser. 1: 195.

———. 1886. "Cocaine in the vomiting of pregnancy." *New York Medical Journal* 44: 420.

Byford, William H., and Henry T. Byford. 1888. *The Practice of Medicine and Surgery Applied to the Diseases and Accidents Incident to Women*. 4th ed. Philadelphia: P. Blakiston.

Califano, Joseph A., Jr. 1992. "Three-headed dog from Hell: The staggering public health threat posed by AIDS, substance abuse and tuberculosis." *Washington Post*, December 21, 1992. Repr. in Program for Second Annual State Systems Development Program Conference, Center for Substance Abuse Treatment, Hot Springs, Arkansas, April 21–23, 1993.

Calkins, Alonzo. 1871. *Opium and the Opium-Appetite*. Philadelphia: J. B. Lippincott.

Cancellaro, Louis A. 1972. "New treatment concepts at the NIMH Clinical Research Center, Lexington, Kentucky." In *Drug Abuse*, ed. Wolfram Keup, 355–367. Springfield, Ill.: Charles C. Thomas.

Carlson, Gregory A., and Joseph Westermeyer. 1988. "Minneapolis–Saint Paul." In *Methadone in the Management of Opioid Dependence: Programs and Policies around the World*, ed. Awin Arif and Joseph Westermeyer, 227–237. Geneva: World Health Organization.

Carr, Caleb. 1994. *The Alienist*. New York: Random House.

Carter, Pamela. 1975. "Being where it hurts." In *Drugs, Alcohol and Women*, ed. Muriel Nellis, 150–151. Washington, D.C.: National Research and Communications Associates.

Cathell, D. W. 1905. *Book on the Physician Himself*. Philadelphia: F. A. Davis. Revised and enlarged by William T. Cathell.

Centers for Disease Control and Prevention. 1993. *HIV/AIDS Surveillance Report. Year End Edition*. Atlanta: Centers for Disease Control.

———. 1994. "Zidovudine for the prevention of HIV transmission from mother to infant." MMWR 43: 285–287.

Chaiken, M. R. 1989. "In-prison program for drug-involved offenders." Washington, D.C.: U.S. Department of Justice, National Institute of Justice.

Chambers, Carl D., Dean V. Babst, and Alan Warner. 1973. "Characteristics of patient retention/attrition." In *Methadone: Experiences and Issues,* ed. Carl D. Chambers and Leon Brill, 109–119. New York: Behavioral Publications.

Chambers, Carl D., and Leon Brill, eds. 1973. *Methadone: Experience and Issues*. New York: Behavioral Publications.

Chambers, Carl D., Walter R. Cuskey, and Arthur D. Moffett. 1970. "Mexican-American opiate addicts." In *The Epidemiology of Opiate Addiction in the United States,* ed. John C. Ball and Carl D. Chambers, 202–221. Springfield, Ill.: Charles C. Thomas.

Chambers, Carl D., and M. S. Griffey. 1975. "Use of legal substances within the general population: The sex and age variables." *Addictive Diseases: An International Journal* 2: 7–19.

Chambers, Carl D., R. Kent Hinesley, and Mary Moldestad. 1970. "The female opiate addict." In *The Epidemiology of Opiate Addiction in the United States,* ed. John C. Ball and Carl D. Chambers, 222–239. Springfield, Ill.: Charles C. Thomas.

Chambers, Carl D., and Arthur D. Moffett. 1970. "Negro opiate addiction." In *The Epidemiology of Opiate Addiction in the United States,* ed. John C. Ball and Carl D. Chambers, 178–201. Springfield, Ill.: Charles C. Thomas.

Chambers, Carl D., and W. J. Russell Taylor. 1973. "The incidence and patterns of drug abuse during maintenance therapy." In *Methadone: Experiences and Issues,* ed. Carl D. Chambers and Leon Brill, 121–129. New York: Behavioral Publications.

Chapman, Chauncey F. 1893. "The bichloride of gold treatment of dipsomania." *Chicago Medical Recorder* 4: 104–111.

Chase, A. W. 1873. *Dr. Chase's Family Physician, Farrier, Bee-Keeper and Second Receipt Book*. Toledo, Ohio: Chase Publishing.

Chasnoff, Ira J. 1989. "Drug use and women: Establishing a standard of care." *Annals of the New York Academy of Sciences* 562: 208–210.

Chasnoff, Ira J., Harvey J. Landress, and Mark E. Barrett. 1990. "The prevalence of illicit-drug or alcohol use during pregnancy and discrepancies in mandatory reporting in Pinellas County, Florida." *New England Journal of Medicine* 322: 1202–1206.

Chatham, Lois R. 1975. "Federal policy." In *Drugs, Alcohol and Women,* ed. Muriel Nellis, 26–27. Washington, D.C.: National Research and Communications Associates.

Chavkin, Wendy. 1990. "Drug addiction and pregnancy: Policy crossroads." *American Journal of Public Health* 80: 483–487.

————. 1991. "Mandatory treatment for drug abuse during pregnancy." *Journal of the American Medical Association* 266: 1556–1561.

————. 1994. "Women and clinical trials." *Journal of the American Medical Women's Association* 49: 99–126.

Chavkin, Wendy, et al. 1993a. "Reframing the debate: Toward effective treatment for inner city drug-abusing mothers." *Bulletin of the New York Academy of Medicine* 70: 50–68.

————. 1993b. "Psychiatric histories of drug using mothers: Treatment implications." *Journal of Substance Abuse Treatment* 10: 445–448.

Chein, Isidor. 1965. "The use of narcotics as a personal and social problem." In *Narcotics,* ed. Daniel M. Wilner and Gene C. Kassebaum, 103–117. New York: McGraw-Hill.

Chein, Isidor, et al. 1964. *The Road to H: Narcotics, Delinquency, and Social Policy.* New York: Basic Books.

Chiasson, Mary Ann, et al. 1991. "Heterosexual transmission of HIV-1 associated with the use of smokable freebase cocaine (crack)." *AIDS* 5: 1121–1126.

"The chloroform habit as described by one of its victims." 1884. *Detroit Lancet* 8: 251–254.

Chu, Susan Y., James W. Buehler, Ruth L. Berkelman. 1990. "Impact of the human immunodeficiency virus epidemic on mortality in women of reproductive age, United States." *Journal of the American Medical Association* 264: 225–229.

Clinical Guidelines for the Use of Zidovudine Therapy in Pregnancy to Reduce Perinatal Transmission of HIV. 1994. New York State Department of Health AIDS Institute. Pamphlet.

Cloyd, Jerald W. 1992. *Drugs and Information Control: The Role of Men and Manipulation in the Control of Drug Trafficking.* Westport, Conn.: Greenwood Press.

Cobbe, William Rosser. 1895. *Doctor Judas: A Portrayal of the Opium Habit.* Chicago: S. C. Griggs.

Cohen, Maimon M., Kurt Hirschhorn, and William A. Frosch. 1967. "In vivo and in vitro chromosomal damage induced by LSD-25." *New England Journal of Medicine* 277: 1043–1049.

Cole, Henry G. 1895. *Confessions of an American Opiate Eater.* Boston: J. H. Earles.

Collins, Charles W., and John Day. 1909. "Dope, the new vice: Part 5, the woe of women." *Everyday Life* 5: 4–5.

Collins, Cornelius F. 1919. "The drug evil and the drug law." *New York City Department of Health Monthly Bulletin* 9: 1–24.

Colten, Mary Ellen. 1979. "A descriptive and comparative analysis of self-perceptions and attitudes of heroin-addicted women." In *Addicted Women: Family Dynamics, Self Perceptions, and Support Systems.* NIDA Services Research Monograph Series. DHEW Pub. No. (ADM) 80–762.

Connaughton, J. F., et al. 1975. "Current concepts in the management of the pregnant opiate addict." *Addictive Diseases* 2: 21–35.

Coontz, Stephanie. 1992. *The Way We Never Were.* New York: Basic Books.

Cooper, James B. 1988. "Methadone treatment in the United States." In *Metha-done in the Management of Opioid Dependence: Programs and Policies around the World*, ed. Awni Arif and Joseph Westermeyer, 139–153. Geneva: World Health Organization.

Cooperstock, Ruth. 1978. "Women and psychotropic drug use." In *The Chemically Dependent Woman*, ed. J. Dowsling and A. MacLennan, 39–48. Toronto: Addiction Research Foundation.

Cooperstock, Ruth, and H. Lennard. 1979. "Some social meanings of tranquilizer use." *Sociology of Health and Illness* 1: 331–347.

Cooperstock, Ruth, and Penny Parnell. 1982. "Research on psychotropic drug use." *Social Science and Medicine* 16: 1179–1196.

Copeland, S. Royal. 1920. "The narcotic drug evil and the New York City Health Department." *American Medicine* 15: 17–23.

Cornell, A. P. 1891. "Is cocaine aphrodisiac?" *Medical Brief* 19: 152.

Cortina, Frank Michael. 1970. *Stroke a Slain Warrior.* New York: Columbia University Press.

Courtwright, David T. 1978. "Opiate addiction as a consequence of the Civil War." *Civil War History* 24: 101–111.

———. 1982a. *Dark Paradise.* Cambridge, Mass.: Harvard University Press.

———. 1982b. "The Female Opiate Addict in Nineteenth-Century America." *Essays in Arts and Sciences* 10: 161–171.

Courtwright, David T., Herman Joseph, and Don Des Jarlais. 1989. *Addicts Who Survived.* Knoxville: University of Tennessee Press.

Coxe, John Redman. 1818. *The American Dispensatory.* 4th ed. Philadelphia: Thomas Dobson and Son.

Crothers, T. D. 1898. "Cocaine-Inebriety." *Quarterly Journal of Inebriety* 20: 369–376.

———. 1899. "Morphinism among physicians." *Medical Record* 55: 784–786.

———. 1910. "Cocainism." *Quarterly Journal of Inebriety* 32: 78–84.

Culbreth, David M. R. 1903. *A Manual of Materia Medica and Pharmacology,* 3d ed. Philadelphia: Lea Brothers.

"Current Drug Use Trends in New York City." 1993. New York State Office of Alcoholism and Substance Abuse Services.

Cushman, P., Jr. 1978. "Detoxification of methadone maintained patients." In *Drug Abuse: Modern Trends, Issues, and Perspectives,* ed. Arnold Schecter, Harold Alksne, and Edward Kaufman, 337–345. New York: Marcel Dekker.

Cushman, P., et al. 1976. "Methadone maintenance treatment of narcotic addictions: A unit of medical care based on over 50,000 patient treatment years." *American Journal of Drug and Alcohol Abuse* 3: 221–233.

Cuskey, Walter R., Arthur D. Moffett, and Happa B. Clifford. 1971. "Comparison of female opiate addicts admitted to Lexington Hospital in 1961 and 1967." *HSMHA Health Reports* 86: 332–339.

Cuskey, Walter R., T. Premkumar, and Lois Siegel. 1972. "Survey of opiate addiction among females in the United States between 1850 and 1970." *Public Health Reviews* 1: 6–39.

Cuskey, Walter R., and Richard B. Wathey. 1982. *Female Addiction*. Lexington, Mass.: Lexington Books.

Dai, Bingham. 1937. *Opium Addiction in Chicago*. Montclair, N.J.: Patterson Smith. Repr. 1970.

Danaceau, Paul. 1973. *Methadone Maintenance: The Experience of Four Programs*. Washington, D.C.: Drug Abuse Council.

"Dangers of giving opiates to children." 1834. *Boston Medical and Surgical Journal*, April 23: 174.

Daniels, Cynthia R. 1993. *At Women's Expense: State Power and the Politics of Fetal Rights*. Cambridge, Mass.: Harvard University Press.

Darling, Lynn. 1995. "Women on drugs." *Bazaar*. April.

Davenport, H. 1889. *Diseases of Women*. Philadelphia: Lea Brothers.

David, William K., ed. 1896. *Secrets of Wise Men, Chemists and Great Physicians*. Philadelphia: William K. David.

Davis, Nathan S. 1884. *Lectures on the Principles and Practice of Medicine*. Chicago: Jansen, McClurg & Co.

Day, Horace, ed. 1868. *The Opium Habit*. New York: Harper and Brothers.

de Crevecoeur, J. Hector St. John. [1782] 1981. *Letters from an American Farmer and Sketches of Eighteenth-Century America*, ed. Albert E. Stone. New York: Penguin Books.

De Leon, George. 1985. "The therapeutic community: Status and evolution." *International Journal of the Addictions* 20: 823–844.

De Leon, George, and Jainchill, Nancy. 1981–1982. "Male and female drug abusers: Social and psychological status 2 years after treatment in a therapeutic community." *American Journal of Drug and Alcohol Abuse* 8: 465–497.

Del Rey, A., et al. 1977. "The therapeutic community as adjunct to methadone maintenance." In *Drug Detoxification: A Comprehensive Examination*, ed. Joyce Lowinson and John Langrod, 158–167. Oceanside, N.Y.: Dabor Science Publications.

Densen-Gerber, Judianne. 1973. *We Mainline Dreams: The Odyssey House Story*. Garden City, N.Y.: Doubleday.

Dicker, Marvin, and Eldin A. Leighton. 1991. "Trends in diagnosed drug problems among newborns: United States, 1979–1987." *Drug and Alcohol Dependence* 28: 151–165.

Didion, Joan. 1961. *Slouching towards Bethlehem*. New York: Noonday Press.

"Diet and drinks of nursing women." 1860. *Godey's Magazine*, December: 558.

Dishotsky, Norman I., et al. 1971. "LSD and genetic damage." *Science* 172: 431–440.

Doberczak, Tatiana M., et al. 1987. "Impact of maternal drug dependency on birth weight and head circumference of offspring." *American Journal of Diseases of Children* 141: 1163–1167.

Douglas, Charles J. 1913. "Morphine in general practice." *New York Medical Journal* 97: 882–883.

Doyle, Kathleen M., et al. 1977. "Restructuring rehabilitation for women: Programs for the female drug addict." *American Journal of Psychiatry* 134: 1395–1399.

Driver, C. W. Chavkin, and G. Higginson. 1987. "Survey of infants awaiting placement in voluntary hospitals, 1986–87." New York: New York City Department of Health.

Drug Abuse Council. 1980. *The Facts about "Drug Abuse."* New York: Free Press.

"Drug addicts in the South." 1919. *Survey* 42: 147–148.

Drug Use in America: Problem in Perspective. 1973. Second Report of the National Commission on Marihuana and Drug Abuse. Washington, D.C.: U.S. Government Printing Office.

Drugs and Crime Facts. 1992. Washington, D.C.: U.S. Department of Justice. Pamphlet NCJ-139561.

Drysdale, H. H. 1915. "Some of the effects of the Harrison Anti-Narcotic Law in Cleveland." *Cleveland Medical Journal* 14: 353–364.

Duncan, H. S. 1885. "The mophia [sic] habit—How is it most usually contracted, and what is the best means to diminish it?" *Nashville Journal of Medicine and Surgery* 35: 246–248.

Dundee, J. W., and P. D. A. McIlroy. 1982. "The history of the barbiturates." *Anaesthesia* 37: 726–734.

DuPont, Robert L. 1975. "New perceptions." In *Drugs, Alcohol and Women,* ed. Muriel Nellis, 7–13. Washington, D.C.: National Research and Communications Associates.

Duvall, Henrietta J., Ben Z. Locke, and Leon Brill. 1963. "Followup study of narcotic drug addicts five years after hospitalization." *Public Health Reports* 78: 185–193.

Earle, Charles W. 1880. "The opium habit: A statistical and clinical lecture." *Chicago Medical Review* 2: 442–446. Repr. in Morgan 1974: 53–61.

Earle, F. B. 1888. "Maternal opium habit and infant mortality." *Medical Standard* 3: 2–4.

Eaton, Virgil G. 1888. "How the opium habit is acquired." *Popular Science Monthly* 33: 663–667.

Eberle, E. G., and F. T. Gordon. 1903. "Report of Committee on Acquirement of Drug Habits." *American Journal of Pharmacy* 75: 474–488.

Edlin, Brian R., et al. 1992. "High-risk sex behavior among young street-recruited crack cocaine smokers in three American cities: An interim report." *Journal of Psychoactive Drugs* 24: 363–371.

"An effect of cannabis indica." 1885. *Medical Age* 3: 107.

Eldred, Carolyn A., and Mabel N. Washington. 1976. "Interpersonal relationships in heroin use by men and women and their role in treatment outcome." *International Journal of the Addictions* 11: 117–130.

Eldridge, William Butler. 1962. *Narcotics and the Law.* New York: American Bar Foundation.

Ellinwood, E. H., W. G. Smith, and G. E. Vaillant. 1966. "Narcotic addiction in males and females: A comparison." *International Journal of the Addictions* 1: 33–38.

Ellis, Benjamin. 1846. *The Medical Formulary.* 8th ed. Philadelphia: Lea and Blanchard.

"Erythroxylon Coca as an antidote to the opium habit." 1880. *Detroit Therapeutic Gazette* 1: 172.

Etheridge, J. H. 1872. "Lectures on chloral hydrate." *Chicago Medical Journal* 29: 521–527.

Ettore, Elizabeth. 1992. *Women and Substance Use.* New Brunswick, N.J.: Rutgers University Press.

Falco, Mathea. 1989. *Winning the Drug War.* New York: Priority Press.

Farr, Clifford B. 1915. "The relative frequency of the morphine and heroin habits." *New York Medical Journal* 101: 892–895.

Faulkner, Thomas, and J. H. Carmichael. 1892. *The Cottage Physician.* Springfield, Mass.: King, Richardson.

Federal Bureau of Investigation. 1965–1976. *Crime in the United States.* Uniform Crime Reports. Washington, D.C.: U.S. Department of Justice.

———. 1992. *Crime in the United States 1991.* Washington, D.C.: U.S. Department of Justice.

Fiddle, Seymour. 1967. *Portraits from a Shooting Gallery.* New York: Harper and Row.

Fidell, Linda S. 1973. "Put her down on drugs: Prescribed drug usage in women." Paper presented at the Western Psychological Association Meeting, Anaheim, Calif., April 12.

Field, Gary. 1989. "The effects of intensive treatment on reducing the criminal recidivism of addicted offenders." *Federal Probation* 53: 51–56.

Finestone, Harold. 1957. "Narcotics and criminality." *Law and Contemporary Problems* 22: 69–85.

Finnegan, L. P., et al. 1972. "Comprehensive care of the pregnant addict and its effect on maternal and infant outcome." *Contemporary Drug Problems* 1: 795–809.

Finnegan, Loretta P., and Stephen R. Kandall. 1992. "Maternal and neonatal effects of alcohol and drugs." In *Substance Abuse: A Comprehensive Textbook,* ed. Joyce H. Lowinson, Pedro Ruiz, Robert B. Millman. Baltimore: Williams and Wilkins.

Firebaugh, Ellen M. 1904. *The Physician's Wife.* Philadelphia: F. A. Davis.

Fischer, Louis. 1894. "The opium habit in children." *Medical Record* 45: 197–199.

Fishburne, Patricia M., Herbert I. Abelson, and Ira Cisin. 1979. *National Survey on Drug Abuse: Main Findings: 1979.* Rockville, Md.: National Institute on Drug Abuse. DHHS Pub. No. (ADM) 80–976.

Fisher, Florrie. 1971. *The Lonely Trip Back.* Garden City, N.Y.: Doubleday.

Flohr, Rinna B. 1975. "Promoting community investment." In *Drugs, Alcohol and Women,* ed. Muriel Nellis, 67–70. Washington, D.C.: National Research and Communications Associates.

Flynn, Patrick M., et al. 1995. "Relationship between drug preference and psychiatric impairment." *American Journal of Drug and Alcohol Abuse* 21: 153–166.

Fort, Joel. 1969. *The Pleasure Seekers: The Drug Crisis, Youth and Society.* Indianapolis: Bobbs-Merrill.

Fort, John P., Jr. 1954. "Heroin addiction among young men." *Psychiatry* 17: 251–259.

Fothergill, J. Milner. 1877. *The Practitioner's Handbook of Treatment.* Philadelphia: Henry C. Lea.

Frank, Blanche, and John Galea. 1992. "Current drug use trends in New York City." New York State Office of Alcoholism and Substance Abuse Services.

Frank, Deborah, et al. 1988. "Cocaine use during pregnancy: Prevalence and correlates." *Pediatrics* 82: 888–895.

Freeland, Jeffrey B., and Richard S. Campbell. 1973. "The social context of first marijuana use." *International Journal of the Addictions* 8: 317–324.

French, James. 1903. *A Textbook on the Practice of Medicine.* New York: William Wood.

Freudenberger, Herbert J. 1978. "The woman in a therapeutic community." In *Drug Abuse: Modern Trends, Issues, and Perspectives,* ed. Arnold Schecter, Harold Alksne, and Edward Kaufman, 176–181. New York: Marcel Dekker.

Frost, C. P. 1869–1870. "Opium: Its uses and abuses." *Transactions of the Vermont Medical Society,* pp. 131–147.

Garb, Solomon. 1965. "Narcotic addiction in nurses and doctors." *Nursing Outlook* 13: 30–34.

Gay, Anne C., and George R. Gay. 1972. "Evolution of a drug culture in an era of mendacity." In *It's So Good, Don't Even Try It Once,* ed. David E. Smith and George R. Gay, 13–31. Englewood Cliffs, N.J.: Prentice-Hall.

Gay, George. 1981. "You've come a long way, baby! Coke time for the new American lady of the Eighties." *Journal of Psychoactive Drugs* 13: 297–318.

Gay, George, John A. Newmeyer, and John J. Winkler. 1972. "The Haight-Ashbury Free Medical Clinic." In *It's So Good, Don't Even Try It Once,* ed. David E. Smith and George R. Gay, 71–85. Englewood Cliffs, N.J.: Prentice-Hall.

Gearing, Frances R. 1971. "Evaluation of methadone maintenance treatment program." In *Methadone Maintenance,* ed. Stanley Einstein, 171–197. New York: Marcel Dekker.

Gearing, Frances R., Dina A. D'Amico, and Freida Thompson. 1978. "What's good about methadone maintenance after ten years?" In *Drug Abuse: Modern Trends, Issues, and Perspectives,* ed. Arnold Schecter, Harold Alksne, and Edward Kaufman, 645–666. New York: Marcel Dekker.

Gerstein, Dean R., and Henrick J. Harwood, eds. 1990. *Treating Drug Problems: A Study of the Evolution, Effectiveness, and Financing of Public and Private Drug Treatment Systems.* Washington, D.C.: National Academy Press.

Glasscote, Raymond M., et al. 1972. *The Treatment of Drug Abuse: Programs, Problems, Prospects.* Washington, D.C.: Joint Information Service of the American Psychiatric Association and the National Association for Mental Health.

Gleason, Mrs. R. B. 1871. *Talks to My Patients.* New York: Wood and Holbrook.

Glynn, Thomas J., Helen Wallenstein Pearson, and Mollie Sayers. 1983. *Women and Drugs.* Rockville, Md.: National Institute on Drug Abuse. DHHS Pub. No. (ADM) 83–1268.

Gold, Mark S. 1992. "Cocaine (and Crack): Clinical aspects." In *Substance Abuse: A Comprehensive Textbook,* ed. Joyce Lowinson, Pedro Ruiz, and Robert B. Millman, 205–221. Baltimore: Williams and Wilkens.

Goldberg, Peter. 1980. "The federal government's response to illicit drugs, 1969–1978." In Drug Abuse Council, *The Facts about "Drug Abuse,"* 20–62. New York: Free Press.

Goldstein, Paul J. 1979. *Prostitution and Drugs.* Lexington, Mass.: Lexington Books.

Goldstein, Paul J., Lawrence J. Ouellet, and Michael Fendrich. 1992. "From bag brides to skeezers: A historical perspective on sex-for-drugs behavior." *Journal of Psychoactive Drugs* 24: 349–361.

Goode, Erich. 1972. *Drugs in American Society.* New York: Knopf.

Gordon, Barbara. 1979. *I'm Dancing as Fast as I Can.* New York: Harper and Row.

Graham-Mulhall, Sara. 1921a. "Experiences in narcotic drug control in the State of New York." *New York Medical Journal* 113: 106–111.

———. 1921b. "The helpless narcotic: A public health menace and a public health responsibility." *American Journal of Public Health* 11: 25–52.

———. 1926. *Opium: The Demon Flower.* New York: Montrose Publishing.

Green, E. M. 1914. "Psychoses among negroes—A comparative study." *Journal of Nervous and Mental Disease* 41: 697–708.

Grinnell, A. P. 1905. "A review of drug consumption and alcohol as found in proprietary medicine." *Medico-Legal Journal.* Cited in Terry and Pellens 1928.

Grinspoon, Lester. 1971. *Marihuana Reconsidered.* Cambridge, Mass.: Harvard University Press.

Grover, George Wheelock. 1894. *Shadows Lifted.* Chicago: Stromberg, Allen.

Haack, Mary R., and Tonda L. Hughes, eds. 1989. *Addiction in the Nursing Profession.* New York: Springer.

Hall, Margaret E. 1938. "Mental and physical efficiency of women drug addicts." *Journal of Abnormal and Social Psychology* 33: 332–345.

Haller, John S., Jr. 1989. "A short history of the quack's materia medica." *New York State Journal of Medicine* 89: 520–525.

Haller, John S., Jr., and Robin M. Haller. 1974. *The Physician and Sexuality in Victorian America.* Urbana: University of Illinois Press.

Hamburger, Ernest. 1969. "Contrasting the hippie and the junkie." *International Journal of the Addictions* 4: 121–135.

Hamlin, F. H. 1882. "The opium habit." *Medical Gazette* 9: 426–431.

Hammond, W. A. 1886a. "Remarks on cocaine and the so-called cocaine habit." *Journal of Nervous and Mental Disease* 13: 754–759.

———. 1886b. "Cocaine and the so-called cocaine habit." *New York Medical Journal* 44: 637–639.

Happel, T. J. 1892. "Morphinism in its relation to the sexual functions and appetite, and its effect on the off-spring of the users of the drug." *Medical and Surgical Reporter* 68: 403–407.

———. 1900. "Morphinism from the standpoint of the general practitioner." *Journal of the American Medical Association* 35: 407–409.

Harper, R. G., et al. 1974. "The effect of a methadone treatment program upon pregnant heroin addicts and their newborn infants." *Pediatrics* 54: 300–305.

Harrison, Patricia Ann, and Carol A. Belille. 1987. "Women in treatment: Beyond the stereotype." *Journal of Studies on Alcohol* 48: 574–578.

Hartwell, B. H. 1889. "The sale and use of opium in Massachusetts." *Annual Report, Massachusetts State Board of Health* 20: 137–158.

Health Systems Agency of New York City, Inc. 1994. "Charting new directions: Planning substance abuse treatment services in New York City." New York: Health Systems Agency.

Hellinger, F. J. 1990. "Updated forecasts of the costs of medical care for persons with AIDS, 1989–93." *Public Health Reports* 105: 1–12.

Helmer, John. 1975. *Drugs and Minority Oppression.* New York: Seabury Press.

Henderson, Alberta L. 1975. Introduction. *Drugs, Alcohol and Women,* ed. Muriel Nellis, 1–2. Washington, D.C.: National Research and Communications Associates.

Hentoff, Nat. 1968. *A Doctor among the Addicts.* New York: Rand McNally.

Herman, Judith L. 1992. *Trauma and Recovery.* New York: Basic Books.

High Times. 1994. *High Times Greatest Hits: Twenty Years of Smoke in Your Face.* New York: St. Martin's.

Hilker, Robert R. J., Fern E. Asma, and Robert L. Ross. 1978. "An industrial approach to drug abuse rehabilitation." In *Drug Abuse: Modern Trends, Issues, and Perspectives,* ed. Arnold Schecter, Harold Alksne, and Edward Kaufman, 408–413. New York: Marcel Dekker.

Hillsman, Julia. 1975. "Finding the positive in people." In *Drugs, Alcohol and Women,* ed. Muriel Nellis, 121–123. Washington, D.C.: National Research and Communications Associates.

Himmelstein, Jerome L. 1983. *The Strange Career of Marijuana: Politics and Ideology of Drug Control in America.* Westport, Conn.: Greenwood Press.

Hindelang, Michael J., et al. 1977. *Sourcebook of Criminal Justice Statistics 1976.* Washington, D.C.: U.S. Department of Justice and Criminal Justice Research Center.

Hirata, Lucie Cheng. 1979. "Chinese immigrant women in nineteenth-century America." In *Women of America: A History,* ed. Carol Ruth Berkin and Mary Beth Norton. Boston: Houghton Mifflin.

Hole, James W. 1880. "Therapeutic Gazette." 1892. Repr. in *The Pharmacology of the Newer Materia Medica,* 393–440. Detroit: G. S. Davis.

Holiday, Billie. 1992. *Lady Sings the Blues.* London: Penguin Books.

Holmes, Oliver Wendell. 1888. "Currents and counter-currents." *Medical Essays: 1842–1882.* Boston: Houghton Mifflin.

hooks, bell. 1981. *Ain't I a Woman: Black Women and Feminism.* Boston: South End Press.

House Committee on the Judiciary. *Establishment of Two Federal Narcotic Farms: Hearing before the Committee on the Judiciary.* 70th Cong., 1st sess., 1928.

Howard, Horton, M.D. 1879. *Domestic Medicine.* Philadelphia: Hubbard Brothers.

Howard, Jan, and Phillip Borges. 1972. "Needle sharing in the Haight." In *It's So Good, Don't Even Try It Once,* ed. David E. Smith and George R. Gay. Englewood Cliffs, N.J.: Prentice-Hall.

Howard, Judy. 1992. "Discussion: Effect of legal stipulations on the conduct of treatment and prevention research." In *Methodological Issues in Epidemiological, Prevention, and Treatment Research on Drug-Exposed Women and Their Children,* ed. M. Marlyne Kilbey and Khursheed Ashgar, 385–393. Rockville, Md.: National Institute on Drug Abuse. DHHS Pub. No. (ADM) 92–1881.

Howard, William Lee. 1904a. "Some facts regarding the morphine victim." *Quarterly Journal of Inebriety* 26: 128–136.

———. 1904b. "Some subjective hints of the morphine habit." *Medical News* 84: 113–114.

Hubbard, Robert L., et al. 1989. *Drug Abuse Treatment: A National Study of Effectiveness.* Chapel Hill: University of North Carolina Press.

Hubbard, S. Dana. 1920a. "Municipal narcotic dispensaries." *Treasury Weekly Public Health Reports, U.S. Public Health Service* 35, part 1, nos. 1–26.

———. 1920b. "New York City Narcotic Clinic and differing points of view on narcotic addiction." *Monthly Bulletin, New York City Department of Health* 10: 33–47.

———. 1920c. "Report of the Special Committee on the Narcotic Drug Situation." *Journal of the American Medical Association* 74: 1959.

———. 1920d. "Some fallacies regarding narcotic drug addiction." *Journal of the American Medical Association* 74: 1439–1441.

Hughes, Helen MacGill, ed. 1961. *The Fantastic Lodge.* Boston: Houghton Mifflin.

Hughes, Patrick H., et al. 1992. "Prevalence of substance use among U.S. physicians." *Journal of the American Medical Association* 267: 2333–2339.

Hull, J. M. 1885. "The opium habit." *Iowa State Board of Health Biennial Report* 3: 535–545. Repr. in part in Morgan 1974: 39–42.

Huncke, Herbert. 1990. "A brief oral history of Benzedrine use in the U.S." *The Drug User: Documents 1840–1960,* ed. John Strasbaugh and Donald Blaise, 57–59. New York: Blast Books.

Hunt, G. Halsey, and Maurice E. Odoroff. 1962. "Followup study of narcotic drug addicts after hospitalization." *Public Health Reports* 77: 41–54.

Hunt, Leon Gibson. 1977. "Prevalence of active heroin use in the United States." In *The Epidemiology of Heroin and Other Narcotics,* ed. Joan Dunn Rittenhouse. NIDA Research Monograph 16. DHEW Pub. No. (ADM) 78–559.

Hunt, Leon Gibson, and Carl D. Chambers. 1976. *The Heroin Epidemics.* New York: Spectrum.

Hutchins, Ellen, and Greg R. Alexander. 1990. "Substance abuse during pregnancy and its effect on the infant: A review of the issues." *HHS Region III Perinatal Information Consortium Technical Report Series.* Booklet PIC-III TRS 90–01. Department of Maternal and Child Health, School of Hygiene and Public Health, Johns Hopkins University.

Hynson, H. P. 1902. "Report of Committee on Acquirement of the Drug Habit." *American Journal of Pharmacy* 74: 547–554.

Iennarella, Ralph, Gay M. Chisum, and Jill Bianchi. 1986. "A comprehensive treatment model for pregnant chemical users, infants and families." In *Drug Use in Pregnancy: Mother and Child,* ed. Ira J. Chasnoff, 42–51. Boston: MTP Press.

Illich, Ivan. 1976. *Medical Nemesis: The Expropriation of Health.* New York: Pantheon Books.

Immarigeon, Russ, and Meda Chesney-Lind. 1992. "Women's prisons—Overcrowded and overused." San Francisco: National Council on Crime and Delinquency.

Implications of the Drug Use Forecasting Data for TASC Programs: Female Arrestees. 1991. Washington, D.C.: Bureau of Justice Assistance Monograph. NCJ 129671.

Inciardi, James A., Dorothy Lockwood, and Anne E. Pottieger. 1993. *Women and Crack-Cocaine.* New York: Macmillan.

Inciardi, James A., and Anne E. Pottieger. 1986. "Drug use and crime among two cohorts of women narcotic users: An empirical assessment." *Journal of Drug Issues* 16: 91–106.

Inciardi, James A., Anne E. Pottieger, and Charles E. Faupel. 1982. "Black women, heroin and crime: Some empirical notes." *Journal of Drug Issues* 12: 241–250.

Isbell, Harris. 1955. "Medical aspects of opiate addiction." *Bulletin of the New York Academy of Medicine* 31: 886–901.

———. 1965. "Perspectives in research on opiate addiction." In *Narcotics,* ed. Daniel M. Wilner and Gene G. Kassebaum, 36–50. New York: McGraw-Hill.

Jackson, Charles O. 1970. *Food and Drug Legislation in the New Deal.* Princeton: Princeton University Press.

Jaffe, Jerome H. 1978. "Reminiscences of a drug czar." In *Drug Addiction and the Public Health Service,* ed. William Martin and Harris Isbell, 281–294. Washington, D.C.: U.S. Department of Health, Education and Welfare. DHEW Pub. No. (ADM) 77–434.

Jahiel, R. I. 1992. "The size of the homeless population." In *Homelessness: A Prevention Oriented Approach,* ed. R. I. Jahiel, 337–359. Baltimore: Johns Hopkins University Press.

James, Jennifer, Cathleen Gosho, and Robbin W. Wohl. 1979. "The relationship between female criminality and drug use." *International Journal of the Addictions* 14: 215–229.

Jarvis, William Chapman. 1884. "Cocaine in Nasal Surgery." *Medical Record,* December 13. 1892. Repr. in *The Pharmacology of the Newer Materia Medica.* Detroit: G. S. Davis.

Johnson, Kit G., et al. 1971. "Survey of adolescent drug use." *American Journal of Public Health* 61: 2418–2432.

Johnston, Lloyd D., Jerald G. Bachman, and Patrick M. O'Malley. 1979. *Drugs and the Class of '78: Behaviors, Attitudes, and Recent National Trends.* Rockville, Md.: National Institute on Drug Abuse. DHEW Pub. No. (ADM) 79–877.

Johnston, Lloyd D., Patrick M. O'Malley, and Jerald G. Bachman. 1987. *National Trends in Drug Use and Related Factors among American High School Students and Young Adults, 1975–1986.* Rockville, Md.: National Institute on Drug Abuse. DHHS Pub. No. (ADM) 87–1535.

———. 1993. *National Survey Results on Drug Use from The Monitoring the Future Study, 1975–1992.* Rockville, Md.: National Institute on Drug Abuse. NIH Pub. No. 93–3598.

———. 1994. *National Survey Results on Drug Use from The Monitoring the Future Study, 1975–1993.* Rockville, Md.: National Institute on Drug Abuse. NIH Pub. No. 94–3810.

Jolly, P., and D. M. Hudley, eds. 1992. *Statistical Information Related to Medical Education.* Washington, D.C.: Association of American Medical Colleges.

Joyce, Theodore, et al. 1995. "The impact of prenatal exposure to cocaine on newborn costs and length of stay." *HSR: Health Services Research* 30: 341–358.

Kaestner, Elizabeth, et al. 1986. "Substance use among females in New York State: Catching up with the males." *Advances in Alcohol and Substance Abuse* 5: 29–49.

Kahn, Robert B., and N. T. Schramm. 1978. "Twenty-one-day outpatient detoxification: An evaluation." In *Drug Abuse: Modern Trends, Issues, and Perspectives,* ed. Arnold Schecter, Harold Alksne, and Edward Kaufman, 301–307. New York: Marcel Dekker.

Kail, Barbara Lynn, Deena D. Watson, and Scott Ray. 1995. "Needle-using practices within the sex industry." *American Journal of Drug and Alcohol Abuse* 21: 241–255.

Kaltenbach, Karol A., and Loretta P. Finnegan. 1992. "Studies of prenatal drug exposure and environmental research issues: The benefits of integrating research within a treatment program." In *Methodological Issues in Epidemiological, Prevention, and Treatment Research on Drug-Exposed Women and Their Children,* ed. M. Marlyne Kilbey and Khursheed Ashgar, 259–270. Rockville, Md.: National Institute on Drug Abuse. DHHS Pub. No. (ADM) 92–1881.

Kandall, Stephen R. (Consensus Panel Chair). 1993. *Improving Treatment for Drug-exposed Infants.* Rockville, Md.: U.S. Department of Health and Human Services. DHHS Pub. No. (SMA) 93–2011.

Kandall, Stephen R., and Wendy Chavkin. 1990. "Between a rock and a hard place: Perinatal drug abuse." *Pediatrics* 85: 223–225.

Kandall, Stephen R., et al. 1976. "Differential effects of maternal heroin and methadone on birthweight." *Pediatrics* 58: 681–685.

Kandall, Stephen R., et al. 1977. "The narcotic-dependent mother: Fetal and neonatal consequences." *Early Human Development* 1/2: 159–169.

Kandall, Stephen R., et al. 1993. "Relationship of maternal substance abuse to subsequent sudden infant death syndrome in offspring." *Journal of Pediatrics* 123: 120–126.

Kandel, Denise, Eric Single, and Ronald C. Kessler. 1976. "The epidemiology of drug use among New York State high school students: Distribution, trends, and changes in rates of use." *American Journal of Public Health* 66: 43–53.

Kane, H. H. 1880. *The Hypodermic Injection of Morphia.* New York: C. L. Bermingham.

———. 1881. *Drugs That Enslave.* Philadelphia: Presley Blakiston.

———. 1882. *Opium-Smoking in America and China.* New York: G. P. Putnam's Sons.

———. 1883. "A hashish-house in New York." *Harper's Monthly* 67: 944–949.

Kaufman, Edward. 1972. "Reality House: A self-help day-care center for narcotic addicts." In *Drug Abuse,* ed. Wolfram Keup, 381–386. Springfield, Ill.: Charles C. Thomas.

Kaufman, Edward, Ron Williams, and Marie Broudy. 1978. "Su Casa: A methadone to abstinence therapeutic community." In *Drug Abuse: Modern Trends, Issues, and Perspectives,* ed. Arnold Schecter, Harold Alksne, and Edward Kaufman, 200–206. New York: Marcel Dekker.

Kaysen, Susanna. 1993. *Girl, Interrupted.* New York: Turtle Bay Books.

The Keeley Institute, White Plains. Undated. New York Academy of Medicine, Pamphlet no. 104167.

Keeley, Leslie E. 1880. *The Opium Habit: Its Proper Method of Treatment and Cure, without Suffering or Inconvenience.* Dwight, Ill. New York Academy of Medicine pamphlet.

———. 1881. "Experiences of recent opium eaters." *The Morphine Eater: Or from Bondage to Freedom.* Dwight, Ill.: C. L. Palmer.

Kellogg, J. H. 1898. "A new and successful method of treatment for the opium habit and other forms of drug addiction." *Modern Medicine and Bacteriological Review* 7: 125–132.

———. 1903. "The treatment of drug addiction." *Quarterly Journal of Inebriety* 25: 30–43.

Kenealy, Arabella. 1899. "A lady doctor on the girl of today." *Medical Record* 55: 719.

Kerr, Barbara. *Strong at the Broken Places: Women Who Have Survived Drugs.* 1974. Chicago: Follett.

Kerr, Norman. 1894. *Inebriaty or Narcomania.* 3d ed. London: H. K. Lewis.

Kiev, Ari. 1975. *The Drug Epidemic.* New York: Free Press.

King, Ellie. 1980. "Sex bias in psychoactive drug advertisements." *Psychiatry* 43: 129–137.

King, Rufus G. 1953. "The Narcotics Bureau and the Harrison Act: Jailing the healers and the sick." *Yale Law Journal* 62: 736–749.

Kingree, J. B. 1995. "Understanding gender differences in psychosocial functioning and treatment retention." *American Journal of Drug and Alcohol Abuse* 21: 267–281.

Kirkland, Gelsey. 1986. *Dancing on My Grave*. New York: Berkley Books.

Kleber, Herbert D. 1971. "The New Haven methadone program." In *Methadone Maintenance*, ed. Stanley Einstein, 103–117. New York: Marcel Dekker.

Kolb, Lawrence. 1925. "Types and characteristics of drug addicts." *Mental Hygiene* 9: 699–724.

———. 1956. "Let's stop this narcotics hysteria." *Saturday Evening Post,* July 28, 1956, p. 19.

———. 1962. *Drug Addiction.* Springfield, Ill.: Charles C. Thomas.

Kolb, Lawrence, and A. G. Du Mez. 1924. "The prevalence and trend of drug addiction in the United States and factors influencing it." *Public Health Reports* 39: 1179–1204.

Kremers, Edward, and Urdang, George. 1976. *History of Pharmacy.* 4th ed. Philadelphia: J. B. Lippincott.

Kuhns, Joseph B., III, Kathleen M. Heide, and Ira Silverman. 1992. "Substance use/misuse among female prostitutes and female arrestees." *International Journal of the Addictions* 27: 1283–1292.

Kunnes, Richard. 1973. "Poly-drug abuse: Drug companies and doctors." *American Journal of Orthopsychiatry* 43: 530–532.

Lambert, Alexander, and Frederick Tilney. 1926. "The treatment of narcotic addiction by Narcosan." *Medical Journal and Record* 124: 764–768.

La Motte, Ellen N. 1924. *The Ethics of Opium.* New York: Century.

Langrod, John. 1977. "Secondary drug use among heroin users." In *Drug Detoxification: A Comprehensive Examination,* ed. Joyce Lowinson and John Langrod, 3–28. Oceanside, N.Y.: Dabor Science Publications.

Langrod, John, Herman Joseph, and Katherine Valdes. 1977. "The role of religion in the treatment of opiate addiction." In *Drug Detoxification: A Comprehensive Examination,* ed. Joyce Lowinson and John Langrod, 168–187. Oceanside, N.Y.: Dabor Science Publications.

Larner, Jeremy, ed. 1964. *The Addict in the Street.* New York: Grove Press.

Lawton, Stephan. 1975. "Promoting responsive commitment." In *Drugs, Alcohol and Women,* ed. Muriel Nellis, 226–228. Washington, D.C.: National Research and Communications Associates.

Leahy, Sylvester R. 1915. "Some observations on heroin habitues." *Psychiatric Bulletin of the New York State Hospitals,* n.s. 8: 251–263.

Lee, Harper. 1960. *To Kill a Mockingbird.* New York: Warner Books.

Levine, David G., Phyllis A. Preston, and Sally G. Lipscomb. 1974. "A historical approach to understanding drug abuse among nurses." *American Journal of Psychiatry* 131: 1036–1037.

Lichtenstein, Perry M. 1914. "Narcotic addiction." *New York Medical Journal* 100: 962–966.

Limiting the Production of Habit-forming Narcotic Drugs and the Raw Materials from Which They Are Made. 67th Cong., 4th sess. H.R. Rept. 1678.

Lindesmith, Alfred R. 1965. "Problems in the social psychology of addiction."

In *Narcotics*, ed. Daniel M. Wilner and Gene G. Kassebaum, 118–139. New York: McGraw-Hill.

Linn, Lawrence S., and Milton S. Davis. 1971. "The use of psychotherapeutic drugs by middle-aged women." *Journal of Health and Social Behavior* 12: 331–340.

Logan, C. A. 1859. "Upon the use of opium in certain conditions of the parturient process." *Atlanta Medical and Surgical Journal* 4: 617.

Loveland, J. A. 1881. "Morphia habit." *Boston Medical and Surgical Journal* 104: 301.

Ludlow, Fitzhugh. 1867. "What shall they do to be saved?" *Harper's Magazine* 35: 377–387. Repr. in Day 1868: 250–284.

Lydon, Susan Gordon. 1993. *Take the Long Way Home*. San Francisco: Harper San Francisco.

Macklin, M. C. 1919. "Morphine addiction." *Bulletin of the Iowa Institute, Des Moines* 21: 171–176.

Maddux, James F. 1965. "Hospital management of the narcotic addict." In *Narcotics*, ed. Daniel M. Wilner and Gene G. Kassebaum, 159–176. New York: McGraw-Hill.

Maddux, James F., and David P. Desmond. 1988. "San Antonio." In *Methadone in the Management of Opioid Dependence: Programs and Policies around the World*, ed. Awin Arif and Joseph Westermeyer, 244–258. Geneva: World Health Organization.

Magid, M. O. 1929. "Narcotic drug addiction in the female." *Medical Journal and Record* 129: 306–310.

Magura, Stephen, Andrew Rosenblum, and Herman Joseph. 1992. "Evaluation of in-jail methadone maintenance: Preliminary results." In *Drug Abuse Treatment in Prisons and Jails*, ed. Carl G. Leukefeld and Frank M. Tims. NIDA Research Monograph Series 118. DHHS Pub. No. (ADM) 92–1884.

Manges, M. 1900. "A second report on the therapeutics of heroine." *New York Medical Journal* 71: 79–83.

Manheimer, Dean I., Glen D. Mellinger, and Mitchell B. Balter. 1968. "Psychotherapeutic drugs." *California Medicine* 109: 445–451.

———. 1970. "Marijuana use among urban adults." *Science* 166: 1544–1545.

Marsh, J. P. 1883. "A case of the opium habit treated with erythroxylon coca." *Therapeutic Gazette*, n.s. 4: 359.

Marshall, Orville. 1878. "The opium habit in Michigan." *Michigan State Board of Health Annual Report* 6: 63–73. Repr. in O'Donnell and Ball 1966: 45–54.

Maternal and Child Health Bureau. 1993. "Prevention of perinatal substance use: Pregnant and Postpartum Women and their Infants demonstration grant program." Arlington, Va.: National Center for Education in Maternal and Child Health.

Maternal Drug Abuse and Drug Exposed Children: A Compendium of HHS Activities. 1992. U.S. Department of Health and Human Services. DHHS Pub. No. (ADM) 92–1948.

Maternal Drug Abuse and Drug Exposed Children: Understanding the Problem.

1992. U.S. Department of Health and Human Services. DHHS Pub. No. (ADM) 92–1949.

Mattison, J. B. 1879a. "Opium habituation." *Medical Record* 16: 332–333. October 4.

———. 1879b. "Chloral inebriety." Read before the Kings County Medical Society, April 15, 1879. New York Academy of Medicine Pamphlet no. 1811.

———. 1883. "Opium addiction among medical men." *Medical Record* 23: 621–623.

———. 1887a. "Cocaine dosage and cocaine addiction." Read before the Kings County Medical Society, February 15, 1887. *Lancet* (London), May 23: 1.

———. 1887b. "Cocaine toxaemia." Read before the American Associates for the Cure of Inebriates, November 8, 1887.

———. 1891. "Cannabis Indica as an anodyne and hypnotic." *St. Louis Medical and Surgical Journal* 61: 266.

———. 1892. "The curability of narcotic inebriety." *Cleveland Medical Gazette,* September: 13. New York Academy of Medicine Pamphlet no. 9174.

———. 1898. "Morphinism among women." *Quarterly Journal of Inebriety* 20: 202–208.

Maurer, David W., and Victor H. Vogel. 1973. *Narcotics and Narcotic Addiction.* 4th ed. Springfield. Ill.: Charles C. Thomas.

McGee, Richard A. 1965. "New approaches to the control and treatment of drug abusers in California." In *Narcotics,* ed. Daniel M. Wilner and Gene C. Kassebaum, 263–273. New York: McGraw-Hill.

McGlothlin, William H., M. Douglas Anglin, and Bruce D. Wilson. 1977. "A follow-up of admissions to the California Civil Addict Program." *American Journal of Drug and Alcohol Abuse* 4: 179–199.

McGlothlin, William H., and David O. Arnold. 1971. "LSD revisited: A ten-year follow-up of medical LSD use." *Archives of General Psychiatry* 24: 35.

McGlothlin, William H., K. Jamison, and S. Rosenblatt. 1970. "Marijuana and the use of other drugs." *Nature* 228: 1227–1229.

McIver, Joseph, and George E. Price. 1916. "Drug addiction." *Journal of the American Medical Association* 66: 476–480.

McKusker, Jane, et al. 1995. "Outcomes of a 21-day detoxification program: Retention, transfer to further treatment and HIV risk reduction." *American Journal of Drug and Alcohol Abuse* 21: 1–16.

Meiselas, Harold. 1965. "The narcotic addiction program of the New York State Department of Mental Hygiene." In *Narcotics,* ed. Daniel M. Wilner and Gene G. Kassebaum, 249–262. New York: McGraw-Hill.

Mellinger, Glenn D., Mitchell B. Balter, Chevy Chase, and Dean I. Manheimer. 1971. "Patterns of psychotherapeutic drug use among adults in San Francisco." *Archives of General Psychiatry* 25: 385–394.

Melody, Roland. 1971. *Narco Priest.* New York: Tower.

Meyer, Roger E. 1972. *Guide to Drug Rehabilitation.* Boston: Beacon Press.

Mezzrow, Mezz, and Bernard Wolfe. 1990. *Really the Blues.* New York: Citadel Underground.

Miller, Brenda A. 1981. "Drug use and criminality among women in detention." *Journal of Psychoactive Drugs* 13: 289–295.

Miller, Edward, M.D. 1798. "Remarks on the cholera or bilious diarrhoea of infants." *Medical Repository* 1:58–65.

Miller, Judith Droitcour. 1983. *National Survey on Drug Abuse: Main Findings 1982.* Rockville, Md.: National Institute on Drug Abuse. DHHS Pub. No. (ADM) 83–1263.

Miller, Richard E. 1984. "Nationwide profile of female inmate substance involvement." *Journal of Psychoactive Drugs* 16: 319–326.

"Minutes of the Clinical Society of the New York Postgraduate Medical School and Hospital Meeting." 1884. *New York Medical Journal* 40: 588.

"Minutes of the New York Neurological Society Meeting." 1886. *New York Medical Journal* 44: 638–639.

Mitchell, Janet L. (Consensus Panel Chair). 1993. *Pregnant, Substance-Using Women: The Recommendations of a Consensus Panel.* Rockville, Md.: U.S. Department of Health and Human Services, Center for Substance Abuse Treatment.

Mitchell, S. Weir. 1888. "Pain and the opium habit." *Doctor and Patient.* Philadelphia: J. B. Lippincott.

M'Meens, R. R. 1860. "Report of the Committee on Cannabis Indica." *Transactions of the Fifteenth Annual Meeting of the Ohio State Medical Society,* pp. 94–95.

"A modern opium eater." 1914. *American Magazine* 77: 31–35.

Moise, Rebecca, et al. 1982. "A comparison of black and white women entering drug abuse treatment programs." *International Journal of the Addictions* 17: 35–49.

"Morbidity and Mortality Weekly Report." 1992. *Summary of Notifiable Diseases, United States* 40: 57.

Morgan, H. Wayne. 1974. *Yesterday's Addicts.* Norman: University of Oklahoma Press.

————. 1981. *Drugs in America: A Social History 1800–1980.* Syracuse: Syracuse University Press.

Morrison, Martha. 1989. *White Rabbit.* New York: Berkley Books.

Mortimer, W. Golden. 1901. *History of Coca.* 1974. Repr. San Francisco: And/Or Press.

Mosher, Elissa H. 1975. "Regional coalition: Reports and initiatives." In *Drugs, Alcohol and Women,* ed. Muriel Nellis, 233–248. Washington, D.C.: National Research and Communications Associates.

Musto, David. 1973. *The American Disease.* New Haven: Yale University Press.

————. 1977. "Historical highlights of American drug use (1800–1940)." In *Americans and Drug Abuse,* ed. C. Krymer and S. P. Strickland, 3–8. Aspen, Colo.: Aspen Institute for Humanistic Studies.

Musto, David, and Manuel R. Ramos. 1981. "Notes on American medical history: A follow-up study of the New Haven morphine maintenance clinic of 1920." *New England Journal of Medicine* 304: 1071–1077.

Nadelmann, Ethan A. 1989. "Drug prohibition in the United States: Costs, consequences, and alternatives." *Science* 245: 939–947.

"Narcotic treatment program standards and methadone in maintenance and detoxification." 1977. *Federal Register* 42, no. 208: 56902.

National Household Survey on Drug Abuse: Main Findings 1985. 1988. Rockville, Md.: National Institute on Drug Abuse. DHHS Pub. No. (ADM) 88–1586.

National Institute on Drug Abuse. 1976. *Heroin Indicators Trend Report.* Rockville, Md.: National Institute on Drug Abuse.

————. 1981. *Drug Abuse Treatment in Prisons.* Rockville, Md. DHHS Pub. No. (ADM) 81–1149.

————. 1994. *1995 Budget Estimate.* N.p.

National Institute on Justice. 1990. *Drug Use Forecasting Annual Report 1989.* Washington, D.C.: U.S. Department of Justice.

Neims, S. 1990. "An overview of Georgia's child protective system." Paper prepared for Clinical and Developmental Research Program, Human Genetics Laboratory, Georgia Mental Health Institute, Atlanta, Ga. Reported in NIDA Research Monograph (ADM) 92–1881.

Nellis, Muriel, ed. 1975. *Drugs, Alcohol and Women.* Washington, D.C.: National Research and Communications Associates.

Nelson-Zlupko, Lani, Eda Kauffman, and Martha Morrison Dore. 1995. "Gender differences in drug addiction and treatment: Implications for social work intervention with substance-abusing women." *Social Work* 40: 45–54.

Newland, Constance A. 1962. *My/Self and I.* New York: Coward-McCann.

Newman, Robert G. 1988. "New York City." In *Methadone in the Management of Opioid Dependence: Programs and Policies around the World,* ed. Awni Arif and Joseph Westermeyer, 238–243. Geneva: World Health Organization.

Newmayer, John A. 1978. "The current status of cocaine use in the San Francisco Bay area." In *Drug Abuse: Modern Trends, Issues, and Perspectives,* ed. Arnold Schecter, Harold Alksne, and Edward Kaufman, 1135–1144. New York: Marcel Dekker.

New York City Department of Health. 1919. *Annual Report.*

————. 1920. *Annual Report.*

————. 1989. "Maternal drug abuse—New York City." *City Health Information* 8, no. 8.

Nolan, D. W. 1881. "The opium habit." *Catholic World* 33: 827–835.

Novick, D. M., I. Khan, and M. J. Kreek. 1986. "Acquired immunodeficiency syndrome and infection with hepatitis viruses in individuals abusing drugs by injection." *Bulletin on Narcotics* 38: 15–25.

O.W. 1930. *No Bed of Roses: The Diary of a Lost Soul.* New York: Sheridan House.

O'Donnell, John A. 1969. *Narcotic Addicts in Kentucky.* Chevy Chase, Md.: National Institute of Mental Health. U.S. Public Health Service Pub. No. 1881.

———. 1974. "The older white addict." In *Towards a Typology of Opiate Users,* ed. William Bates and Betty Crowther, 21–48. Cambridge, Mass.: Schenkman.

O'Donnell, John A., and John C. Ball. 1966. *Narcotic Addiction.* New York: Harper and Row.

Oliver, F. E. 1872. "The use and abuse of opium." *Massachusetts State Board of Health, Third Annual Report,* 162–177. Repr. in Morgan 1974: 43–52.

"Opium eating." 1833. *Boston Medical and Surgical Journal* 9: 66–67.

"The opium habit." 1878. *Medical and Surgical Reporter* 38: 40.

Osler, William. 1894. *The Principles and Practice of Medicine.* New York: D. Appleton.

———. 1901. *The Principles and Practice of Medicine.* 4th ed. New York: D. Appleton.

———. 1913. *The Principles and Practice of Medicine.* 8th ed. New York: D. Appleton.

Palmer, Cynthia, and Michael Horowitz, eds. 1982. *Shaman Woman, Mainline Lady.* New York: William Morrow.

Paltrow, Lynn. 1990. "When becoming pregnant is a crime." *Criminal Justice Ethics,* Winter/Spring: 41–47.

Paone, D., et al. 1995a. "Operational issues in syringe exchanges: The New York City tagging alternative study." *Journal of Community Health* 20: 111–123.

Paone, D., et al. 1995b. "Sex, drugs and syringe exchange in New York City: Women's experiences." *Journal of the American Medical Women's Association* 50: 109–114.

Parke, Davis and Company. 1885. *Coca Erythroxylon and Its Derivatives.* Detroit and New York: Parke, Davis.

Parry, Hugh J. 1968. "Use of psychotropic drugs by U.S. adults." *Public Health Reports* 83: 799–810.

Patch, Vernon D., et al. 1978. "The efficacy of detoxification as a treatment for polydrug abusers." In *Drug Abuse: Modern Trends, Issues, and Perspectives,* ed. Arnold Schecter, Harold Alksne, and Edward Kaufman, 316–329. New York: Marcel Dekker.

Paton, Stewart. 1905. *Psychiatry: A Text-book for Students and Physicians.* Philadelphia: J. B. Lippincott.

Peak, Jeanie L., and Peter Glankoff. 1975. "The female patient as booty." In *Developments in the Field of Drug Abuse,* ed. Edward Senay, 509–512. Cambridge, Mass.: Schenkman.

Pepper, William, ed. 1886. *A System of Practical Medicine by American Authors.* Philadelphia: Lea Brothers.

Pescor, Michael J. 1942. "Physician drug addicts." *Diseases of the Nervous System* 3: 2–3.

———. 1944. "A comparative study of male and female drug addicts." *American Journal of Psychiatry* 100: 771–774.

Pettey, George E. 1902–1903. "The heroin habit another curse." *Alabama Medical Journal* 15: 174–180.

———. 1913. *Narcotic Drug Diseases and Allied Ailments.* Tennessee: J. A. Davis.

Phibbs, Ciaran S., David A. Bateman, and Rachel M. Schwartz. 1991. "The neonatal costs of maternal cocaine use." *Journal of the American Medical Association* 266: 1521–1526.

Pickard, Madge E., and R. Carlyle Buley. 1946. *The Midwest Pioneer: His Ills, Cures, and Doctors.* New York: Henry Schuman.

Pierce, Joseph. 1894. "The medical abuse of opium." *Medical Age* 12: 631.

Pierce, R. V. 1895. *The People's Common Sense Medical Adviser in Plain English.* Buffalo: World's Dispensary.

Pollard, Thomas. 1858. "Use of opium in children." *Atlanta Medical and Surgical Journal* 4: 129–134.

Poplar, Jimmie F. 1969. "Characteristics of nurse addicts." *American Journal of Nursing* 69: 117–119.

Prather, Jane, and Linda S. Fidell. 1975. "Sex differences in the content and style of medical advertisements." *Social Science and Medicine* 9: 23–26.

———. 1978. "Drug use and abuse among women: An overview." *International Journal of the Addictions* 13: 863–885.

Prescribing and Dispensing of Narcotics under the Harrison Narcotic Law. 1966. U.S. Bureau of Narcotics, Treasury Pamphlet No. 56. Washington, D.C.: U.S. Government Printing Office.

President's Advisory Commission on Narcotic and Drug Abuse: Final Report. 1963. Washington, D.C.: U.S. Government Printing Office.

Price, Richard H., et al. 1991. "Outpatient drug abuse treatment services, 1988: Results of a national survey." In *Improving Drug Abuse Treatment*, 63–92. Rockville, Md.: National Institute on Drug Abuse. DHHS Pub. No. (ADM) 91–1754.

Price, Thomas. 1975. "Linking the religious community." In *Drugs, Alcohol and Women*, ed. Muriel Nellis, 212–213. Washington, D.C.: National Research and Communications Associates.

"Property right versus public health." 1912. *Journal of the American Medical Association* 58: 706.

Ramos, Maria C., Patricia Howard, and Catherine K. Forrest. 1978. "Sex-related differences in drug abuse treatment: Implications for clinical practice." In *Drug Abuse: Modern Trends, Issues, and Perspectives*, ed. Arnold Schecter, Harold Alksne, and Edward Kaufman, 866–874. New York: Marcel Dekker.

Rape in America: A Report to the Nation. 1992. Arlington, Va.: National Victim Center and National Crime Victims Research and Treatment Center.

Rasor, Robert W., and H. James Crecraft. 1955. "Addiction to meperidine (Demerol) hydrochloride." *Journal of the American Medical Association* 157: 654–657.

Rayburn, Carole A. 1975. "Young students of crime." In *Drugs, Alcohol and Women*, ed. Muriel Nellis, 98–99. Washington, D.C.: National Research and Communications Associates.

Reed, Beth Glover. 1985. "Drug misuse and dependency in women: The meaning and implications of being considered a special population or minority group." *International Journal of the Addictions* 20: 13–62.

Reed, Beth Glover, and Edward Leibson. 1981. "Women clients in special women's demonstration drug abuse treatment programs compared with women entering selected co-sex programs." *International Journal of the Addictions* 16: 1425–1466.

Reed, Beth Glover, and Rebecca Moise. 1979. "Implications for treatment and future research." In *Addicted Women: Family Dynamics, Self Perceptions, and Support Systems,* 114–130. NIDA Services Research Monograph Series, DHEW Pub. No. (ADM) 80–762.

Reed, Beth Glover, et al. 1980. "The many faces of addicted women: Implications for treatment and future research." In *Drug Dependence and Alcoholism,* ed. Arnold Schecter, 833–847. New York: Plenum.

Reforming New York City's Response to Homelessness. 1993. New York: Department of Homeless Services.

Rehabilitating the Narcotic Addict. 1966. Washington, D.C.: U.S. Department of Health, Education and Welfare, Vocational Rehabilitation Administration.

"Report on drug addiction." 1955. *Bulletin of the New York Academy of Medicine* 31: 592–607. Repr. in O'Donnell and Ball 1966: 188–195.

Reynolds, J. Russell. 1876. *A System of Medicine.* 3d ed. London: Macmillan.

Ricci, Jean M., Rita M. Fojaco, and Mary Jo O'Sullivan. 1989. "Congenital syphilis: The University of Miami/Jackson Memorial Medical Center experience, 1986–1988." *Obstetrics and Gynecology* 74: 687–693.

Rich, Kenneth C. 1992. "Perinatal substance abuse and AIDS: Subject selection, recruitment, and retention." In *Methodological Issues in Epidemiological, Prevention, and Treatment Research on Drug-Exposed Women and Their Children,* ed. M. Marlyne Kilbey and Khursheed Ashgar, 166–182. Rockville, Md.: National Institute on Drug Abuse. DHHS Pub. No. (ADM) 92–1881.

Richards, Louise G., ed. 1981. *Demographic Trends and Drug Abuse, 1980–1985.* National Institute on Drug Abuse. NIDA Research Monograph 35. DHHS Pub. No. (ADM) 81–1069.

Richman, Alex, Marcus A. Feinstein, and Harold L. Trigg. 1972. "Withdrawal and detoxification in New York City heroin users." In *Drug Abuse,* ed. Wolfram Keup, 424–433. Springfield, Ill.: Charles C. Thomas.

Robinson, Bernard F. 1961. "Criminality among narcotic addicts in the Illinois State Reformatory for Women." *Illinois Medical Journal,* pp. 320–326.

Rodino, Peter W. 1975. "National legislation—The Congressional view." In *Drugs, Alcohol and Women,* ed. Muriel Nellis, 30–36. Washington, D.C.: National Research and Communications Associates.

Roeth, A. Gaston. 1886. "Cocaine in trachelorrhaphy." *American Practitioner and News* 1: 37.

Rosenbaum, Marsha. 1979. "Difficulties in taking care of business: Women addicts as mothers." *American Journal of Drug and Alcohol Abuse* 6: 431–446.

———— 1981a. *Women on Heroin.* New Brunswick, N.J.: Rutgers University Press.

———— 1981b. "Sex roles among deviants: The woman addict." *International Journal of the Addictions* 16: 859–877.

———— 1981c. "Women addicts' experience of the heroin world: Risk, chaos, and inundation." *Urban Life* 10: 65–91.

Rosenbaum, Marsha, and Murphy, S. 1981. "Getting the treatment: Recycling women addicts." *Journal of Psychoactive Drugs* 13: 1–13.

Rosenthal, A. M. 1996. "The poisoned babies." *New York Times,* Jan 16.

Rosenthal, Barry J., et al. 1979. "Drug treatment outcomes: Is sex a factor?" *International Journal of the Addictions* 14: 45–62.

Rothenberg, Richard, et al. 1987. "Survival with the acquired immunodeficiency syndrome: Experience with 5833 cases in New York City." *New England Journal of Medicine* 317: 1297–1302.

Ruiz, Pedro, et al. 1977. "Social rehabilitation of addicts: A two-year evaluation." In *Drug Detoxification: A Comprehensive Examination,* ed. Joyce Lowinson and John Langrod, 197–205. Oceanside, N.Y.: Dabor Science Publications.

Rush, Benjamin. 1789. "An inquiry into the case of the cholera infantum." *Medical Inquiries and Observations.* Vol. 1. Philadelphia: Pritchard and Hall.

Russell, Ira. 1887. "Opium inebriety." *Medico-Legal Journal* 5: 144–152.

Rutlin, Malaika. 1975. "Thrice oppressed." In *Drugs, Alcohol and Women,* ed. Muriel Nellis, 136–137. Washington, D.C.: National Research and Communications Associates.

Sainsbury, Harrington. 1909. *Drugs and the Drug Habit.* New York: E. P. Dutton.

Sanchez, Jose E., and Bruce D. Johnson. 1987. "Women and the drugs-crime connection: Crime rates among drug abusing women at Rikers Island." *Journal of Psychoactive Drugs* 19: 205–216.

Sander, Ellen. 1973. *Trips.* New York: Charles Scribner's Sons.

Sandmaier, Marian. 1980. *The Invisible Alcoholics: Women and Alcohol Abuse in America.* New York: McGraw-Hill.

Sanger, William. 1858. *The History of Prostitution: Its Extent, Causes, and Effects throughout the World.* New York: Harper and Brothers.

Sansone, Janet. 1980. "Retention patterns in a therapeutic community for the treatment of drug abuse." *International Journal of the Addictions* 15: 711–736.

Sapira, Joseph D., John C. Ball, and Emily Cotrell. 1973. "Methadone as a primary drug of addiction." In *Methadone: Experience and Issues,* ed. Carl D. Chambers and Leon Brill, 87–93. New York: Behavioral Sciences Press.

Schaumberg, Ron. 1993. "The pediatric grind: Setup for substance abuse?" *Pediatric Management,* June: 25–30.

Scheffel, Carl. 1918. "The victims of habit-forming drugs, from a medical-sociological and legal point of view." *Medico-Legal Journal* 35: 17–20.

Scheppegrell, W. 1898. "The abuse and dangers of cocain." *Medical News* 73: 417–422.

Schertzer, A. T. 1870. "Excessive opium eating." *Boston Medical and Surgical Journal,* n.s. 5: 56.

Schlissel, Lillian. 1982. *Women's Diaries of the Westward Journey.* New York: Schocken Books.

Schlosser, Eric. 1994a. "Reefer madness." *Atlantic Monthly,* August.

———. 1994b. "Marijuana and the law." *Atlantic Monthly,* September.

Schultz, Ardelle Poletti. 1975. "Staff makes the difference." In *Drugs, Alcohol and Women,* ed. Muriel Nellis, 145–147. Washington, D.C.: National Research and Communications Associates.

Seeger, C. L. 1833. "Opium eating." *Boston Medical and Surgical Journal* 9: 117–120.

Seidenberg, Robert. 1971. "Drug advertising and perception of mental illness." *Mental Hygiene* 55: 21–31.

Selden, Anne M. 1992. "Measures of pregnant, drug-abusing women for treatment research." In *Methodological Issues in Epidemiological, Prevention, and Treatment Research on Drug-Exposed Women and Their Children,* 194–211. Rockville, Md.: National Institute on Drug Abuse. DHHS Pub. No. (ADM) 92–1881.

Sells, S. B., et al. 1978. "Evaluation of present treatment modalities: Research with DARP admissions, 1969–1973." *Annals of the New York Academy of Sciences* 311: 270–280.

Shapiro, Sam, and Baron, Seymour H. 1961. "Prescriptions for psychotropic drugs in a noninstitutional population." *Public Health Reports* 76: 481–488.

Sharp, Sharon A. 1986. "Folk medicine practices: Women as keepers and carriers of knowledge." *Women's Studies International Forum* 9: 243–249.

Shearn, Regina. 1975. "The female and criminality." In *Drugs, Alcohol and Women,* ed. Muriel Nellis, 47–49. Washington, D.C.: National Research and Communications Associates.

Sheffet, Amiram, et al. 1978. "The role of detoxification in treatment of heroin addiction." In *Drug Abuse: Modern Trends, Issues, and Perspectives,* ed. Arnold Schecter, Harold Alksne, and Edward Kaufman, 346–358. New York: Marcel Dekker.

Shipman, E. W. 1890. "The promiscuous use of opium in Vermont." *Transactions of the Vermont Medical Society,* pp. 72–77.

Silver, Gary, ed. 1979. *The Dope Chronicles (1850–1950).* San Francisco: Harper and Row.

Silverman, Ira J. 1982. "Women, crime and drugs." *Journal of Drug Issues* 12: 167–183.

Simon, Carleton. 1924. "Survey of the narcotic problem." *Journal of the American Medical Association* 82: 675–679.

Simon, William. 1975. "Issue orientation." In *Drugs, Alcohol and Women,* ed. Muriel Nellis, 4–6. Washington, D.C.: National Research and Communications Associates.

Simonton, Thomas G. 1903. "The increase of the use of cocaine among the laity in Pittsburgh." *Philadelphia Medical Journal* 11: 556–560.

Simpson, D. Dwayne, and S. B. Sells. 1982. "Effectiveness of treatment for drug abuse: An overview of the DARP research program." *Advances in Alcohol and Substance Abuse* 2: 7–29.

Simrell, Earle V. 1970. "History of legal and medical roles in narcotic abuse in the U.S." In *The Epidemiology of Opiate Addiction in the United States*, ed. John C. Ball and Carl D. Chambers, 22–35. Springfield, Ill.: Charles C. Thomas.

Singer, Mark I., et al. 1995. "The psychosocial issues of women serving time in jail." *Social Work* 40: 103–113.

Smith, Brenda. 1991. "Legal and policy issues affecting the research and treatment of alcohol and other drug addiction among pregnant and parenting women." Policy paper, National Women's Law Center.

Smith, David E., and George R. Gay, eds. 1972. *It's So Good, Don't Even Try It Once.* Englewood Cliffs, N.J.: Prentice-Hall.

Smith, Mickey C. 1991. *A Social History of the Minor Tranquilizers: The Quest for Small Comfort in the Age of Anxiety.* New York: Haworth Press.

Smith, William G. 1832. "On opium, embracing its history, chemical analysis and use and abuse as a medicine." M.D. diss., University of the State of New York.

Snell, Tracy J. 1992. "Women in Jail 1989." *Bureau of Justice Statistics Special Report.* Washington, D.C.: U.S. Department of Justice. Doc. NCJ-134732.

———. 1994. "Women in Prison: Survey of State Prison Inmates." *Bureau of Justice Statistics Special Report.* Washington, D.C.: U.S. Department of Justice. Doc. NCJ-145321.

Spillane, Joseph F. 1994. "Modern drug, modern menace: The legal use and distribution of cocaine in the United States, 1880–1920." Ph.D. diss., Carnegie Mellon University.

Stanley, L. L. 1915–1916. "Morphinism." *Journal of the American Institute of Criminal Law and Criminology* 6: 586–593.

———. 1918. "Morphinism and crime." *Journal of the American Institute of Criminal Law and Criminology* 8: 749–756.

———. 1919. "Drug addictions." *Journal of the American Institute of Criminal Law and Criminology* 10: 62–70.

Starks, Michael. 1982. *Cocaine Fiends and Reefer Madness: An Illustrated History of Drugs in the Movies.* New York: Cornwall Books.

Starr, Karen. 1975. "Collective growth and service." In *Drugs, Alcohol and Women*, ed. Muriel Nellis, 191–192. Washington, D.C.: National Research and Communications Associates.

Starr, Paul. 1982. *The Social Transformation of American Medicine.* New York: Basic Books.

State of California, Division of Substance Abuse. 1975. *Drug Abuse Treatment in California Federally Funded Units 1975.*

Stein, Michael D., et al. 1991. "Differences in access to zidovudine (AZT) among symptomatic HIV-infected persons." *Journal of General Internal Medicine* 6: 35–40.

Stockwell, Adrienne. 1993. "Cost versus benefits: The legal and economic implications of different approaches to drug treatment." *Clearinghouse for Drug Exposed Children Newsletter* 4, no. 2.

Stockwell, G. Archie. 1877. "Erythroxylon Coca." *Boston Medical and Surgical Journal* 96: 399–404.

Stone, Nannette, Marlene Fromme, and Daniel Kagan. 1984. *Cocaine: Seduction and Solution.* New York: Clarkson N. Potter.

Strasbaugh, John, and Donald Blaise, eds. 1991. *The Drug User: Documents 1840–1960.* New York: Blast Books.

Strauss, M. E., et al. 1974. "Methadone maintenance during pregnancy: Pregnancy, birth, and neonate characteristics." *American Journal of Obstetrics and Gynecology* 120: 895–900.

Strumpell, Adolf. 1888. *A Text-Book of Medicine.* New York: D. Appleton.

Suffet, Frederic, David Hutson, and Richard Brotman. 1984. "Treatment of the pregnant addict: A historical overview." In *Pregnant Addicts and Their Children,* ed. Richard Brotman et al., 14–30. New York: Center for Comprehensive Health Practice, New York Medical College.

Sullivan, Eleanor J. 1987. "Comparison of chemically dependent and nondependent nurses on familial, personal and professional characteristics." *Journal of Studies on Alcohol* 48: 563–568.

Sullivan, Eleanor J., LeClair Bissell, and Doris Leffler. 1990. "Drug use and disciplinary actions among 300 nurses." *International Journal of the Addictions* 25: 375–391.

Sullivan, Eleanor J., LeClair Bissell, and Etta Williams. 1988. *Chemical Dependency in Nursing.* Menlo Park, Calif.: Addison-Wesley.

Susann, Jacqueline. 1966. *Valley of the Dolls.* New York: B. Geis Associates.

Swaine, George D. 1918. "Regarding the luminal treatment of morphine addiction." *American Journal of Clinical Medicine* 25: 610–612.

Taylor, Henry S. 1869. *Our Family Doctor.* Philadelphia: John E. Potter.

Taylor, Walter C. 1872. *A Physician's Counsels to Woman.* Springfield, Ill.: W. J. Holland.

Terry, C. E. 1913. *Annual Report, Board of Health, Jacksonville, Florida.*

———. 1921. "Some recent experiments in narcotic control." *American Journal of Public Health* 11: 25–52.

Terry, C. E., and Mildred Pellens. 1928. *The Opium Problem.* Bureau of Social Hygiene. 1970. Repr. Montclair, N.J.: Patterson, Smith.

Thobaben, Marshelle, Linda Anderson, and Harold G. Campbell. 1994. "Chemical dependency in home healthcare nurses." *Home Healthcare Nurse* 12: 67–69.

Thomas, Charles Herman. 1885. "Some uses of cocaine in gynecology." *Medical and Surgical Reporter* 53: 649–650.

Thomas, T. Gaillard. 1879. "Clinical lecture on diseases of women." *Medical Record* 16: 316.

———. 1880. *A Practical Treatise on the Diseases of Women.* 5th ed. Philadelphia: Henry C. Lea's Son.

Tjio, Joe-Hin, Walter N. Pahnke, and Albert A. Kurland. 1969. "LSD and chromosomes: A controlled experiment." *Journal of the American Medical Association* 210: 849–856.

Todd, Suzanne W. 1975. *Methadone Maintenance Treatment in New York City.*

New York: Committee on Youth and Correction, Department of Public Affairs, Community Service Society.

"Toward Preventing Perinatal Abuse of Alcohol, Tobacco, and Other Drugs." 1993. Rockville, Md.: U.S. Department of Health and Human Services, Center for Substance Abuse Prevention. CSAP Tech. Rept. 9. DHHS Pub. No. (SMA) 93–2052.

Towns, Charles B. 1912. "The peril of the drug habit and the need of restrictive legislation." *Century Magazine* 84: 580–587.

"Traffic in narcotic drugs." 1918. *Report of Special Committee of Investigation Appointed by the Secretary of the Treasury.* Washington, D.C.

Transactions of the Medical Society of Virginia, November 1887: 212–226.

Trussell, Ray E. 1971. "Treatment of narcotic addicts in New York City." In *Methadone Maintenance,* ed. Stanley Einstein, 1–7. New York: Marcel Dekker.

Turnbull, Laurence. 1885. "Coca and cocaine." *Therapeutic Gazette* 1: 226–228.

Twelve Steps and Twelve Traditions. 1952. New York: Alcoholics Anonymous World Services.

Tyler, Joanna, and Greg H. Frith. 1981. "Primary drug abuse among women: A national study." *Drug and Alcohol Dependence* 8: 279–286.

Tyler, Joanna, and Marian Thompson. 1980. "Patterns of drug use among women." *International Journal of the Addictions* 15: 309–321.

Tyson, James. 1900. *The Practice of Medicine.* 2d ed. Philadelphia: P. Blakiston's Son.

Tyson, James, and M. Howard Fussell. 1913. *Practice of Medicine.* 6th ed. Philadelphia: P. Blakiston's Son.

Vaillant, George E. 1966. "A twelve-year follow-up of New York narcotic addicts. I. The relation of treatment to outcome." *American Journal of Psychiatry* 122: 727–737.

Vandor, Maria, Patti Juliana, and Rose Leone. 1991. "Women and illegal drugs." In *Alcohol and Drugs Are Women's Issues.* Vol. 1. *A Review of the Issues,* ed. Paula Roth, 155–160. Metuchen, N.J.: Women's Action Alliance/Scarecrow Press.

Volkman, Rita, and Donald R. Cressey. 1963. "Differential association and the rehabilitation of drug addicts." *American Journal of Sociology* 69: 129–142.

Wagner, Janet D., Edna M. Menke, and Janet K. Ciccone. 1993. "Homeless pregnant mothers who abuse chemical substances: What the primary care physician should know." *Substance Abuse* 14: 148–158.

Waldorf, Dan, Martin Orlick, and Craig Reinarman. 1974. *Morphine Maintenance: The Shreveport Clinic, 1919–1923.* Washington, D.C.: Drug Abuse Council.

Waldorf, Dan, Craig Reinarman, and Sheigla Murphy. 1991. *Cocaine Changes.* Philadelphia: Temple University Press.

Walker, Le Roy Pope. 1884. "A few clinical facts regarding cocaine hydrochlorate, the new anesthetic." *New York Medical Journal* 40: 459–460.

Walker, William O., III. 1981. *Drug Control in the Americas.* Albuquerque: University of New Mexico Press.

Wallach, Robert C., Eulogio Jerez, and George Blinick. 1969. "Pregnancy and menstrual function in narcotics addicts treated with methadone." *American Journal of Obstetrics and Gynecology* 105: 1226–1229.

Wallen, Jacqueline. 1992. "A comparison of male and female clients in substance abuse treatment." *Journal of Substance Abuse Treatment* 9: 243–248.

Walter, Peter V., Barbara K. Sheridan, and Carl D. Chambers. 1973. "Methadone diversion: A study of illicit availability." In *Methadone: Experiences and Issues*, ed. Carl D. Chambers and Leon Brill, 171–176. New York: Behavioral Publications.

Ward, Mary Jane. 1946. *The Snake Pit*. New York: Grosset and Dunlap.

Waterhouse, E. R. 1886. "Cocaine debauchery." *Eclectic Medical Journal* (Cincinnati) 56: 464–465.

Weber, Ellen Marie. 1992. "Alcohol- and drug-dependent pregnant women: Laws and public policies that promote and inhibit research and the delivery of services." In *Methodological Issues in Epidemiological, Prevention, and Treatment Research on Drug-Exposed Women and Their Children*, ed. M. Marlyne Kilbey and Khursheed Ashgar, 349–365. Rockville, Md.: National Institute on Drug Abuse. DHHS Pub. No. (ADM) 92–1881.

Weed, Maria. 1895. *A Voice in the Wilderness*. Chicago: Laird and Lee.

Weibel, W. W., et al. 1990. "HIV-1 seroconversion in a cohort of street intravenous drug users in Chicago." Paper presented at Sixth International Conference on AIDS, San Francisco, June. Abstract F.C. 556.

Weil, Andrew. 1972. *The Natural Mind*. Boston: Houghton Mifflin.

Weissman, James C., and Karen N. File. 1978. "Criminal behavior patterns of female addicts: A comparison of findings in two cities." In *Drug Abuse: Modern Trends, Issues, and Perspectives*, ed. Arnold Schecter, Harold Alksne, and Edward Kaufman, 1082–1096. New York: Marcel Dekker.

Wellisch, Jean, M. Douglas Anglin, and Michael L. Prendergast. 1993. "Numbers and characteristics of drug-using women in the criminal justice system: Implications for treatment." *Journal of Drug Issues* 23: 7–30.

Wenger, Lynn D., and Marsha Rosenbaum. 1994. "Drug treatment on demand— Not." *Journal of Psychoactive Drugs* 26: 1–11.

Wharton, Edith. 1984. *The House of Mirth*. New York: Bantam Books.

White House Conference on Narcotic and Drug Abuse. September 27–28, 1962. Washington, D.C.: U.S. Government Printing Office.

Whittaker, James T. 1885a. "Cocaine in the treatment of the opium habit." *Nashville Journal of Medicine and Surgery* 36: 403.

——— . 1885b. "Cocaine for the opium habit." *Medical and Surgical Reporter* 53: 177–178.

Wholey, C. C. 1912. "Morphinism in some of its less commonly noted aspects." *Journal of the American Medical Association* 58: 1855–1856.

——— . 1913. "Psychopathologic phases observable in individuals using narcotic drugs in excess." *Pennsylvania Medical Journal* 16: 721–725.

Wieland, William F., and Carl D. Chambers. 1973. "A comparison of two stabilization techniques." In *Methadone: Experiences and Issues*, ed. Carl D. Chambers and Leon Brill, 95–108. New York: Behavioral Publications.

Wilbert, M. I. 1908. "Some early botanical and herb gardens." *American Journal of Pharmacy* 80: 426.

———. 1915. "The number and kind of drug addicts." *American Journal of Pharmacy* 87: 415–420.

Wilkerson, David. 1963. *The Cross and the Switchblade*. Grand Rapids, Mich.: Chosen Books.

Williams, Edward Huntington. 1914. "The drug habit menace in the South." *Medical Record* 85: 247–249.

Williams, Joyce E., and William M. Bates. 1970. "Some characteristics of female narcotic addicts." *International Journal of the Addictions* 5: 245–256.

Williams, Terry. 1989. *The Cocaine Kids*. Reading, Mass.: Addison-Wesley.

———. 1992. *Crackhouse*. New York: Penguin Books.

Wilmarth, Stephen S., and Avram Goldstein. 1974. *Therapeutic Effectiveness of Methadone Maintenance Programs in the USA*. Geneva: World Health Organization.

Wilner, Daniel M., and Gene G. Kassebaum. 1965. *Narcotics*. New York: McGraw-Hill.

Wilson, James C. 1886. "The opium habit and kindred affections." In *System of Practical Medicine*, ed. William Pepper, 647–660. Philadelphia: Lea Brothers.

Wilson, J. C., and A. A. Eshner. 1896. *An American Text-book of Applied Therapeutics*. Philadelphia: W. B. Saunders.

Winick, Charles. 1959–1960. "The use of drugs by jazz musicians." *Social Problems* 7: 240.

———. 1965. "Epidemiology of narcotics use." In *Narcotics*, ed. Daniel M. Wilner and Gene C. Kassebaum, 3–18. New York: McGraw-Hill.

Winick, Charles, and Paul M. Kinsie. 1971. *The Lively Commerce: Prostitution in the United States*. Chicago: Quadrangle Books.

Winterburn, George W. 1882. "A seductive drug." *Medical Tribune* 4: 509.

"Women and drug abuse." 1994. *NIDA Capsules*, June.

"Women and prescription drugs." 1978. *NIDA Capsules*, April.

Women's Drug Abuse Treatment Programs. 1979; rev. 1980. Rockville, Md.: National Clearinghouse for Drug Information. Alcohol, Drug Abuse, and Mental Health Administration. DHHS Pub. No. (ADM) 80–852.

Wood, George B., and Franklin Bache. 1834. *The Dispensatory of the United States of America*. 2d ed. Philadelphia: Grigg and Elliot.

Wood, Horatio C., Jr. 1869. "On the medical activity of the hemp plant as grown in North America." *Proceedings of the American Philosophical Society* 11: 226–232.

———. 1893. "Opium." *Boston Medical and Surgical Journal* 128: 638–639.

Wood, Roland W. 1966. "California Rehabilitation Center." In *Rehabilitating the Narcotic Addict*. Washington, D.C.: U.S. Department of Health, Education and Welfare, Vocational Rehabilitation Administration.

Wood-Allen, Mary. 1905. *What a Young Woman Ought to Know*. Philadelphia: Vir Publishing.

Worth, Dooley. 1991. "American women and polydrug abuse." *Alcohol and*

Drugs Are Women's Issues. Vol. 1. *A Review of the Issues,* ed. Paula Roth, 1–9. Metuchen, N.J.: Women's Action Alliance/Scarecrow Press.

Wright, Hamilton. 1910. Report on International Opium, Opium Problem. 61st Cong., 2d sess., Feb. 21. S. Doc. 377.

Yablonsky, Lewis, and Charles E. Dederich. 1965. "Synanon: An analysis of some dimensions of the social structure of an antiaddiction society." In *Narcotics,* ed. Daniel M. Wilner and Gene C. Kassebaum, 193–216. New York: McGraw-Hill.

Yolles, Stanley. 1969. *Narcotics Legislation.* Hearings before the Subcommittee to Investigate Juvenile Delinquency of the Committee on the Judiciary. U.S. Senate, 91st Cong., 1st sess., Sept. 17. Washington, D.C.: U.S. Government Printing Office.

Young, Iris. 1994. "Punishment, treatment, empowerment: Three approaches to policy for pregnant addicts." *Feminist Studies* 20: 33–57.

Young, James Harvey. 1961. *The Toadstool Millionaires.* Princeton: Princeton University Press.

———. 1967. *The Medical Messiahs.* Princeton: Princeton University Press.

Zinn, Howard. 1980. *A People's History of the United States.* New York: HarperCollins.

Zuckerman, Barry, et al. 1989. "Effects of maternal marijuana and cocaine use on fetal growth." *New England Journal of Medicine* 320: 762–768.

INDEX